Sustainability

To all the future generations

Sustainability

Essentials for Business

Scott T. Young | Kanwalroop Kathy Dhanda

DePaul University | *DePaul University*

Los Angeles | London | New Delhi
Singapore | Washington DC

Los Angeles | London | New Delhi
Singapore | Washington DC

FOR INFORMATION:

SAGE Publications, Inc.
2455 Teller Road
Thousand Oaks, California 91320
E-mail: order@sagepub.com

SAGE Publications Ltd.
1 Oliver's Yard
55 City Road
London EC1Y 1SP
United Kingdom

SAGE Publications India Pvt. Ltd.
B 1/I 1 Mohan Cooperative Industrial Area
Mathura Road, New Delhi 110 044
India

SAGE Publications Asia-Pacific Pte. Ltd.
3 Church Street
#10-04 Samsung Hub
Singapore 049483

Acquisitions Editor: Patricia Quinlin
Editorial Assistant: Katie Guarino
Production Editor: Libby Larson
Copy Editor: Megan Markanich
Typesetter: C&M Digitals (P) Ltd.
Proofreader: Dennis W. Webb
Indexer: Jean Casalegno
Cover Designer: Michael Dubowe
Marketing Manager: Liz Thornton

Copyright © 2013 by SAGE Publications, Inc.

Printed in the United States of America

Library of Congress Cataloging-in-Publication Data

Young, Scott T.

Sustainability : essentials for business/Scott T. Young, DePaul University, Kanwalroop Kathy Dhanda, DePaul University.

pages cm
Includes bibliographical references and index.

ISBN 978-1-4129-8284-9 (pbk.)

1. Management—Environmental aspects. 2. Industries—Environmental aspects 3. Sustainable development. I. Dhanda, Kanwalroop Kathy, 1970- II. Title.

HD30.255.Y67 2013
658.4'083—dc23   2012043302

This book is printed on acid-free paper.

12 13 14 15 16 10 9 8 7 6 5 4 3 2 1

Brief Contents _____

Detailed Contents _____

Preface _____

This book represents a collaboration of two like minds aided by a team of committed publishing professionals at SAGE. Any book begins with an idea that there is some need, some niche that needs to be addressed, and that is where this book started—the desire to have a text with the necessary information to teach a course in sustainability.

We come to sustainability from different approaches, so we will start with our own paths. Scott originally taught at the University of Utah, where protection of the wilderness is a big issue. Scott is a lover of the outdoors, a distance runner who loved communing with nature along the trails of the Wasatch Front and was reluctant to sacrifice nature for commercial pursuits. In 2002, Scott developed a course called Business and Nature, which explored those concerns. Another influence was a friend named James Alto, a consultant who introduced Scott to the sustainability issues of the mining industry. James introduced Scott to the current literature and increased his excitement to study the intersection between business and the environment.

Fast forward a few years. Scott moved to Chicago to teach at DePaul University, where he recruited Kathy Dhanda, who grew up in India, where the culture is deeply respectful of nature yet is one that, in current times, sacrifices conservation to development. In her dissertation, Kathy mathematically modeled a market akin to Kyoto whereby nations trade permits to meet a previously set cap on emissions. Her work led to a book titled *Environmental Networks: A Framework for Economic Decision-Making and Policy Analysis* (with Edward Elgar). From this point on, Kathy's research focused on modeling and design of environmental topics. After Kathy took the reins of the course in sustainability, she developed and taught the course with a number of readings since there was a dearth of comprehensive texts in this area. Kathy had conversations with Scott, and they decided to write a book that could be used to educate business students about sustainability. The early materials were gathered in 2008, and the book took final shape over the next 4 years.

This book is aimed at students who are interested in sustainability. Many colleges and universities offer courses that focus on or are related to sustainability. This book could be offered to students in a variety of settings ranging from an interdisciplinary course in the liberal arts to an advanced undergraduate or graduate course in business.

This book is the first business text to offer an in-depth exploration of the relationship of environmental science to business. This book has a focus upon the triple bottom line (TBL) of business. The sections are broken up into the three categories of (1) natural capital (planet), (2) the human capital (people), and (3) the financial capital (profits). In addition, it offers material across business functions—operations, marketing, and, in particular, strategy. Controversial topics such as global warming are presented with both sides of the current debate so that students can have rich classroom discussion. Each of the chapters in the book offers a selection of websites for further information and exploration. The chapters also contain suggested case studies for intensive treatment of topics.

The authors would like to thank editors Patricia Quinlin and Lisa Shaw, associate editors Maggie Stanley and Eve Oettinger, editorial assistant Katie Guarino, and the publishing staff at SAGE. We would also like to thank our students and staff for their immeasurable help in assisting with the book: Erin Nelson, Nell Bochenek, Ronak Jain, and Rita Zakusilo. We would like to thank our colleagues at the college and the dean, Ray Whittington. Last but not least, we would like to thank our spouses (Luciana and Adrian) and our children (Gabriella [Gabi], Gianna [Gigi], Reggie, Galen, Ariana, and Arman) for putting up with us as we worked on the book.

The authors and the staff at SAGE Publications would like to thank the following reviewers:

Lynne Andersson, Temple University

Eric J. Arnould, Professor of Consumer Marketing, School of Management, University of Bath Visiting Professor of Marketing, Department of Marketing and Management, Southern Denmark University

Pratima Bansal, Ivey Business School, Western University

Phillip E. Barnes, PhD, School of Earth, Ocean and Environment, Environment and Sustainability Program, University of South Carolina

Sushil Bhatia, Suffolk University, Sawyer Business School

Asayehgn Desta, PhD, Dominican University of California

J. Marshall Eames, PhD, Loyola University Chicago

John Hardman, Regenerative Organizations or Department of Educational Leadership & Research Methodology, Florida Atlantic University

Jill Beth Jacoby, PhD, University of Wisconsin, Superior

Chonnikarn Fern Jira, Doctoral Candidate, Harvard Business School

Robert Kistler, Bethel University

Tom Landgraf, School of Business, Real Estate and Urban Land Economics, University of Wisconsin–Madison

Sylvia Maxfield, PhD, Simmons School of Management

Christopher D. Merrett, Illinois Institute for Rural Affairs, Western Illinois University

Thalia M. Mulvihill, Professor of Social Foundations and Higher Education, Ball State University

Will O'Brien, Visiting Assistant Professor, Clark University, Graduate School of Management, Worcester, Massachusetts

Melinda Phillabaum, Indiana University–Purdue University Indianapolis

Rhonda Phillips, Arizona State University

Gordon Rands, Western Illinois University

Clint Relyea, Arkansas State University

Jonathan M. Scherch, PhD, Core Faculty, Graduate Program in Environment & Community, Antioch University Seattle

Robert Sroufe, Duquesne University MBA Sustainabilty Program

Pablo Toral, Beloit College

Gregory P. Trudeau, University of Wisconsin

David Warner, Winthrop University

PART I

Sustainability—Essentials for Business

Introduction _____

Global forces such as the energy crisis, recession, and climactic catastrophies have resulted in the **sustainability** movement's growth in importance. With its origins from environmental management, the field of sustainability has emerged as a new business discipline—one that must find its way into the curriculum of business schools.

The position of the organization within the context of the natural world has caused a new awareness of our collective need for a sustainability emphasis. This book represents an introduction to the field. It will introduce the key business interactions with sustainable development while providing a basic background on environmental science.

What Is Sustainability? _____

Sustainability is difficult to define since it is an evolving concept. Similar to other concepts like democracy and globalization, sustainability is one of the most "ubiquitous, contested and indispensable concepts of our time" (Tavanti, 2010). In a very general sense, the term *sustainability* means to endure. Hence, in ecology, sustainability pertains to "how biological systems remain diverse and productive over time" (Tavanti, 2010). For human beings, sustainability is about the "potential for long-term maintenance of well-being, which in turn depends on the maintenance of the natural world and natural resources" (Bromley, 2008).

There are more than 500 definitions of sustainability, and most of these pertain to the specific discipline or field—for example, sustainable community or sustainable design. Despite the varied definitions of sustainability, the concepts include these basic precepts:

- Living on earth has environmental limits.
- Humans have the responsibility of preventing or cleaning up pollution.
- The economy, environment and society are interconnected and interdependent (Tavanti, 2010).

The most common definition of sustainability is one from the area of sustainable development provided by the World Commission on Environment and Development (WCED), also known as the **Brundtland Report,** that states, "Sustainable development is the development that meets the needs of the present without compromising the ability of future generations to meet their own needs" (WCED, 1987).

Sustainability-Related Definitions

Sustainable university: "A higher education institution, as a whole or as a part, that addresses, involves and promotes, on a regional or a global level, the minimization of environmental, economics, societal, and health negative effects in the use of their resources in order to fulfill its main functions of teaching, research, outreach & partnership, and stewardship among others as a way to helping society make the transition to sustainable life styles" (Velazquez, Munguia, Platt, & Taddei, 2006, p. 812).

Sustainable education: "Sustainable education involves active participation to create economic and social development programs and goals that will help balance and generate long standing improvements of a nation's basic quality of life standards and needs. This can help generate empowerment to the nation's citizens" (United Nations Educational, Scientific, and Cultural Organization [UNESCO], 2002).

Sustainable city: "Sustainable urban development is improving the quality of life in a city, including ecological, cultural, political, institutional, social and economic components without leaving a burden on the future generations. A burden which is the result of a reduced natural capital and an excessive local debt. Our aim is that the flow principle, that is based on an equilibrium of material and energy and also financial input/output, plays a crucial role in all future decisions upon the development of urban areas" (Anastasiadis & Metaxas, 2010).

Sustainable community development: "Sustainable community development is the ability to make development choices which respect the relationship between the three 'E's'—economy, ecology, and equity: Economy—Economic activity should serve the common good, be self-renewing, and build local assets and self-reliance. Ecology—Human are part of nature, nature has limits, and communities are responsible for protecting and building natural assets. Equity—The opportunity for full participation in all activities, benefits, and decision-making of a society" (Mountain Association for Community Economic Development, n.d.).

Sustainable food: "Food that is healthy for consumers and animals, does not harm the environment, is humane for workers, respects animals, provides a fair wage for the farmer, and supports and enhances rural communities" (MeetGreen, n.d.).

Sustainable agriculture: "[Sustainable agriculture is] an agriculture that can evolve indefinitely toward greater human utility, greater efficiency of resource use, and a balance with the environment that is favorable both to humans and to most other species" (Harwood, 1990).

Sustainable design: "Sustainable design is the set of perceptual and analytic abilities, ecological wisdom, and practical wherewithal essential to making things that fit in a world of microbes, plants, animals, and entropy. In other words, (sustainable design) is the careful meshing of human purposes with the larger patterns and flows of the natural world, and careful study of those patterns and flows to inform human purposes" (Orr, 1992).

Sustainable society: "A sustainable society is one which satisfies its needs without diminishing the prospects of future generations" (Brown, 1981).

Sustainable value: "As a value, it refers to giving equal weight in your decisions to the future as well as the present. You might think of it as extending the Golden Rule through time, so that you do unto future generations as you would have them do unto you" (Gilman, 1991).

Sustainable processes: "A transition to sustainability involves moving from linear to cyclical processes and technologies. The only processes we can rely on indefinitely are cyclical; all linear processes must eventually come to an end" (Henrik-Robert, 2010).

Sustainability ethics: "A thing is right when it tends to preserve the integrity, stability, and beauty of the biotic community. It is wrong when it tends otherwise" (Leopold, 1948).

Sustainability in commerce: "Leave the world better than you found it, take no more than you need, try not to harm life or the environment, make amends if you do" (Hawken, 1984).

Sustainable economy: "A sustainable economy is one in which resources are not used up faster than nature renews them. It also marks a thriving climate for business that balances environmental, social, and economic vitality" (Oregon Environmental Council, 2010).

Environmental sustainability: "Sustainability means using, developing and protecting resources at a rate and in a manner that enables people to meet their current needs and also provides that future generations can meet their own needs" (Duncan, 2001).

Government sustainability: "A sustainable society needs local and central government to lead the way by consuming differently, and by planning effectively and efficiently in order to integrate sustainable practices in the services it provides to citizens, and throughout its estates and workforce" ("Public Sector Sustainability," 1999).

More definitions of sustainability and sustainable development can be found at Sustainable Measures (2010).

History of the "Green" Movement

Modern civilization has seen a dramatic shift in technology, science, and the way we live. The world has gone from a primarily agrarian society a mere 150 years ago, to a highly mechanized, industrialized, and urbanized society.

The industrialization of society made work easier and less labor intensive, but as we progressed with technology and production, jobs shifted to cities and with it brought pollution and crime.

History reveals a pattern: We create new technologies only to discover that they lead to health complications. Then we solve the problem with science. In the 19th century, cities and towns relied on horses for transporting and shipping. The automobile was designed to eliminate these problems.

We have a tendency to find out much too late that modern living is also killing us—for example, asbestos, chemicals, the food we eat, air pollution. We drove for many years before the smog accumulated through exhaust fumes was identified as harmful to your lungs. Meanwhile the tobacco and automobile industries became two of our biggest economies, with a legal force behind them to fight any threat.

The sustainability movement is not at all new, but it grows increasingly important with the cost and scarcity of fuel for energy. Its prominence today is caused by a perfect storm:

- Increased energy costs
- A number of calamities—some caused by man, others by nature
- The increasing attention paid to the green movement
- Economic recession

History of Pollution

Throughout history, raw sewage and industrial waste have been dumped into our rivers and streams, leading to outbreaks of cholera. The **Clean Water Act of 1972 (CWA)** prohibited discharge into waterways, helping improve the quality of our drinking water.

The use of coal to heat caused deadly smog to envelop London in 1880, killing 3,000 people, and again in 1952, killing 4,000 people. This led to the passing of the Clean Air Act of 1956. Similarly, a deadly fog killed 1,063 in

Glasgow, Scotland, in 1909. The death toll goes way beyond the immediate counts, due to the daily breathing of toxic materials. A grandmother of one of the authors of this book, a nonsmoker, died of lung cancer in 1946, most likely caused by her living and breathing the air in Glasgow, Scotland.

In 1977, rainfall in a community in New York resulted in corroding underground containers full of chemical waste. The resultant pollution leaked its way into homes and schools, leading to cancer, birth defects, and miscarriages. The Love Canal scandal exposed the damage caused by toxic waste and the care that must be taken in its disposal.

History is full of catastrophic events that cause immediate changes in process once the damage has already been done. In 1984, a Union Carbide plant in India released chemical gases into the air that killed thousands of people. In 1989, the **Exxon Valdez** tanker spilled oil off the coast of Alaska, decimating the ecostructure of the area. Twenty-four years later, an even costlier spill by British Petroleum (BP) wreaked havoc with the Gulf Coast. In 1986, a nuclear reactor in the Ukraine exploded. Combined with an incident in the United States at Three Mile Island, Pennsylvania, nuclear energy as a source of fuel became threatened, if not discarded.

Urbanization

The increasingly urban global population also creates added concerns for pollution control (see Table 0.1). Congregating automobiles in one city, with limited urban transit available, adds emissions into the air, causing health and breathing problems.

Naturalists and Environmentalists

While the world has become awash with pollution and natural resources are depleted, there have been key defenders of nature whose words and deeds have influenced legislation and thinking.

There are days which occur in this climate, at almost any season of the year, wherein the world reaches its perfection; when the air, the heavenly and the earth, make a harmony, as if nature would indulge her offspring; when, in these bleak upper sides of the planet, nothing is to desire that we have heard of the happiest latitudes, and we bask in the shining hours of Florida and Cuba; when everything that has life gives sign of satisfaction, and the cattle that lie on the ground seem to have great and tranquil thoughts. (Emerson, 1983)

There are many points in history that one could point to as a beginning of the sustainability movement. The transcendentalists of the 19th century,

Table 0.1 Urban Proportions 1950–2030				
Country	1950	1980	2010	2030
Afghanistan	5.8	15.7	24.8	36.3
Australia	77	85.8	89.1	91.9
Brazil	36.2	67.4	86.5	91.1
Canada	60.9	75.7	80.7	84.4
China	13	19.6	44.9	60.3
Finland	31.9	59.8	61.6	68.8
France	55.2	73.3	77.8	82.9
Italy	54.1	66.6	68.4	74.6
Japan	34.9	59.6	66.8	73.7
United Kingdom	79	87.9	90.1	92.2
USA	64.2	73.7	82.3	87

Source: Brown (2009).

including Ralph Waldo Emerson, Henry David Thoreau, Bronson Alcott, and Margaret Fuller, emphasized the interaction of man and nature in their writings and saw the world in a holistic sense.

Emerson's essays made him an influential figure in his lifetime, which was not the case of his young protégé, Henry David Thoreau (1854), whose famous work *Walden* would not receive acclaim until many years after his death. Thoreau's venture, to spend 2 years in a cabin, primarily living off the land, was a total immersion in nature and solitude and was an important work in influencing such future leaders as Mahatma Gandhi. His friend Bronson Alcott, the father of Louisa May Alcott, started one of the first communes—Fruitlands, an idealistic effort to live off the land and live as vegetarians.

Thoreau (1854) wrote this in *Walden*:

I went to the woods because I wished to live deliberately, to front only the essential facts of life, and see if I could not learn what it had to teach, and not, when I came to die, discover that I had not lived. I did not wish to live what was not life, living is so dear; nor did I wish to practice resignation, unless it was quite necessary. I wanted to live deep and suck out all the marrow of life, to live so sturdily and Spartan like as to put to rout all that was not life, to cut a broad swath and shave close, to drive life into a corner, and reduce it to its lowest terms, and if it proved to be mean, why then to get the whole and genuine meanness of it, and publish its meanness to the world; or if it were sublime, to know it by experience, and be able to give a true account of it in my next excursion.

John Muir

The Scottish immigrant John Muir was an important figure in taking a stance for protection of the wilderness. Muir helped found the Sierra Club and was instrumental in the designation of Yosemite as a national park. Muir, like Thoreau, was a long-distance hiker, once chronicling his walk from Indiana to the Gulf as "A THOUSAND MILE WALK TO THE GULF." The Muir Woods and Muir Beach in California were named for him in appreciation of his efforts to protect forests.

Today, the Sierra Club still maintains a strong presence in lobbying efforts to protect the wilderness, plus sponsoring eco-friendly tours.

John James Audubon

John James Audubon was a 19th-century French immigrant naturalist/painter who catalogued his drawings into the opus *Birds of America,* a collection of over 400 illustrations of North American birds. The Audubon Society was formed in 1905 with the goal "To conserve and restore natural ecosystems, focusing on birds, other wildlife, and their habitats for the benefit of humanity and the earth's biological diversity."

The Wilderness Society

Four individuals formed the Wildness Society in 1935: (1) Robert Sterling Yard, who helped create the National Park Service; (2) Benton MacKay, the father of the Appalachian Trail; (3) Robert Marshall, chief of recreation for the Forest Service; and (4) Aldo Leopold, an ecologist at the University of Wisconsin. These men helped steer the Wilderness Act through Congress in 1964.

WILDERNESS, in contrast with those areas where man and his own works dominates the landscape, is hereby recognized as an area where the earth and its community of life are untrammeled by man, where man himself is a visitor who does not remain. ("What Is Wilderness?," 2009).

Rachel Carson

Rachel Carson, a naturalist and scientific writer, wrote the book *Silent Spring,* which pointed out the harm caused to plants and wildlife by pesticides.

The initial reaction to her book was that it was unfounded nonsense, but further research validated her arguments, and the government acted to halt the use of DDT.

Carson's (1962) book was the beginning of awareness that consumers should be more careful about what they put into their bodies. For many years, the populace had been operating under the assumption that as long as they ate the recommended diet approved by the USDA, their health was safe. Although Carson cannot be considered the first environmentalist, she probably had the most impact.

Gaylord Nelson

Gaylord Nelson (1970), a U.S. senator from Wisconsin, had witnessed how the timber industry had entered his region's white pine forest and "wiped it out in an eyewink of history and left behind fifty years of heartbreak and economic ruin." He came to be known as the "conservation governor" for his efforts to preserve the natural resources of his state. Inspired by the teach-ins across colleges to protest the Vietnam War, he came up with the idea of Earth Day. The first Earth Day was held in 1970 and attracted 20 million participants. Each year since then, Earth Day has been observed around the world (Wilderness Society, 2012).

Ten Myths About Sustainability

1. Nobody knows what sustainability really means. The UN (Brundtland Report) definition states that sustainable development is "development that meets the needs of the present without compromising the ability of the future generations to meet their own needs" (WCED, 1987). People everywhere realize there is a future price to pay if we do not take care now.

2. Sustainability is all about the environment. The focus of the original UN commission was to help poor nations catch up. Poverty often contributes to environmental degradation—that is, economies that survive by cutting the rain forest or slaughtering endangered species. However, inefficient resource use and emissions of greenhouse gases (GHGs) are also problematic since the ramifications might be irreversible.

3. *Sustainable* is a synonym for *green*. The term *green* usually suggests a preference of natural over artificial. However, in order to meet the needs of our population, there is a heavy reliance on technology.

4. It's all about recycling. Recycling, by itself, is a small part of the larger issue as energy and transportation are the biggest aspects of sustainability.

5. Sustainability is too expensive. Although sustainability efforts may require an initial capital outlay, it has a significant long-term impact. W. Edwards Deming fought the same battle with quality. Detractors argued that quality was expensive. Deming argued that not having quality is more expensive.

6. Sustainability means lowering our standard of living. It will mean a shift of employment, as withering industries lose employment to green industries.

7. Consumer choices and grassroots activism, not government intervention, offer the fastest, most efficient routes to sustainability. Since transportation and energy are key factors in sustainability and powerful lobbies exist in both areas, governmental legislation helps keep these companies active.

8. New technology is always the answer. There are cases where a creative business model might offer a better solution.

9. Sustainability is ultimately a population problem. Not quite, though the best way to curb population is by educating women and raising the standard of living. However, a larger focus needs to be placed on less waste of precious resources.

10. Once you understand the concept, living sustainably is a breeze to figure out. A practice cannot be termed sustainable without a complete life-cycle analysis of all the costs involved. (Lemonick, 2009)

Within business schools, academic majors are organized around the traditional major functional disciplines: management, marketing, finance, accounting, economics, and operations management. Where does sustainability fit within business schools—and further, within the organizational structure of the firm?

In terms of the organization, we see the eventual place for sustainability as a distinct function, equal with operations, accounting, and the others. Since sustainability is strategic in nature, its home may be found either in the business strategy domain, or, since it is very involved with process and maintenance, within operations management.

In the business school curriculum, it should have a similar evolution. As it grows in importance, it brings more students and more courses. Some would argue that sustainability is a topic within business ethics, but that implies that operating in a sustainable way is an ethical choice. It is not a choice. Business ethics is a topic that crosses all functional boundaries. We do not get into business ethics in sustainability until we have a case in which ethics is breached.

The Case for Being Sustainable

What forces companies to think about sustainability? The most obvious one is the link to profitability. The other reasons are image enhancement, response to shareholders, and business strategy among others.

Profitability

Businesses that focus on sustainability can be more innovative and see an increase in profits. A report from BT and Cisco states that sustainability can create commercial success and lead businesses to develop new products and services. The 10 steps that can be taken by companies to become sustainability driven are as follows:

1. Make innovating for sustainability part of an overall corporate vision.

2. Formulate a strategy with sustainability at its heart.

3. Embed sustainability in every part of your business.

4. Emphasize actions, not words.

5. Set up effective board-level governance to make sustainability matter.

6. Set firm rules.

7. Bring stakeholders on board by engaging them.

8. Use people power through recruitment, staffing, training and rewards.

9. Join networks focused on sustainability.

10. Think beyond reporting—align all business systems with the company's sustainability vision. (GreenBiz Staff, 2008)

Stakeholders want to know more about what companies are doing to improve the world and lessen their impact on the world. Though profit is still important, it is not the sole criterion upon which companies are ranked.

Linking Profitability to Development

Companies can contribute to global sustainable development through their core businesses so that they are both profitable and help development (World Business Council for Sustainable Development [WBCSD], 2009). The report by WBCSD provides perspectives on key challenges and opportunities for the poor countries. The key messages from the report are as follows:

1. The lives of people can be improved via direct employment, purchasing from local suppliers, and delivery of affordable products and services.

2. Companies can offer vocational training and capacity building, invest in energy infrastructure and renewable energy solutions, support healthcare initiatives and education, reduce dependence on scarce raw materials, create new businesses to preserve ecosystems, and help governments embed good governance.

3. Establish policies and legislation that establish the necessary framework conditions.

4. Government must show commitment by investing in core infrastructure and encourage investment and involvement from large corporations. (WBCSD, 2009)

Competitiveness

Another reason is that companies need to be competitive. The **Carbon Beta and Equity Performance** report by Innovest (Murray, 2007) states that companies with comprehensive climate change strategies are outperforming their competitors over the past 3 years. This study was done on 1,500 companies, and it discovered that there was a strong correlation between industrial companies' sustainability in general and climate change in particular. The report states that the information reported by companies on their environmental initiatives is inadequate, and they find it hard to identify the companies with the lowest climate risk (Murray, 2007).

Consumer Loyalty

Consumers are also providing a big push for companies to become sustainable. Specifically, the consumers worried about sustainability are seeking more environmentally friendly products and telling companies to lessen their impact on the planet. The Grocery Manufacturers Association/Food Products Association (GMA/FPA) argues that incorporating sustainable supply chain practices would be good because it will increase profit, help the industry work with government agencies to create regulations, and build consumer loyalty (GreenBiz Staff, 2007a).

Global Warming Concerns

There is more interest in sustainability/green construction because of concerns on global warming and oil prices. It is estimated that only 6% of commercial developments are certified as "sustainable" or have applied for LEED (Leadership in Energy and Environmental Design) certification. It is expected that by 2010 it will be 10%. People in Japan are expected to have grass on their roof, computerized light systems, and an HVAC system. Prologis plans to create minimum design standards for new developments so that it meets the requirements for environmental certification. The company Simon has reduced $18 million a year in operating costs by green retrofitting and other projects. It reduced 110,000 metric tons of carbon dioxide emissions per year. The U.S. Environmental Protection Agency (EPA) encourages green environment measures by providing a free software tool called Portfolio Manager. The benefits of green buildings are lowering consumption and costs, attracting more tenants, tax credit, and insurance discounts (Marino, 2007).

International Pressures

The European Commission new biofuels target for the European Union is increasing pressure on tropical forests and peatlands. The UN Food and Agriculture Organization plans to develop bioenergy guidelines, and Ecole Polytechnique Fédérale de Lausanne plans to draft global standards on sustainable biofuels. There is concern that growing more palm oil in Asia for bioenergy and food use will increase emissions of GHGs ("Sustainability Moves Centre-Stage," 2007).

Public Exposure

The Massachusetts Institute of Technology (MIT) awards an annual Lemelson–MIT Prize and the Lemelson–MIT Award for Sustainability. The Lemelson–MIT Prize is given to inventors who make a product or process that can offer significant value to society. The sustainability award is given to inventions that work to expand economic opportunity and community well-being in developing and developed countries (GreenBiz Staff, 2007b).

Greening the Supply Chain

A survey conducted by eyeforprocurement showed that more than 50% of companies have policies on greening their supply chain. The survey asked 188 procurement professionals about their companies' practices, policies, and plans on reducing the environmental impact of the materials used. The survey showed that two thirds of the professionals are practicing green procurement to support their companies' environmental or sustainability strategies. About 49% said that they are practicing green in order to respond to customers' interest in eco-friendly products and services. Companies responded that green purchasing continues to expand and customers' demands are increasing (GreenBiz Staff, 2007c).

Minimizing Waste

Sonoco plans to help manufacturing companies save money eliminating and reusing waste streams. Sonoco Sustainability Solutions' (S3) goal is to reduce the amount of waste entering landfills. Sonoco plans to develop custom programs for their customers to reduce the amount of waste generated. S3 will find new ways to use the waste to generate a new revenue stream (GreenBiz Staff, 2007d).

However . . . a Note of Caution

In spite of all the progress made by corporations and organizations, one needs to be careful. A lot of companies are being criticized for *greenwashing,* a practice of appearing green without incorporating actual, measurable goals that lead toward sustainability.

Real sustainability is complicated and more positive in that it aims to have humans and other life flourish on the planet forever. Sustainability is gained when everything is working well with everything else. A primary reason why the environment can't be fixed easily is consumption. Even though companies have created programs to reduce waste they are continuing to feed the beast. Companies need to offer products and services that help consumers to restore and maintain their ability to care, flourish, and be aware. Sustainability will help stop the addiction by providing carefully designed products and services that lead people toward responsible choices (Ehrenfeld, 2006).

Why Sustainable Strategy? _____

The increase in the price of fuel, concern over global warming, and increased consumer demand for environmentally friendly products are just some of the factors that have made sustainability a strategic focal point in industry after industry. All organizations, whether for- or not-for-profit, compete for customers, and increasing awareness has altered the competitive landscape. All one needs to do is compare the websites in any industry—automobile manufacturing, hospitality, publishing, pharmaceutical, food products, even ice cream—and it is quite easy to see a growing emphasis on sustainability. Given the strategic importance of this area, we have devoted an entire chapter (Chapter 6) to reviewing the various frameworks that try to define and classify sustainability.

As with any trend, there are the skeptics who are doubtful and resistant to the trend. Then, there are the early adopters who embrace the trend and incorporate it within their organizations. Sustainability is no different; it has its share of believers and skeptics. As this trend unfolds, we shall see organizations that will be skeptical and do as much of the minimum as possible. There will be other organizations that will not want to be perceived as laggards and will attempt to be more engaged. But there will also be the organizations that will truly walk the talk and will embrace the concept and incorporate it throughout the ranks.

Peter Senge (2008) wrote a book titled *The Necessary Revolution* that discusses how organizations and individuals can work together to create a sustainable world. Indeed, there are plenty of organizations that are huddled together in paralysis and inaction. Rather than being proactive, these organizations think that doing nothing is the safe way to go. However, there are other organizations that believe that in order to survive in the future they need to incorporate sustainability into their long-term goals. How does sustainability become a priority for organization leaders? The initial step is to change the view, refocus the vision. The traditional, accepted industrial-age view is one wherein the largest and most important circle is the economy that contains smaller subareas of society and environment. The only way to change this view is to shift priorities and integrate sustainability into the organization. This can be done by reconsidering the traditional view. In the new way of looking at the world, the largest circle is the environment, within which is contained a circle of human activity. The circle representing the economy, the industrial systems, is the smallest circle within (see Figure 0.1).

The economy is the wholly owned subsidiary of nature, not the other way around.

—U.S. Senator Gaylord Nelson,
quoted by Ray Anderson (Senge, 2008)

Figure 0.1   The Real, Real World

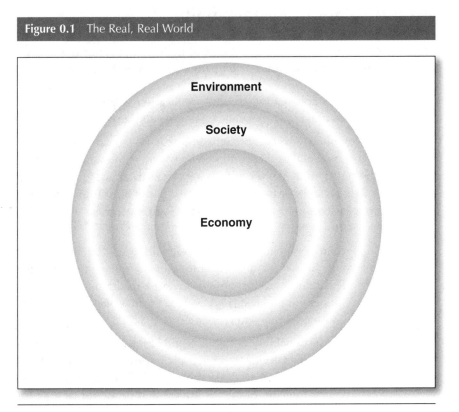

Source: Adapted from Senge (2008).

It is known that all the stakeholders of an organization—from customers to suppliers, employees to shareholders—care about the environment and social issues. With information being instantly disseminated on the web blogs and Internet, the organizations have no place to hide. Indeed, organizations that ignore sustainability issues run the risk of losing market share, losing talented employees, and incurring damage to their reputations. For those organizations that want to be on the front lines, there needs to be enough evidence for opportunities from embracing sustainability. The following is a small list of benefits:

- Gaining competitive advantage from goodwill
- Preference of green brands by consumers
- Recruiting and retaining good employees
- Saving money from efficiency and waste reduction
- Making money from creative forms of waste re-generation
- Sustainability as point of differentiation
- Shaping future of industry
- Becoming preferred supplier
- Providing competitive edge to customers
- Changing image and brand (Senge, 2008).

Five Stages on the Path to Sustainability

For any organization, there are five stages to go from noncompliance to full integration of sustainability into a company's strategy and purpose.

Stage 1 is noncompliance where an organization is essentially getting fined for not complying with local emission regulations.

Stage 2 is compliance where, perhaps in a reaction to external pressure from nongovernmental organizations (NGOs) and regulators, the organizations begin to comply but the actions are primarily aimed at compliance so as not to incur fines or taxes. At this point, the organization is meeting minimum legal requirements with regards to air emissions, water effluents, or toxic waste emissions.

Stage 3 is beyond compliance. Organizations discover that savings and payoffs of going further than compliance can far outweigh the initial investments. This reinforces the win-win scenario, or the snowball effect, wherein reinvestment of initial savings leads to positive gains including an improvement in brand value and reputation.

Stage 4 is where sustainability is fully integrated into strategy. This happens when organizations decide to proactively integrate sustainability factors into every aspect of their business strategy. In addition, sustainability is also factored into the core of the investment and decision-making process across the organization. Numerous companies from Alcoa, General Electric (GE), Wal-Mart, and DuPont have made the move to Stage 4.

Stage 5 is where organizations stepped into without passing through other stages, usually due to a mission of making a change or to contribute to society. Examples are Patagonia, Seventh Generation, The Body Shop, and several others. Ray Anderson, the CEO of Interface the carpet tile company, set out to make his company a restorative enterprise "a sustainable operation that takes nothing out of the earth that cannot be recycled or quickly regenerated, and that does no harm to the biosphere" (Dean, 2007). More organizations move to Stage 5 as their mission begins incorporating sustainability. A movement from Stage 4 to 5 can also be the result of a natural progression as the leaders can learn from the experiences of launching new initiatives that get positive feedback from employees (Senge, 2008, pp. 114–117).

Triple Bottom Line

Triple bottom line (TBL) states that the success of a company needs to be measured along three lines—(1) economic, (2) social, and (3) environmental. It also goes by the term *3P,* which stands for people, planet, and profits; it states that companies need to measure their impacts not only on the bottom line (profits) but also on the community (people) and the environment (planet). The phrase was first used in 1989 by John Elkington, cofounder of a consultancy focused on sustainability.

The TBL is a form of reporting that states that the business's responsibility extends to all of its stakeholders, not merely to its shareholders. In other words, it takes into account the impact of the business in terms of social and environmental values along with financial returns. Whereas traditional models were about making money and garnering profits, TBL accounting recognizes that without satisfied employees and a clean environment, business is doomed to be unsustainable in the long run (Green Living Tips, 2010).

People: This is also known as **human capital,** and it relates to fair and beneficial business practices toward labor and the community and region in which a corporation conducts its business. In simplest terms, it means treating your employees right. In addition, businesses should not only pay fair wages but also reinvest some of its gains into the surrounding community through sponsorships, donations, or projects that go toward the common good (Green Living Tips, 2010).

Planet: This is **natural capital,** and it refers to the company's environmental practices. A business will strive to minimize its ecological impact in all areas—from sourcing raw materials, to production processes, to shipping and administration. It's a *cradle to grave* approach and in some cases *cradle to cradle* (C2C)—that is, taking some responsibility for goods after they've been sold such as offering a recycling or take-back program. In addition, a TBL business will also not be involved in the production of toxic items (Green Living Tips, 2010).

Profit: "This is more about making an honest profit than raking a profit at any cost—it must be made in harmony with the other two principles of People and Planet." The profit aspect is the real economic value created by the company, one that deducts the cost of all inputs (Green Living Tips, 2010).

The Importance of Triple Bottom Line

Of the 100 largest economies in the world, 51 are businesses and the other 49 are countries. In terms of financial power, "General Motors is now bigger than Denmark; DaimlerChrysler is bigger than Poland; Royal Dutch/Shell is bigger than Venezuela; IBM is bigger than Singapore; and Sony is bigger than Pakistan" (Anderson & Cavanagh, 2000).

> Instead of being an award, accreditation or a certification, the Triple Bottom Line is an ongoing process that just helps a company in running a greener business and demonstrates to the community at large they are working not just towards riches, but the greater common good. Green business is simply good business [in practice]. (Green Living Tips, 2010)

Figure 0.2 Triple Bottom Line

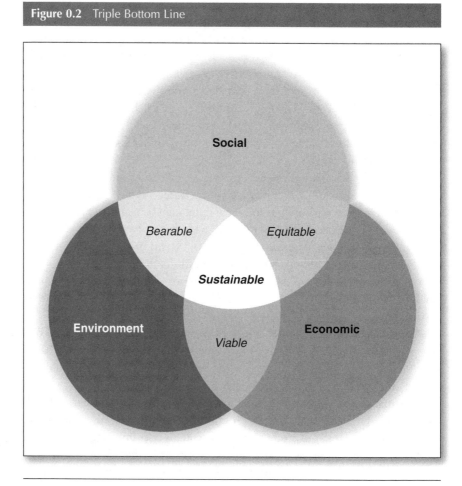

Source: Dreo (2006).

Chapter Outline

The purpose of this book is to provide a comprehensive treatment of the relationship between business and sustainability. Our goal is that this book serves as a key source for instructors and students wanting to learn about sustainability within a business context. The opening chapters of this book address the major issues confronting our natural resources. It is important to get a grounded perspective on these critical issues before addressing the strategic issues of the firm. Businesses must have a clear understanding of the consequences of wasted resources and polluted environments. Therefore, we begin the book with a basic overview of the concerns surrounding resources (see Figure 0.2).

The approach that we take in this book is to start with Part II: Renewable Resources and discuss the natural resources such as air, water, forests, soil, and biodiversity. This discussion provides a starting point so that the later chapters on environmental challenges can be framed within an appropriate context. We also include a chapter on energy and fuel that discusses conventional forms of energy along with renewable, clean sources of energy. The next section of the book is Part III: Stakeholder Interest and Choices. The first chapter in this section provides a comprehensive discussion of strategies and frameworks used to understand and implement sustainability. The rest of this section presents various stakeholder perspectives such as the role of consumers (what people buy), the role of corporations (what companies sell), and the role of governments and NGOs (how people organize and govern). This section also presents the concept of ecological footprint and illustrates how to compute an individual carbon footprint. The last section of the book is Part IV: Strategies for a Sustainable Future. This section of the book presents chapters on reporting and measurement, carbon markets, the design of sustainable cities, and green marketing.

Part I: Renewable Resources

The first bottom line is the one that concerns the planet. The planet is our **natural capital**, and together we need to preserve the planet and its resources. In this section, we will present the renewable resources that the planet has offered to its inhabitants. Can we, as consumers, hope to preserve nature while we make use of its goods and services? This section will contain numerous chapters as listed next.

Chapter 1: Air and Climate Issues

In this chapter, we will do the following:

- Explain the basic causes and outcomes of air pollution.
- Discuss the UN 27 principles of sustainability.
- Discuss the goals of the Kyoto Protocol.

- Discuss Agenda 21.
- Discover the effects of indoor air quality (IAQ).
- Determine the measurement of air quality.
- Research local air quality information.
- Discover the potential problems caused by global warming.

Chapter 2: Water Issues

In this chapter, we will do the following:

- Explain the problems created by plastic water bottles.
- Describe the major causes of water pollution.
- Explain the importance of conserving water.
- Discuss the impact water legislation acts have at the national and state level.
- Develop sustainable water protection and conservation strategies.

Chapter 3: Sustainable Agriculture and Food

In this chapter, we will do the following:

- Discuss sustainable agriculture.
- Discuss the foods we eat.
- Recognize the differences between natural and organic foods.
- Examine companies involved in the food industry, including McDonald's, Wal-Mart, and Monsanto.
- Discuss malnutrition.

Chapter 4: Forests, Wildlife, and Biodiversity

In this chapter, we will do the following:

- Discuss the relationship between the forest and climate.
- Discuss the various methods of tree cutting.
- List the certification programs for sustainable forestry.
- Understand the importance of urban forests.
- Explain the importance of preserving wilderness.
- Discuss the Endangered Species Act of 1973 (ESA).
- Research the issues concerning economics and biodiversity.

Chapter 5: Alternative Clean Energy and Fuels

In this chapter, we will do the following:

- Discuss the need for clean energy.
- Present the four types of conventional energy.
- Explain the different types of renewable energy.
- Compare and contrast solar and wind energy.
- Evaluate the promise of plant-based energy from ethanol to wood waste.

- Discuss other forms of energy, such as tidal to geothermal.
- Evaluate the most viable alternative energy and fuel sources for businesses today.

Part III: Stakeholder Interest and Choices

In this section, the focus of the book moves away from renewable resources to issues faced by stakeholders. At what level are the various stakeholders impacted by degradation of our natural resources? Are some communities or some nations at a higher risk than other, more affluent communities or nations? What can consumers, organizations, and governments do in order to prepare for a sustainable future? The second bottom line concerns the people that inhabit the planet. The people as a collective is our human capital and, similar to the natural capital, this human capital also needs to be treated in a way that is fair and beneficial to the entire community. In this section, we will present some of the strategies and frameworks used to understand sustainability. In addition, this section will discuss the role of consumers, the role of the corporation, and the role of NGOs and governments.

Chapter 6: Sustainability Strategies and Frameworks

In this chapter, we will do the following:

- Explain the concept of sustainable value creation.
- Understand the precepts of natural capitalism.
- Examine activities via the natural step.
- Discover examples of industrial ecology and biomimcry.
- Compare and contrast the principles of the cradle to cradle (C2C) approach with biomimicry.
- Explain environmental management system (EMS) and environmental stewardship.
- Compare and contrast various tools and processes used for sustainable strategies.

Chapter 7: Role of the Consumer

In this chapter, we will do the following:

- Discuss consumption and its link to ecosystem services.
- Evaluate the link between consumption and environment.
- Detail the sustainable choices in food, drink, housing, clothing, and transportation.
- Explain the role of consumers.
- Discuss the ecological footprint and compute carbon footprint.
- Elaborate on the role of business in promoting sustainable consumption.
- Examine the future of consumption.

Chapter 8: Role of the Corporation

In this chapter, we will do the following:

- Present the chrysalis economy.
- Discuss why sustainability is more than green.
- Define corporate social responsibility (CSR) and link it to sustainability.
- Understand the phases of CSR and how to make a case for CSR.
- Discuss the benefits and challenges of CSR.
- Explain green supply chains and sustainable value chains.
- Examine the role of logistics, transportation, and green procurement.
- Map out a business case for sustainability.

Chapter 9: Role of Governments and Nongovernmental Organizations

In this chapter, we will do the following:

- Understand the role of governments in promoting sustainability.
- Present the role of the EPA.
- Explain Agenda 21 and the role of local governments.
- Discuss the history, growth, and funding of NGOs.
- Expand on the role of NGOs in social development, community development, and sustainable development.
- Explore NGOs and business partnerships.
- Discuss the role of NGOs and sustainable consumption.
- Present the five types of environmental NGOs.

Part IV: Strategies for a Sustainable Future

The third bottom line concerns the profits that are derived from the operations of the corporations. The basic idea is that corporations ought to be focused on making an honest profit than raking a profit at any cost—it must be made in harmony with the other two principles of people and planet. The profit aspect is the real economic value created by the company—one that deducts the cost of all inputs. This section focuses on the role of transparency and reporting along with discussing carbon markets and green marketing.

Chapter 10: Transparent Reporting, Measurement, and Standards

In this chapter, we will do the following:

- Understand the need for reporting and transparency.
- Present voluntary reporting on sustainability.

- Discuss the role of the Global Reporting Initiative (GRI).
- Compare and contrast the various ISO 14001 standards.
- Explain ISO 26000 standards.
- Discuss the UN Global Compact.
- Present some other reports, repositories, and indexes.

Chapter 11: Carbon Markets

In this chapter, we will do the following:

- Present the concept of carbon neutrality.
- Explain the Kyoto Protocol.
- Discuss the details of carbon markets.
- Compare and contrast the various types of offsets.
- Present the market standards.
- Discuss proceedings of Conference of the Parties (COP17) Durban.

Chapter 12: Designing Sustainable Cities and Communities

In this chapter, we will do the following:

- Discuss the sustainability plan highlights of major cities across the world.
- Understand the components of a sustainability city plan.
- Discuss the city's contribution to corporate sustainability.

Chapter 13: Green Marketing

In this chapter, we will do the following:

- Know the basic rules of green marketing.
- Understand greenwashing: trying to pass a company off as green when it is questionable.
- Explain the "five green Ps."
- Discuss the consumer groups that marketers target.

Appendix: Green Jobs

This appendix is an excerpt from the *one* report on green employment.

Conclusion

This book will explore ideas and concepts for a future that is more sustainable. The range of ideas are multipronged—investing in alternative energy sources, going back to the old methods of purchasing seasonal food from local farms, designing our communities to encourage people to work and live in common areas, encouraging walking and public transportation, and aiming development globally with a vision for reducing poverty and population hot spots.

KEY WORDS

Brundtland Report

Carbon Beta and Equity Performance

Clean Water Act of 1972 (CWA)

Exxon Valdez

Human capital

Natural capital

Sustainability

Triple bottom line (TBL)

DISCUSSION QUESTIONS

1. What is sustainability?

2. Why is sustainability important?

3. What are the sustainability practices of companies you are familiar with?

4. Is sustainability the same as green?

5. Do a cost–benefit analysis of a hybrid automobile compared to the same non-hybrid model.

6. If all automobiles were hybrids in the United States, what would be the cumulative effect?

7. Is there any evidence of a sustainability program at your college or university?

RECOMMENDED WEBSITES

www.naturalstep.org/

www.sustainablemeasures.com/

www.un-documents.net/wced-ocf.htm

www.unesco.org/new/en/unesco/

www.worldwatch.org/

PART II

Renewable Resources

1

Air and Climate Issues

LEARNING OBJECTIVES

By the end of this chapter, you should be able to do the following:

- Explain the basic causes and outcomes of air pollution.
- Discuss the UN 27 principles of sustainability.
- Discuss the goals of the **Kyoto Protocol.**
- Discuss **Agenda 21.**
- Discover the effects of **indoor air quality (IAQ).**
- Determine the measurement of air quality.
- Research local air quality information.
- Discover the potential problems caused by **global warming.**

Chapter Overview

In 1974, scientists announced that there was a "hole in the ozone" caused primarily by the use of household products. F. S. Rowland of the University of California found that the **chlorofluorocarbons** (CFCs) used in such products as deodorant, hair spray, refrigerators, and air conditioners, was thinning the **ozone layer.**

The average citizen was about to get some understanding of what this meant. The ozone layer resides 6 miles above the earth's surface, above what is called the **troposphere,** which is the air around us. Above the ozone layer is the stratosphere, which extends another 30 miles into the air.

Ozone is a molecule that filters ultraviolet rays. The U.S. Environmental Protection Agency (EPA) estimated that ozone depletion would cause an additional 300,000 cases of skin cancer and 1.6 million additional cases of cataracts every year. So here is a case in which the products we used offered the potential to harm our health. As a result, in 1978, the United States banned CFCs in spray cans (but not in refrigerators and air conditioners). The question is whether that action was in time. Other nations did not begin to follow suit for a decade.

Man had caused a problem that upset the balance of nature. We set about to correct the problem, but the implications of our actions can cause additional problems that will impact our future generations. Why should we care about global citizens far into the future? They are the children perhaps of your grandchildren that will suffer the consequences.

An issue today is global warming, and there are debates about its existence. Should we ignore the scientific studies? Should we assume that this is merely a meteorological cycle that will correct itself? Should we prepare for it? Should we prevent it from happening? In this chapter, we will discuss the scenarios presented by global warming.

This chapter will review the critical matters of the air and climate that organizations need to consider in their workplace planning. There are many reasons that businesses should be concerned about air quality. They are major contributors to pollution and thus have some control over their emissions. Also, the IAQ should be monitored. Air quality has been linked to illness and disease, thus increasing health care costs. We will review the basics of air pollution and pollution prevention and what global warming is all about.

A Primer on Air Pollution

The biggest pollutant in the air is **carbon monoxide,** comprising 48% of the total pollutants (U.S. Census Bureau, 2012). Most of the carbon monoxide comes from natural sources, such as the decay of marshland. About 7% of the carbon monoxide comes from automobiles, but this volume is highly concentrated over major cities with thousands of automobiles. If you live in rural Montana, you don't have much carbon monoxide. You get most of yours from cow dung. Major industry contributes around one third of the air pollution in the form of **sulfur dioxide, nitrogen dioxide,** and **suspended particulates.**

The brownish haze that envelops some cities in summer is a photochemical smog: ozone. This smog is accentuated whenever a temperature inversion exists, a condition that traps air near the surface until the air finally moves out. Anyone who has experienced an inversion in cities like Los Angeles, Denver, and Salt Lake City knows it does not make a pretty picture.

Long-term exposure to breathing this air can cause a variety of health problems: chronic bronchitis, emphysema, lung cancer, and in some cases death (Pope, 1989). Lung disease is four times more common in urban areas than in rural towns (Portney & Mullahy, 1990). Air pollution is the most likely cause of this phenomenon. A study in Salt Lake City saw upper respiratory ailments more than double in days of high pollution, compared to days with lower levels of pollution (Love, Lan, & Shy, 1982).

Air pollution causes damage to fruits, plants, trees, and flowers. **Acid rain,** created by precipitation passing through polluted air, causes damage to buildings and metal structures.

Air pollution can alter local climates (Bernard, Samet, Grambsch, Ebi, & Romieu, 2001; Swart, Amman, Raes, & Tuinstra, 2004). Particulates from industry and power plants are blown into the air and seed clouds downwind of major cities. Increased rainfall in areas 50 miles from major cities have been attributed to this tendency.

Smokers are six times more likely to die from pulmonary diseases, 10 times more likely to die from lung cancer, and nearly twice as likely to die from heart disease (Feenstra van Genugten, Hoogenveen, Wouters, & Rutten-van Molken, 2001). Secondhand smoke, breathed by those in the proximity of smokers, also puts health at risk (Raoh et al., 2004).

The **Clean Air Act** in the United States established car, industrial, and urban emissions standards. This act imposes penalties and taxes on standards violators.

The EPA lists 19 sources of air pollution:

- Aerosols
- Asbestos
- Carbon monoxide
- CFCs
- Criteria air pollution
- Ground level ozone
- Hazardous air pollution
- Hydrofluorocarbons (HFCs)
- **Lead**
- Mercury
- Nitrogen dioxide
- **Particulate matter**
- Propellants
- Radiation
- Radon
- Refrigerants
- Sulfur dioxide
- Toxic air pollution
- Volatile organic compounds (VOCs)

From this list, the National Ambient Air Quality Standards list six of the common air pollutants that are harmful to health.

1. *Ground level ozone:* At ground level, ozone is created by a chemical reaction between oxides of nitrogen and VOCs. Automobile exhaust, gasoline vapors, and industrial exhaust are examples of chemicals in the air that form ozone. The effect is accentuated by heat and sunlight. The mix creates smog and is harmful to breathe.

2. *Particulate matter:* Small particles of nitrates, sulfates, organic chemicals, metals, and dust create a mixture that is hazardous to the health. There are two categories: (1) inhalable coarse particles, usually dirt and dust; and (2) fine particles, which are gases emitted from smoke and haze.

3. *Carbon monoxide:* This is a colorless gas caused by combustion. At high levels, it can cause death. Campers have lost their lives by heating their tents with a propane tank. People have lost their lives by leaving their automobiles running in a closed garage or not turning off the gas to the stove.

4. *Sulfur dioxide:* These are reactive gases that come primarily from power plants and industrial facilities. They are known to be hazardous to the respiratory system.

5. *Nitrogen dioxide:* This is a reactive gas created from emissions in the air such as vehicle exhaust combined with power plant emissions and off-road equipment. It contributes to ground-level ozone and is a health hazard.

6. *Lead:* The switch to unleaded gasoline for automobiles dramatically reduced the lead in the air. Lead emissions are now primarily found near metals processing plants.

Pollution Control

Industrial pollution control devices are a major dampening factor in reduction and vary according to the nature of the industry. While smokestack industries may require one type of control, chemical industries require another.

The fight against automotive exhaust is aided with the catalytic converter, which converts carbon monoxide into less harmful carbon dioxide and water. In situations where smog is excessive, additional controls may be required.

The Air Pollution Control Technology Center (APCTC), of the Air Pollution Prevention and Control division of the EPA, verifies technologies that attempt to reduce indoor air pollutants. The categories they verify include diesel engine emission controls, baghouse filtration products, nitrogen oxides controls, VOC controls, dust suppression, soil stabilization, and paint arrestors.

Pollution Effects

Acid Rain

Acid rain is a term for atmospheric deposits containing nitric and sulfuric acids. Volcanoes, decayed vegetation, and emissions containing sulfur dioxide and nitrogen oxides cause it. When these gases react with water in the atmosphere, the result is acids falling to the ground in rain, snow, fog, or mist. The same effect can happen without moisture, in dry weather, because the acids reach the ground and a subsequent rainfall can activate the acids.

Acid rain damages trees, soil, and buildings and decays statues and sculptures. It is measured using a scale called pH. The National Atmospheric Deposition Program measures and monitors pH. The EPA and research scientists work toward reducing acid rain.

A major approach to reduction is to cut the exhaust from smokestacks and exhaust pipes. Coal accounts for most of the sulfur dioxide and nitrogen oxides emissions, and much of this comes from power plants. Switching fuels to natural gas would reduce the emissions. They can also "scrub" the smokestacks to remove the sulfur dioxide (Chiras, Reginald, & Owen, 2002). These methods are costly, however.

Other sources of power such as nuclear, wind, hydropower, geothermal, and solar that do not rely upon coal would greatly reduce the problems caused by acid rain.

The EPA suggests a process called **liming** would help bring back lakes and streams to their natural acidic composition (www.epa.gov/acidrain/reducing/index.html). This process adds lime to offset the acidity. It does not harm fish and has been used successfully in Norway and Sweden.

The EPA studies the economic costs and benefits. A division of EPA, the Air Economics Group, statistically models the effects of air pollution and produces a number of reports and analysis of the trade-offs of alternative technologies.

Health Effects

About one in three people in the United States is at a high risk of having ozone-related health issues (www.airnow.gov). Ozone exposure can have the following effects:

- Irritate the respiratory system, resulting in coughing and having chest pain.
- Reduce lung function; the volume of air breathed in is diminished. This becomes a problem for outdoor workers and athletes.
- Aggravate asthma; allergens are made more sensitive by the ozone.
- Damage lung lining; damaged cells may cause long-term health effects.
- Aggravate chronic lung disease; those with bronchitis and emphysema should reduce exposure to ozone.
    Most at risk are the following populations:
- Children: Children are more prone to asthma and respiratory illnesses, and their vigorous outdoor activity can increase their risk.
- Outdoor-active adults: Runners and bikers can actually do more harm to their lungs exercising in a smoggy environment than any benefits they might normally experience.
- People with respiratory disease: People with asthma and respiratory illness are more vulnerable.
- People with unusual susceptibility to ozone: There are some individuals who are more sensitive to ozone.

Heat Island Effect

Cities with populations over 1 million have an average temperature increase of from 1.8 to 5.4 degrees Fahrenheit annually, compared to surrounding areas (Chiras et al., 2002). This phenomenon is called the **heat island effect**. In the summertime, this results in increased air-conditioning use and electricity bills. Large cities must find ways to reduce this effect.

Legal Enforcement

The Clean Air Act was written in 1963. Although it is a federal law, the act relies greatly upon state and local governments for enforcement. The act has resulted in a 50% reduction of the six common air pollutants in the period from 1970 to 2011. Industrial air pollutants have been reduced by 70% in that time period. Cars built in 2012 burn 90% cleaner fuel than they did in 1970, and production of ozone-depleting chemicals has been banned.

During that same 40-year time period, energy consumption increased by 50% and vehicle use by 200%.

Indoor Air Quality

The EPA provides information on its website, www.epa.gov, to show all the possible sources of indoor air pollution. The major sources are as follows:

- Smoking
- Carbon monoxide—kitchen and fireplace
- Pet dander
- Dust mites—bedroom
- Mold—bathroom and basement
- **Radon**—basement
- VOCs—kitchen and basement

Radon is a radioactive gas that leaks in through cracks in the walls and ceilings. Smoking and secondhand exposure to smoke have been found to be a cause of cancer and lung disease. Radon can also cause cancer. Carbon monoxide poisoning can be fatal.

Sick building syndrome (SBS) is when a great number of individuals either living or working in the same building experience all sorts of health issues that are traced to the air quality of the building they inhabit. Indicators of SBS include headaches; eye, nose, and throat irritation; cough; itchy skin; dizziness; nausea; and fatigue.

One of the causes for SBS is poor ventilation. Buildings have a standard of approximately 15 cubic feet per minute of outside air per occupant. Smoking lounges in airports require 60 cubic feet per minute of outside air.

Chemical contaminants—such as VOCs, carbon monoxide, and formaldehyde—and biological contaminants—such as mold, bacteria, and pollen—can cause SBS. Increasing air ventilation, cleaning the air, and removing the sources of pollutants reduce SBS. It is not an uncommon phenomenon.

Mobile Sources

The EPA monitors pollution from all sources of transportation: airplanes, automobiles, motorcycles, trucks, trains, and boats. Since airplanes still use leaded fuel, efforts are underway to try to reduce emissions from that source.

Locomotive engines received new guidelines in 2004 in the Clean Air Nonroad Diesel Rule, which specified that allowable levels of sulfur must be reduced by 99%. The new legislation cuts emissions as much as 90%. Newly built locomotive engines will use high-efficiency catalytic aftertreatment technology beginning in 2015, cutting emissions even further.

Boats are addressed through their fuels and emissions. Fuel improvements that started in 2007 are designed to cut sulfur by 99%. New engines have stricter requirements to reduce emissions with a goal of cutting emissions by 80%.

Air Quality Index

An **air quality index** consists of measures of specific pollutants in urban areas, interurban air quality, and an index of industrial emissions—primarily in rural areas.

Rogers and colleagues (1997) established a comprehensive air quality index, measured as an index of sulfur dioxide; suspended particulate matter; and coefficient of haze, carbon monoxide, total oxidants, and oxides of nitrogen.

The U.S. EPA uses ground level ozone, particulate matter, carbon monoxide, sulfur dioxide, and nitrogen dioxide. The EPA has established a standard index of 100, above which air quality is considered to be unhealthy (see Tables 1.1 and 1.2).

These tables only represent a 1-day snapshot, a day in which Denver most likely had an air inversion. That same day on Causeway Bay, Hong Kong, the reading was 67.

Don't think for a moment that this pollution is limited to cities. Air currents take pollution hundreds of miles. Pollution from Los Angeles drifts into Sequoia National Park, more than 100 miles away. Pollution from Atlanta and Birmingham drifts into the Great Smoky Mountains, which averages 20 unhealthy air quality days per year.

Table 1.1   Environmental Protection Agency Air Quality Index Levels

AQI Value	Conditions	Color
0–50	Good	Green
51–100	Moderate	Yellow
101–150	Unhealthy for sensitive groups	Orange
151–200	Unhealthy	Red
201–300	Very unhealthy	Purple
301–500	Hazardous	Maroon

Source: Adapted from "Understanding the AQI" (n.d.).

Table 1.2   Environmental Protection Agency Air Quality Index for Several Cities in April 2011

Here are air quality index readings for several cities on November 4, 2011.

City	Air Quality Index on November 4, 2011
Atlanta	16
Boston	35
Chicago	29
Denver	50
Jacksonville	19
New York City	42
Phoenix	53
Salt Lake City	12

Source: Adapted from AirNow (n.d.).

Air Pollution in Cities

Six out of 10 Americans live in urban areas where air pollution can cause health problems (see Table 1.3).

The U.S. EPA offers a helpful website for citizens and students (www.epa .gov). On the opening webpage, you can access environmental information for every state.

Table 1.3 Most Polluted Cities

Most Polluted U.S. Cities (by Short-Term Particle Pollution)	Cleanest Cities
1. Bakersfield, CA	1. Santa Fe, NM
2. Fresno, CA	2. Cheyenne, WY
3. Hanford, CA	3. Prescott, AZ
4. Los Angeles, CA	4. Tucson, AZ
5. Modesto, CA	5. Albuquerque, NM
6. Pittsburgh, PA	6. Redding, CA
7. Salt Lake City, UT	7. Colorado Springs, CO
8. Logan, UT	8. Flagstaff, AZ
9. Fairbanks, AK	9. Anchorage, AK
10. Merced, CA	10. Boise, ID

Source: Adapted from State of the Air, American Lung Association (2012a, 2012b).

Note: These are the most polluted cities as of July 31, 2012.

In the state of Illinois, we can find the air quality index every day for every zip code. On November 4, 2011, Chicago had an air quality index of 29, which was given a good score.

The Illinois Pollution Control Board (IPCB) offers an e-library with helpful resources.

Global Sustainability Conferences

Rio Conference on Sustainability 1992

In 1992, the UN Conference on Environment and Development convened in Rio de Janeiro. The conference resulted in a number of proclamations and the setting of Agenda 21 for all nations.

The published documents begin with these principles:

Principle 1

Human beings are at the centre of concerns for sustainable development. They are entitled to a healthy and productive life in harmony with nature.

Principle 2

States have, in accordance with the Charter of the United Nations and the principles of international law, the sovereign right to exploit their own resources pursuant to their own environmental and developmental policies, and the responsibility to ensure that activities within their jurisdiction or control do not cause damage to the environment of other States or of areas beyond the limits of national jurisdiction.

Principle 3

The right to development must be fulfilled so as to equitably meet developmental and environmental needs of present and future generations.

Principle 4

In order to achieve sustainable development, environmental protection shall constitute an integral part of the development process and cannot be considered in isolation from it.

Principle 5

All States and all people shall cooperate in the essential task of eradicating poverty as an indispensable requirement for sustainable development, in order to decrease the disparities in standards of living and better meet the needs of the majority of the people of the world.

Principle 6

The special situation and needs of developing countries, particularly the least developed and those most environmentally vulnerable, shall be given special priority. International actions in the field of environment and development should also address the interests and needs of all countries.

Principle 7

States shall cooperate in a spirit of global partnership to conserve, protect and restore the health and health and integrity of the Earth's ecosystem. In view of the different contributions to global environmental degradation, States have common but differentiated responsibilities. The developed countries acknowledge the responsibility that they bear in the international pursuit of sustainable development in view of the pressures their societies place on the global environment and of the technologies and financial resources they command.

Principle 8

To achieve sustainable development and a higher quality of life for all people, States should reduce and eliminate unsustainable patterns of production and consumption and promote appropriate demographic policies.

Principle 9

States should cooperate to strengthen endogenous capacity building for sustainable development by improving scientific understanding through exchanges of scientific and technological knowledge, and by enhancing the development, adaptation, diffusion and transfer of technologies, including new and innovative technologies.

Principle 10

Environmental issues are best handled with the participation of all concerned citizens, at the relevant level. At the national level, each individual shall have appropriate access to information concerning the environment that is held by public authorities, including information on hazardous materials and activities in their communities, and the opportunity to participate in decision-making processes. States shall facilitate and encourage public awareness and participation by making information widely available. Effective access to judicial and administrative proceedings, including redress and remedy, shall be provided.

Principle 11

States shall enact effective environmental legislation. Environmental standards, management objectives and priorities should reflect the environmental and developmental context to which they apply. Standards applied by some countries may be inappropriate and of unwarranted economic and social cost to other countries, in particular developing countries.

Principle 12

States should cooperate to promote a supportive and open international economic system that would lead to economic growth and sustainable development in all countries, to better address the problems of environmental degradation. Trade policy measures for environmental purposes should not constitute a means of arbitrary or unjustifiable discrimination or a disguised restriction on international trade. Unilateral actions to deal with environmental challenges outside the jurisdiction of the importing country should be avoided. Environmental measures addressing transboundary or global environmental problems should, as far as possible, be based on an international consensus.

Principle 13

States should develop national law regarding liability and compensation for the victims of pollution and other environmental damage. States shall also cooperate in an expeditious and more determined manner to develop further international law regarding liability and compensation for adverse effects of environmental damage caused by activities within their jurisdiction or control to areas beyond their jurisdiction.

Principle 14

States should effectively cooperate to discourage or prevent the relocation and transfer to other States of any activities and substances that cause severe environmental degradation or are found to be harmful to human health.

Principle 15

In order to protect the environment, the precautionary approach shall be widely applied by States according to their capabilities. Where there are threats of serious or irreversible damage, lack of full scientific certainty shall not be used as a reason for postponing cost-effective measures to prevent environmental degradation.

Principle 16

National authorities should endeavor to promote the internationalization of environmental costs and the use of economic instruments, taking into account the approach that the polluter should, in principle, bear the cost of pollution, with due regard to the public interest and without distorting international trade and investment.

Principle 17

Environmental impact assessment, as a national instrument, shall be undertaken for proposed activities that are likely to have a significant adverse impact on the environment and are subject to a decision of a competent national authority.

Principle 18

States shall immediately notify other States of any natural disasters or other emergencies that are likely to produce sudden harmful effects on the environment of those States. Every effort shall be made by international community to help States so afflicted.

Principle 19

States shall provide prior and timely notification and relevant information to potentially affected States on activities that may have a significant adverse transboundary environmental effect and shall consult with those States at an early stage and in good faith.

Principle 20

Women have a vital role in environmental management and development. Their full participation is therefore essential to achieve sustainable development.

Principle 21

The creativity, ideals and courage of the youth of the world should be mobilized to forge a global partnership in order to achieve sustainable development and ensure a better future for all.

Principle 22

Indigenous people and their communities and other local communities have a vital role in environmental management and development because of their knowledge and traditional practices. States should recognize and duly support their identity, culture, and interests and enable their effective participation in the achievement of sustainable development.

Principle 23

The environment and natural resources of people under oppression, domination and occupation shall be protected.

Principle 24

Warfare is inherently destructive of sustainable development. States shall therefore respect international law providing protection for the environment in times of armed conflict and cooperate in its further development, as necessary.

Principle 25

Peace, development and environmental protection are interdependent and indivisible.

Principle 26

States shall resolve all their environmental disputes peacefully and by appropriate means in accordance with the Charter of the United Nations.

Principle 27

States and people shall cooperate in good faith and in a spirit of partnership in the fulfillment of the principles embodied in this Declaration and in the further development of international law in the field of sustainable development. (UN Agenda 21, accessed on 6/2012 at http://www.un.org/esa/dsd/agenda21/ © United Nations. Reproduced with permission.)

The United Nations established the Division for Sustainable Development, the Economic and Social Development Division for Sustainable Development. The following is an excerpt from their stated objectives:

Objectives

9.11. The basic and ultimate objective of this programme area is to reduce adverse effects on the atmosphere from the energy sector by promoting policies or programmes, as appropriate, to increase the contribution of environmentally sound and cost-effective energy systems, particularly new and renewable ones, through less polluting and more efficient energy production, transmission, distribution and use. This objective should reflect the need for equity, adequate energy supplies and increasing energy consumption in developing countries, and should take into consideration the situations of countries that are highly dependent on income generated from the production, processing and export, and/or consumption of fossil fuels and associated energy-intensive products and/or the use of fossil fuels for which countries have serious difficulties in switching to alternatives, and the situations of countries highly vulnerable to adverse effects of climate change. (UN Agenda 21, Sec II, chapter 9, article 9.11 accessed on 6/2012 at http://www.un.org/esa/dsd/agenda21/res_agenda 21_09.shtml © United Nations Reproduced with permission.)

To achieve these objectives, the United Nations made recommendations that governments cooperate in finding environmentally sound energy sources and develop the methodologies to make environmental and policy decisions that contributed to sustainable development.

The United Nations advocated the promotion of research and development to improve energy efficiency in all sectors, industrial, commercial, and residential. It also encouraged increased educational activity in pursuit of knowledge of sustainable development practices.

The United Nations was created after World War II, primarily to promote peacekeeping across the globe. The United Nations provides peacekeeping in times of conflict, and humanitarian relief. Its power to fulfill these principles lies in a unified effort of nations.

The UN statement of principles in 1992 was a collection of idealistic notions about the way the world should be. The members of the United Nations' intention in having sustainable development conferences is to create a better tomorrow for global citizens.

Kyoto Protocol

In 1997, the United Nations convened in Kyoto, Japan, seeking commitments to reduction of greenhouse gases (GHGs), proactively seeking ways to slow global warming. The Kyoto Protocol set a target for industrialized nations to reduce emissions by 5% from the 1990 levels during the period of 2008 to 2012. Countries that fail to meet the standards may attempt emissions trading with cleaner nations.

The Kyoto Protocol is a legally binding agreement under which industrialized countries will reduce their collective emissions of greenhouse gases by 5.2% compared to the year 1990 (but note that, compared to the emissions levels that would be expected by 2010 without the Protocol, this target represents a 29% cut). The goal is to lower overall emissions from six greenhouse gases—carbon dioxide, methane, nitrous oxide, sulfur hexafluoride, HFCs and PFCs—calculated as an average over the five-year period of 2008–12. National targets range from 8% reductions for the European Union and some others to 7% for the US, 6% for Japan, 0% for Russia, and permitted increases of 8% for Australia and 10% for Iceland. ("A Survey of Organizations, Providers and Research," n.d.)

The biggest emitter of these gases, the United States, did not ratify the protocol by a vote in the Senate of 95 to 0. U.S. politicians viewed it as cost prohibitive and objected to the exemption of China and India.

Approximately 197 other nations have ratified the protocol, including Japan, Canada, France, Italy, Germany, and every major industrialized country other than the United States.

Then-president George W. Bush was quoted as saying, "This is the American position because it's right for America. . . . We will not do anything that harms our economy, because first things first are the people who live in America." The deciding factor in the U.S. rejection of Kyoto was the perceived prohibitive costs required to meet the standards, and neither major political party endorsed its ratification.

Johannesburg Earth Summit

The United Nations convened in Johannesburg, South Africa, for the **Earth Summit** in 2002. The intention of the Earth Summit was to strengthen commitments on sustainable development. The United States continued its stance on the Kyoto Protocol. Other commitments sought included goals in health, poverty, and water.

The UN Earth Summit of 2012 was held in Rio de Janeiro, Brazil, and it continues to advance its objectives in sustainable development across the globe.

Industry Efforts

Steel Industry

Tim Timken, chairman of the Timken Company, said the following:

The industry has already reduced energy use per ton of steel shipped by 27 percent since the Kyoto baseline year of 1990, which also puts reduction by America's steel sector of greenhouse gas emissions far below Kyoto standards. We are not complacent, however. We are actively investing in research and new technologies to sustain significant progress. (Steelworks, 2007)

Several industries are considered "dirty"—the nature of their production methods contributes to air pollutants. Historically, the iron and steel industry has been responsible for a great portion of the emissions into the atmosphere. This industry accounted for 19% of energy use and about 25% of direct carbon dioxide emissions from the industry sector.

In the United States, the American Iron and Steel Institute joined Climate Vision, a Department of Energy voluntary program, and its efforts paid off. From 1994 to 2003, GHG emissions were reduced by 25%, despite an increase in production. However, Russia and the Ukraine's steel industry continue to use inefficient open-hearth furnaces.

Automobile Industry

The automobile industry has the dilemma of producing cars that consumers want to buy while meeting calls to produce more fuel-efficient vehicles. While SUVs rose in demand, so did complaints of their fuel consumption. Auto manufacturers produce what sells, so until customers vote with their dollars and increase the demand for alternative automobiles, we will not see any dramatic change in automakers' portfolios. Strategically, the auto companies must consider the possibility of a paradigmatic shift in consumer thinking. Whatever their own feelings about the environment, they are ultimately selling consumer goods. The following section discusses the sustainability efforts of several leading automobile manufacturers.

Ford Motor Company

All the automobile manufacturers have sustainability programmatic efforts featured on their websites. The Ford Motor Company distinctively lists its considerations for climate change. Their efforts included the following:

- Launch of the first Ford electric vehicle
- A reduction of carbon dioxide emissions in the United States from 2006 to 2010 by 10.5% and in Europe by 8.1%

- Increased production of EcoBoost fuel-saving engines to 1.5 million
- Four models offered that operated on 40 miles per gallon (mpg) or better
- Eighteen models offered in Europe that were below a threshold of 130 grams per kilometer of carbon dioxide emissions

Efforts in improving automobile fuel efficiency were accompanied by major efforts to reduce the energy consumption in manufacturing plants, and this resulted in a 3% improvement from 2010 to 2011. Ford achieved the goal set forth by the Chicago Climate Exchange (CCX) to reduce emissions between 2000 and 2010 by 6%.

Ford introduced a Product Sustainability Index (PSI) to design their automobiles and was vigilant about increasing the use of recycled materials ("2009/10 Blueprint for Sustainability: The Future at Work," 2010).

General Motors

General Motors (GM) offers 12 vehicles that exceed 30 mpg on the highway. They have vehicles that are powered by gas, diesel, biofuels, and electricity.

The Chevrolet Volt gets 94 mpg when operating on electricity and 40 mpg on gas. The Silverado Hybrid pickup gets 23 mpg on the highway, one of the leading pickups for fuel efficiency.

GM claims the following:

We're committed to alternative fuels and believe biofuels are the most significant near-term solution to reduce petroleum dependence and carbon dioxide emissions. We're the global leader in producing FlexFuel vehicles that operate on both gasoline and E85 ethanol, and offer more of these models than anyone else. ("General Motors Sustainability Report," n.d.)

GM's hybrid models include the Chevrolet Silverado and Tahoe, GMC Sierra and Yukon, and Cadillac Escalade. An eAssist technology increases fuel efficiency by 25%. GM is presently testing a number of vehicles that will operate on fuel cells that release water vapor rather than carbon dioxide emissions (General Motors Sustainability Report, n.d.).

Toyota

Toyota offers the best-selling hybrid, the Prius, which was introduced in 2000. Approximately 10% of Toyota's sales in the United States are hybrids, where 75% of hybrids are sold. The Prius contains carbon-neutral plastics known as "ecological plastics" that emit less carbon dioxide than petroleum-based plastics.

Toyota's efforts to make use of the 5 Rs (refine, reduce, reuse, recycle, and recover energy) include the following:

- A reduction of water usage per vehicle by 20% since 2003 with continued efforts to improve water management
- A reduction of landfill waste by 96% since 1999, accomplished through waste management and recycling
- Continued use of renewable materials such as plastic made from corn. They have introduced a soy oil-based polyurethane foam used for passenger seats in the Corolla and Lexus RX.
- The end-of-life vehicle (ELV) recovery rate exceeds 90%, and the goal is 95% by 2015.
- Metal returnable shipping containers saved over 30 million pounds of wood, 10 million pounds of cardboard, and $20 million in shipping costs since 2003. ("Toyota 2010 North America Environmental Report," 2010)

Land Rover UK

The British-manufactured Land Rover as a company has a target of a 25% reduction in carbon dioxide emissions and a 10% water consumption reduction from 2010 to 2012. Every Land Rover is 95% recoverable and reusable, with 85% recyclable. Land Rover offers carbon offset programs for its customers to offset their fuel consumption. "CO2 offsetting allows us to take action now, to reduce our impact on the environment, as part of an integrated carbon management plan" (Land Rover, n.d.).

Honda Motor Company

Honda introduced the most fuel-efficient engine at the time in 1974, the Civic CVCC engine. Honda sold the first hybrid vehicle in North America in 1999 and the first certified fuel-cell car.

The FCX Clarity FCEV emits no carbon dioxide and was released in Southern California in 2011. It emits water vapor, uses hydrogen, and is a certified zero-emission vehicle (ZEV). This vehicle is not in full production due to limited fueling options. As these options become more widely available, Honda will ramp up production to meet demand ("2011 North American Environmental Report Highlights," 2012).

Climate and Global Warming

Evidence for Global Warming

The biggest environmental debate concerns global warming. Some argue that it does not exist. Others fear its catastrophic repercussions.

The discussion on global warming begins with the evidence. From 1900 to 2000, there was a demonstrable increase in global temperature. The United Nations commissioned a study by the Intergovernmental Panel on Climate Change, which predicted that by 2100 the increase in North America would be from 3 to 6 degrees Celsius (5 to 10 degrees Fahrenheit) (Pachauri & Reisinger, 2007).

This increase is attributed to the increase in carbon dioxide in the atmosphere. This increase is partly natural and partly man-made, the man-made factor being the release of CFCs into the atmosphere.

Two human activities—(1) the burning of fossil fuels and (2) tropical deforestation—have had a big impact. The clearing and burning of the tropical rain forests releases approximately 25% as much carbon into the air as the burning of fossil fuels.

According to scientific studies, an increase in GHG emissions is leading to an increase in the earth's temperature that, in turn, leads to an increase in the intensity and duration of extreme weather phenomena like hurricanes and tornadoes. Over the past 100 years, the increase in average surface temperature has been about 1 degree Fahrenheit, and this increase most likely has impacted the loss of snow cover and ice packs (The Global Warming Statistics, n.d.).

This study clearly indicates that an increase in GHG emissions is causing the extreme weather episodes that have been occurring globally.

What are the effects of global warming? Chiras and colleagues (2002) and Craven (2009) listed the benefits:

1. The cost of heating might decline.

2. The far north would become more habitable (i.e., Northern Canada, Alaska).

3. Increased rainfall in some areas would increase the growing season for agriculture.

4. The rate of photosynthesis would increase, benefiting the yields of rice, corn, and wheat.

The list of harmful effects:

1. Summer cooling expenses would increase.

2. An increase in the melting of the polar ice cap would raise ocean levels. Cities highly vulnerable to such a shift include Boston, Philadelphia, New York City, Baltimore, and Washington, D.C., and could result in billions of dollars of flood damage.

3. Many rice-growing areas would be flooded out, including Pakistan, China, and Bangladesh.

4. There would be an increase in hurricanes and tropical storms.

5. Changing weather patterns would make the midwestern United States drier and less fertile.

6. Droughts in the Great Plains would trigger dust storms.

7. Carbon dioxide buildup would cost billions of dollars. New irrigation systems, dams, and levees would be required.

8. Many plants and animals would become extinct.

9. Diseases found in the tropics would spread northward.

10. Floods and droughts would cause serious health problems. (pp. 509–510)

Arguments Against Global Warming

Bjorn Lomborg (2001), a statistician from Sweden, challenged the prevailing arguments about global warming, questioning the following:

The way in which future scenarios have been arrived at and finds that forecasts of climate change of 6 degrees by the end of the century are not plausible. I shall argue that the limitations of computer modeling, the unrealistic nature of the basic assumptions made about technological change and political value judgments have distorted the scenarios being presented to the public. (p. 259)

Lomborg acknowledged that global warming is real but took issue with some of the dire forecasts. He argued that it would be more expensive to cut carbon dioxide emissions than to pay the costs of adaptation.

Business Implications

Outdoor air quality and IAQ are not the sole concern of the government. Businesses and individuals have a very real stake in this issue. For the individual, poor air can contribute to illness and disease. For the business, poor air can contribute to the poor health of its employees and the local community, thus increasing health care costs.

The beauty and aesthetics that nature provides are spoiled with smog and pollution, and the quality of life for citizens is degraded. Although one manufacturing plant or one home might consider efforts to reduce emissions insignificant, the cumulative effect is what the local community must breathe.

Conclusion

The air we breathe includes our own exhaust—the energy used to heat and cool our homes and buildings, to run our plants, and to mow our lawns all rises into the atmosphere and contributes to pollution. Those who live in cities suffer from poorer air quality than those in small towns and rural communities. The lure of jobs, entertainment, and city living results in traffic congestion and diminished air quality that can harm our health. Corporations, nonprofit organizations, and individual citizens all have a role in what goes into the air. It affects our economy and quality of life. Legislation has made strident efforts to clean up the air, and companies that fail to meet standards and do not make a serious effort to clean up their act should be more publicized. If consumers stopped buying the products of companies that missed standards, it might have a desirable impact.

Companies must monitor not only the pollutants their plants put into the air and local water supply but the energy and water consumption in their own workplaces. New standards for buildings have emerged that require a thorough examination of the use of energy and reduction of waste. But IAQ is also important to the health of employees, and proper air ventilation and the removal of pollutants are important actions.

Individual citizens often have a choice of modes of transportation. They may minimize their fuel consumption by taking public transportation. It obviously pays to conserve energy within the home. Air quality is affected by geography and air currents, sometimes the concentration of industry, and is related to the number of cars on the streets. Finding ways to economize on fuel and economize on actual miles driven can aid in the effort to improve air quality. Modes of public transportation also must be active in reducing emissions. Buses and trains also must pursue alternative energy sources.

This chapter reviewed the major issues of air quality, air pollution, and the potential impact of climate change.

KEY WORDS

Acid rain	Lead
Agenda 21	Liming
Air quality index	Nitrogen dioxide
Carbon monoxide	Ozone
Chlorofluorocarbons (CFCs)	Ozone layer
Clean Air Act	Particulate matter
Earth Summit	Radon
Global warming	Sick building syndrome (SBS)
Heat island effect	Sulfur dioxide
Indoor air quality (IAQ)	Suspended particulates
Kyoto Protocol	Troposphere

DISCUSSION QUESTIONS

1. How do air issues impact a business located in a large city? In a rural community?

2. What is today's air quality index in your location?

3. What does the Clean Air Act accomplish?

4. Which of the UN principles of sustainability are not environmental?

5. Why did the United States decline to ratify the Kyoto Protocol?

6. How could global warming affect your community? Would there be any positive effects?

7. How does smoking affect IAQ?

8. Determine the safety of exercising outside on a day of poor air quality.

9. Are there any environmental issues related to the building in which you work or study?

10. Some communities have outlawed burning leaves. Why?

11. Compare the sustainability reports of some major automobile manufacturers. How are they alike, and how do they differ?

RECOMMENDED WEBSITES

www.corporate.honda.com/environment/2011-report/statement.aspx

www.earthsummit2002.org

www.epa.gov/airtrends

www.fordmotorcompany.com

www.global-greenhouse-warming.com

www.gmsustainability.com

www.kyotoprotocol.com

www.landrover.com

www.stateoftheair.org

www.sustainable-steel.org

www.toyota.com/about/environmentreport2010/splash.html

www.un.org/esa/dso/agenda21/

2

Water Issues

Chapter Overview

Water is our lifeblood. It keeps us alive, flows through our bodies, and exudes from our pores. Water is our economy. It runs into our businesses, provides **drinking water**, lubricates industry, and stimulates the growth of the food we eat. Water provides spirituality and tranquility, as nothing soothes the soul as the sight of a sunset over the ocean. Finally, water can destroy; when in a torrential rage, it beats down upon us and destroys entire towns.

This chapter concerns all aspects of water that affect us—drinking water, irrigation systems, sewage systems, water pollution, and water conservation. The major issues about water are pollution and consumption. Individuals must consume water and have a certainty that they are drinking **purified water** that will not cause illness. Water is not only for drinking; it has recreational and industrial aspects. We have an expectation that the beauty of lakes, rivers, and oceans will not be spoiled by pollution, waste, and spillage. Fish make up an important proportion of our diet, and there has to be a certainty that what we are eating has not been tainted. In many areas of the world, scarcity and purity are immediate concerns.

Legislation is in place to protect our waters, and it is the responsibility of citizens and businesses to abide by these laws. Businesses cannot be irresponsible when it comes to water use, and fines can be imposed when they are detected polluting the local water.

Drinking Water

The **water cycle** or **hydrological cycle** is the endless process of evaporation of water into the atmosphere and returning as precipitation. About 30% of the precipitation we receive finds its way into lakes, rivers, ponds, and oceans (Chiras, 2010, p. 246). The rest either evaporates back into the atmosphere or transpires through plants and trees. When water evaporates back into the atmosphere, it forms clouds and moves with air currents until it may recur as rain miles away. Roughly 97% of the earth's water is in the oceans; the rest is freshwater (Chiras, 2010, p. 246).

The entire United States averages 30 inches of rain per year, but the different climate zones have a radically different distribution. While the Pacific Northwest and the Southeast receive tremendous amounts of rain, many parts of Arizona, Utah, and Nevada suffer from lack of rain.

Chiras, Reginald, and Owen (2002) noted that the average glass of drinking water has passed through eight humans before it got to you. Therefore, we better trust that our water treatment plants are doing the job.

If you live near a lake, you probably drink lake water that has been filtered and chlorinated. Water from rivers is dammed to form a reservoir of water. Other areas draw the water supply from groundwater pumped from wells.

However in Mexico, because the groundwater is close to the surface, it is easily contaminated by garbage. Impure water contains parasites that can take up residence in someone's intestines for some time, creating havoc on the bowels and stomach. The **Centers for Disease Control and Prevention (CDC)** lists a number of countries/regions where the water is unsafe to drink: most of Africa, Asia, the Middle East, Eastern Europe, Russia, South Africa, Argentina, Chile, Haiti, and the Dominican Republic. When traveling to these areas, one should drink bottled water, never include ice in a drink, brush teeth with bottled water, and be careful not to ingest water during a shower. International travelers should consult the CDC website prior to a visit to ascertain the safety of the drinking water and other local diseases.

Bottled Water

Louaillier (2008) listed the top five myths about bottled water:

1. Bottling plants are beneficial for communities—although they do provide jobs, they TAKE water. The average bottling plant employs

only 24 people (www.foodandwaterwatch.org) at primarily low-paying jobs. In India, a local bottling plant draws from the ground-water enough water to serve 75,000 people a day.

2. Bottled water tastes better. In one blind taste, two thirds of the participants preferred tap water to bottled brand names.

3. Bottled water is inexpensive—it still costs hundreds of thousands more than tap water.

4. Bottled water is cleaner and safer than tap water—less than 40% are actually regulated by the U.S. Food and Drug Administration (FDA). About 20% come from the same water source that tap water does and contains no additional filtration.

5. Bottled water doesn't negatively impact the environment. U.S. bottle production requires 17 million barrels of oil, enough to fuel 1 million cars. 86% of plastic bottles are never recycled.

According to ACNielsen, the United States spent about $9 million on bottled water in 2008, and the sales continue to grow.

According to the Mayo Clinic, people should drink water before and during exercise, with every meal, and between meals. Although various publications have recommended drinking eight glasses of water per day, the Mayo Clinic's advice is that if you are not thirsty, you are drinking an adequate amount (Mayo Clinic Staff, 2011).

Bottled water is regulated by the FDA and requires bottlers to identify the type of water.

Water Pollution

Water pollution is a significant global problem. Water that becomes contaminated with chemicals, whether from industrial spills or improperly purified waste, not only kills fish and water life but also endangers human health, as well. In poor countries, it may be found that water purification is too expensive, and contaminated drinking water can lead to infectious diseases and infant mortality. The six countries with the highest infant mortality rate are Angola (17.5% of infants die in the first year of life), Afghanistan (14.9%), Niger (11.2%), Mali (11.1%), Somalia (10.5%), and South Sudan (10.2%); all are countries with polluted drinking water ("Country Comparison," 2012).

Water pollution causes citizens to raise questions. They may start to question if their water is safe to drink. Is it safe to swim in a lake? Can they eat the fish they catch? What are the causes and sources of local water pollution? How does the water quality of this lake or river compare to others?

Sewage

Sewage is one major contributor to water pollution. Companies are required by law to install water purification systems prior to discharging water into a stream. However, violators exist and the dumping of industrial waste jeopardizes not only drinking water but also the ecosystem as a whole.

Sewage treatment is an essential matter for public health. Sewage goes through two stages of treatment. The primary treatment acts like a sieve to filter out large objects and place the remaining sludge in a tank. The second stage removes and treats organic matter. The remaining liquid is chlorinated prior to distribution into lakes or streams.

Turk (1989) described the cycle that dumping sewage into a stream:

In a natural system, the growth of all organisms is controlled by the quantity of the nutrients available. The system is delicately balanced. If the supply of any essential ingredient is increased or decreased, the entire system may be upset. Imagine a clean, cool, flowing river that supports a healthy population of trout and salmon. The fish share the stream ecosystem with populations of plankton, larger plants, microorganisms, small aquatic worms, and many other types of organisms. Now suppose that someone dumps some sewage into this stream. The sewage doesn't poison aquatic plants and animals. To the contrary, sewage is loaded with nutrients. Plankton and algae will grow faster, and the fish that eat the plankton will be nourished as well. Yet the introduction of sewage may lead to severe ecological disruptions. In general, populations of small animals grow faster than populations of microscopic organisms, small worms, and larger sludge worms will expand. Algae will also grow rapidly. The problem is that all these organisms consume large quantities of oxygen. If their growth is rapid enough, they will use up most of the oxygen in the water, and fish will eventually suffocate and die.

It is important to emphasize that the sewage, by itself, does not kill fish. In fact, it nourishes them. But the sewage supports the growth of other forms of life that consume oxygen. It is the lack of oxygen that kills fish. (pp. 309–310)

Another source of water pollution is seepage into groundwater from chemical or industrial waste. Over time, improper disposal of materials can seep into the groundwater and will find its way into the drinking water. Iowa discovered that half of its city wells were polluted with pesticides.

When tests revealed toxic pollutants in Morris, Illinois, suspicion naturally arose that the water was the cause of every ailment the citizens nearby experienced. The tests in local wells discovered "dangerously high" levels of arsenic, selenium, lead, thallium, antimony, and other chemicals. One home tested extremely unsafe drinking water containing arsenic.

Blame was placed on Envirotech, which operates a landfill for nonhazard-ous waste. However, the **U.S. Environmental Protection Agency (EPA)** could not lay the blame on Envirotech and noted other potential pollutant sources: local agriculture and three local nuclear power plants.

Morris's conflict is one of jobs versus safety. The town needs the landfill, whether it is the source of pollution or not. The landfill provides jobs for a community with 13% unemployment. Additional tests on the water revealed lower levels of the chemical, suggesting this was a one-time spike, but the EPA was unable to discover the source of the pollution. Meanwhile, people have switched to drinking bottled water rather than putting their health at stake. These are the issues caused by pollution of the groundwater.

Ocean Pollution

The oceans absorb almost a quarter of all carbon emissions, which increases the acidity and endangering species. The rate of acidity has increased 30% in the past 250 years, but projections call for a doubling of the acidity in the next 40 years.

The increased acidity affects ocean life in several ways. First, it harms coral reefs, shells, and shellfish. The weaker shells also harm lobsters, mussels, and many smaller organisms that larger fish feed upon. Coral reefs offer protection to coastal communities against severe storms and hurricanes, and the weakening of the reefs would increase the danger for these areas. It would also cause problems for fishing and tourism.

Offshore drilling also puts oceans at risk with potential oil spills bringing damaging losses to local businesses. The 2010 British Petroleum (BP) spill described later in this chapter caused severe economic problems to the state of Louisiana.

Beachgoers experiencing pollution can receive ear infections, stomach flu, and rashes from polluted beach water. Beaches should be made safe through frequent testing and efforts to protect the water. Coastal communities must have a strategic vision to protect the future of their beaches, as in the case of Florida.

Florida's Coastal and Ocean Future

The threat of pollution to Florida's beaches resulted in the report "Florida's Coastal and Ocean Future," which was endorsed by 160 coastal and ocean businesses.

The report's principal author, Julie Hauserman (2007), introduced her topic:

Nothing defines Florida more than its coast. People come from around the world to swim, boat, scuba dive, surf, fish, and kayak, enjoy our beaches, and see our unique coastal wildlife. The coast is Florida's economic engine. But alarming changes are taking place, from plummeting fish catches to outbreaks of harmful algae, dying marine life, and beach closures. (p. 6)

In 2005, tourists were greeted with algae-covered beaches and dead fish, dolphins, sea turtles, and manatees washing ashore. Hemmed in by development, our beaches are eroding and our reefs and fisheries continue to decline. Florida's next governor can—and must—boldly act to stop this alarming decline and to reform coastal management policies before we lose the natural resources that fuel our economy and our identity as Floridians.

A retiree trying his luck fishing off a pier in Pensacola described one of the problems plainly: "'Twelve years ago, you could catch three coolers (of fish) in three hours,' he said. 'Now, you're lucky to get a cooler in three days'" (Hauserman, 2007, p. vi).

Hauserman's (2007) report listed six main areas to address:

1. Strengthening controls on coastal development.

2. Reducing the pollution that degrades Florida's waters, and maintaining, if not improving, water quality standards.

3. Keeping offshore oil drilling away from Florida's economically valuable beaches.

4. Ending overfishing and preserving marine and coastal ecosystems.

5. Helping Florida become a leader in reducing pollution sources, especially carbon dioxide emissions that contribute to sea level rise and more intense hurricanes.

6. Strengthening governance by establishing unified, coordinated leadership for ocean and coastal resources. (p. vii) (Reprinted with permission from the National Resources Defense Council.)

As Florida has grown, development has threatened the beaches. As Hauserman (2007) put it, "Coastal development is increasingly moving seaward, while the sea is moving landward." Florida's population has grown from 2 million in the 1940s to 16 million, with 3 million added in the 1990s. Florida is soon to surpass New York as the third largest state (after California and Texas), and growth projections are for 26 million by 2030.

This development has resulted in loving the beaches to death, with 38% of the beaches considered to be in a state of critical erosion. To protect the coast against storms, seawalls are built—on the one hand protecting homes, on the other eroding the beaches that bring tourists and help the economy.

A number of sources add to the pollution. Sixty-two Superfund sites threaten to contaminate public waters. Radioactive and nutrient-filled wastewater sits in large pits, and a hurricane can distribute this toxic water all around the state.

Leaks from sewage disposal systems are problematic as are runoff from agriculture. Another source of pollution is cruise ships, which can hold 5,000 people. A typical cruise generates 25,000 gallons of sewage from toilets and 143,000 gallons from sinks, kitchens, and showers ("Cruise Ship Pollution: Overview," n.d.).

These cruise ships are not regulated by the Clean Water Act of 1972 (CWA), which allows discharge beyond 3 miles from shore.

The Hauserman (2007) Florida report recommends the following actions to protect the state from ocean pollution:

1. Halt the state's misguided efforts to weaken water quality standards.

2. Require developers who apply for Environmental Resource Permits (ERP) to prove they have first made all efforts to avoid impacts to the state's water resources.

3. Include an enforceable nitrogen standard in the Everglades Restoration Plan.

4. Strengthen watershed-based planning to protect springs and sinkholes, which feed coastal waters.

5. Upgrade the state's stormwater regulations.

6. Require at a minimum that adequate capacity and infrastructure for sewage and stormwater treatment exists prior to issuing permits for new development.

7. Require that any waste injected underground be treated to advanced nutrient-stripping levels.

8. Use energy efficiency, renewable and other clean energy technologies to meet growing energy needs.

9. Bring polluting industrial facilities, such as paper mills and power plants, into compliance with modern pollution regulations.

10. Update management plans for the 41 aquatic preserves.

11. Develop a comprehensive program to treat, regulate, and reduce wastes from the many cruise ships and gambling boats that dock in the state's ports. (pp. 11–12) (Reprinted with permission from the National Resources Defense Council.)

Overfishing

An important issue to the sustainability of our oceans is the preservation of marine ecosystems. We sometimes forget that environmental management applies to the sea as well as the land. We are eating more than the ocean can replenish. In **overfishing,** many of the fish we eat today may become a thing of the past if trends continue.

The leading causes of overfishing is not really our appetites for fish but the combination of overcapacity in marine fisheries—high levels of "bycatch." Fishermen discard between 25% and 30% of their catches and cause habitat damage.

Hauserman's (2007) Florida report made a number of recommended actions for the protection of marine ecosystems and fisheries including the following:

1. Focus on managing special places and ecosystems.

2. Redefine the principal objective of marine fishery policy to be the protection of marine ecosystems.

3. Achieve an integrated and adaptive ecosystem management framework that includes marine fisheries.

4. Establish partnerships between the Florida Fish and Wildlife Conservation Commission and federal ecosystem-based fishery management efforts through the South Atlantic Fishery Management Council.

5. Use innovative management tools, including marine protected areas and no-take/no-fishing marine reserves.

6. End overfishing in the several fisheries in the South Atlantic and Gulf of Mexico where that destructive practice is now occurring and rapidly rebuild depleted fish populations to healthy and abundant levels. (pp. 17–18) (Reprinted with permission from the National Resources Defense Council.)

Water Scarcity

The world has enough water for its population—just not always in the right places. While one area complains about its chronic rainfall, another area has not seen rain for months. Lake Baikal, in Siberia, Russia, is the largest lake in the world and contains 20% of the freshwater in the world. It is larger than all the Great Lakes of the United States put together. However, the lake is surrounded by mountains, and the frigid winters result in a sparse population. This one lake could easily quench the thirst of the entire continent of Africa.

The following table (Table 2.1) illustrates the major differences in water consumption across the globe. The quantities are listed in cubic kilometers per year. Consumption is listed as cubic meters per person per year. Of the countries listed, only the United States, Canada, and Australia exceed 1,000 per person per year.

Six countries (Brazil, Canada, China, Colombia, Indonesia, and Russia) contain more than half of the world's freshwater. Meanwhile, the United Nations predicts that by the year 2025 forty-eight countries will face water scarcity.

Table 2.1 The World's Water Consumption in Cubic Kilometers Per Year (2008–2009)

Country	Annual Renewable Water Resources (km3/yr)	Freshwater Withdrawal	Per Capita Withdrawal (m3/p/yr)
Kenya	30.2	1.58	46
Nigeria	286.2	8.01	61
South Africa	50.0	12.50	264
Canada	3300	44.72	1386
Haiti	14	0.99	116
Mexico	457.2	78.22	731
USA	3069	477.	1600
Brazil	8233	59.3	318
Colombia	2132	10.71	235
Peru	1913	20.13	720
Afghanistan	65	23.26	779
Bahrain	0.1	0.3	411
China	2829.6	549.76	415
India	1907.8	645.84	585
Japan	430.0	88.43	690
Italy	175.0	41.98	723
Australia	398.0	24.06	1193
France	189.0	33.16	548
Germany	188.0	38.01	460

Source: Gleick et al. (2008).

Meanwhile, the average U.S. resident uses 150 gallons of water per day for domestic and municipal purposes, compared to 3 gallons per day in Kenya and 30 gallons per day in the United Kingdom. This consumption was in the face of a major drought in the Southeast United States, which saw 2007 set records for the driest year on record for Georgia, North Carolina, and Tennessee.

Water Conservation

Approximately 95% of the U.S. surface freshwater comes from the Great Lakes, and 20% of the demand for water supply comes from the Chicago-to-Milwaukee corridor, making water conservation an important consideration. Weighing the threat of a drying groundwater that flows into the lakes—with an average population increase of 4.4%—Chicago has embarked on a $620 capital improvement program that replaces 50 miles of leaking water mains each year. This improvement yields 120 million gallons of water each year. Water usage actually decreased from 1990 to 2001 from 780 million gallons per day in 1990 to 638 million gallons per day in 2001 due to the vigilance of the city's water districts.

A City Water Agenda: Chicago

In 2003, Chicago outlined a comprehensive water agenda. It was appropriate that Chicago should note the importance of water, as it depends upon Lake Michigan for drinking water, recreation, and fishing.

The Chicago Water Agenda (2003) has the following prelude:

WATER—OUR GREATEST NATURAL TREASURE

Throughout history, great cities have always had one thing in common: water. Chicago's world-class status is owed largely to its position at the confluence of the Chicago River and Lake Michigan. These waterways signified transportation and trade to Chicago's settlers and continue to attract millions of visitors to our city every year.

Beyond the Lake Michigan shoreline, our water resources extend throughout, and beneath, the City. They are the Chicago River, Lake Calumet, the Calumet River, thousands of acres of wetlands, creeks, streams and lagoons, as well as canals and channels. Equally important are the thousands of miles of pipes, man-made tributaries that have—for over 100 years—delivered drinking water and helped us manage storm water.

These resources are critical to our public health, safety, economy, and quality of life. They provide recreational opportunities like boating, fishing, and swimming, our waterways provide natural experiences in an urban setting. We are fortunate to live near some of the cleanest drinking water in the world.

With nearly 20 percent of the Earth's, and 95 percent of the nation's, fresh surface water supply, a walk along the Great Lakes shoreline suggests our waters are vast and inexhaustible.

They are not. We must not take these resources for granted.

Chicagoans before us lifted the City out of a swamp, reversed the Chicago River to protect the drinking water supply, and connected us to the Mississippi River. Now the region is building one of the nation's largest public works projects to manage stormwater. These engineering fixes are not enough. The challenges ahead will once again require us to lead by example and demonstrate new ways of thinking about water.

Nearly a century ago, Chicago introduced the first land use plan for a modern city. Now we must again be forward thinking and chart a course for our important water resources. We must take actions now that will benefit citizens who follow.

Chicago's Water Agenda 2003 outlines a strategy for caring for our water resources as a whole. Understanding that our water resources work as a complex and connected system, the agenda calls for a comprehensive approach to the City's treasured waterways to ensure that they are conserved for future generations, protected and improved, and managed so that water can continue to sustain us, connect us as neighbors and define our community's role nationally and internationally. (Copyright City of Chicago. All rights reserved. Used with permission of the City of Chicago.)

Examples of conservation efforts include the following:

- Ensuring that all new drinking fountains have on/off controls.
- Upgrading 43 swimming pools so that they safely re-circulate water.
- Installing splash fountains that re-circulate water.
- Disconnecting downspouts that connect to the sewer system on Park District facilities so that stormwater is used for irrigation and for recharging groundwater.
- Examines the Building Code for opportunities to allow for more efficient fixtures, like waterless urinals and dual flush toilets.
- Explore the potential of installing gray water systems to irrigate landscaping or for flush toilets in public buildings.
- Plant native species that are drought tolerant to reduce the need for watering.
- Recover and recycle water in industrial processes.
- Repair or install cooling towers.
- Upgrade valves on process machines.
- Savings identified to date from 12 audits = 130 million gallons of water per year.
- The City will develop a plan to ensure that everyone pays for water based on usage. (The Chicago Water Agenda, 2003. Copyright City of Chicago. All rights reserved. Used with permission of the City of Chicago.)

Chicago's main waterway is the Chicago River, which snakes through the city, its currents reversed by an early 20th-century engineering feat. This river is traveled by more than 50,000 commercial and passenger boats each year and sustains such fish as yellow perch, sunfish, bass, and trout, and birds like ducks, kingfishers, herons, and blackbirds.

Challenges to the waterways are listed as follows:

- Effectively dealing with municipal storm and wastewater
- Keeping our beaches safe and open for swimming
- Addressing pollution that is buried on our river and lake bottoms
- Reducing the pollution that enters our waterways from the air
- Ensuring that recreational users are being good stewards
- Eliminating the introduction of harmful invasive species
- Reducing the environmental and health risks associated with international shipping
- The Chicago Park District, which manages the City's beaches, uses the most aggressive testing schedule of any community in the region.
- Chicago has inspected and repaired all sewer infrastructure within one half mile of the Lake Michigan shoreline.
- The Park District will continue to explore the effectiveness of a filter netting to prevent excessive bacteria from entering the swimming area.
- The City will conduct a pilot study on equipment that will reduce the time needed for bacteria test results.
- The City will work with the United States Geological Survey to create a computer model that can predict when bacteria levels at the beaches will be unsafe. (The Chicago Water Agenda, 2003. Copyright City of Chicago. All rights reserved. Used with permission of the City of Chicago.)

Water Legislation

The U.S. government has created legislation to assure that all citizens have the confidence that water is safe to drink. Failure to abide by these laws results in fines and penalties and negative public relations.

The Clean Water Act

The CWA requires that states develop water standards for bodies of water within their boundaries. This act dictates the acceptable volume of pollutants that can be discharged into our lakes and rivers. The EPA monitors these measurements. The major source of water pollution is "nonpoint source" runoff, which comes from a number of sources.

Each state tests the water and must report to the EPA where there are excessive pollution spots. States determine total maximum daily loads (TMDLs), the amount of acceptable pollutants that can be discharged.

TMDLs are determined by adding nonpoint source pollution to point source pollution, plus a safety buffer. States must report any sources of pollutants—that is, industry sources—determine why these pollutions have exceeded the standards, and provide a plan for reducing the pollution.

The EPA lists the following areas that contribute to **nonpoint pollution,** which is pollution carried by rain or snowmelt away from the source (see Table 2.2).

The CWA established a system for water discharge: the **National Pollutant Discharge Elimination System (NPDES),** which requires permits for pollution discharge. When industrial facilities discharge into the sewer system, termed **publicly owned treatment works (POTW),** the discharge must be treated.

Safe Drinking Water Act

The **Safe Drinking Water Act (SDWA),** established as law in 1974, covers all water used for human consumption, thus including bathwater, cooking

Table 2.2 Nonpoint Pollution Sources

Industry	Nonpoint
Agriculture	Animal waste
	Contour farming
	Crop rotation
	Buffer strips
	Livestock exclusion
	Fertilizer management
Construction	Disturbed area limits
	Soil stabilization
	Runoff detention/retention
Urban areas	Flood storage
	Runoff detention/retention
	Street cleaning
Forestry	Ground cover maintenance
	Limiting disturbed areas
	Log removal techniques
	Construction of haul roads
	Removal of debris

Source: "What Is Nonpoint Source Pollution?" (n.d.).

water, and anything that comes out of the household faucet. The average American uses 8 liters a day for drinking and cooking, but one flush of a toilet uses 20 liters.

The act established maximum contaminant levels of such toxic elements as mercury, cyanide, benzene, and aluminum. The act prohibited lead pipes, solder, or flux for use in human consumption water. The importance of monitoring these levels is illustrated by the discovery that benzene leaked into a water supply from underground gasoline tanks led to increased risk of cancer.

State Water Protection

States must work with the EPA in order to do as follows:

1. Ensure rivers, streams, and lakes support all uses for which they are designated, including protection of aquatic life, recreation, and drinking water

2. Ensure safe drinking water

3. Protect groundwater for drinking and other beneficial uses

The EPA's website, www.epa.gov, provides local information state by state concerning issues facing that community. The EPA is divided into regional districts that enforce regulations.

Typical questions that citizens want to know about their water include the following:

1. Is it safe to swim in this lake?

2. Can I eat the fish I caught?

3. How does the water quality of this lake or river compare to others?

4. Is the water safe to drink?

5. If buying lakefront property, how does the water quality of this lake compare to others?

6. What are the causes and sources of local water pollution?

Water Disasters

The following cases illustrate the serious national problems that water disasters can cause. Some are man-made and others are from natural disasters. In every case, businesses in these communities are forced to abandon, forsaking a lifetime's work. The lessons learned from these cases emphasize the need for community water and disaster planning.

Mismanaged Water: The Story of the Aral Sea

The importance of a rational national plan is illustrated by the impact of a Russian government decision 50 years ago. The Russian government was pressured to divert water to farmland, and canals were constructed to divert water from the Aral Sea. If there was an environmental impact study performed, it must have been ignored because economics guided the decision. In 1956, the old Soviet Union opened the Kara Kum Canal, intended to divert water for farming. Three more canals were constructed, intended to irrigate the Uzbek and Kazakh deserts. What followed was what author Marq de Villiers (2001) termed, "Without any exaggeration, the Aral Sea has become the greatest man-caused ecological catastrophe our benighted planet has yet seen, an awful warning of the consequences of hubris, greed, and the politics of ignorance."

One village, Muynak, was originally an island in the Amu Darya Delta. By 1970, the sea was 10 kilometers away. By 1980, 40 kilometers, and by 1998, 75 kilometers (1 kilometer = 0.62 miles). The salinity of the Aral increased tenfold. The commercial fishing industry, which had provided 50,000 tons of fish per year and employed 60,000 people, was shut down completely.

Wildlife disappeared from the region. Soviet agriculture never discontinued the use of DDT, and the pesticides built up in the sea. The dried-up seabed was heavy with pesticide residue, and toxic chemicals and dust storms carried poisonous fumes across the region.

De Villiers (2001) wrote the following:

> If you stand on what had been the shore of this once great lake, you can see the salts in the air. Throat cancer, the local doctors say, has reached epidemic proportions. So have kidney and liver diseases, arthritis, chronic bronchitis, typhoid, and hepatitis A. It is worst in the Amyu Darya Delta, a region called Karakappakstan, where the bioaccumulation of toxins is so great that mothers have been advised not to breast-feed their babies, and infant mortality has climbed past one hundred deaths per thousand births. (p. 110)

Unfortunately, the collapse of the Soviet Union coincided with plans to rescue the Aral Basin, and the sea appears to be headed for oblivion.

Oil Spills: Exxon Valdez and British Petroleum

The importance of clean water is magnified during instances of natural and man-made disasters. Oil spills, hurricanes, and earthquakes put people in situations where clean water becomes a scarce resource. In 1989, the ship Exxon Valdez was grounded off Prince William Sound in Alaska, spilling 10.9 million gallons of oil.

The spill damaged 1,100 miles of coastline and required 11,000 personnel and 1,400 boats in repair efforts. The economic loss was calculated as ranging from $4.9 to $7.2 billion.

The spill killed at least 1,000 sea otters, 302 seals, and 250,000 birds. Exxon was fined $150 million by the U.S. government, of which 125 was forgiven due to the costs incurred by Exxon in the cleanup.

The *Encyclopedia of Earth* (Cleveland, 2010) listed five lessons to be learned from the *Exxon Valdez* disaster:

1. Clean-up attempts can cause more damage than the oil. There can be a strong reaction from the chemical methods used to clean.

2. The oil can resurface years later on the beaches and harm nearby animals.

3. Rocky shores should have high priority for the cleanup due to the slow penetration of the oil on this terrain.

4. Prolonged exposure to the oil will have continued impact on sea birds and mammals. The initial destruction is devastating, but there is an aftereffect.

5. Exposure of fish embryos to the oil has long-term consequences on reproduction and mortality.

The BP spill in 2010 was so massive that every 4 days it spilled the equivalent of the Exxon Valdez spill. A blowout in the *Deepwater Horizon* oil rig spilled 4.9 billion barrels of oil, or 170 million gallons, into the Gulf of Mexico, almost 20 times the amount spilled by the Valdez.

As oil and gas reserves have been nearly depleted close to shore, drilling has increased in the deepest depths of the Gulf of Mexico. The Gulf accounts for 30% of U.S. oil production, and two thirds of the oil now comes from depths exceeding 1,000 feet (Bourne, 2010, p. 44). With deepwater drilling comes increased difficulty of controlling any blowouts that may occur (Bourne, 2010, p. 44).

Eleven workers lost their lives in the Deepwater blowout, which had the following statistics:

- 130 miles long and 70 miles wide—size of the oil slick in the Gulf.
- 436,000 gallons of dispersant sprayed on the oil spill for clean up.
- 50,000 barrels of mud to stop the flow of leaking oil.
- 1.6 billion—confirmed cost of the spill to BP, as of 6/14/2010.
- $75 million—government mandated cap on oil company liability.
- $1.5 billion—amount the spill will cost insurers.
- $62 million—claims paid to 26,500 Gulf residents as of 6/14/2010.
- 27—offshore gulf drilling operations approved for operation since the BP spill. ("The BP Gulf of Mexico Oil Spill Update," n.d.)

Katrina

The worst natural disaster in the history of the United States was Hurricane Katrina and its devastation of New Orleans, Louisiana. Katrina caused 1,800 deaths and tens of billions of dollars in damage. Because New Orleans is an important port for shipping lanes, responsible for as much as one third of all gas passes through this port, rebuilding New Orleans was the only option.

New Orleans continues to be in danger due to the chance of flooding of the Mississippi River, the disappearance of surrounding wetlands, and the deteriorating levees.

Costanza, Mitsch, and Daly (2006) prescribed seven principles for the restoration of New Orleans:

1. Let the water decide. Since New Orleans is built below sea level, creating wetlands inside the levees would be helpful. Future building should consider construction that can accommodate floods if and when they occur.

2. Avoid abrupt boundaries between deepwater systems and uplands. The levees cause abrupt boundaries and the authors suggest a multiple line of defense that would include barrier islands, wetlands, and natural ridges.

3. Restore natural capital. The restoration of the wetlands is paramount to New Orleans, not only for storm protection, but also for economic reasons.

4. Use the resources of the Mississippi River to rebuild the coast, changing the current system that constrains the river between levees. This measure includes reconnecting the river to the deltaic plain, barrier island restoration, use of dredged sediments, and canal and bank removal.

5. Restore New Orleans with high-performance green buildings and a car-limited urban environment. Rebuilding a city brings the opportunity to make ecological choices.

6. Rebuild New Orleans with 21st century standards of diversity, tolerance, fairness, and justice. Katrina revealed New Orleans to be a city of the haves and have-nots. As the population returns to the city, all efforts should be made to eliminate racism and classism.

7. Restore the Mississippi River Basin to minimize coastal pollution and the threat of river flooding. Consideration of farming practices along the river should include sustainable agriculture.

Thailand—The Tsunami

On December 26, 2004, the Indian Ocean tsunami that hit 11 countries caused 150,000 dead. This was a natural disaster that could not be prevented.

An earthquake at the bottom of the ocean floor sent a wave as far as 3,000 miles. Immediately prior to the arrival of the wave in Phuket, Thailand, the ocean's edge rapidly receded and curious spectators walked far out into the beach to see what was going on.

One resident in a local village had seen a *National Geographic* special on tsunamis and warned his village to seek cover, saving 1,500 lives. Those who ventured out on the beach were swallowed up within a few minutes by a wave judged as high as 50 feet. From Thailand to Africa, this tsunami wreaked devastating damage.

But the aftereffects of the tsunami were just as serious, since there was no clean water to drink. A massive humanitarian aid effort was undertaken. Tsunamis are rare, but hurricanes are not. In any case of natural disaster, the damage to the water systems creates an unsanitary and deadly situation.

Drought of Lake Lanier

Lake Lanier, 60 miles northeast of Atlanta, is the main water source for over 5 million people in Georgia and the Southeast. In 2007, the lake was so low that it faced running out of water—this for a lake that is 38,000 acres.

Mayor of Atlanta Shirley Franklin called for water restrictions, including an indefinite ban on new rezoning. Developers could not build. Two of the largest water consumers in the state, Coca-Cola and Gatorade, grew increasingly concerned, as the drought had gone on for 3 years.

The governor of Georgia, Sonny Perdue, blamed the U.S. Army Corps of Engineers for releasing water to Florida. The drought happened as the population in greater Atlanta continued to climb as one of the fastest growing cities in the United States.

Plans to introduce Snow Mountain, an artificial ski hill in Stone Mountain Park, were put on hold. Then, the rains finally came back, and by 2009, the lake had recovered to prior depths. But in that period, the arguments from neighboring states about Georgia's water consumption exemplified how the scarcity of water can lead to conflict, both political and real.

Company Water Policies

Company sustainability reports should include information on the following:

- Goals statement
- Environmental report card
- Community and charitable activities
- Ethics and compliance statement

- Social responsibility activities
- Health and wellness activities
- Responsible marketing statement
- Product safety and quality activities
- Supplier partnerships

A study analyzed corporate social responsibility (CSR) and sustainability reports from 139 large companies in 11 water intensive industry sectors and found that though water reporting is becoming standard practice, some inconsistencies remain. Some of these are that water measurement is inconsistent, the supply chain issues are not considered, and the data on water recycling and water-related risks are not reported (Morikawa, Morrison, & Gleick, 2007).

Principles for Building Water Consciousness _____

Today's businesses must instill water awareness, both in practice and in policy. Although water conservation is an important contributor to the bottom line as it is a resource that is often wasted, it must be appreciated as an important source of employee and community health.

The disposal of industrial waste must be carefully considered so that it does not pollute and all legislative standards are met. Citizens take it for granted that the local drinking water is safe, and they are dependent on local governments and businesses to guarantee that certainty.

In the book *Water Consciousness*, Tony Clarke (2008) offered eight principles to build a new water consciousness:

1. *Water integrity:* Indigenous cultures have an appreciation of the sacredness of water and its power. An appreciation for the value of water is a starting point for its appreciation and conservation.

2. *Water commons:* Sharing with people and nature, water *belongs* to people and nature.

3. *Water sovereignty:* Water should be controlled by not-for-profit organizations.

4. *Water equity:* Water services should also be provided by public institutions.

5. *Water conservation:* We should only use the water we need and not be wasteful.

6. *Water quality:* Since clean water is a major health concern, all efforts should be made to avoid pollution and provide clean drinking water.

7. *Water security:* Water rights have been known to cause wars, so sharing among bordering countries, states, etc., is important.

8. *Water democracy:* "The operating principles of developing water consciousness include the recognition that water belongs first and foremost to people and nature, that it is deeply personal, and that it is local." (p.167)

Fourteen Actions You Can Take to Protect Our Water

Individuals can participate actively in many ways to assure safe and clean water. Since our planet depends so mightily upon water, taking an active role in its conservation is a worthwhile occupation.

1. Find out how much water you use.
2. Stop drinking bottled water.
3. Help create a clean water trust fund (www.foodandwaterwatch.org/water/trust-fund).
4. Conserve water inside.
5. Conserve water outside.
6. Don't pollute your watershed.
7. Learn about your watershed.
8. Help keep your watershed healthy.
9. Clean up agriculture.
10. Protect groundwater from depletion and degradation.
11. Learn about dams in your area. Oppose construction of new dams.
12. Reduce your energy use.
13. Support the right of water for everyone.
14. Help spread the word. (Lohan, 2008)

Business Implications

Businesses and organizations must pay more attention to water consumption than the mere paying of the water bill. In old buildings, the water pipe infrastructure must be updated to prevent cracks that can introduce contamination. The health of their employees is a major concern, and a safe drinking water environment at work should be guaranteed.

Vending machines are undoubtedly stocked with plastic water bottles, so recyclable bins should be placed in highly visible locations. Further efforts might be to encourage employees to drink from reusable containers.

Employees should be educated on water conservation. This is especially important in manufacturing operations that consume massive amounts of water for production.

Conclusion

In this chapter, we have reviewed the basic workings of the water cycle. We studied the ways we get our drinking water and the pros and cons of bottled water. Water is plentiful in some countries and a valued, rare commodity in others. In areas of water scarcity, water conservation is a practice that many of us do not practice.

Water has brought us many tragedies with the power and devastation caused by hurricanes and typhoons and at the other end of the spectrum, drought. Since it is so critical to our livelihood, so, too, must it not be taken for granted.

KEY WORDS

Centers for Disease Control and Prevention (CDC)

Drinking water

U.S. Environmental Protection Agency (EPA)

Hydrological cycle

National Pollutant Discharge Elimination System (NPDES)

Nonpoint pollution

Overfishing

Publicly owned treatment works (POTW)

Purified water

Safe Drinking Water Act (SDWA)

Water cycle

DISCUSSION QUESTIONS

1. Investigate your state's water policies. What actions is your state taking to reduce water pollution and water consumption? Could further action be taken?

2. Describe the types of water.

3. What defines safe drinking water?

4. Compare and contrast the pros and cons of water bottles. Does one outweigh the other? Explain your answer.

5. Describe the various ways sewage impacts the ecosystem.

6. What are the major processes involved in sewage treatment?

7. What are the major contributors to ocean pollution?

8. What are the most viable ways industries and businesses can reduce their water waste?

9. How do ocean liners contribute to pollution?

10. Name three important water legislation acts. Describe the main standards established by each.

11. Is the United States doing enough at the federal level to protect oceans, establish drinking standards, and reduce consumption? Why or why not?

12. How can businesses reduce their water consumption?

13. Name one company that is making strides toward more sustainable water practices. What are the strengths of the plan, and what are its weaknesses?

RECOMMENDED WEBSITES

www.eoearth.org

www.epa.gov

www.epa.state.il.us/water/

www.geology.com

www.mayoclinic.com

www.nrdc.org/oceans/

3

Sustainable Agriculture and Food

LEARNING OBJECTIVES

In this chapter, we will do the following:

- Discuss **sustainable agriculture.**
- Discuss the foods we eat.
- Recognize the differences between **natural** and organic foods.
- Examine companies involved in the food industry, including McDonald's, Wal-Mart, and Monsanto.
- Discuss malnutrition.

Chapter Overview

The food industry is one of the largest industries in the world. In the United States alone, 17% of the labor force is employed in the various segments of the food industry, which includes grocery stores, restaurants, food and beverage manufacturers, and agriculture. Its importance to the global economy cannot be understated. Sustainability issues within this industry include the production of safe and healthy food and healthy nutrition. This chapter begins with the current state of sustainable agriculture and contrasts that to organic farming. The next section reviews food consumption patterns in several countries. We discuss food safety and animal welfare issues. After a discussion on what we eat, we review the plight of the malnourished. Then, we look at several corporate approaches to sustainability, including Monsanto, McDonald's, Wal-Mart, and Cargill.

Farmers have the challenge of presenting bright and shiny fruits and vegetables to the market, because they sell a lot better than worm-eaten, sundamaged produce. Thus, food sellers often use chemicals to enhance the appearance of the produce.

We will then review the issues surrounding health and safety of our food consumption. Pesticides cause 200 to 1,000 deaths in the United States each year, with 45,000 serious poisonings. Those affected are usually farm workers.

Sustainable Agriculture

Sustainable agriculture embraces the same principles as the triple bottom line (TBL)—to achieve environmental, economic, and social goals. Farmers work by the old saying, "Make hay while the sun shines." In other words, they sometimes experience extreme swings in feast and famine. One year the crops are plentiful, and then years of drought may follow. Therefore, the farmer must budget for those lean times or else risk bankruptcy.

The environmental aspects of agricultural sustainability relate to the following:

- *Water conservation:* The message here is to use just what is needed and find ways to conserve through irrigation. Irrigation systems are available on the same principle as reduced volume showerheads—less water is released.
- *Water quality:* The two main issues are **salinization**—when salt content from crops damages the soil—and **contamination** from pesticides. Methods of improving quality include the use of salt-tolerant crops and reducing the use of pesticides.
- *Energy:* Agriculture requires fuel to sustain and thus the use of oil. Seeking alternative energy sources such as wind and solar help reduce the dependency on oil.
- *Air:* Farms generate dust, smoke, and pesticide drift. The UC Davis School of Agriculture recommends the use of windbreaks and covering crops with perennial grasses.
- *Soil:* Erosion is always the concern of the farmer.
- *Selection of site and diversity:* Location of crops in relation to optimal soil conditions and raising a variety of crops aids the sustainability of the farm.
- *Soil management:* The use of cover crops, compost, and manures and reducing tillage are methods of maintaining healthy soil.

Obviously, farms need to make a sustained profit over time. Federal assistance notwithstanding, the competition from large conglomerate farms makes it increasingly difficult to stay in business.

Social considerations include offering a fair and equitable wage to farm workers and including health benefits and accommodations. The poultry industry, for example, has the reputation of using illegal aliens as labor. This brings with it a number of ethical issues. Although their employment is illegal, they still must be treated with good working conditions and wages that are fair. These are jobs that are hard to fill. No one wants them except for the direly poor and desperate.

The U.S. Department of Agriculture (USDA) has grappled with sustainability for quite some time. David Glickman, the Secretary of Agriculture, stated in 1996 that the USDA was committed to economic, environmental, and social sustainability (Glickman, 1996).

The 1990 U.S. Farm Bill defined sustainable agriculture as an integrated system that will do the following:

- Satisfy human food and fiber needs;
- Enhance environmental quality and the natural base upon which the agricultural economy depends;
- Make the most efficient use of nonrenewable resources and on-farm resources and integrate, where appropriate, natural biological cycles and controls;
- Sustain the economic viability of farm operations; and
- Enhance the quality of life for farmers and society as a whole (Sustainable Agriculture, 2009).

The USDA cited these major ecological, economic, and social concerns:

- Decline in soil productivity due to erosion
- Source of nonpoint water pollution due to chemicals and fertilizer pollutants
- Overconsumption of water
- Insect and pest infestation
- Link to global climate change
- Wide discrepancy in farmer income
- Many farms have had to leave the industry due to financial losses (Gold, 1999).

Organic Farming

Organic farming can be considered sustainable agriculture, but sustainable agriculture is not necessarily organic. Organic farms do not use pesticides, artificial fertilizer, or **biotechnology.** They do not use genetically modified seeds or treat seeds or food with **irradiation.** Research has shown that organic produce is healthier for the human body than nonorganic produce. Nestle (2006) cited studies that have shown that farmers who converted from traditional to organic methods had lower crop yields, but these losses were offset by reduced fuel costs. Organic poultry and beef must also meet strict standards set by the USDA to attain that label. Their feed must be organic, they must not be injected with antibiotics or growth hormones, and they must not be confined all of the time. **Free range** means that the bird is not in a coop and was raised in an open environment.

The food we eat as humans has as much to do with sustainability as the air we breathe. We expect it to be safe to consume. We expect the animals that we eat have been raised in a clean and hygienic environment. Yet that is not always the case.

According to the Environmental Working Group (Epicurious Staff, 2006), the 12 fruits and pesticides that expose one to an average of 20 pesticides per day are as follows:

1. Peaches

2. Apples

3. Sweet bell peppers

4. Celery

5. Nectarines

6. Strawberries

7. Cherries

8. Pears

9. Grapes (imported)

10. Spinach

11. Lettuce

12. Potatoes

The "cleanest 12" are fruits and vegetables with the lowest exposure to pesticides:

1. Onions

2. Avocados

3. Sweet corn (frozen)

4. Pineapples

5. Mangoes

6. Asparagus

7. Sweet peas (frozen)

8. Kiwi fruit

9. Bananas

10. Cabbage

11. Broccoli

12. Papaya (Epicurious Staff, 2006)

Buy Local

The average distance that produce travels to the typical U.S. grocery store is 1,500 miles. This is 27 times higher than produce bought from local sources, like the neighborhood farmer's market. Approximately 40% of the fruit in the grocery store is produced overseas.

The website www.sustainabletable.org has an article that detailed the economics of produce:

> Annually, Americans consume more than $600 billion in food. In most communities today food is purchased entirely at a grocery store or market, with only about 7% of local food dollars staying in the community. The other 93% of the modern food dollar travels to pay processors, packagers, distributors, wholesalers, truckers, and the rest of the infrastructure that a global food system demands, a stark comparison to 40% in 1910 by contrast. ("Why Buy Local?" 2009)

The website www.organiclinker.com calculates the *food miles* that your food travels from the farm to plate. Distance the food travels, of course, is not the only consideration in purchasing food. One still must consider how a food item is grown or harvested and not base purchasing decisions totally on distance. A study by the British government's Department of the Environment concluded that a single indicator was inadequate in considering the cost of food transport and should aggregate the carbon emissions of the transportation mode into the fuel and labor expenses (Watkiss, 2005).

What We Eat

The label **certified organic** means that produce has been grown according to the principles of the Organic Foods Production Act of 1990. A USDA inspection must qualify the designation, which can read, 100% Organic, Organic, and Made with organic ingredients. If the produce contains 73% or less organic ingredients, it can only list the ingredients on the information panel.

Chicken Surpasses Beef

In the United States, in 2008, the average person consumed the following, compared to 1980 ("Profiling Food Consumption in America," 2009):

	2008	1980 (estimates)
Poultry	72.6 pounds	41.0
Beef	61.2 pounds	77.0
Pork	46.0 pounds	43.0
Fish/shellfish	16.0 pounds	16.0
All vegetables	392.7 pounds	340.0
All fruits	250.9 pounds	250.0
Fresh vegetables	187.7 pounds	150.0
Fresh fruits	126.8 pounds	105.0

In 2008, the average person drank the following:

	2008	1990 (estimates)
Soft drinks	46.9 gallons	46.0
Bottled water	28.5 gallons	10.0
Milk	20.7 gallons	26.0
Fruit juices/drinks	19.8 gallons	17.0

The shift from beef to chicken is reflective of the health concerns about red meat. Health concerns also are shown in the increase in vegetable consumption. The increase in bottled water consumption can generally be attributed to successful marketing practices.

The United States entered a campaign against childhood obesity with its campaign "Let's Move," spearheaded by Michelle Obama (www.lets move.gov). Critics argued that government had no business interfering with the health and eating habits of its citizens. Proponents argued that with accelerating health care costs, it had a very real stake in reducing obesity.

Consumption in Canada

Table 3.1 shows a comparison of the meat consumption of Canada and the United States:

| Table 3.1 | Meat Consumption by Canada and the United States in 2008 vs. 1980 | | | |

Meat	2008 Canada	2008 USA	1980 Canada	1980 USA
Poultry	83.7	72.6	49.3	41.0
Beef	66.7	61.2	88.4	77.0
Pork	51.7	46.0	70.7	43.0

Source: "Poultry Marketplace" (n.d.); "Profiling Food Consumption in America" (2009).

Canadian consumption of poultry overtook beef consumption in 1999. The biggest decline was in 1993, during the mad cow disease scare. The consumption patterns of the two North American countries are similar. Canadians increased their poultry consumption by 34 pounds in the 28-year period, and United States citizens increased their consumption by 31 pounds. Beef declined 22 pounds in Canada in that period and 16 pounds in the United States. Pork dropped 19 pounds in Canada but increased by 3 pounds in the United States due to successful marketing campaigns for "the other white meat."

As third world economies evolve, meat consumption increases. Table 3.2 illustrates the meat consumption per capita in selected countries.

| Table 3.2 | Meat Consumption Per Capita (in Kilograms Per Year) | | |

Country	2002	1980	1961
Argentina	97.6	114.4	103.6
Austria	94.1	94.7	65.6
Bahrain	70.7	58.9	15.4
Bangladesh	3.1	2.4	3.2
Brazil	82.4	41.7	27.8
Canada	108.1	100.9	81.7

Country	2002	1980	1961
China	52.4	14.6	3.8
Denmark	145.9	84.9	56.7
Egypt	22.5	13	10.8
France	101.1	101.6	77.7
Germany	82.1	95.9	63.8
Greece	78.7	67.8	21.9
Haiti	15.3	11.8	10.4
India	5.2	3.7	3.7
Ireland	106.3	74.7	55.5
Israel	97.1	51.6	30
Italy	90.4	75	30.5
Japan	43.9	30.6	7.6
Liberia	7.9	10.3	10.8
Mexico	58.6	37.5	25.4
New Zealand	142.1	141.6	113.5
South Africa	39	35.6	32.9
United Kingdom	79.6	71	69.8
United States	124.8	108.1	89.2

Source: Brown (2009).

The table shows that wealthy countries (Denmark, New Zealand, etc.) have increased meat consumption, as have poor countries. However, some countries whose economies have sunk even farther over time have seen a decline in meat consumption (Liberia).

Livestock account for 8% of greenhouse gas (GHG) emissions, primarily methane from the digestive process of cows (Macmillan, 2007). In other words, the cows are farting emissions. While the United Kingdom seeks ways to lower emissions by cutting meat consumption, poor countries try to put more meat on their plates. In 2000, the world ate 229 million tons of meat. By 2050, the United Nations estimates that consumption will double.

Globally, poultry consumption equaled beef consumption by 1995. Beef consumption increased worldwide from 1995 to 2005 despite declines in the United States. See Table 3.3.

Table 3.3 Commodity Consumption in Metric Tons

Commodity	1995 (million metric tons)	2005
Poultry		
World	54.2	82.8
USA	13.8	18.4
China	8.7	14.8
Beef		
World	54.2	60.1
USA	11.6	11.3
Brazil	5.7	7.8
China	3.6	6.8
Pork		
World	80.1	102.8
China	33.4	51.2
USA	8.1	9.4

Source: Food and Agricultural Organization (2007).

Where's the Beef?

In the early 1990s, 150 people in Great Britain died of mad cow disease, formally known as bovine spongiform encephalopathy (BSE). Hundreds of thousands of cows caught the disease and were destroyed. Proteins that are "misfolded" cause BSE. It is believed that the cows got the disease by eating sheep brains infected with a variant of the disease. The British beef industry learned the lesson: Never feed meat and bone meal from parts of the brain, nervous system, or by-products of animals that could have this protein disease.

Mad cow disease brought meat safety front and center into the consumer's consciousness. The USDA inspects meat, but it is still possible to contain bacteria. Recalls are listed on the USDA website (www.fsis.usda.gov). In the first 3 months of 2010, nineteen recalls were listed. The typical reasons for a recall are salmonella, E. coli, or listeria.

Bacteria spread from animal waste in crowded feedlots and slaughterhouses. Typically, the bacteria contaminate the outer surface of cuts of meat, but sometimes it will penetrate the interior.

A controversial method of killing the bacteria is the use of irradiation—zapping the meat with X-rays. Author Marian Nestle (2006) protested that this process allows meat companies to produce dirty meat and then fix it by zapping. Consumers are urged to read the safe handling messages on the packages of meat, protecting the meat producers from liability. Keep refrigerated. Keep raw meat and poultry separate from other foods. Keep hot foods hot. Refrigerate leftovers immediately or discard.

Organic Beef

The USDA has a number of requirements for all meat to be certified as organic:

- Not be fed by-products from other animals
- No antibiotics or hormones
- Fresh air, sunlight, and freedom of movement
- Grass fed (beef)
- Organic grain (beef and pork)
- Inspected by USDA (n.d.)

Organic differs from *natural* simply in that it meets all the previously given definitions. The designation of natural has three requirements: (1) no artificial flavors, colors, or preservatives; (2) minimal processing, and (3) a labeled definition of natural, be it absence of antibiotics, organic grain-fed, and so forth.

Nestle (2006), in her book *What to Eat,* stressed the advantages of grass-fed beef over grain-fed beef:

- Lower levels of E. coli
- Fewer bacteria in the feces of the cows, a source of contamination
- Cows are sick less often and require fewer antibiotics (p. 177)

Afowl of Fowl

Health concerns have driven the movement of consumers from beef to chicken. If one looks closely at the poultry industry, one may find it difficult to eat any kind of meat at all.

The life of most chickens we eat cannot be more miserable. They are housed in rectangular barns with no sunlight, stuffed full of hormones and antibiotics, and fed until they are so fat they can hardly walk. Then their lives end after around 45 to 50 days.

Here is an excerpt on the treatment of chickens from www.chicken industry.com:

Such fast growth causes chickens to suffer from a number of chronic health problems, including leg disorders and heart disease. According to one study, 90 percent of broilers had detectable leg problems, while

26 percent suffered chronic pain as a result of bone disease. Two researchers in *The Veterinary Record* report, "We consider that birds might have been bread to grow so fast that they are on the verge of structural collapse." (Compassion Over Killing, n.d.)

Industry journal *Feedstuffs* ("Chicken Industry Report," 1997) reported that "broilers now grow so rapidly that the heart and lungs are not developed well enough to support the remainder of the body, resulting in congestive heart failure and tremendous death losses."

Broiler chickens are confined in long warehouses, called **grower houses,** which typically house up to 20,000 chickens in a single shed at a density of only 130 square inches of space per bird. Such shocking densities make it impossible for most birds to carry out normal behaviors and cause the chickens to suffer from stress and disease. As two industry researchers wrote, "Limiting the floor space gives poorer results on a bird basis, yet the question has always been and continues to be: What is the least amount of floor space necessary per bird to produce the greatest return on investment" (Compassion Over Killing, n.d.).

After the industry average of 45 days in the grower shed, chickens are transported to slaughter without food, water, or shelter from extreme temperatures. Standard industry practices cause chickens to experience both acute and chronic pain. The treatment of these animals would be illegal if anti-cruelty laws applied to farm animals. But profits have taken priority over animal welfare. One industry journal asked the following:

> Is it more profitable to grow the biggest bird and have increased mortality due to heart attacks, and leg problems, or should birds be grown slower so that birds are smaller, but have fewer heart, lung and skeletal problems? A large portion of growers' pay is based on the pound of saleable meat produced, so simple calculations suggest that it is better to get the weight and ignore the mortality." (Compassion Over Killing, n.d.)

Turkeys suffer a similar plight. Turkeys reach slaughter weight in 14 to 16 weeks if they are female and 17 to 21 weeks if they are male. The birds live in barns that can hold as many as 10,000 hens or 7,000 tom turkeys. The birds are debeaked and detoed to avoid pecking and clawing, but these procedures are painful and can lead to excessive bleeding, infections, and death. Like chickens, the birds are fed to an uncomfortable weight that puts strain on their legs.

While some consumers feel more at ease by purchasing a free range turkey, Farm Sanctuary wrote the following:

> Thanksgiving shoppers buying an "organic" or "free-range" turkey have no way of knowing just how natural a life that turkey actually led. Compassionate consumers must remember that even on so-called

"free-range" farms, animals are subjected to inhumane treatment, and ultimately their lives are ended prematurely. (Consider the Turkey, 2010).

The top states for chicken fryer production are Georgia with 1.4 billion, Arkansas with 1.1 billion, Alabama with 1 billion, and Louisiana with 0.8 billion, with over half of the U.S. totals centered in these four states. Turkey's biggest states are Minnesota with 45.5 million, North Carolina with 37.5 million, Arkansas with 28 million, and Missouri with 21 million. These four states also make up more than half of the turkeys raised to eat in the United States. The states with the most chicken eggs produced are Iowa with 14.4 billion, Ohio with 7.3 billion, Pennsylvania with 6.5 billion, Indiana with 6.4 billion, and Texas with 4.9 billion (Lasley, Jones, Easterling, & Christensen, 1988).

These industries pretty much cannot survive without illegal immigrant labor. The natures of the unpleasant working conditions make jobs in this industry difficult to staff. The film *Food, Inc.* revealed that some of the poultry farms routinely allow federal raids on their workers, who are deported, only to be replaced by a new crew.

The Omnivore's Dilemma

Author Michael Pollan has written a series of books studying the food we eat. In *The Omnivore's Dilemma* (Pollan, 2006), he posed this basic question: What should we eat for omnivores—that is, humans—since we can eat practically anything edible. He attempted to trace corn from the farm to the market and pointed out that humans eat so much corn that we are almost made of corn by the corn syrup that goes into our soft drinks, the corn feed that the animals we eat consume, and all the various by-products of corn.

The dilemma is that we have to make choices—ethical choices, health choices. Do we eat organic? Do we eat only fair trade? Do we become vegans or vegetarians? Should we eat red meat? Should we eat carbohydrates? Should we eat more fat? Pollan (2006) noted that the French are healthier on average than Americans, despite consuming more chocolates, wines, and cheeses, and that is because of the amount of food Americans consume.

Pollan (2006) investigated the plight of the small farmer. By focusing upon a small farm in Iowa of 470 acres, he discussed the difficulty of competing with the large conglomerates that dominate agriculture. A 470-acre farm produces enough to feed 129 people yet still struggles to survive.

Food, Inc.

The film *Food, Inc.* (Kenner, 2010) was based upon *The Omnivore's Dilemma*. The film was directed by Robert Kenner and narrated by Michael Pollan and Eric Schlosser (2005), author of *Fast Food Nation*. In this film, the production of chicken, beef, and pork are shown and described as inhumane and unsustainable.

The legal clout of the large food conglomerates is discussed, with extensive coverage of Monsanto. After viewing the film, film critic Roger Ebert (2009), of the *Chicago Sun-Times*, wrote the following:

> Food labels depict an idyllic pastoral image of American farming. The sun rises and sets behind reassuring red barns and white frame farmhouses and contented cows graze under the watch of the Marlboro Cowboy. This is a fantasy. The family farm is largely a thing of the past. When farmland comes on the market, corporations outbid local buyers. Your best hope of finding real food grown by real farmers is at a local farmer's market.

At the conclusion of his review, Ebert (2009) stated the following:

> It's times like these I'm halfway grateful that after surgery I can't eat regular food anymore and have to live on a liquid diet out of a can. Of course, it contains soy and corn products, too, but in a healthy form.

Monsanto

Easily the biggest player in the agriculture industry is Monsanto. Monsanto has the largest market share of the seeds and pesticides used in agriculture. *Forbes Magazine* named Monsanto its "Company of the Year" in 2010, with 18% growth in the years 2005 to 2009, a time of a down economy.

Originally a chemical company, Monsanto got into the crop biotech industry in 1981. This became their primary industry, and the chemical business was finally sold.

Monsanto's first genetically engineered product was bovine growth hormone, released in 1994 to increase milk production. Many consumers unknowingly drank milk from cows pumped full of this hormone, the bovine equivalents to steroids.

Monsanto has a three-pronged approach to increasing food production (Monsanto, n.d.). According to their website, the amount of food needed in the next 40 years will surpass the food needed in the past 10,000 years combined. These figures are likely based on everyone in the world getting a complete diet, which has never been the case.

The three approaches that Monsanto is taking to reach the increased needs of food production are **breeding**, which involves combining two plants to produce a new one. For example, a sweet potato could be crossbred with a regular potato to produce, perhaps, a semisweet potato!

The second prong is biotechnology, which involves transferring DNA applications. Geneticists work in Monsanto's laboratories to improve the traits of such crops as corn and soybeans. Biotechnology is also used to reduce the reliance on pesticides and herbicides.

Finally, **agronomic practices** involve fungicides to increase yields, advanced GPS technology to maximize yield mapping, and seed treatments to protect the plant's nutrients.

Monsanto has not been without its critics. Genetically modified crops are banned in much of Europe, although they allow importation of the genetically modified produce. Zambia once rejected a cargo donation of genetically modified corn, although it was experiencing a famine (Mahara & Mukwita, 2002).

Monsanto's market position has created a monopolistic situation. They have the top-selling herbicide, Roundup, and then genetically engineer seeds that are "Roundup ready," unlike the competition's seeds. The idea came from trying genes from bacteria in the wastewater near the Roundup plant. However, the patent on Roundup-ready soybean seeds, a $500 million annual business, expires in 2014, and DuPont is expected to release a competitive product.

Raj Patel (2007), in his book *Stuffed and Starved*, wrote that in 1995, the Indian state of Andhra Pradesh (population 75 million) banned Monsanto from licensing its genetically modified cottonseed on the grounds that they had been ineffective. "Yields were lower, and more prone to disease, than non-genetically modified crops" (Patel, 2007).

So Monsanto's quest to help feed a growing population is not without its detractors. Arguments in favor of **genetically modified foods** would include the ability to feed malnourished populations in a less costly manner and the ability to engineer foods that are resistant to allergens.

Diet and Health

As we have noted, one of the sustainability issues pertaining to food is nutrition. The World Health Organization (WHO) of the United Nations considers nutrition and the prevention of malnutrition as fundamental to human development. In that regard, WHO ("Global Strategy on Diet, Physical Activity, and Health," n.d.) made specific dietary recommendations:

- Limiting fat
- Shifting consumption from saturated and trans-fatty acids to unsaturated fats
- Increasing consumption of fruits, vegetables, legumes, whole grains, and nuts
- Limiting sugars
- Limiting salt
- Practicing weight control
- Engaging in physical activity
- Controlling tobacco use

In an article relating to Canadian health and food, authors Cash, Goddard, and Lerohl (2006) listed the key positions of Canadian nongovernmental organizations (NGOs):

- Up to 30% of cancer is related to diet.
- Consumption of fruits and vegetables can reduce cancer and cardiovascular disease.
- Large serving sizes are an impediment to a better diet.
- Cardiovascular disease is responsible for 38% of the total deaths of Canadian men and 35% of Canadian women.
- Obesity is on a par with tobacco smoking as a health risk.
- Almost half of Canadians are overweight or obese, and two thirds are either overweight or smokers.
- Urban planning should promote exercise and public health.
- Childhood obesity is related to inadequate consumption of fruits and vegetables.

Malnutrition

While citizens of the rich countries of the world struggle with issues of obesity and rush to one fad diet after another in search of a thin figure, close to 800 million global citizens are *undernourished*; in other words, they do not eat the minimal number of food calories required for health. Of these, approximately 110 million are Chinese. More than half of Central Africa is undernourished. Other countries with severe hunger problems affecting over half the population include Somalia (75%), Burundi (66%), the Democratic Republic of the Congo (64%), Afghanistan (58%), Eritrea (57%), Haiti (56%), Mozambique (54%), and Angola (51%).

Malnutrition is a socioeconomic fact of life. As incomes lower to poverty levels, the chance of malnutrition increases. Food prices are directly influenced by the price of fuel. Increases in oil prices lead to increases in the prices of fertilizers and agricultural chemicals, the cost of running farm equipment, and an increase in transportation costs. When food prices increase and incomes either decline or stay static, food scarcity ensues, leading to undernourishment, malnourishment, and death.

According to the World Bank ("Population Growth Rate," 2001), the world population is currently growing at 1.2% per year (1% in the United States), with projections calling for a doubling of the world's 6.4 billion population by the year 2060. An issue will be the food supply. Corn and other cereal grains comprise 80% of the world's food supply, and the rate of growth in production is not projected to keep up.

Factors affecting food production include soil degradation and erosion, an inadequate water supply for irrigation, pollution, and fuel availability.

Malnutrition is the direct cause of 300,000 deaths per year; worldwide, 53% of the deaths of children under 5 years of age are due to malnutrition.

Approximately 852 million people were classified as undernourished in 2002. Malnutrition is the result of a deficiency in iron, iodine, vitamin A, and zinc. Poverty is the main cause of malnutrition. People are too poor to purchase adequate food. This leads to chronic infections and early death.

Ready-to-use therapeutic foods (RUTF) have proven to help treat malnutrition. Malnourished patients in Maradi, Africa, received these foods and 6,200 were cured, while 1,000 died.

Sustainability at Food Companies

McDonald's

The documentary film *Super Size Me* depicted a man who ate at McDonald's every day for a month and gained 28 pounds. He could have just as easily eaten at McDonald's and lost weight by changing his selections; however, the film-maker honed in on the most caloric items on the menu. The lesson McDonald's learned was to no longer encourage customers to increase the size of the order, which was their usual practice. Super sizing the French fries increases the calories and the price. McDonald's took a public relations hit as the result of the film. Companies like McDonald's, Wal-Mart, and Coca-Cola must often deal with public backlash when their business practices are called into question.

Examining these companies, you do find that the corporate attitude is moving in the direction of sustainability.

McDonald's has as a corporate value: "We're determined to continuously improve our social and environmental performance. We work hard, together with our suppliers and independent restaurant franchisees, to strive toward a sustainable future—for our company and the communities in which we operate" ("Getting to Know Us," 2012).

Within the McDonald's values, one clearly finds a subscription to the TBL.

Animal Welfare

McDonald's is one of the largest buyers of beef, chicken, and pork in the world and has a policy that dictates humane treatment of these animals. Some of their involvement includes the following:

- Finding ways to reduce the distress of poultry at the point of slaughter.
- Support the phasing out of gestation crates for pigs. These crates were so small that pigs spent their lifetimes in a cage, unable to turn around. The movement is to larger crates, enabling movement. (Sow Housing, 2012)

Restaurant Level Efforts

At McDonald's restaurants, three main areas highlight the sustainability efforts: (1) energy efficiency, (2) sustainable packaging and waste management, and (3) green restaurant design. In 1990, McDonald's established its Global Environmental Commitment, focusing on continuous improvement in these areas ("Environmental Responsibility," n.d.).

Cargill

Cargill, a company producing food, agricultural, and industrial products with annual earnings of $116 billion, offers a sustainability section on their webpage, Cargill.com. Somewhat like Monsanto, Cargill has a noble mission: to help meet the growing food needs of the global population.

Cargill lists four environmental innovation examples:

1. *Process optimizers:* helping customers save energy and water use

2. *Converting methane:* a program to convert methane from landfills and waste water treatment plants into usable energy sources

3. *Anaerobic digester:* converts cow effluent into more than 2 megawatts of power per year

4. *Comprehensive footprint:* Partnered with McDonald's in France to create a carbon footprint for its chicken meat supply chain. This led to a 10% reduction in GHG emissions ("Environmental Sustainability," n.d.).

Cargill is a big believer in developing the local communities it serves. It contributed $58 million in 2009 to help these communities; $10 million went to CARE to fight poverty in Brazil, Ghana, Cote d'Ivoire, Honduras, and Guatemala ("In Classrooms, Not Fields," 2011).

Kraft Foods

A Chicago-based food company with $48 billion annual revenue, primarily from snacks, confectionary, and cheese products, set some ambitious environmental goals in 2005. Table 3.4 shows their 2011 goals versus their 2005 accomplishments.

In 2009, Kraft received an award from the U.S. Environmental Protection Agency (EPA) for ozone protection. Since Kraft is a major buyer of agricultural products across the world, it has a strong interest in sustainable agriculture.

Wal-Mart

Wal-Mart, the world's largest retail chain, with worldwide sales in 2009 of $405 billion—$258 billion in the United States—is very involved in a

Table 3.4 Kraft Foods Goals and Accomplishments

	Goals 2005–2011	As of 2009
Plant energy usage	−25%	−15%
Plant emissions	−25%	−17%
Plant solid waste generation	−15%	−30%
Plant water consumption	−15%	−32%
Packaging reduction	−150 million pounds	−174 million pounds

Source: "Kraft Foods Sustainability Goals" (2011).

sustainability program and publishes an annual progress report. Their approach is called Sustainability 360 and involves their 100,000 suppliers; 2 million employees; and customers ("Global Responsibility Report," 2012). Their broad goals are to be supplied 100% by renewable energy, create zero waste, and sell products that sustain people and the environment. New stores are designed to be 25% to 30% more energy efficient with a goal of a 20% reduction in GHGs ("Climate and Energy," n.d.).

Wal-Mart found ways to make shipping more efficient. Although they shipped 77 million more cases in 2009 than they did the year before, they reduced the miles driven by 100 million in that one year. They accomplished this by loading trailers more efficiently. In 2010, efficiency was further improved by increasing deliveries by 57 million more cases, while driving 49 million fewer miles. This is the equivalent of taking 7,600 cars off the road ("Logistics," n.d.).

Recycling efforts resulted in 1.3 million pounds of aluminum, 120 million pounds of plastics, 11.6 million pounds of paper, and 4.6 billion pounds of cardboard. They have started an experimental program with reusable bags to reduce the waste of plastic bags. In 2010, plastic bag waste was reduced by 3.5 billion bags, a 21% reduction from 2007. ("Zero Waste," n.d.).

Wal-Mart also looks at the products on its shelves to make sure they are in keeping with their sustainability products. Among their moves in this regard are the following:

- Purchases 25% wood items that have received third-party certification
- Seeks phosphate-free detergents
- Started a Direct Farm Program to purchase produce directly from local farmers
- Offers Fair Trade Certified bananas
- Wrote a Best Practices Guide for its clothing manufacturers
- Joined the Unilever–Greenpeace Sustainable Palm Oil Coalition to shift sourcing of palm oil to sustainable sources

Beyond their products, Wal-Mart was active in many other ways that promote sustainability:

- Protected 624,000 acres of habitat in the Acres for America program
- Provided 1.5 million of financial support to the relief efforts after the Haiti earthquake
- Started a program in Bharti, India, to ensure that 100% of the households have toilets
- Donated 1.6 million in Chile to alleviate poverty
- Conducted a Christmas drive in Brazil that yielded 490 tons of food; 163,000 books; 118,000 winter clothing items; and 12,000 toys

Whole Foods

Whole Foods is a grocery chain specializing in "healthy" foods and products. Thus, it emphasizes dealing with ethical suppliers and offers a large assortment of organic food items. On their website, they include sustainability in their Values & Actions section. Below are excerpts from their website (www.wholefoodsmarket.com):

Seafood Sustainability

Whole Foods lists their following practices:

- Source as much Marine Stewardship Council (MSC) certified **sustainable seafood** as possible
- When MSC-certified options are not available, give customers transparent information, let them vote with their dollars, and commit to further change
- Set the bar high with Responsibly Farmed seafood ("Seafood Sustainability," n.d.).

We need sustainable seafood because "...80 percent of fisheries are fully exploited, overfished, depleted, or recovering from depletion" ("Seafood Sustainability," n.d.). With seafood growing in demand, it is critical that sustainable fishing practices are followed.

Genetically Engineered Foods

In terms of genetically modified foods, Whole Foods Market offers customers options for avoiding foods that are intentionally grown from genetically engineered seeds. For example, it offers many organic choices. Producers who supply products that are certified organic are not permitted to use genetically engineered seeds to produce those crops. Whole Foods Market also requires vendors who produce its 365 Everyday Value products to source plant ingredients from non-GMO sources. It also supports the work of the Non-GMO Project, a nonprofit organization dedicated to promoting the use of non-GMO ingredients. Many of Whole Foods Market's 365 Everyday Value products have been evaluated by the Non-GMO Project and include the Non-GMO Project seal ("Genetically Engineered Foods," n.d. Courtesy of Whole Foods Market. "Whole Foods Market" is a registered trademark of Whole Foods Market IP, L. P.).

Sustainability and Our Future

Whole Foods Market's vision of a sustainable future means our children and grandchildren will be living in a world that values human creativity, diversity, and individual choice. Businesses will harness human and material resources without devaluing the integrity of the individual or the planet's ecosystems. Companies, governments, and institutions will be held accountable for their actions. People will better understand that all actions have repercussions and that planning and foresight coupled with hard work and flexibility can overcome almost any problem encountered. It will be a world that values education and a free exchange of ideas by an informed citizenry; where people are encouraged to discover, nurture, and share their life's passions.

At Whole Foods Market, we are starting to implement this new vision of the future by changing the way we think about the relationships between our food supply, the environment, and our bodies. ("Sustainability and Our Future," n.d.)

Starbucks

Starbucks has divided its sustainability site into the following categories: recycling and reducing waste, energy conservation, water conservation, building greener stores, and tackling climate change.

- *Recycling and reducing waste:* Starbucks recycles in stores that have community recycling. It also offers discounts for customers who bring their own mug and has a goal of offering 25% reusable cups by 2015.
- *Energy conservation:* The goal by the end of 2010 is to reduce energy consumption by 25% and to obtain 50% of energy from renewable sources. New lighting and improved heating, ventilation, and cooling systems are planned.
- *Water conservation:* The water use goal is a drop of 15% by 2012. One water reduction technique is the use of high-pressure water blasts rather than using an open tap.

- *Building greener stores:* All stores built from late 2010 on will attempt to achieve LEED certification, the certificate for buildings that meet the highest standards.
- *Tackling climate change:* One of the ironies of Starbucks' quest to help climate change is that some of the rain forest is being denuded in favor of coffee plantations. Their efforts focus on the use of renewable energy and energy conservation. ("Environmental Stewardship," n.d.).

Conclusion

The agriculture industry is, of course, responsible for the food that goes into our bodies. Ultimately, the whole concept of sustainability revolves around health and hygiene. We take for granted that the food we consume is safe and rely upon the government to fix standards that will protect us. The diets of developed and emerging countries are much different from third world, impoverished countries. Their concern is simply to avoid malnourishment and hunger.

This chapter covered the critical aspects of sustainable agriculture. We reviewed the principles that go into organic food and studied some of the practices that put meat on the table. The intelligent consumer should be aware of how their food arrives at the table. Knowledge of this process may alter one's dietary practices.

A review of the sustainability practices of a number of food and food-related companies showed the seriousness with which this subject is taken at the corporate level. Whole Foods, for example, owes its very existence to the commercialization of healthy and organic foods. Fast-food giant McDonald's is not naive about its contribution to diet and health and has gone to great lengths to get away from the image of the company that wanted to *super size* your plates.

KEY WORDS

Agronomic practices

Biotechnology

Breeding

Certified Organic

Contamination

Free range

Genetically modified foods

Grower houses

Irradiation

Natural

Salinization

Sustainable agriculture

Sustainable seafood

DISCUSSION QUESTIONS

1. Visit your supermarket and find foods that are labeled *natural*. Determine how they qualify for that designation.

2. Is there evidence of sustainable seafood at your local fish counter?

3. How does the quality of the soil differ from one region of the United States to another?

4. What are the main crops in your state or region? What evidence of sustainability practices can you find in local growers?

5. The poultry industry is known to employ illegal workers. Comment on the ethics of this practice.

6. How can a small farm succeed in today's market?

7. Why do you believe there has been a drop in the consumption of red meat in the United States?

8. Some countries have seen declines in meat consumption; other countries have seen increases. What are the driving forces in meat consumption?

9. A national politician recently criticized the U.S. government's program to combat obesity. Why would a government pursue a program like this?

10. What could be done to reduce cases of malnutrition across the world?

RECOMMENDED WEBSITES

www.advocacy.brittanica.com/

www.ewg.org

www.foodethicscouncil.org

www.foodnews.org

www.guardian.co.uk

www.monsanto.com

www.worldhunger.org

www.worldwatch.org

4

Forests, Wildlife, and Biodiversity

LEARNING OBJECTIVES

By the end of this chapter, you will be able to do the following:

- Discuss the relationship between the forest and climate.
- Discuss the various methods of tree cutting.
- List the certification programs for sustainable forestry.
- Understand the importance of urban forests.
- Explain the importance of preserving wilderness.
- Discuss the Endangered Species Act of 1973 (ESA).
- Research the issues concerning economics and biodiversity.

Chapter Overview

This chapter deals with three topics that often intertwine: (1) the fate of the trees in the forest, (2) the relationship with wildlife and economics, and (3) the importance of biodiversity to nature. Many people fail to see the importance of these issues if they live in an urban environment. However, urban forests also play a critical role in ecosystems. There are economic consequences arising from sustainable development decisions. We cut down trees, and it accentuates global warming. Without trees, we have no paper and no new houses. Without new houses, we lose jobs. It is this dilemma—the need for economic gain versus the protection of our natural resources—that we discuss in this chapter.

The Spotted Owl Controversy

In 1991, a federal judge protected the forest habitat of the northern spotted owl from logging. The protection of the spotted owl, an **endangered species,** brought howls of protests from the logging industry. It made no sense to them to protect a bird at the cost of revenues to the industry. The incident is key in understanding the conflict between the need for resources and the protection of endangered species.

It is difficult to understand that these cases have an impact on all of us—not just those who live in the Pacific Northwest—because the interrelationships between nature and humans often clash with ways to make more money.

The spotted owl has a range from British Columbia to northern California and resided in "old-growth" forests, primarily nesting in the cavities of tree trunks. About 2,000 spotted owls exist today.

The court protected at least 40% of old growth forest found within a 1.3-mile radius of a known spotted owl nest. The importance of the spotted owl to environmentalists, ecologists, and forest managers is that it is what is called an **indicator species,** a barometer of the health of an entire ecosystem. A second reason is that the forests provide aesthetic value to be enjoyed by hikers, backpackers, and bird-watchers.

The timber industry's counterargument is one of economics and jobs. They argued that 28,000 jobs would be lost and that old growth must be cut to plant new trees to perpetuate their industry. Environmentalists argued that at the current rate of tree cutting, there would be no trees to cut down by the year 2020.

Economists discovered that 8 years after the federal ban on logging the spotted owl's habitats, the Northwest was able to replace jobs. Wood products employment dropped 27,000 jobs between 1979 and 1989 and another 21,000 by 1996 after the reduction of the old growth forests took effect. Approximately 9,300 were directly attributed to the old growth forest protection (Kirschner, 2010).

These losses were offset by the addition of Hyundai and Sony plants in Oregon and the continued strength of Nike.

The Rain Forest

The **tropical rain forest** is important because it absorbs carbon dioxide, which helps reduce global warming. However, the rate at which it is being cut down at 32 million acres per year—the size of the state of Washington—could denude the globe of the entire rain forest in 100 years. With the death of the rain forest, we will see the demise of thousands of species and a change in global rainfall patterns (Chiras, 2010).

Brazil cleared much of its rain forest in favor of agriculture, viewing the revenues from coffee, rubber, and chocolate as more lucrative than protecting its forests. However, clearing the forest exposes the soil to heavy rains, which fill the streams and rivers with sediment. Chiras (2010) pointed out that the soil beneath rain forests is typically poor for farming.

Naturalist E. O. Wilson (2002) described the destruction of the rain forest in his book *The Future of Life*:

The tearing down of a tropical rainforest follows a typical sequence. First, a road is cut deep into the interior for logging and settlement. Trails and forest camps are built along the way, and hunters fan out to furnish game—"bushmeat"—for the work crews. The land, depleted of the best timber and in declining condition, is next sold in lots to ranchers and small farmers. They build small roads laterally off the main route, creating the fishbone pattern seen, for example, along the highways west through Rondonia and north from Manaus to Boa Vista near the Guyana border. The settlers topple most of the rest of the trees, use some for lumber, and let the rest dry out. A year later they burn the debris. The ash that settles on the barren soil is enough for several years of good harvest. As the ground nutrients wash away, the settlers either make the best of a worsening situation or else move on to occupy new land closer to the frontier. Some are lucky enough to find tracts of deeper, more persistent and fertile soil. Repeating the ruinous cycle endlessly, the human wave is rolling up the Amazon forest like a gigantic carpet. (pp. 63–64)

Some of the rain forest has been cleared to make way for coffee plantations, which offer a source of revenue for farmers.

Forest Management

Forest managers have to consider the trees, soil, streams, plants, animals, and insects. All life in the forest is a holistic ecosystem.

Trees represent a commodity when harvested. While still standing, they represent a capital good. Forest managers must decide the optimal point at which to harvest the trees.

Types of Tree Harvesting

There are several ways trees are harvested either to clear the land for other purposes or to turn the timber into paper or wood products.

Clear-cutting is a method in which loggers cut down 40 to 200 acres of forest and then burn the ground and tree remnants. This method is found to be the cheapest and fastest method for clearing trees; however, it brings with it several disadvantages:

- Creates an unsightly scar in the forest
- Fragments or destroys wildlife habitats
- Destroys plants
- Causes soil erosion, which can be serious

Strip-cutting is when loggers cut in much smaller strips—usually from 1 to 5 acres. Private landowners may cut 1.5 acres without permission of the U.S. Forest Service. This technique reduces the devastation to soil, plants, and species that can be found with clear-cutting.

Selective-cutting is when specific types of trees are removed from the forest— maple, for example—reducing visual scarring of the forest and protecting the forest from disease and insects. However, selectively cutting from the forest is costly.

Shelter-wood cutting is a technique in which poor quality trees are removed, while healthy trees protect the new seedlings until they are of sufficient height to remove the high quality trees. This method is a superior method for protecting species and the visual aspects of the forest, although is still quite costly when compared to clear-cutting.

Sustainable Forestry

The Montreal Process, a 1993 follow-up to the Earth Summit, listed the following criteria for sustainable forest management:

1. Conservation of biological diversity including ecosystem diversity, species diversity, and genetic diversity.

2. Maintenance of productive capacity of forest ecosystems.

3. Maintenance of forest ecosystem health and vitality.

4. Conservation and maintenance of soil and water resources.

5. Maintenance of forest contribution to global carbon cycles.

6. Maintenance and enhancement of long-term multiple socioeconomic benefits to meet the needs of societies, including production and consumption, recreation and tourism, investment in the forest sector, cultural, social, and spiritual needs and values, and employment and community needs.

7. Legal, institutional, and economic framework for forest conservation and sustainable management including a legal framework, institutional framework, economic framework, a means to measure and monitor changes, and to conduct and apply research and development. (Montreal Process Working Group, 1999)

There are three major certification bodies for sustainable forests: (1) the Programme for the Endorsement of Forest Certification (PEFC) in Europe, (2) the Forest Stewardship Council (FSC), and (3) the Sustainable Forestry Initiative (SFI).

PEFC employs the theme "Think global—act global" in its governance efforts and is primarily applied in Europe and North America. It relies on intergovernmental agreements and internationally recognized processes, although the national standards are independently developed. PEFC has been tailored to family- and community-owned forests.

The PEFC (n.d.) process sets requirements in the following areas:

- Biodiversity of forest ecosystems
- The range of ecosystem services is sustained: provisioning services for food, fiber, biomass, and wood; regulatory services as part of the water cycle; capturing and storing carbon; and preventing soil erosion; support services that provide habitats for people and wildlife; and cultural services for spiritual and recreational benefits.
- Chemicals are substituted with natural alternatives and their use is minimized
- Workers' rights and welfare are protected
- Local employment is encouraged
- Indigenous peoples' rights are respected
- Operations are undertaken within the legal framework and follow best practices.

FSC (n.d.) claims to be the strictest certification process and is based upon 10 principles:

Principle 1: Compliance with all applicable laws and international treaties

Principle 2: Demonstrated and uncontested, clearly defined, long-term land tenure and use rights

Principle 3: Recognition and respect of indigenous peoples' rights

Principle 4: Maintenance or enhancement of long-term social and economic well-being of forest workers and local communities and respect of workers' rights in compliance with International Labour Organisation (ILO) conventions

Principle 5: Equitable use and sharing of benefits derived from the forest

Principle 6: Reduction of environmental impact of logging activities and maintenance of the ecological functions and integrity of the forest

Principal 7: Appropriate and continuously updated management plan

Principle 8: Appropriate monitoring and assessment activities to assess the condition of the forest, management activities and their social and environmental impacts

Principle 9: Maintenance of High Conservation Value Forests (HCVFs) defined as environmental and social values that are considered to be outstanding significance or critical importance

Principle 10: In addition to compliance with all of the above, planta-tions must contribute to reduce the pressures on and promote the res-toration and conservation of natural forests.

FSC offers three types of certificates: **forest management, chain of cus-tody,** and **controlled wood.** The forest management certification applies to those directly involved with forestry. The chain of custody is for companies in the supply chain involving forest products that must demonstrate the use of responsibly produced raw materials. Controlled wood is for companies to be able to sell to certified chain of custody companies.

SFI is similar in structure, with three certifications involving forest, chain of custody, and fiber sourcing.

Forest Ethics

Forest Ethics, a politically active environmental organization based in Canada, protects forests in a number of ways. It lobbies corporations to be more sustainable, protect the forest, and reduce waste. Since 2009, it has been on a campaign to protect the Canadian Boreal Forest, primarily by fighting the Canadian tar sands oil refinery, which is the dirtiest fuel in North America.

The organization is upset with the SFI-certified logging in the Sierra Nevada Mountains, which they label as **greenwashing**—that is, giving license to decimate the forest and feel good about it because the logging is certified.

Forest Ethics was instrumental in protecting the Great Bear Rainforest in British Columbia. The group combined with the forest industry, the Canadian government, the Coastal First Nations, Home Depot, and Lowe's to success-fully protect 5 million acres from logging.

About $120 million was set aside for the First Nation community to develop alternative conservation economies in compensation for the lost revenues the community received from logging. This is an economic fact of life: Aboriginal groups yield their forests to logging as a way to sustain their community. Thus, incentives must be provided for them to seek other ways to thrive. That is a definite action that illustrates the sustain-ability mindset.

The group also releases an annual list of companies that are naughty or nice with their mail distribution to consumers (Alter, 2007).

Nice list:

Timberland	REI	Macy's	Crate and Barrel
Patagonia	Bloomingdale's	Dell	Victoria's Secret
JCPenney	L.L.Bean	J.Crew	

Naughty list:

Sears	Neiman Marcus	Eddie Bauer	Citibank
Chase			

Urban Forests

Since 80% of the U.S. population resides in urban areas, most people are concerned with the trees in their own backyard. Urban forests include city parks, tree-lined avenues, public gardens, greenways, wetlands, and nature preserves. The US Forest Service (U.S. Department of Agriculture Forest Service, n.d.) maintains these forests and lists their benefits:

- Urban forests are dynamic ecosystems that provide environmental services by cleaning air and water that help control stormwater and conserve energy.
- They add beauty and structure to urban noise.
- They reduce noise and provide places to recreate.
- They strengthen social cohesion.
- They add economic value.

A research study in Finland by Tyrvainen, Silvennoinen, and Kole (2003) looked at whether ecological values could be combined in the management of Helsinki forests. They discovered that Helsinki citizens preferred managed forests, but there were significant differences in support. Groups that favored managed forests were younger, had more education, and actively used the forests. Showing less support were older respondents who were less educated and non-users of the forests.

A comprehensive study of urban forestry was conducted in Chicago in 1994. The Chicago Urban Forest Climate Project revealed that the urban forest of Chicago consisted of 51 million trees (McPherson, Nowak, & Rowntree, 1994). Trees in Chicago removed an estimated 17 tons of carbon monoxide, 93 tons of sulfur dioxide, 98 tons of nitrogen dioxide, 210 tons of ozone, and 234 tons of particulate matter. The study concluded that the tress coverage improved air quality by approximately 15% during the mid-day hours.

Further, the study concluded that a "large street tree growing to the west of a typical brick residence" reduced air-conditioning expenses by 2% to 7%. Finally, the cost benefits per tree came to $402 in its life span—more than twice the tree's cost (Jonnes, 2011).

Other cities that have actively pursued tree planting to increase urban forests include New York, where Mayor Bloomberg invested $31 million to fund Million Trees NYC, and Los Angeles, with Million Trees LA, each city committing to plant one million trees in a period of 10 years.

Business and Wood

Home Depot established the Sustainable Cities Institute as a philanthropic organization funded by its foundation. Home Depot is one of the largest retailers of wood and wood products in the United States. The website outlines its Eco Options program, which highlights more energy efficient products for its buyers.

Not to be outdone, Home Depot's biggest competitor, Lowe's, states that in order to operate more sustainably, Lowe's (n.d.) will do the following:

- Provide customers with environmentally-responsible products, packaging and services at everyday low prices;
- Educate and engage employees, customers and others on the importance of conserving resources, reducing waste and recycling;
- Use resources—energy, fuel, water and materials—more efficiently and responsibly to minimize our environmental footprint;
- Establish sustainability goals and objectives;
- Review and communicate progress made toward achieving established goals and objectives; and
- Engage on public policy issues related to sustainability.

Office Depot (n.d.), a retailer that sells paper and paper goods, offered this information on its website:

The purpose of Office Depot's policies on responsible forest management are to promote well managed production forests in concert with forest and biodiversity conservation and to promote stewardship by implementing policies that encourage the use, distribution and sale of environmentally preferable products and services.

Since Office Depot is in a business that goes through a lot of paper, it is important to convey to customers that they are aware of paper's impact on the environment and intend to be proactive on the issue.

Paper Use

Although you would expect with the popularity of e-mail and the web that paper use has diminished, that is hardly the case. Roughly 42% of the harvested wood goes into paper production. The United States is the largest consumer, with 92,000 metric tons, followed by China with 36,000, and Japan at 31,000. Industrialized nations, with 20% of the world's population, consume 87% of the printing and writing paper.

The United States consumes 4 million tons of copy paper, 2 billion books, 350 million magazines, and 25 billion newspapers per year. Paper makes up 40% of solid waste.

The U.S. Environmental Protection Agency (EPA) reports that one third of paper comes from trees, one third from recycled paper, and one third from wood chips and scraps. Approximately 39% of recycled paper is exported from the United States (U.S. EPA, 2003).

Harack and Laskowski (2010) offered the following suggestions for reducing paper use:

- Distribute memos via e-mail.
- Share internal documents through the Intranet.
- Bookmark webpages instead of printing them out.
- Use electronic business forms.
- Store office records on CD-ROMS.
- Request electronic or CD-ROM versions and share subscriptions.
- Share one master copy of hard documents, and edit draft documents on a single circulating draft.
- Adjust page settings.
- Print letterhead directly from computers.
- Consolidate similar forms.
- Eliminate commercial junk mail.
- Replace fax cover sheets with stick-on labels.
- Send and receive faxes via personal computers to avoid printing.
- Print fax confirmation sheets only when there is a failed transmission.
- Set copiers and printers to duplex as a default.
- Print two or more pages per side of a sheet
- Use scrap paper for drafts or note paper.
- Eliminate cover or divider pages.

The Wilderness

Joni Mitchell (1970), in her song "Big Yellow Taxi," sang the following:

> Don't it always seem to go, that you don't know what you've got till its gone. They paved Paradise and put up a parking lot. They took all the trees, put them in a tree museum. And they charged the people a dollar and a half just to see 'em.

Approximately 4% of the United States is designated as *wilderness* and receives government protection. U.S. law defines wilderness as "an area where the earth and its community of life are untrammeled by man, where man is himself a visitor who does not remain."

Of the 107 million acres of land protected by the Wilderness Act of 1964, about 57 million acres are in Alaska. The act prohibits logging, motorized vehicles, and motorboats. The purpose is to leave nature in its pristine state, for outdoor enthusiasts to enjoy communing away from urban traffic and pollution. However, even the wilderness, like national parks, is in danger of being loved to death. Overcrowding on trails and at campsites has increased garbage and damage to plants. Chiras (2010) recommended seven steps to reduce environmental degradation caused by backpackers and campers:

1. Educate campers on ways to lessen their impact.

2. Restrict access to overused areas.

3. Issue permits to control the number of users.

4. Designate campsites.

5. Increase the number of wilderness rangers to monitor use.

6. Disseminate information about infrequently used areas.

7. Improve trails to promote use of underutilized areas.

The Wilderness Society

In 1935, five individuals formed the **Wilderness Society,** a group whose stated purpose was as follows: "All we desire to save from invasion is that extremely minor fraction of outdoor America which yet remains from mechanical sights and sounds and smells."

The group consisted of Robert Marshall, known for his advocacy of Alaskan wilderness; Aldo Leopold, author of *The Sand County Almanac* and a naturalist known for his ethical treatment of the land; Benton Mackaye, the acknowledged *father* of the Appalachian Trail; Robert Sterling Yard, a protector and advocate for the national park system; and Harvey Broome, a conservationist based in the Smoky Mountains. Their efforts led to the passing of the 1964 Wilderness Act.

The current issues the society is involved in are as follows:

- *Wilderness:* Protection of the last untouched wild places
- *Energy:* Defending the land from irresponsible energy development by pushing cleaner and sustainable energy policies
- *Roadless forests:* Protecting pristine forests from development and preserving resources for wildlife and humankind
- *Global warming:* Protecting public lands from the effects of global warming
- *Stewardship:* Restoring public lands to their "full splendor," and protecting them from threats (The Wilderness Society, n.d.).

Managing Biodiversity

Forest managers have more to do than supervise the trees. Their jobs include all the plants, streams, ponds, and animals found within the forest. Brenda McComb (2008) put it this way:

We manage habitat for various reasons such as personal goals, corporate objectives, and legal requirements. Policies in the United States, such as the Endangered Species Act and National Forest Management Act, require people in various agencies to manage habitat. But why do we have these policies? Why should we spend time and money managing habitat for species that occur in our forests? Quite simply, we do or do not manage habitat because society either cares about these resources or does not, respectively. Wildlife are public resources that occur on both public and private lands. If society placed no value on a species or group of species, then we would not manage their habitat. Values that society places on animals evolve over time and from culture to culture. (p. 7)

But why do we care about biodiversity? Hunter (1999) categorized the values for maintaining biodiversity as economic, spiritual, scientific and educational, ecological, strategic, realized versus potential, and genetic.

The economic values include outdoor recreation and the economic values of the resources—that is, wood—and the medicines derived from plants. Many people find spiritual uplifting when surrounded by the forest and the wild. The scientific value comes from the research provided by a diverse setting. The ecological value derives from the study of the ecosystem and its interrelationships. The strategic value is noticeable in the efforts of nongovernmental organizations (NGOs) to market themselves using symbols of the wild. Hunter (1999) noted that many species have not yet realized their potential value and may never. Finally, the genetic value is in maintaining species to avoid extinction.

Those who doubt the value of maintaining biodiversity point to the survival of the fittest: If left alone and unprotected, many species will die away. Approximately 99% of all the species that have lived on Earth are now extinct. Biological conservationists believe that the rate of extinction is increasing rapidly, aided by man. At that rate, will we see a day when only man is left standing?

Special Species

Forest managers must pay special attention to certain types of species. These have importance to maintaining the biodiversity of the forest.

Ecologically important species have special meaning because of their places within the *food web*. These species are called **keystone species;** "if removed from a system [they] would have a disproportionally large impact on that system (Power et al., 1996). This definition also includes plants. Thompson and Angelstam (1999) provided the example of the reduction of the wolf population in Norway, Sweden, and Newfoundland, all resulting in increased moose populations and decreased tree and plant species.

Thompson and Angelstam (1999) also noted that beavers, ants, and earthworms act as keystone species. Beavers hold importance for damming trees to create habitats for aquatic and semiaquatic species. Ants and earthworms redistribute seeds and spores for plants, mix and aerate the soil, and decompose wood.

The case of the spotted owl illustrates how some species are area-sensitive and require certain characteristics within a habitat. The spotted owl needed to find old-growth forests for its habitat. Caribou require several hundred square kilometers of old-growth forest. Where logging cuts into their territory, it exposes the caribou to wolf populations.

Some species have migratory patterns that must be considered. There has been controversy in Mexico over the habitat of the monarch butterfly. This butterfly has a pattern of wintering either in Mexico or California and then migrating to northern climates in the United States and Canada to lay eggs in the summer. It is its winter habitat in the Mexican forests that is under siege by loggers who want to cut the trees from what is now an ecological preserve.

Endangered species are those that are found in a small area and are at low density within that area. Once a species becomes noticeably endangered, intervention or protection becomes necessary.

The International Union for the Conservation of Nature (IUCN) ("The IUCN Red List of Threatened Species," 2012) lists the following classes of extinction:

1. *Critically endangered:* Risk of immediate extinction

2. *Endangered:* Very high risk of extinction

3. *Vulnerable:* High risk of extinction in the medium term

4. *Conservation dependent:* The focus of continuing habitat conservation programs

5. *Near threatened:* Close to being vulnerable

6. *Least concern:* Not conservation-dependent or close to being vulnerable

Indicator species are representative of the health of an ecosystem. Forest managers may select several species, and their health and population are representative of the system as a whole.

Causes of Extinction

Biologists group the factors endangering species into the acronym **HIPPO:**

- Habit destruction
- Invasive species
- Pollution
- Population
- Overharvesting

Commercial development often leads to an alteration of habitat for a number of species. The destruction of the rain forest has led to the disappearance of many species. Destruction of coral reefs and wetlands has been a factor in the loss of many species. Roughly 90% of the wetlands in New Zealand and Australia have been overtaken by human development, as have 75% of the mangrove swamps in India, Pakistan, and Thailand. With these areas went a number of species.

Hunting has reduced a number of species to the endangered status. The whale population was once estimated at 2.6 million. Killing whales became a popular industry, providing oil and meat. Currently, the estimated whale population stands at 1.5 million, but two thirds of these numbers are the minke whale. The sperm whale population is one fourth of what it used to be, and the fin whale is only 10% of its prior standing.

Bison was once the food staple for Native Americans, but once they were slaughtered for their hides, the numbers put them on the brink of extinction. It was estimated that as many as 60 million bison once roamed the United States. Now there are approximately 500,000, and close to 70% are intended for human consumption as meat. Only 15,000 can be considered roaming the wild.

Illegal hunting is calling **poaching**, and that applies to hunters who kill game for economic gain. The African elephant numbered 2.5 million in 1970. Today the population is less than 600,000. Tusks are harvested for ivory and are particularly valuable in Asia. Similarly, the rhinoceros has found itself endangered as hunters kill them for ivory.

The introduction of a foreign species to a habitat can drive another species out and into endangerment. Other causes of endangerment include pests, viruses, pollution, and human collection.

A controversial clash over the ESA happened in 1975 when a federal court halted construction of a dam that would have destroyed the habitat of the **snail darter,** a minnow that measured 3 inches in length. The U.S. Supreme Court upheld this decision. However, Congress eventually ordered an exemption, and the dam was completed. Fortunately, the snail darter was successfully transplanted to another habitat.

This case illustrated the basic conflict between nature and human progress. While some would question the common sense of protecting a tiny snail darter at the expense of a dam, others would argue about the importance of maintaining biodiversity and that we should find alternative solutions.

Why Should We Care?

E. O. Wilson (2002) wrote the following:

We, Homo sapiens, have arrived and marked our territory well. Winners of the Darwinian lottery, bulge-headed paragons of organic evolution, industrious bipedal apes with opposable thumbs, we are chipping away the ivorybills and other miracles around us. As habitats shrink, species decline wholesale in range and abundance. They slip down the Red Line ratchet, and the vast majority depart without special notice. Being distracted and self-absorbed, as is our nature, we have not yet fully understood what we are doing. But future generations, with endless time to reflect, will understand it all, and in painful detail. As awareness grows, so will their sense of loss. (p. 105)

Reintroduction of the Wolves

In 1995, thirty-one wolves were captured and released in Yellowstone National Park, and another 36 in Idaho after an absence from the region of 70 years. The intention was to return the wolves to a natural habitat that they had been driven from by man. Ranchers in the area, who were concerned about the safety of their cattle, greeted the news of the wolf's reintroduction with horror. Here was a case of conservationists advocating a return to the natural balance of the wilderness at the expense of some local citizens' livelihood.

The wolf population has grown from that original group of 66 to 663, with 271 residing in Yellowstone, 284 in Idaho, and 108 in Montana. This has reduced their status from endangered to *threatened*.

In 2002, wolves killed 52 cattle, 99 sheep, nine dogs, and five llamas. Ranchers shot and killed 46 wolves in the same period. Ranchers are compensated by the federal government for their losses. In 2008, the Bush administration authorized wolf hunting in this region.

The clash in the West over the reintroduction of wolves is an example of the conflict between nature and economics. In 2008, the U.S. government published a rule that permitted the killing of wolves despite their classification as an endangered species. Conservationists immediately sued to block the rule (Zumbo, n.d.).

The Silence of the Bees

Another example of the critical relationship between man and nature is the disappearance of bees in the winter of 2006 and 2007. For most of us, a bee appears to be nothing more than an annoying pest to smash against a wall. However, the bee serves an important role in nature, pollinating one third of all our fruits and vegetables.

That winter, approximately 25% of the bee population in the United States disappeared, vanished. Simultaneous disappearances were reported in Europe and South America. It was discovered that the bees that grew sick with a virus would leave the hive and die. The disease was called **colony collapse disorder**, and after much study, it was linked to a virus that had been imported by bees that hailed from Australia, and the virus was traced to Israel.

This virus held the threat of total annihilation, and in some hives, only the queen bee survived. There was an obvious economic loss to beekeepers who made money by transporting their bees to pollination zones, but the loss of a quarter of the pollinators of fruits and vegetables led to an agricultural loss as well (PBS, n.d.).

Biodiversity Action Plans

The Earthwatch Institute (n.d.) has a website (www.businessandbiodiversity .org) that addresses how businesses can have an action plan for biodiversity.

- *Stage 1: Assess your impacts:* This starts with an ecological survey of the habitats and species on site. Following a site analysis, an investigation of the entire supply chain would make this a thorough assessment.
- *Stage 2: Prioritization:* A risk analysis will determine which projects take the most priority in immediate action.
- *Stage 3: Management schedule and monitoring:* A project schedule should set out the critical path of activities that must be accomplished across multiple projects, noting milestones and budgets.
- *Stage 4: Targets and performance indicators:* Realistic target dates and outcomes should be established.
- *Stage 5: Monitor, review, and report:* A regular review of the action plan should help monitor how the plan is working and if adjustments to the plan and schedule must be made.

One example of a full-fledged biodiversity action plan is BP's plan for Indonesia. Their actions took steps that supported a plan for the local nature reserve, supported a conservation fund, and required a biodiversity awareness program for employees. "Our challenge is to transcend the apparent trade-off between energy supply and the environment. To show that energy can be produced and used without destroying biodiversity" (Browne, 2000).

Deep Ecology

Deep ecology is a school of thought of environmentalism that believes humans are part of nature but all other species have equal standing. It was first proposed in 1972 by Arne Naess. It is termed *deep* because "assumptions about the value of nature and the relationship between humans and the natural world, for instance, shape the way we view and interact with nature. . . . It reflects critically on those fundamental assumptions" (Barnhill, 2006).

An understanding of this movement is important because businesses have to consider radical points of view in many cases. Deep ecologists are important stakeholders in the environmental movement.

Naess (1989) and Sessions (1995) laid out eight principles for the movement:

1. The well-being and flourishing of human and nonhuman life on earth have value in themselves. These values are independent of the usefulness of the nonhuman world for human purposes.

2. Richness and diversity of life forms contribute to the realization of these values and are also values in themselves.

3. Humans have no right to reduce this richness and diversity except to satisfy vital needs.

4. The flourishing of human life and cultures is compatible with a substantial decrease of the human population. The flourishing of nonhuman life requires such a decrease.

5. Present human interference with the nonhuman world is excessive, and the situation is rapidly worsening.

6. Policies must therefore be changed. These policies affect basic economic, technological, and ideological structures.

7. The ideological change is mainly that of appreciating life quality rather than adhering to an increasingly higher standard of living.

8. Those who subscribe to the foregoing points have an obligation directly or indirectly to try to implement the necessary changes.

Barnhill (2006) wrote the following:

One of the common characteristics of deep ecology is the valorization of wilderness. Since nature is being destroyed by human exploitation and manipulation, the ideal is to be found in areas in which there has been virtually no such use and control. In wilderness areas, we see how nature works without human interference, flourishing with a complex and spontaneous order. In addition, we recognize ourselves as but a small part o the vast richness of the natural world. For some deep ecologists, this has led to a critical attitude toward agriculture as another instance of humans manipulating the Earth for their own ends.

Estuary Protection

Estuaries, which are partially enclosed bodies of water along the coast where freshwater from rivers meets salt water from the ocean, are natural habitats to a number of endangered species. Coastal watershed counties provide 69 million jobs and are sources of recreation and natural beauty, and protection is important.

The EPA gave these reasons for the importance of estuaries:

Estuaries provide us with a suite of resources, benefits, and services. Some of these can be measured in dollars and cents, others cannot. Estuaries provide places for recreational activities, scientific study, and aesthetic enjoyment. Estuaries are an irreplaceable natural resource that must be managed carefully for the mutual benefit of all who enjoy and depend on them.

Thousands of species of birds, mammals, fish, and other wildlife depend on estuarine habitats as places to live, feed, and reproduce. And many marine organisms, including most commercially important species of fish, depend on estuaries at some point during their development. Because they are biologically productive, estuaries provide ideal areas for migratory birds to rest and re-fuel during their long journeys. Because many species of fish and wildlife rely on the sheltered waters of estuaries as protected spawning places, estuaries are often called the "nurseries of the sea." (U.S. EPA, 2012)

Business Implications

Economic development often comes into conflict with the conservation and preservation of nature. While a new housing development brings employment and economic gain, it also can threaten an important ecosystem and upset the balance of nature. Many question why we should care about the fate of a snail darter or a spotted owl, a species so minute in the greater scale of things that their disappearance would hardly be noticed. The counter to this philosophy is that we are all interrelated; man and nature and must respect the earth.

The overarching theme of sustainable development, however, is to act today as if tomorrow mattered, and a beautiful tomorrow would include pristine lakes, ponds, and forests. This is precisely the theme of Dr. Seuss's (1971) *The Lorax*: decimating a forest to make money can have such a devastating effect.

Conclusion

In this chapter, we reviewed issues concerning forests, wilderness, wildlife, and biodiversity. These issues all pertain to the natural balance of the planet. It is important to understand these relationships and interdependencies when pursuing a course of sustainable development.

When a firm chooses to use paper or wood products, it is making a sustainability decision. When one drinks his or her cup of coffee in the morning, sustainability issues go into that cup—where the coffee is from, what sort of cup holds the coffee, and what type of labor was involved in getting it into your cup.

When that individual on the street stops and asks you to donate to save the whales, you wonder why you should care. What good does a whale ever do for you? And what business is it of ours that wolves were driven out of their habitats? After all, you might say this is a survival of the fittest world, and humans, having the greatest intellect, ultimately win.

The issues in this chapter point out the conflict that can arise between nature and economics. All too often, nature loses the conflict.

KEY WORDS

Chain of custody

Colony collapse disorder

Controlled wood

Deep ecology

Endangered species

Forest Ethics

Forest management

Forest Stewardship Council (FSC)

Greenwashing

HIPPO

Indicator species

Keystone species

Montreal Process

Poaching

Programme for the Endorsement of Forest Certification (PEFC)

Selective-cutting

Shelter-wood cutting

Snail darter

Strip-cutting

Sustainable Forestry Initiative (SFI)

Tropical rain forest

Wilderness Society

DISCUSSION QUESTIONS

1. Discuss the relationship between climate and the rain forest.

2. What are the major methods for tree cutting?

3. Much controversy has centered upon how much land should be protected as wilderness. What is the focus of both sides of the argument?

4. Why do we enact laws to protect endangered species?

5. Discuss the role biodiversity plays in nature.

6. How do the various forest certification programs differ?

7. Wood certification programs have been criticized for their relationship with corporations. Research the controversy over certification.

8. What are the issues in the debate over hunting wildlife from airplanes?

9. It is a practice to destroy wildlife (i.e., bears) that have attacked human beings. Why is this practiced?

10. If trees are cleared for growing coffee, how do coffee providers justify their environmental policies?

RECOMMENDED WEBSITES

www.businessandbiodiversity.org

www.environmentalpaper.org

www.eoearth.org

www.forests.org

www.fs.fed.us

www.fsc.org

www.iucnredlist.org

www.pbs.org

www.pefc.org

www.sfiprogram.org

www.woodconsumption.org

www.yellowstonenationalpark.org

5

Alternative Clean Energy and Fuels

LEARNING OBJECTIVES

By the end of this chapter, you will be able to do the following:

- Discuss the need for clean energy.
- Present the four types of conventional energy.
- Explain the different types of **renewable energy.**
- Compare and contrast solar and **wind energy.**
- Evaluate the promise of plant-based energy from **ethanol** to wood waste.
- Discuss other forms of energy, such as tidal to geothermal.
- Evaluate the most viable alternative energy and fuel sources for businesses today.

Chapter Overview

There is a growing public interest in finding sustainable, alternative sources of energy and fuel. Fortunately, a whole spectrum of alternative options does exist in the form of renewable energy sources that can be harnessed from natural sources such as the wind, sun, earth, and ocean. Renewable fuels derived from plants and vegetable oil produce fewer emissions than coal and are viable resources for organizations wishing to reduce their coal and oil consumption. This chapter presents conventional energy and its challenges and discusses the next generation of alternative fuels and energy options. We will also discuss the benefits and challenges associated with each of these alternative sources of energy and fuel and evaluate implications of clean energy.

The Need for Clean Energy

Energy poses one of the biggest challenges to sustainability. The need for energy is ever-increasing. Residents of affluent nations like Germany; developing worlds like China; or struggling, underdeveloped countries like Haiti all rely on some form of energy. The energy economy of the past was fueled by oil, coal, and **natural gas.** Concerns about global warming and the rising cost of fuel have spurred interest in a new energy economy less dependent upon **fossil fuels.** This new energy economy is powered by wind, solar, and other forms of clean and renewable sources (Brown, 2009).

In recent years, the natural resources have been depleted at an unprecedented rate (Worldwatch Institute, n.d.), and continued rates of extraction will deplete this store of the natural capital. Fossil fuels have been the dominant source of the world's energy since the beginning of industrial revolution, accounting for 82% of energy demand in the United States (U.S. Energy Information Administration [EIA], 2010). As illustrated in Figure 5.1, approximately 45% of electricity is generated from burning coal. This fossil fuel consumption releases carbon dioxide emissions into the atmosphere that, in turn, warms the planet. The Energy Information Administration (EIA) expects global emissions of carbon dioxide from the fossil fuel sources to rise by more than 12 billion tons, a gain of almost 40% by 2035 (Gardner, 2010). In addition, China's economic growth has led to carbon dioxide emissions from industrial sources from 2000 to 2004, increasing at a rate over three times the rate during the 1990s (Vergano, 2007). Switching to alternative sources of power, such as clean and renewable energy, will

Figure 5.1   U.S. Electric Power Industry Net Generation, 2009

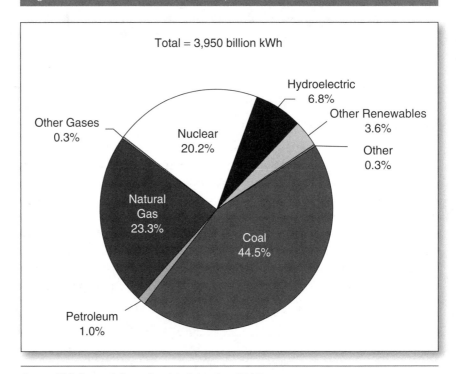

Source: U.S. Energy Information Administration (2010).

reduce the amount of carbon dioxide released in the atmosphere. In the next decade, an 80% cut in carbon dioxide emissions would be possible only by replacing coal- and oil-fired electricity generation with renewable sources (Brown, 2009).

Conventional Sources of Energy

There are primarily four sources of conventional energy: (1) coal, (2) oil, (3) natural gas, and (4) nuclear. Another energy source—**hydropower**—is also conventional, but it is renewable as well. Hence, hydropower will be discussed later in the chapter.

Coal

Coal energy accounts for 22% of U.S. production, and almost 90% of coal is used to generate electricity. Coal has had a long history and was widely used in the Middle Ages for forges, breweries, and smithies. Coal helped fuel the physical and industrial expansion of the United States as coal-fired steam generators produced electricity in 1880s. At present, the United States produces more coal than any other country, with the exception of China, and the production of coal exceeds the demand (Berinstein, 2001).

Advantages

Coal energy is affordable and reliable. The plants are flexible in that they are capable of burning coal, oil, and **biomass.** Coal is fairly efficient, and the newer plants have installed filters that eliminate 99% of smoke particles and 95% of the carbon released ("Coal Energy," n.d.). Coal energy is not dependent on the weather, and its reserves are more abundant than oil and natural gas (Fossil Fuel, n.d.).

Disadvantages

Coal is in limited supply, and there are environmental detriments to coal production and consumption. In terms of coal production, there are numerous concerns such as land subsidence from underground mining, disruption of habitats from strip mining, gas and particulate emissions from power plants, waste piles accrued in mining, acid mine drainage that leaks into waterways, methane emissions from mines, and so on. Coal contains 70% carbon, and its consumption creates more carbon dioxide than other conventional sources such as oil or natural gas. The sulfur in coal becomes sulfur dioxide that in turn causes corrosion in boilers (Berinstein, 2001). In addition, smoke from coal can cause adverse health effects such as emphysema.

Clean Coal

Clean coal technologies refers to a plethora of options to reduce the environmental impact of coal energy generation. Some of these options include the following: chemically washing the impurities and minerals contained in coal; using gasification whereby organic materials are converted into carbon dioxide, hydrogen, carbon monoxide, and methane; treating the flue gases with steam to reduce sulfur dioxide; using coal liquefaction to convert coal into liquid fuels; utilizing fluidized bed combustion in which low quality coal is burned on a bed of limestone to absorb carbon dioxide; and using carbon capture technologies to store the carbon dioxide from flue gases and treating brown coal to improve the efficiency of conversion from coal to electricity (Berinstein, 2001).

Duke Energy received stimulus funds to build a $2.35 billion carbon capture and sequestration plant in Indiana. The new plant will cook the coal into a fuel gas and then clean the gas thoroughly before burning it in a jet engine. The next step would be to capture the carbon dioxide by storing it in a deep well on the site (Wald, 2009). However, there is concern that the risks of underground storage are too high.

Oil

Crude oil or petroleum has been around for a long time, but its demand increased dramatically during the Industrial Revolution. The world uses millions of barrels of oil each day. Crude oil, or petroleum, remains an important ingredient for many of the products we use daily, from plastics to gasoline, as well as energy.

Advantages

Petroleum is readily available, efficient, and relatively affordable, though price per barrel of oil continues to change due a variety of factors. Oil generates less carbon dioxide than coal when burned.

Disadvantages

Petroleum is formed from organic matter that was buried millions of years ago and was subjected to extreme temperature and pressure. Its supply is limited and will eventually run out. The costs of extraction continue to rise, and fuel costs are projected to rise over time. The extraction of oil is environmentally damaging, and crude oil needs to be transported to refineries via pipelines or tankers. The accidents from tanker ships have caused damage to marine life as witnessed by the ExxonMobil spill and the British Petroleum (BP) spill. Furthermore, the usage of oil causes emissions of carbon dioxide, carbon monoxide, nitrogen oxide, and hydrocarbons (Berinstein, 2001; Fossil Fuel, n.d.).

Natural Gas

Natural gas was most likely formed by the remains of decayed plant and animal matter that was under pressure over millions of years. It comprises mostly methane, ethane, propane, and other hydrocarbons. It is used for heating, cooling, electricity generation, powering appliances, and in fuel cells (Berinstein, 2001; Fossil Fuel, n.d.).

Advantages

Natural gas is considered clean compared to other fossil fuels since its use results in minimal emissions of carbon monoxide and hydrocarbons and almost no emissions of sulfur dioxide. It is relatively inexpensive when compared to coal. Due to the highly efficient combustion process, natural gas produces very few by-products (Berinstein, 2001; Fossil Fuel, n.d.).

Disadvantages

Natural gas is highly flammable, and its production needs to be managed carefully. It is colorless and odorless, and it can be difficult to find potential leaks. A drilling method—**hydrofracking**—carries significant environmental risks. A series of documents obtained by the *New York Times* report that dangers from the wastewater, an output of hydrofracking, contain radioactive materials that may pollute rivers (Urbina, 2011).

Nuclear

Nuclear energy is the potential energy of atoms and is derived from the splitting of uranium atoms in a process called fission. "In a power plant, this fission process is used to generate heat for producing steam, which is used by a turbine to generate electricity" (Westinghouse, n.d.). Nuclear energy is considered a good solution because it emits far fewer greenhouse gases (GHGs) than coal or other power generation resources (Presidio Buzz, 2009). However, it is also a somewhat dangerous and hazardous source as illustrated by the March 2011 nuclear crisis at the Fukushima Daiichi power plant. The discussion about using nuclear power is focused on weighing the risks against the rewards, both of which are discussed next.

Advantages

Nuclear power generation emits a relatively low amount of greenhouse emissions. The operating costs are relatively low, and the technology is known and developed. In addition, the large power-generating capacity can meet industrial and urban demands. Furthermore, it is possible to reduce nuclear waste through recycling and reprocessing (Presidio Buzz, 2009).

Disadvantages

The biggest challenge is how to dispose of or store the radioactive waste. High risk is another challenge, and accidents happen even with high security standards. The energy source for nuclear energy is uranium, the supply of which is extremely scarce and is estimated to run out in 30 to 60 years (Time for Change, n.d.). Given an accident, there are also concerns of meltdown and radiation, both of which were worrisome in the nuclear crisis at Fukushima Daiichi power plant in 2011. Nuclear energy is neither renewable nor sustainable since the disposal of nuclear waste and the retirement of nuclear plants contradicts the basic tenet of sustainability, which says that the present generations consumption should not impact the consumption for future generations.

An Overview of Renewable Energy

Renewable energy, such as the sun, the wind, plants, and water, use natural and virtually inexhaustible sources of power and are clean since these sources do not cause air, soil, or water pollution. Renewable energy accounted for 18% of global electricity generation in 2006; however, it is projected to overtake natural gas as the largest source of electricity after coal by 2015 (International Energy Agency [IEA], 2008).

In terms of energy supply, renewable energy technologies are fastest growing, outdoing new coal, nuclear, and oil plants (Sturgis, 2009). Renewable sources of energy climbed to 11.37% in the United States as of 2010 (U.S. EIA, 2010). Renewable energy technologies are attractive since these have the potential to strengthen our nation's economy by not relying on foreign oil and improve environmental quality (U.S. Department of Energy, 2011f).

We will discuss the most viable alternative energy sources available for business today: **solar energy**, wind energy, hydropower, plant-based energy, and other sources of renewable energy. There are other forms of energy derived from tides and oceans that can be used to generate electricity. Unfortunately, most of these forms suffer significant disadvantages that restrict their potential. The less feasible options will be presented later in the chapter.

Renewable energy sources account for a very small portion of the global energy supply portfolio. The primary reason for this is that the developed countries are the largest consumers of energy with fully established energy production infrastructure dependent upon fossil fuels. Changing this system of energy production over to a renewable supply would require billions of dollars. In the case of developing countries lacking a power infrastructure, switching over to renewable energy sources sounds ideal. However, the fact is that using fossil fuels is also cheap—*especially* where there are abundant deposits of coal or oil. The initial investment for renewable energy sources is prohibitive for some of the developing countries. As a result, these developing countries choose inexpensive fuels like coal when they embark on the path to development.

It should be pointed out that harnessing renewable energy sources is not perfect since these alternative energy sources have their own set of issues or limitations.

Solar Energy

The earth is blessed with another incredible supply of a renewable energy: sunlight. Solar energy is used by plants and animals as a primary energy source. The energy provided by the sun in 1 hour is sufficient to supply the human civilization's energy needs for 1 year (Morton, 2006). Solar energy is attained from collecting sunlight and converting it to energy using different technologies. These range from heating water using solar collectors to direct conversion of sunlight to electrical energy using solar panels, mirrors, or photovoltaic cells. Some of the newer technologies include thin film, nanotechnology, solar paint, and more efficient batteries to store **solar power** (see Figure 5.2).

Though solar energy is a free and inexhaustible natural resource, harnessing it is a relatively new idea. Solar power is obtained by harvesting solar radiation energy and converting that energy into electricity. There are two ways to harvest solar energy. The first, **photovoltaics**, involves the use of solar panels.

Figure 5.2   Solar Potential in the United States

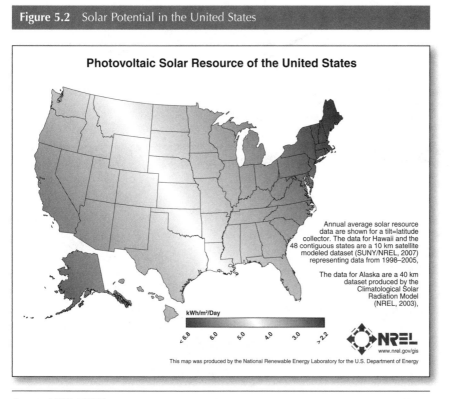

Source: NREL (2008).

These panels collect the solar energy and store it for later use. An example of photovoltaics is the solar powered calculator in which light energy is used to power the small battery located in the calculator. Photovoltaics is a clean source of energy and is relatively maintenance free. Solar panels have a very long life and require almost no maintenance after installation ("Advantages of Solar Energy," n.d.). The other way to harvest solar energy is by concentrating solar power (CSP) on a closed container and using the resultant energy to boil water that in turn generates power. The concept is similar to that of a steam engine. With enough heat, water is converted to steam, and this steam can then be used to drive turbines and create energy (Brown, 2009).

Please see Figures 5.3, 5.4, and 5.5 for images of solar energy technologies:

Figure 5.3   Parabolic Trough System

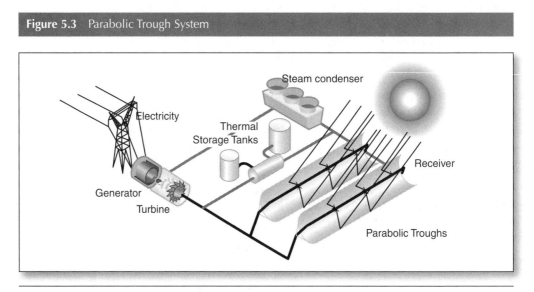

Source: http://www.eere.energy.gov/basics/renewable_energy/linear_concentrator.html

Figure 5.4   Linear Fresnel Reflector System

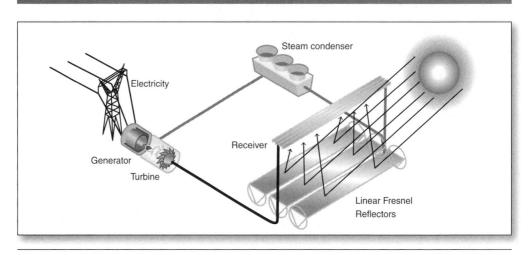

Source: http://www.eere.energy.gov/basics/renewable_energy/linear_concentrator.html

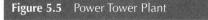

Figure 5.5 Power Tower Plant

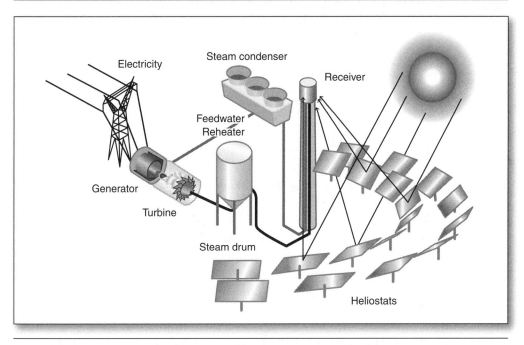

Source: http://www.eere.energy.gov/basics/renewable_energy/power_tower.html

Newer Technologies

There are some other technologies that are helping make solar energy more efficient and less expensive. Some of these are discussed here.

Thin film solar cells use a layer of semiconducting material to harvest electricity. A number of manufacturing companies (Global Solar, HelioVolt, Nanosolar) employ a copper indium gallium selenide (CIGS) to make thin film solar cells to produce photovoltaic cells. The challenges to this technology are cost, efficiency, and reliability (Biello, 2008).

Using *nanotechnology*, the energy collecting materials are printed onto rolls of thin foil. This foil or spray can then be applied to any surface to collect solar energy. Earlier solar panels had to be pointing towards the sun to collect energy. With nanotechnology, the spray contains layers of rods that filter and redirect sunlight for maximum absorption (Affordable-Alternative-Energy.com, n.d.).

Work is being done to create a paint that absorbs sunlight: *solar paint*. This paint is coated onto the surface of aluminized mylar in order to conduct electricity. Furthermore, it is coated with a clear layer of indium tin oxide that covers the paint and conducts electricity. This technology is still under development and is supposed to work like a solar panel but at a reduced cost (Affordable-Alternative-Energy.com, n.d.).

Scientists have developed a *new solar cell technology* that absorbs up to 96% of incident light. Early experiments indicate that these cells operate at

90% efficient rate. Since these cells are made of plastic, there is a potential of reduced costs (Huff, 2011). In other projects, utilities are working with residential customers to install *solar photovoltaic systems* with *smart grid* and *energy storage capabilities*. This technology is being tested in a pilot study in Sacramento, California (U.S. Department of Energy, 2012a).

Advantages of Solar Energy

Solar energy produces no emissions and requires very little maintenance since there are no movable or breakable parts. It has a significant life span of 20 to 30 years and the operation costs are low. It does not require large-scale installation or any specific supervision. It is also a scalable technology in that the systems can be small or large, depending upon the needs of the community. Solar energy systems operate silently, do not have moving parts, and do not require any fuel. The solar power generators are distributed to homes, schools, or businesses. The assembly of these generators does not require any extra development or land area, and the functioning of these systems is safe and quiet. The technology is flexible in that more solar energy capacity can be added as needed.

In developing countries, solar energy is also gaining popularity. Indeed, developing countries are the fastest growing segment of the photovoltaics market. Since the solar technology is modular and decentralized, it is highly suited for remote areas. Solar energy is much more practical than the extension of expensive power lines into remote areas. This is applicable for communities not yet connected to an electrical grid (Brown, 2009). Often, in these cases, it is cheaper to install photovoltaic panels rooftop by rooftop than to build a central power plant (IEA, 2006). When a villager in a remote area purchases a solar photovoltaic system, there is no fuel cost and very little maintenance required. To help with the initial cost, credit systems have been set up with the assistance of the World Bank and the United Nations Environment Programme (UNEP). For example, a World Bank assisted 50,000 homeowners in Bangladesh to obtain solar cell systems (de La Hamaide, 2007).

In developing countries, solar power is abundant and can be tapped at a reasonable market price. Solar energy costs approximately 30 cents per kilowatt-hour in developed countries, which is about 3.5 times the average rate paid by residents for conventional electricity (Foroudastan & Dees, 2006). The costs are higher because the electricity generated from the solar power has to be connected in to the grid. There are no grids in remote areas, and there is no linkup required to tie the solar power to an energy grid. Hence, the cost per kilowatt-hour drops to 0.6 times the average household. This fact makes the potential of solar energy in developing countries very attractive (Foroudastan & Dees, 2006). Nations from Algeria to China and India are investing in solar energy (Brown, 2009).

It is estimated that solar photovoltaic manufacturing companies can install systems that produce electricity for 12 cents a kilowatt-hour in Spain and 18 cents a kilowatt-hour in southern Germany by 2010 ("PV Costs Down Significantly From 1998–2007," 2009; "PV Costs Set to Plunge for 2009/10," 2008). China might join Israel, Spain, and Portugal in mandating that all new buildings incorporate rooftop solar water heaters (Nelson, 2007).

Challenges of Solar Energy

The primary challenge to solar energy is the initial, up-front cost to install a system. Despite the tax credits, this energy is still more expensive than electricity derived from conventional sources of energy. Solar panels require a lot of space for installation, and this might pose another challenge. Furthermore, the amount of sunlight varies from high solar intensity areas found in Africa, Asia, Latin America, and the Southwest United States to low solar intensity areas in Northern Europe. The payback period for solar energy also varies depending upon the complexity of the installed system, to solar intensity, to tax incentives. This time ranges from 3 or 4 years to 10 or more years (House-Energy, n.d.).

Business and Global Implications

The natural question is how to make solar energy more economically attractive for businesses. There are two ways to accomplish this: (1) government incentives and (2) energy cost savings. As an example, the government allows companies to receive tax breaks if solar energy technology is implemented, and a 30% corporate investment tax credit is offered for the amount of cost incurred in installing a solar energy system. There is also the Modified Accelerated Cost Recovery System that reduces depreciation time of the system so that companies get back some of their investment. This system allows for companies to use the money saved for reinvestment. Solar energy can also be used to offset energy cost. Power is more expensive during the peak office time in the day, and energy companies use differential pricing and charge higher rates in peak times. An installed solar system would let companies use solar energy in peak capacity times when energy costs are more expensive.

In 2008, photovoltaic installations went up to 5,600 megawatts worldwide, increasing total installations to nearly 15,000 megawatts. Solar photovoltaic production is one of the world's fastest-growing energy sources (European Photovoltaic Industry Association [EPIA], 2009).

Another method to harness solar energy is to use reflectors, a solar thermal technology, often referred to as concentrated solar power (CSP). Though the United States was the first to construct a CSP on a large scale, many other nations are entering this arena from Algeria to Spain. CSP also holds great promise for India where CSP plants in the desert could satisfy most of India's electricity needs.

There has been a rapid expansion in solar water and space heating in industrialized countries. In China and India, solar water heaters will reduce the need for new coal-fired power plants. These solar water and space heaters are economical in that these systems pay for themselves from electricity savings in fewer than 10 years (Nelson, 2007).

Wind Energy

Wind offers a clean, renewable manner in which to generate electricity. Wind energy is a sustainable solution because it is abundant, low cost, widely distributed, and does not generate atmospheric emissions or pollution. Wind energy has the potential to reduce our dependence on fossil fuels since the United States has enough land that can be used to produce wind energy. In the United States, the Department of Energy estimates that wind power could account for 20% of the nation's electricity supply within 20 years (*The New York Times*, 2012).

The National Renewable Energy Laboratory has identified offshore capacity sufficient to power the U.S. economy (Archer & Jacobson, 2003). Given present day technology, wind energy can provide 20% of America's electricity on very small allocations of land (Fettig, 2007). At present, wind energy accounts for less than 0.5% of all energy produced in America (Fettig, 2007). However, given the right infrastructure, wind energy can supply up to 150% or more of the *entire* U.S. energy demand (Fettig, 2007). The implication is that if wind energy can be ramped up with efficient infrastructure, the need for fossil fuel would be significantly reduced.

Advantages of Wind Energy

Wind is a natural resource of nature that is available all over the world. The conversion of wind power to wind energy is relatively inexpensive and is produced at a fraction of the cost from other power sources. **Wind turbines** are highly efficient as well, and the areas covered by **wind farms** can also be used for other uses such as farming and ranching. Wind energy produces minimal waste over the course of its life span and results in economic gain in cases where the extra energy can be sold back. Small communities, like those in southwestern Minnesota, can pool resources to build wind farms for power generation. The excess power is sold to the local energy companies for a profit (Fettig, 2007).

Windmills can be built anywhere there is wind, and wind turbines can be planted on interior farmlands, coastal boundaries, and in deep sea wind currents. Small wind turbines are designed for simplicity, ruggedness, and low maintenance and are primarily used for household and small farm or business applications. Most modern windmills are operated by computers at central command locations and need occasional repairs or upgrades. Wind turbines work according to air speed and do not consume additional power in order to generate electricity. For most turbines, the cost has a return on investment after about 10 years. The initial cost for the installation of a small turbine is about $40,000 and results in average savings of 40% on energy utlies whereas the initial cost of a large turbine is more than $1 million and results in average savings of 70% to 100% on energy utilities (Gipe, 2004). Utilities offer wind-generated electricity at a premium of 2 to 3 cents per kilowatt-hour. A household that uses wind power for 25% of its energy needs would spend an additional $4 or $5 per month.

Challenges of Wind Energy

There are two major challenges in the way of wind development. First, wind is sporadic, so there is a need for backup power (often fueled by natural gas) to supplement. Hawaii plans to install a 15-megawatt battery to smooth out the flow at a 30-megawatt wind farm in Oahu where the wind can be gusty and erratic. The battery system offers an additional functionality of storing energy for arbitrage. The second challenge is that of wind location. For example, in Texas the winds are strongest in the western part of the state, and expensive transmission lines would need to be set up to transmit the energy to Dallas and Houston (*The New York Times*, 2012). Another solution is to build wind farms offshore. The wind blows harder, and offshore turbines can be located close to the coasts. There are some concerns about the turbines detracting from the view of the coastline. The two projects under consideration are the Cape Wind project, which would be the nation's first offshore wind farm, and the Atlantic Wind Connection (*The New York Times*, 2012).

Business and Global Implications

A wind turbine constructed in an acre of corn land in Iowa can produce $300,000 of electricity per year. If corn were to be planted on this land, it would yield 480 gallons of ethanol worth $960, making a wind farm a much more attractive investment (Brown, 2009).

The turbines occupy only 1% of the land covered by a wind farm, thus enabling the farmers and ranchers to grow grain and graze cattle. These farmers and ranchers typically receive $3,000 to $10,000 a year in royalties for each wind turbine without any up-front investment (Brown, 2009; Union of Concerned Scientists, 2003).

Wind farms also hold promise for rural communities because wind farms yield local jobs, royalties from wind turbines, and additional tax revenue.

Wind turbines can be mass produced on assembly lines. The idle capacity from the U.S. automobile industry is enough to manufacture these wind turbines. In addition to the idle plants, skilled workers are eager to retool their skill set and return to work (Brown, 2009; World Resources Institute, 2003).

In the United States, numerous states require that a portion of their energy production come from renewable sources. From the perspective of utilities, long-term fixed-price contracts are preferable to natural gas and coal-fired power, fuels that come with volatile price and uncertainty (Brown, 2009).

In terms of future growth, wind energy is highly promising. In 2008,wind accounted for 36% of new generating capacity in the European Union compared with 29% for natural gas, 18% for photovoltaics, 10% for oil, and only 3% for coal (European Wind Energy Association [EWEA], 2009). In the United States, new wind-generating capacity has exceeded coal by a wide margin each year since 2005 (Shuster, 2009). It is predicted that further growth can especially be expected in China, the United States, Germany, Spain, and India and in other countries in Eastern Europe, Asia, and Latin America. It is expected that African nations will also turn to wind projects (World Wind Energy Association, 2009).

Wind power is the world's fastest growing energy source and is also becoming one of the most rapidly expanding industries. The United States is the world's leader in total capacity followed by Germany, Spain, China, and India (Global Wind Energy Council [GWEC], 2009). In terms of acquisition of wind energy, Germany, the United States, Spain, Denmark, and India are among the world's leading nations. In terms of wind as a share of national electricity, Denmark is the leader at 21%. Both Spain and France are expanding their wind capacity; Spain is aiming for 20,000 megawatts by 2010, and France, a relative newcomer to wind energy, is looking to develop 25,000 megawatts of wind by 2020 (GWEC, 2009).

China has about 12,000 megawatts of wind-generating capacity. However, in anticipation of future need, China's Wind Base program plans to manufacture six megacomplexes of wind farms. When completed, these complexes will have a generating capacity of 105 gigawatts, equal to the worldwide wind power in 2008. (GWEC, 2009).

Hydropower

Hydropower refers to using water, the most common renewable source of energy in the United States. Similar to wind, this form of energy has been around for thousands of years. The ancient Greeks used water wheels, which picked up water in buckets around a wheel. The weight of the water caused the wheel to turn, and this mechanical energy was used for grinding grain and pumping water. Hydropower became a source for generating electricity during the late 19th century. In 1979, the first **hydroelectric power** plant was built at Niagara Falls in 1979, and 2 years later, the city streetlamps were powered by hydropower.

A hydropower plant comprises three parts: (1) an electric plant where the electricity is produced, (2) a dam to control water flow, and (3) a reservoir where water can be stored. The flow of water behind the dam powers the blades in a turbine, which in turn spins a generator to produce electricity. The electricity is then transported over long-distance electric lines to homes, factories, and businesses (Berinstein, 2001).

Almost one fifth of world's electricity comes from hydropower. The five largest producers of hydropower are China, Canada, Brazil, the United States, and Russia. One of the world's largest hydropower plants is at Three Gorges on China's Yangtze River Dam and is 1.4 miles wide and 607 feet high. The Grand Coulee Dam on the Columbia River (northern Washington) is the biggest hydropower plant in the United States.

Advantages of Hydropower

Hydropower is the most inexpensive way to generate electricity today. Once a dam has been constructed and the equipment installed, the energy source derived from flowing water is free. It is renewable yearly by snow and rainfall. There is no pollution or waste released in the production of hydropower, and fossil fuels are not required to produce the electricity. Hydropower is readily available since the engineers can control the flow of water through the turbines to produce electricity. Furthermore, since water is a naturally recurring resource, there is no worry of price fluctuations, production strikes, issues of transportation, or other national security issues. In addition, reservoirs may offer recreational opportunities, such as swimming and boating ("Hydropower," 2012).

Challenges of Hydropower

Dams are highly controversial for numerous reasons. Containing rivers within dams may disrupt wildlife and other natural resources. For instance, salmon may be prevented from swimming upstream to spawn. Though fish ladders help salmon go over dams and enter spawning areas, the dams can change the migration patterns of fish. Dams can also cause low dissolved oxygen levels in the water that, in turn, is harmful to river habitats ("Hydropower," 2012). An even more problematic issue pertains to the forcible eviction of people from their land as witnessed in China and Chile in recent years. The construction of a new dam requires an open area, and the people living in this area are asked to move and give up their former lifestyles. This becomes very controversial, especially if a community has maintained a particular way of life on the land for generations. For example, in Chile, the indigenous Pehuenche are fighting construction of the Ralco Dam on the Biobio River (570 megawatt-hour and U.S. $500,000,000). The Pehuenche regard the upper Biobio as their ancestral home. The construction of the five dams would result in the relocation of 1,000 Pehuenches, about one fifth of the survivors of this ancient culture (Aylwin, 2002).

There are also public debates between preserving rivers for their natural beauty versus producing electricity to meet energy needs. Indeed, the only undammed river in the United States is the Yellowstone.

Business and Global Implications

The five countries that account for more than half of the world's hydropower production are Brazil, Canada, China, Russia, and the United States ("Hydropower Development," 2010).

There is a correlation between hydropower development and a country's economic development. Norway was one of Europe's poorest countries a century ago, and it has become a highly industrialized, self-reliant, and wealthy nation. Almost 99% of Norway's electricity supply comes from hydropower plants, and the resultant efficiencies aided Norway's economic development and overall expansion ("Hydropower Development," 2010).

In the poverty-ridden country of Bhutan, there is vast potential for hydropower generation. Experts estimate Bhutan's hydropower capacity to exceed 30,000 megawatts. With capital-intensive hydropower projects, Bhutan stands to improve its economic standing ("Hydropower Development," 2010).

In 2006, dams with a combined 6,000 megawatts of capacity were built in rural areas of China. Many other countries are building small-scale dams. In addition, there is growing interest in turbines that do not need a dam and are less environmentally damaging ("Rural Areas," 2007).

Plant-Based Energy

Another source of energy that has been gaining attention is plant-based energy. This source includes biomass, forest industry by-products, sugar industry by-products, and urban tree and yard waste among others.

Biomass

This refers to the use of organic materials as fuel. One of the most common uses of biomass energy is the burning of wood. This energy has a lot of potential in the United States but is not very widely used because of a lack of infrastructure to grow energy crops. The largest contributor to biomass fuels comes from organic waste material that contains energy that can be used as fuel. The industrial wastes include bark, chipped wood, logging residues, and agricultural wastes like plant debris and leaves. The municipal waste can contain 60% of organic material, and the material not recycled can be used for energy. The paper and pulp industry also supplies waste termed *black liquor*, which is residue from wood that is chemically pulped (Berinstein, 2001).

Crop-Based Fuels

Crops were used to produce 19 billion gallons of fuel ethanol and 4 billion gallons of **biodiesel** for automotive fuel worldwide in 2009. About half of the stock of ethanol comes from the United States, one third from Brazil, and the rest from a dozen other countries, led by China and Canada. In terms of biodiesel, Germany and France lead the world's output, each responsible for 15%; the other major producers are the United States, Brazil, and Italy (Licht, 2009).

Biodiesel is a renewable fuel that can be manufactured from vegetable oils, animal fats, or recycled restaurant waste grease. It is also nontoxic, biodegradable, and a cleaner-burning replacement for diesel fuel. The most common biodiesel blend found in the United States is the B20 that is comprised of 20% biodiesel and 80% petroleum diesel. The main advantage of using B20 is that is does not require engine modifications on the vehicle. In addition, B20 performs well in cold weather.

The B100 stands for 100% biodiesel and can be used in some engines provided the parts such as hoses and gaskets are made with biodiesel-compatible material. Besides yielding lower energy content per gallon, there are some other concerns with B100 such as "potential issues with impact on engine warranties, low-temperature gelling, solvency/cleaning effect if regular diesel was previously used, and microbial contamination" (U.S. Department of Energy, 2011c).

Ethanol is another renewable fuel made from corn, sugarcane, or cellulosic feedstocks. The production of ethanol from corn is controversial since it has the potential to drive up corn prices. There have also been concerns about producing ethanol from sugarcane since sugarcane production is correlated to the deforestation of the Amazon in Brazil. The most preferable option would be to produce ethanol from feedstocks—such as grass, wood, crop residues, or old newspapers. However, this process is more cumbersome as the cellulosic material needs to ferment into component sugars (U.S. Department of Energy, 2011d).

Internal combustion engines work well using ethanol as a fuel. In most cases, ethanol is blended with gasoline in various amounts for use in vehicles. E10 (10% ethanol, 90% gasoline) is a low-level blend and can be used in any gasoline-powered vehicle whereas E85 (85% ethanol, 15% gasoline) can be used in vehicles designed as flexible fuel vehicles. The advantage of the 15% gasoline content in E85 is that the flexible fuel vehicles can operate normally under cold conditions. Using a pure ethanol (E100) fuel can lead to issues in cold-weather conditions. There is no perceptible difference between E85 versus gasoline. E85 is priced lower than gasoline and yields about 27% less energy per gallon than gasoline. Hence, the two fuels are comparable.

Challenges of Crop-Based Fuels

Initially, crop-based fuels were considered to be a feasible alternative to oil. However, recent studies have revealed glaring disadvantages. The main concern is that increase in ethanol production will drive up food prices globally. The biodiesel refiners in Europe gets much of their palm oil from Malaysia and Indonesia, where the rain forest is cleared to make way for palm plantations (Guerin, 2007; Licht, 2009). Recent studies have illustrated that conversion of rain forests or grasslands to corn, soybean, or palm oil biofuel production leads to a net carbon emissions increase that is termed as a "biofuel carbon debt" (Fargione, Hill, Tilman, Polasky, & Hawthorne, 2008; Searchinger et al., 2008).

There are many studies that indicate that switchgrass and hybrid poplars could produce relatively high ethanol yields, but there is no low-cost technology available (Hill, Nelson, Tilman, Polasky, & Tiffany, 2006; Perlack et al., 2009; Schmer, Vogel, Mitchell, & Perrin, 2006; U.S. Department of Energy, 2012b).

Business and Global Implications

Waste has been used to generate electricity in the forest industry, including both sawmills and paper mills. The forest waste is burnt to generate electricity for sale to local utilities, providing 11,000 megawatts of electrical generation in the United States (Overend & Milbrandt, 2007).

Furthermore, urban areas also use wood waste for combined heat and power production. In Sweden, nearly half of all residential and commercial buildings are served with district heating systems. In 1980, imported oil supplied over 90% of the heat for these systems but, by 2007, this oil had been replaced by wood chips and urban waste (Swedish Energy Agency, 2008).

The city of Saint Paul, Minnesota, built a combined heat and power plant to use tree waste. The plant utilizes 250,000 tons of waste wood per year and supplies district heating to about 80% of the downtown area. This shift to wood waste mostly replaced coal and cut down carbon emissions by 76,000 tons per year (Rydaker, 2007).

The cane-based ethanol distilleries in Brazil realized the potential of burning bagasse, the fibrous material left after syrup is extracted. Bagasse is burnt to heat the fermentation process and to generate electricity. The sugar industry has begun to burn cane waste to cogenerate heat and power (World Alliance for Decentralized Energy, 2004).

Other Sources of Renewable Energy and Fuel

Our energy needs have been met by coal, oil, and gas industries that have provided humankind with cheap fuel while ignoring the associated pollution and climate change costs. One of the consequences of this reliance has been that there has been scant investment in alternative renewable energies. Besides the previously discussed renewables such as wind, solar, hydropower, and plant-based energy, there are numerous other sources available ranging from geothermal to **wave energy.** Some of these alternatives are discussed next.

Geothermal

Geothermal power comes from the heat contained inside the earth. Some geothermal systems are formed when hot magma near the surface directly heats rocks or groundwater, and this heat flows toward the surface as volcanoes, geysers, and hot springs. Most of the **geothermal energy** is trapped under the earth's crust. Geothermal is not strictly renewable since this resource can be depleted. However, given the amount of this resource, a complete exhaustion is highly unlikely. According to a report financed by the U.S. Department of Energy, advanced geothermal power could theoretically produce as much as 60,000 times the nation's annual energy usage (Glanz, 2009).

Geothermal energy can be used in geologically active areas of the earth, but the concentration of geothermal energy must be quite high in order to make heat extraction feasible. Most of these regions are located in geologically active areas, and these hot spots are found in the western United States, Iceland, New Zealand, the Philippines, and South America.

There are environmental concerns with regards to geothermal energy. The tapping of shallow steam beds can cause small earthquakes. In order to tap the larger reserves of geothermal energy, engineers need to dig deeper in the core. Since large earthquakes tend to originate at great depths, breaking rock that far down carries much more serious risk. The technique to tap geothermal energy requires injecting water at great pressure down drilled holes to fracture the deep bedrock and the subsequent opening of each fracture is akin to a tiny earthquake (Glanz, 2009).

Geothermal Heat Pumps

These pumps use the earth's constant temperature as the exchange medium instead of the outside air temperature. This allows the geothermal heat pumps (GHPs) to operate at high efficiencies (300% to 600%) on the cold winter nights, compared to 175% to 250% for air-source heat pumps on cool days ("Geothermal Heat Pumps," 2011).

There are extreme seasonal variations ranging from blistering heat in the summer to icy cold in the winter. However, a few feet below the earth's surface the ground remains at a relatively constant temperature. These ground temperatures range from 45 degrees Fahrenheit (7 degrees Celsius) to 75 degrees Fahrenheit (21 degrees Celsius) depending on latitude. In the winter, this ground temperature is warmer than the air above it and, conversely, in the summer the ground temperature is cooler than the air above. The GHPs utilize a ground heat exchanger to exchange heat with the earth.

The installation price of a geothermal system can be expensive. However, the additional costs are returned in energy savings in 5 to 10 years. The system life is estimated at 25 to 50 years. In the United States, there are 50,000 GHPs installed each year ("Geothermal Heat Pumps," 2011).

Oceanic Energy

There has been discussion on other forms of renewable energy that include tidal energy, wave energy, and **ocean thermal energy.** About 70% of the earth's surface is comprised of oceans that produce mechanical energy in the form of waves and tides. Ocean thermal energy taps into the thermal energy from the sun. The heat energy stored in the ocean is used to generate electricity using a process called *ocean thermal energy conversion* (OTEC). In the tropical regions, there is a temperature difference between the colder layers at the bottom and the warmer layers at the top. A temperature difference of at least 36 degrees Fahrenheit, or 20 degrees Celsius, is required to form a thermodynamic cycle. The two challenges to this technology are cost and location. There is a huge initial investment required to make this technology a reality, and there are only a few hundred land-based sites in the tropics where OTEC plants can be developed (U.S. Department of Energy, 2011e).

Tide energy utilizes lunar power in the form of high tides and low tides to harness energy. The sheer scale of tidal energy holds great potential. For example, Canada's Bay of Fundy can potentially produce over 4,000 megawatts (Palmer, 2008). In a period of 24 hours, coastal areas witness high tides and low tides. If the difference between these two tides is at least 16 feet, or 5 meters, a dam can be built to block the tide and channel the pressure of the water to feed into a turbine that turns an electric generator. Tidal energy potential is limited to 10 hours per 24-hour period due to the inherent time difference between tides. Hence, this option cannot be used to supply power at a constant rate. The initial construction cost of this technology is high though the operation costs of tidal energy would be reasonable. There are also environmental ramifications of this enery as the dams and silt buildup can impact local ecosystems. With all the drawbacks, tidal energy does not seem to be promising (U.S. Department of Energy, 2011g).

Wave energy is used to obtain energy from surface waves or from pressure fluctuations that exist just below the surface. Once collected, wave energy can be converted into electricity by onshore or offshore systems. This energy can be used in areas with strongest winds such as western coasts of Scotland, southern Africa, northern Canada, and Australia as well as the northeastern and northwestern coasts of the United States. The critical aspect of this technology is to find a site suitable for collection of the energy and yet maintain pristine scenic beaches. There are a few demonstration plants operating globally, but none of these produces a significant amount of energy. Research and development of this technology has been discussed by some European government agencies, but the cost of this technology is not competitive with traditional energy sources at present. However, this technology does have potential since the fuel—in this case, seawater—is abundant and free (U.S. Department of Energy, 2011h).

The first wave farm is operating off the coast of Portugal. Other projects are planned off the coasts of Ireland and the United Kingdom (Brown, 2009). In the United States, the utility company Pacific Gas and Electric Company (PG&E) has filed a plan to develop a 40-megawatt wave farm. In addition, permits have been issued for projects off California's coast (Brown, 2009; Zeller, 2009).

Hydrogen and Hydrogen Fuel Cells

Hydrogen and hydrogen fuel cells are promising since hydrogen is the most abundant element. Pure hydrogen is a colorless, odorless gas, but most hydrogen on Earth is found in the form of water and organic compounds (U.S. Department of Energy Hydrogen Program, n.d.). When hydrogen is used as a fuel, the only combustion by-product is water. In addition, hydrogen can be used in fuel cells to power an electric motor.

As a fuel, hydrogen has many advantages. In addition to being abundant and nontoxic, it produces energy cleanly and efficiently. However, it is energy intensive (and therefore expensive) to produce. Pure hydrogen is a highly flammable gas, and safety is a consideration during transport and storage.

The United States produces about 9 million tons of hydrogen a year, but only a small fraction of that is used for energy (U.S. Department of Energy, 2011b). About 95% of U.S. hydrogen is made by treating natural gas with high temperature steam, which breaks down the methane gas molecules and releases hydrogen (U.S. Department of Energy, 2010a). The purest hydrogen comes from electrolysis, a process that uses electricity to break water into its component elements of hydrogen and oxygen. However, electrolysis is very energy intensive even though the by-product is simply gaseous water.

To make hydrogen more cost effective, researchers are investigating solar-derived electricity and hydroelectric power to fuel the electrolysis process, biological processes that harness certain strains of algae, bacteria, or enzymes to "crack" seawater, and using biomass as a source instead of natural gas (U.S. Department of Energy Hydrogen Program, n.d.).

Fuel cells are electrochemical energy devices that convert stored chemical energy into electricity. **Hydrogen fuel cells** do this by combining hydrogen and oxygen into water, producing heat and electricity.

If hydrogen can be produced and transported efficiently, fuel cells can be a very green technology. Unlike fossil fuel engines, hydrogen fuel cells don't produce any GHGs or hazardous particle emissions. Hydrogen itself is not toxic. Combustion engines in vehicles convert only 20% of the chemical energy of gasoline into usable power, and combustion power plants are about 35% efficient. Fuel cells can convert 40% to 60% of the stored chemical energy into electricity, and their combined heat and power efficiencies can range up to 90% (U.S. Department of Energy, 2010a).

Fuel cells are also highly scalable and have few or no moving parts to maintain or repair. Because they are quiet, clean, and reliable, they can be located anywhere and are especially suited for dense urban areas but also are good options for rural areas, vehicles and portable devices, and spaceflight.

To make hydrogen a workable fuel for vehicles, scientists are studying ways of absorbing and binding hydrogen to a variety of materials for more efficient storage at room temperature. These materials include metal hydrides and carbon-based materials, and these chemical storage methods may provide a stable way to store hydrogen more compactly than liquid hydrogen (U.S. Department of Energy, 2011a).

Viable Options for Businesses Today?

From the detailed discussion on the various sources of energy, it is evident that wind, solar, and fuel from cellulosic material (e.g., wood waste) holds most promise for businesses and consumers. Some of the other sources like hydrogen, tidal, and wave energy sound very promising but are not scalable to the point of commercial use. Still, other sources like hydropower and nuclear energy are highly damaging to the environment and, hence, cannot be considered sustainable.

Conclusion

There are many renewable energy alternatives to the traditional source of energy: coal-fired power plants. Renewable energy sources are attractive since most of these resources are available in nature and are clean sources of energy. Wind energy requires coverage that is extensive enough to yield power in a significant amount, and solar energy is limited by the availability of sunlight; these two sources both hold great promise once the costs of implementing these technologies becomes competitive. Hydroelectric and biomass energy hold promise but also come with a set of environmental issues. Other alternatives such as geothermal, wind, and oceanic energy are restricted to areas where such resources exist. The potential of hydrogen, fuel cells, and other alternative fuels available, such as biodiesel and ethanol, is promising.

KEY WORDS

Biodiesel

Biomass

Clean coal technologies

Coal energy

Ethanol

Fossil fuels

Geothermal energy

Hydroelectric power

Hydrofracking

Hydrogen fuel cells

Hydropower

Natural Gas

Nuclear energy

Ocean thermal energy

Photovoltaics

Renewable energy

Solar energy

Solar power

Tide energy

Wave energy

Wind energy

Wind farms

Wind turbines

DISCUSSION QUESTIONS

1. Why are the primary challenges with the "business as usual" approach in using conventional forms of energy? Discuss in detail.

2. Why is there a need for clean, renewable energy? What are the challenges posed by the way we derive energy at present?

3. What are the issues to incorporating renewable energy in developed world? Developing nations?

4. Wind power is one of the fastest growing energy sources today; however, there are some drawbacks. Discuss the major issues concerning this renewable energy.

5. How do the advantages of solar energy compare to disadvantages? Does one outweigh the other?

6. Why can't plant-based energy replace our current dependence on coal, oil, and natural gas?

7. Governments oftentimes create subsidies and other projects to help industries take off. What sort of role can the government have in encouraging the use and development of clean energy?

8. Which form of renewable energy do you think has the greatest potential to become adaptable in everyday use? Why?

9. Of the other renewable energy sources listed, such as geothermal, oceanic, tidal, and wave energy, which source holds the greatest potential in the United States? Use the Internet to research this question.

10. What are some of the challenges and obstacles involved in switching to a clean energy source?

11. Why is nuclear energy not sustainable? Despite this, what is the allure of nuclear energy for nations that are investing in nuclear energy?

12. What is the controversy surrounding clean coal? Should the United States invest in clean coal technologies?

RECOMMENDED WEBSITES

www.altenergy.org

www.awea.org/

www.eere.energy.gov/

www.gwec.net/

www.solarenergy.org/

PART III

Stakeholder Interest and Choices

6

Sustainable Strategies and Frameworks

Chapter Overview

This chapter will discuss the overall strategies and frameworks that are employed by organizations focused on sustainability. The chapter will start by why organizations desire to pursue sustainability followed by the concept of **sustainable value creation** followed by a discussion of natural capitalism. Next, the chapter will move into a section on the various frameworks available such as the natural step, **industrial ecology,** C2C, biomimicry, and so on. This chapter will also present some other tools used by organizations to develop strategies focused on sustainability.

The topics covered will include natural capitalism, **life cycle assessment (LCA)**, natural step, industrial ecology, C2C, biomimicry, environmental stewardship, EMS, **sustainable operating system (SOS)**, sustainable value stream mapping, and **Sustainability Balanced Scorecard (SBSC)**.

Why Sustainable Strategy?

Given that our world is facing dual pressures of increased demand from an expanding population and declining natural resources of basic ecological stores, it is but a natural response that sustainable strategy be the paradigm for consumption and production. Due to the strategic importance of this area, we have devoted this chapter to reviewing the various frameworks that attempt to define, classify, and embed sustainability.

Sustainable Value Creation

A model of **shareholder value** was developed by Stuart Hart and Mark Milstein (2003). As shown in Figure 6.1, the vertical axis of this model represents time, and this axis reflects the organization's management of current business while simultaneously creating future technology and markets. The horizontal axis represents space, and this axis reflects the organization's need for growth and to protect the internal organization's capabilities while simultaneously incorporating new perspectives and knowledge from outside. The concept is to balance the need to stay focused on core capabilities while being aware of fresh, external perspectives. Putting both the time and space dimensions yields a matrix of four distinct areas—(1) risk reduction, (2) reputation, (3) innovation, and (3) growth—wherein each is critical in the goal of generating shareholder value.

Figure 6.1   Shareholder Value

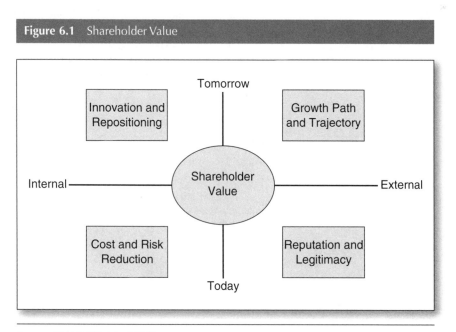

Source: Hart & Milstein (2003).

The sustainable value creation is built around the same two dimensions—(1) time and (2) space—from the shareholder value creation. In addition, as shown in Figure 6.2, this framework includes social and environmental challenges as well.

Global Drivers of Sustainability

There are four sets of drivers that need to be addressed for global sustainability. The first set of drivers relates to the negative impact of industrialization—namely, pollution, waste, and material consumption. The second set relates to groups like nongovernmental organizations (NGOs) and their growing impact on society. The third set of drivers includes the emerging disruptive technologies, such as genomics, nanotechnology, biomimicry, renewable energy, and so on, which have the potential to make the energy and material-intensive industries obsolete. The fourth set of drivers relates to global concerns of increase in population, poverty, and inequity arising from globalization.

According to the sustainable value framework, each **driver** and its strategies and business practices correspond to a dimension of shareholder value. For the lower left quadrant of Figure 6.2, organizations can create

Figure 6.2   Sustainable Value Model

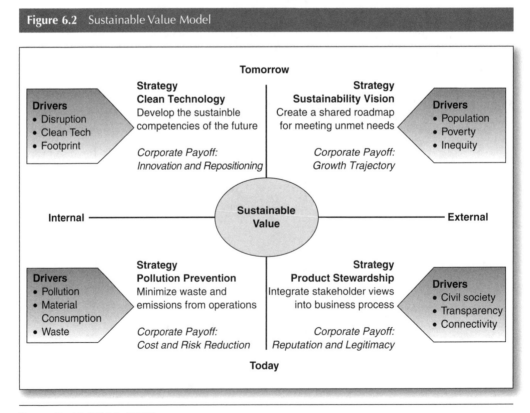

Source: Hart & Milstein (2003).

value by following a strategy of pollution prevention by minimizing emissions and waste. The immediate payoff is one of cost and risk reduction. Indeed, empirical evidence shows that companies pursuing pollution prevention and waste reduction increase profits (Christmann, 1998; Sharma & Vredenburg, 1998). Some industry examples are Dow Chemical's Waste Reduction Always Pays (WRAP), Chevron's Save Money and Reduce Toxins (SMART), 3M's Pollution Prevention Pays (3P), and so on. (Hart & Milstein, 2003).

For the lower right quadrant of Figure 6.2, organizations can increase confidence by engaging stakeholders. The ideal strategy for a company would be to integrate stakeholder views into business processes in order to gain a payoff of reputation and legitimacy. Some actions to take are cause-related marketing, life cycle management, industrial ecology, and so on. As an example of the latter, organizations can convert wastes into inputs. In 1997, Collins and Aikman Floorcoverings, now called Tandus Flooring, Inc., converted old carpet into new carpet backing. This product, ER3 (environmentally redesigned, restructured, and reused), has helped an increase of market share for the company (Buffington, Hart, & Milstein, 2002). Another example is from Nike, who faced a growing backlash regarding its labor and environmental practices and made a turnaround by engaging stakeholders to address social and environmental issues (Hart & Milstein, 2003).

For the upper left quadrant of Figure 6.2, organizations would develop the sustainable competencies of the future for a resultant payoff of innovation and repositioning. Companies that can engage disruptive technologies that address the needs of the society will drive economic growth. Firms that fail to lead in such technologies are not likely to be future market players (Hamel, 2000). For example, British Petroleum (BP) and Shell invested in renewable technologies; Toyota and Honda incorporated hybrid power systems in their cars; General Electric (GE), Honeywell, and United Technologies are investing in small-scale energy systems; and Cargill and Dow are developing biologically based polymers that will enable renewable feedstocks. Another commendable example is of DuPont that transformed itself from a gunpowder and explosives manufacturer to a chemical company in late 1800s and then transformed to renewable resource company focused on sustainable growth in the 1990s (Holliday, 2001). Firms that invest in clean solutions create organizational structures that support the innovative process (Hart & Milstein, 2003).

For the upper right quadrant of Figure 6.2, organizations ought to create a shared road map for meeting unmet needs for a resultant payoff of sustainable growth trajectory. In other words, firms that create a compelling sustainability vision have the potential to unlock future markets. An example is Grameen Bank, which opened a new pathway for business growth (Counts, 1996). Another example of a multinational corporation is Hindustan Unilever Limited (HLL), which developed products specifically aimed at the rural poor in India and was able to provide affordable soaps and shampoos to this market (Balu, 2002). In another example, Hewlett-Packard (HP) created an R & D lab in India to understand this burgeoning market. Other companies like Johnson & Johnson, Dow, DuPont, Coca-Cola, and Procter & Gamble are attempting to leverage their skills to meet the basic needs of the world's poor (Hart & Milstein, 2003).

In conclusion, the opportunity to create sustainable value is huge but unexploited. Organizations do have an option to choose the best strategy on the sustainable value framework and work toward the achievement of sustainable goals.

Ladder of Sustainability

Sustainability can be designed into any area of an organization. The **ladder of sustainability** contains numerous rungs, each of which represents an area of the organization. The idea is to take progressive steps toward attaining TBL (Holmes, n.d.). The rungs are listed as follows:

1. *Products or services:* This is the first area that should be looked into. Are the products made using toxic materials? Are renewable materials used in the products?

2. *Processes:* Are the processes efficient in that they use minimal resources? Is the process geared toward the entire life cycle (C2C versus cradle to grave)?

3. *Business model:* A model of leasing might be more sustainable than selling. In the case of Interface, the reuse of carpet was not aligned with profit when it used to sell the carpet. Once the model was changed to leasing carpet, there was an incentive to collect old carpets and reuse the material.

4. *Company focus:* All the employees of the company need to be on board in order to focus on innovation required for sustainability to become a reality.

5. *Brand identity of company:* Sustainability can be a great branding tool and can be used to create a market niche. Companies like The Body Shop and Ben and Jerry's were highly successful in this area.

6. *Supplier web & value chain:* The commitment to sustainability can extend to all its partners, suppliers, and other members of the value chain. In the case of Wal-Mart, the entire value chain needs to align with the new goals of sustainability.

7. *Industry leadership & advocacy role:* Once a company has succeeded in the first six areas, it can become an advocate for the movement. (Holmes, n.d.)

Players Within the Organization

For internal success of any initiative, it is imperative for all the employees to be involved. The TBL goals call for teams of people who can deliver results. The three groups of people are the (1) leaders, (2) stakeholders, and (3) the change support group.

Leaders: A company needs at least one executive-level sponsor to execute a TBL strategy. The role of the executive-level sponsor is to give or get authorization, support, and resources for necessary activities.

Stakeholders: This group is responsible for implementing a TBL plan. Education and training is required to attain buy-in at this level and to build capability among the group.

Change support: Since the change can be large and complex, a change support team is required to enable a broad-scale migration. This team acts as facilitators, gathering resources and spotting and solving problems (Holmes, n.d.).

Some of the sustainability gurus like McDonough and Braungart and Amory Lovins call for the next Industrial Revolution to be sustainability in business. The goal of the Industrial Revolution was to create financial value; the challenge in this next era is to simultaneously create financial, social, and ecological value.

Natural Capitalism

Our global economy is dependent on natural resources and ecosystem services. The Industrial Revolution, which began in middle 18th century, gave rise to modern industrial capitalism, and it opened up immense possibilities for material development. However, the gains of the Industrial Revolution came at a great cost to nature with resultant loss of topsoil, fall of water tables, and a loss of species and biodiversity.

The three authors Amory Lovins, Hunter Lovins, and Paul Hawken state that we need a new approach, natural capitalism. Amory and Hunter Lovins cofounded the Rocky Mountain Institute, a nonprofit think tank that analyzes the efficient and restorative use of resources. Amory Lovins is considered to be an authority on energy policy and was named as one of the world's 100 most influential people in 2009 by *Time Magazine*. Paul Hawken is an environmentalist, entrepreneur, and author who has written about the impact of commerce on living systems and has served as a consultant on industrial ecology and environmental policy.

By definition, natural capital is the store of commodities produced by nature in its 3.8 billion-year development process. These are the everyday commodities ranging from water and minerals to soil and air. In addition, it includes all living systems from grasslands to rain forests and oceans to coral reefs. These living systems supply the nonrenewable resources and, in addition, also replenish the basic services in nature, such as regeneration of atmosphere, flood management, water storage and purification, soil fertilization, waste processing, and buffering against extremes of weather (Marx, 2001).

The present rates of use and degradation are unsustainable in that there will be little left by the end of the next century. This is of great concern since the decline of this stock of natural capital will impact the vital life-giving services as well. Natural capitalism addresses the "critical interdependency between the production and use of human-made capital and the maintenance and supply of natural capital." A particular economy needs four types of capital to function properly:

1. Human capital, in the form of labor and intelligence, culture, and organization

2. Financial capital, consisting of cash, investments, and monetary instruments

3. Manufactured capital, including infrastructure, machines, tools, and factories

4. Natural capital, made up of resources, living systems, and ecosystem services (Lovins, Lovins, & Hawken, 2000).

Our economy is based upon the first three forms of capital—(1) human, (2) financial, and (3) manufactured—to convert natural capital into items needed for basic living: food, shelter, transportation, and so on. This industrial system does not assign any value to natural resources and the social and cultural systems that are the basis of human capital. Hence, natural capitalism calls for an expanded set of values that would include accounting for natural and human capital. It proposes four central strategies or shifts in business practices so that the ecosystem services are truly valued (Lovins et al., 2000).

Shift #1: Radical resource productivity: Using resources more effectively means getting more product out of each ton of natural material extracted. This step can result in slowing resource depletion, lowering pollution, and providing employment.

Shift #2: Biomimcry: Industrial systems can be redesigned using principles from nature. This idea is focused on the elimination of waste and toxicity in the system. The models of production ought to emulate nature, wherein waste from any system is food for another system.

Shift #3: Service and flow economy: In traditional goods-based business models, consumers acquire goods, consumer them and discard them.

In a solutions-based business model, the producer owns the goods and encourages "take back" when the productive life is over, resulting in incentives for remanufacturing and recycling. A shift to leasing models can lead to decline of material flow and waste.

Shift #4: Investment in natural capital: Businesses need to take leadership to restore, sustain, and expand the planet's ecosystems for future provision of products and services. Without this investment, natural capital stocks will decline and ecological problems will increase, leading to societal pressures through costly and inefficient governmental actions (Senge, 2000).

Natural Step

The Natural Step was developed by Swedish oncologist Dr. Karl Henrik-Robert in 1989 and is a systems-thinking-based framework that combines environmental problems within ecological principles. The framework consists of three parts:

1. the **four system conditions**

2. the funnel

3. strategies for action

Dr. Henrik-Robert worked with children battling leukemia, and he began to suspect environmental causes as sources of cancer. He worked with other scientists to find a set of irrefutable scientific principles on which to base his work. This work led Dr. Henrik-Robert to develop the four system conditions for sustainability.

Four System Conditions for Sustainability

In a sustainable society, nature is not subject to systematically increasing:

1. *concentrations of substances extracted from the earth's crust*

    The first system condition states that in order to convert to a sustainable society, there must be no more extraction of metals, minerals, fossil fuels, etc. from the earth's crust. The build-up of these extractive materials invariably leads to other environmental problems.

2. *concentrations of substances produced by society*

    The second system condition calls for an elimination of synthetic chemicals and compounds, especially those that do not break down easily. Chemicals such as DDT are very hard to get rid of, especially once these leach into the food chains and water tables.

3. *degradation by physical means*

The third system condition calls for an end to the degradation and destruction of natural environments. Examples would be the over-fishing of the oceans, the overharvesting of forests and the decline of biodiversity.

4. *and, people are not subject to conditions that undermine their ability to meet their needs*

The fourth system condition calls for meeting the needs of all people and species in a fair manner. For example, paying farmers low wages to grow cash crops such as cocoa would violate this condition. ("The Four System Conditions," n.d.)

In short, The Natural Step addresses what we take from nature, what we make that impacts nature, what we maintain in nature, and how and what we share with others. In The Natural Step framework, the four system conditions act as a compass that can guide companies or organizations toward sustainability practices.

The Funnel

As a metaphor, The Natural Step uses a "funnel" to describe the current situation and the goal of sustainability. Please refer to Figure 6.3a for a description of the funnel.

The funnel needs to be visualized from the left hand side. The upper wall of the funnel represents the availability of natural resources and the ability of the ecosystem to provide these resources. The lower wall of the funnel represents the increasing demand for these natural resources that are needed to provide our basic needs such as food, shelter, clothing, transportation, etc. Looking into the mouth of the funnel leads to a visualization that, given the increase in population and consumption levels, the demand for ecosystem resources is growing while the nature's ability to regenerate ecosystems is declining.

The two walls of the funnel indicate that human demand is outstripping the supply of natural resources. In order to be sustainable, the shape of this funnel must be opened up by a decrease in our impacts and a restoration of the life support systems. The walls of the funnel can only be opened up with innovative and creative solutions to achieving sustainability. ("The Funnel," n.d.)

Figure 6.3a TNS Resource Funnel

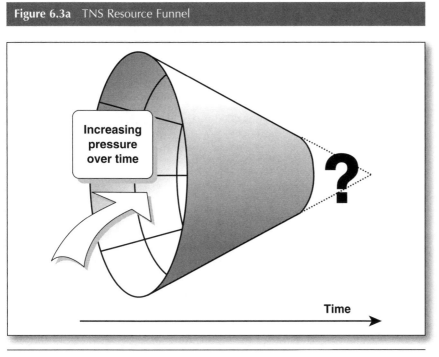

Source: The funnel (n.d.).

Strategies for Action

The Natural Step's strategies for action include four elements referred to as ABCD. Please refer to Figure 6.3b.

1. *Awareness and visioning:* Articulating a common understanding of sustainability within an organization and envisioning what the organization would look like in a sustainable future

2. *Baseline mapping:* Conducting a sustainability "gap analysis" to see which of the organization's activities are counter to principles of sustainability. Mapping current operations allows an organization to identify critical sustainability issues and the business implications of these.

3. *Creative solutions:* People are asked to brainstorm potential solutions to the issues identified in the previous step. In a technique termed *backcasting*, people begin with the end in mind and move toward a shared vision of sustainability with each action moving toward further improvement.

4. *Decide on priorities:* Prioritizing measures to move the organization toward sustainability. Backcasting is employed to determine whether decisions and actions are moving the organization toward the desired steps outlines in Step A. (Applying the ABCD Method, n.d.)

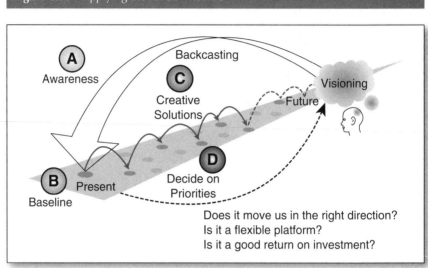

Figure 6.3b Applying the ABCD Method

Source: Applying the ABCD Method (n.d.).

Some of the companies that have employed The Natural Step include McDonald's Sweden, Nike, and Ikea. More details on the functioning of this organization can be found on The Natural Step's website: www.natural step.org.

Industrial Ecology

Industrial ecology is a "scientific discipline that promotes a *systemic approach* to human problems, integrating technical, environmental and social aspects" (Industrial Ecology, 2009). It is sometimes also referred to as "the Science of Sustainability" in that it promotes a broad scientific solution to sustainability problems. One of the basic tenets of industrial ecology is "the shifting of industrial process from linear or open loop systems, in which resource and capital investments move through the system to become waste, to a closed loop system where wastes become inputs for new processes" (Garner & Keoleian, 1995).

Industrial ecology utilizes systems analysis to frame the interaction between industrial systems and natural systems. The key concepts of industrial ecology are as follows:

Systems Analysis

The systems view, or approach, is integral to understanding the relationship between human activities and environmental problems since this viewpoint recognizes the interrelationships between industrial and natural systems. As an example, a manufacturer of a certain product would look at product life cycle stages and analyze the impact of the product on the consumer and the ecosystem. With this viewpoint, the manufacturer can design the product keeping both its consumption and disposal constraints.

Material and Energy Flows and Transformations

An environmental impact analysis entails "material and energy flows and their transformation into products, byproducts, and wastes throughout the industrial system." (Garner & Keoleian, 1995). For example, a material flow diagram of a battery might illustrate how much of the product becomes scrap. Further efforts can be made to use this waste as an input for some other process within the industrial system. This process would result in reducing the negative environmental impact and in improving the efficiency of the system. The ultimate goal is to reduce the overall environmental burden of an industrial system (Garner & Keoleian, 1995).

Multidisciplinary Approach

Since environmental problems are complex by nature, a variety of fields—from economics, public policy, law, ecology, business, and engineering—can be utilized to solve these problems. In addition, in the case where current technologies are upgraded, these need to be matched by changes in consumer behavior and changes in public policy and legal standards.

Analogies to Natural Systems

Over millions of years of evolution, the natural system has evolved from "linear (open) system to cyclical (closed) system in which there is a dynamic equilibrium between the various biological, physical, and chemical processes in nature" (Garner & Keoleian, 1995). The system is cyclical since all the organisms feed and pass on wastes that, in turn, are consumed by other organisms. There exists a high degree of integration and interconnectedness within the natural system along with a complex system of feedback mechanisms that trigger reactions in case certain limits are reached (Garner & Keoleian, 1995).

Linear (Open) Versus Cyclical (Closed) Loop Systems

In a linear system, resources are consumed and wastes are disposed into the environment whereas in a cyclical system, resources and wastes are constantly recycled and reused within the system. A central concept in industrial ecology is the evolution of the industrial system from a linear system to a cyclical system.

The *Type I* system portrays a linear process whereby materials and energy enter the system and are transformed into products and wastes before they exit the system. Refer to Figure 6.4 for an illustration of Type I system. This system needs a large and constant supply of raw materials since there is no recycling or reuse taking place. This system is unsustainable since it needs an infinite supply of raw materials and energy and has limited space to accommodate the wastes.

The *Type II* system portrays the industrial system at present wherein some wastes are recycled or reused whereas a majority of the wastes still leave the system. Refer to Figure 6.5 for an illustration of Type II.

Figure 6.4 Type I System

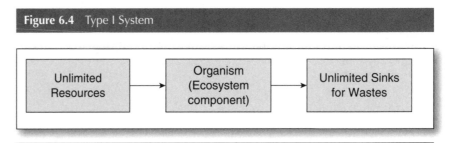

Source: Allenby (1992).

Figure 6.5 Type II system

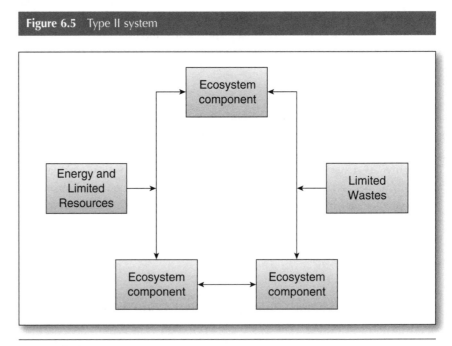

Source: Allenby (1992).

The *Type III* system portrays the ideal dynamic equilibrium state of eco-logical systems, wherein energy and wastes are recycled and reused by other organisms and processes within the system. Refer to Figure 6.6 for an illus-tration of Type III system. A perfect closed industrial system would only require solar energy, and all the by-products would be reused. This Type III system represents a sustainable state, and it epitomizes the ideal goal of industrial ecology.

In terms of geography, the entire earth can be viewed as a natural/physical environmental system within which humans are mere players who have had and continue to have an impact. An essay from Brown (n.d.) includes infor-mation about the earth as a natural system, energy in the system (open sys-tem), matter in the system (closed system), and the evolution of the environment (Brown, n.d.).

Figure 6.6 Type III System

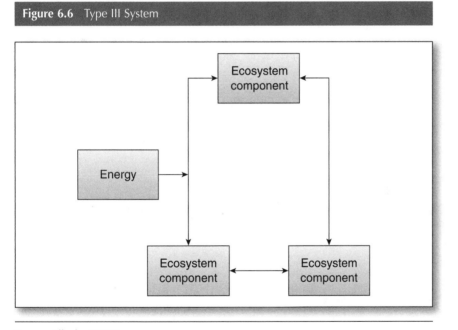

Source: Allenby (1992).

Examples of Industrial Ecology

Barceloneta, Puerto Rico

In Barceloneta, Puerto Rico, a symbiotic relationship exists mainly amongst pharmaceu-tical companies, a waste management firm, and a water treatment plant (see Figure 6.7). The relationship began in the 1970s, as Puerto Rico's lower taxes attracted several pharma-ceutical firms to the island. Around that time, the U.S. Environmental Protection Agency (EPA) also mandated that firms have a water treatment plant to manage the wastewater coming from the various production plants (Ashton, 2008). In response to this need, the firms pooled their funds together to share the operating costs of the treatment plant. This also allowed them to recover solvents from their processes. Furthermore, an exchange of solvents developed from this process, as firms realized that they may benefit from one firm's "wasted" solvent that can be recovered (Ashton, 2008). The ecosystem grew richer with the entrance of a waste management firm in the 1970s as well. This firm was able to make use of many of the solvents that were of no use to the pharmaceutical companies. This company would sell the recovered resources to other companies on the island—companies that were not directly linked to the pharmaceutical plants' water treatment symbiosis (Ashton, 2008). Furthermore, fermentation residue from the pharmaceutical plants benefited farmers' development of animal feed. Also, the treated sludge from the water treatment plant would be used by hay farmers to grow hay (Ashton, 2008).

Kouvola, Finland

Another strong example of an industrial ecosystem exists in Kouvola, Finland (see Figure 6.8). Kouvola's main industry is the UPM-Kymmene Corporation's paper and pulp mill (Sokka, 2010). The Kymi mill was established in 1874 and over time has grown to be the center of the industrial ecosystem. The mill interacts with a power plant, three chemical plants, a water treatment plant, and a sewage plant. The power plant utilizes wood and residual waste from the mill in order to provide the mill with electrical

Figure 6.7   Barceloneta, Puerto Rico

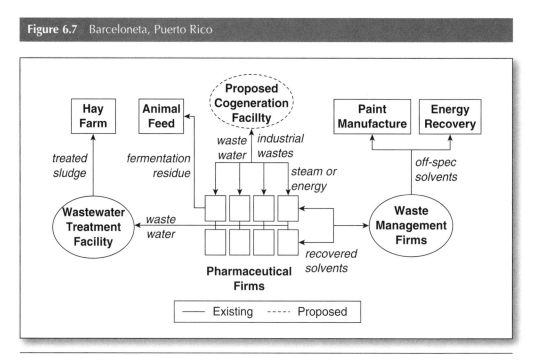

Source: Ashton (2008).

power. Moreover, the output from the power plant also provides the entire town of Kouvola with its electricity and heat (Sokka, 2010). The three chemical plants providing resources to Kymi are powered by Kymi. The Kymi mill also provides the chemical plants with purified water and other resources for their processes. Specifically, the calcium carbonate plant takes in the carbon dioxide given off by Kymi for its own chemical processes (Sokka, 2010). In another process within the ecosystem, a sewage plant provides sludge to a water treatment plant, which receives wastewater from Kymi. The sludge acts as an expedient for purifying the wastewater (Sokka, 2010). This ecosystem not only benefits the participating firms but also the local municipality's residents, as they receive electricity and heat due to the efficient operation of the industrial ecosystem.

Cape Charles, Virginia

Within the United States, an attempt to build the first eco-industrial park occurred at Cape Charles, Virginia (see Figure 6.9). An eco-industrial park is similar to an industrial ecosystem, in the sense that the participating firms are acting toward reducing waste and conserving resources as a responsible global citizen. However, unlike an industrial ecosystem, it does not appear that the participants need to work together as they would in a "food web"-like ecosystem. The Cape Charles Sustainable Technology Park project began around 1996. The park serves the local community as a preserved wetland,

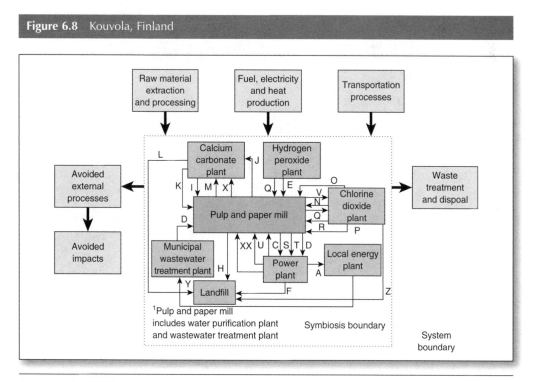

Figure 6.8   Kouvola, Finland

Source: Sokka (2010).

where industries and residential homes can coexist with the natural ecosystem. The pavement of the park is porous, reducing water runoff during a storm. Basically, the park utilizes the natural wetland environment as a water retention system (Duran, n.d.). Furthermore, one of the companies in the park—a water purification company—has designed its building with eco-friendly features. The building consists of several solar panels for assisting with providing electricity to the building. Also, it has additional insulation for heat and cooling energy savings (Duran, n.d.). A German wind power company is planning on installing large windmills in the park to power not only the firms within the park but also the 3,000 nearby homes. The park not only has benefited the environment but has also brought upon more employment in the town (Duran, n.d.). As an incentive to maintain and increase ecological responsibility in the park, lease rates decrease as a company reduces its carbon footprint. The park manages an environmental responsibility scorecard for each company participating. The scores are not only based on eco-friendly measures but also on local employment, thus enhancing the local economy and environment (Duran, n.d.).

Life Cycle Assessment

One of the tools used to support industrial ecology is the LCA, which provides a methodology of analyzing the environmental consequences of product or process from *cradle to grave*. In other words, an LCA is used to determine the total environmental impact of a product. This impact involves accounting for all the inputs and outputs from the birth to the

Figure 6.9   Cape Charles, Virginia

Source: Duran (n.d.).

death of the product including stages of design, raw material extraction, material production, assembly, usage, and final disposal.

The LCA framework comprises four stages: (1) goal definition and scoping, (2) inventory analysis, (3) impact assessment, and (4) interpretation. Refer to Figure 6.10 for an illustration. In the goal definition and scoping stage, the product or process is defined along with the boundaries of assessment. In the second stage—inventory analysis—all the inputs and outputs in the product's life cycle are examined including usage of energy and materials. The next stage is impact analysis in which the environmental impacts of the first stage are evaluated. Next comes the interpretation stage in which the results of the previous two stages are evaluated ("Life Cycle Assessment: Principles and Practice," 2006).

Figure 6.10   Life Cycle Assessment Framework

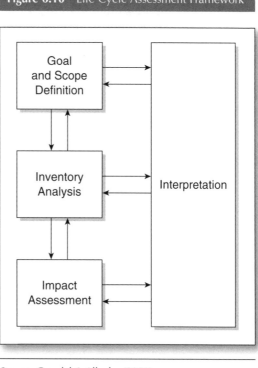

Source: Graedel & Allenby (2009).

The life cycle approach has also been used a lot in international discussions and negotiations around sustainable development. Indeed, the plan for implementation that came out of World Summit on Sustainable Development (WSSD) calls for scientific approaches, like the LCA, in order to develop production and consumption policies while mitigating the environment and health impacts ("Life Cycle Initiative Publications," n.d.).

Cradle to Cradle and Biomimicry

Two other concepts can also provide a new way of thinking about sustainability. The first concept is C2C, taken from design stating that products ought to be designed so that there is no waste or that the wastes produced can be used by another production process. The second, biomimicry, is taken from biology and states that nature is the best teacher for sustainability.

Cradle to Cradle

This concept is derived from the book titled *Cradle to Cradle,* written by William McDonough and Michael Braungart in 2002. The C2C framework

(McDonough & Braungart, 2002) calls for a new way of designing human systems in order to solve the conflicts between economic growth and environmental health. The framework identifies three key design principles in the intelligence of natural systems, which can inform human design:

1. *Waste equals food:* In nature, waste does not exist because the processes of each organism contribute to the health of the whole ecosystem. One organism's waste is food for another, and nutrients flow indefinitely in C2C cycles of birth, decay, and rebirth. In other words, waste equals food. Engineers and designers can use this principle to select safe materials and optimize products and services, creating closed-loop material flows that are safe and sustaining (McDonough & Braungart, 2002).

2. *Use current solar income:* Living things thrive on the energy of the sun, and trees and plants manufacture food from sunlight. C2C systems, ranging from buildings to manufacturing, can use solar energy, a renewable resource (McDonough & Braungart, 2002).

3. *Celebrate diversity*: Natural systems also thrive on diversity. Healthy ecosystems are made up of complex communities of living things, where each organism fits within a system. The engineers can use this principle by considering this C2C maxim: "All sustainability is local." The principle is that optimal sustainable design solutions need to get information locally, must draw on local energy and material flows, and, ultimately, must "fit" within local natural systems (McDonough & Braungart, 2002).

Biomimicry

Biomimicry is the "conscious emulation of life's genius to solve human problems" in design, industry, and elsewhere, according to Janine Benyus (1997), who wrote a book on the topic. The basic assumption is that over 4 billion years, natural selection and evolution have given us sustainable, diverse, complex, and efficient solutions to energy use and population growth. At present, humankind has the technology to understand how these solutions in nature work and these can be applied to current problems. Examples range from mimicking spider silk and applying ideas from prairies and forests to agriculture. Rather than simply exploit nature's design, biomimicry advocates learning from nature. The three precepts are as follows:

1. Nature is a model for sustainable designs and processes.

2. Nature is the measure for successful solutions.

3. Nature is our mentor.

In short, living things have done everything we want to do, without guzzling fossil fuel, polluting the planet, or mortgaging their future. What better models could there be? . . . This time, we come not to learn about nature so that we might circumvent or control her, but to learn from nature, so that we might fit in, at last and for good, on the Earth from which we sprang . . . [That ingenuity displays recurrent] laws, strategies, and principles. Nature runs on sunlight. Nature uses only the energy it needs. Nature fits form to function. Nature recycles everything. Nature rewards cooperation. Nature banks on diversity. Nature demands local expertise. Nature curbs excesses from within. Nature taps the power of limits. (Benyus, 1997)

Benyus combined biomimicry with industrial ecology to come up with 10 principles of an economy that would mimic nature:

1. *Use waste as a resource:* All waste is food. All living things use energy from sunlight and give up by-products of energy in the form of heat.

2. *Diversify and cooperate to fully use the habitat:* Symbiosis and specialization can help businesses collaborate on energy efficiency, remanufacturing, etc.

3. *Gather and use energy efficiently:* Use fossil fuels more efficiently while shifting to solar and renewables in the long run.

4. *Optimize rather than maximize:* Focus on quality over quantity.

5. *Use materials sparingly:* Reduce packaging and switch to businesses providing services rather than selling products.

6. *Don't foul the nests:* Reduce toxins, and decentralize production.

7. *Don't draw down the resources:* Invest in ecological capital, reduce use of renewable feedstocks so as to permit regeneration.

8. *Remain in balance with the biosphere:* Limit greenhouse gas (GHG) emissions and other pollutant emissions that disrupt climate cycles.

9. *Run on information:* Create feedback loops, and reward good environmental behavior.

10. *Shop locally:* Use local resources, and reduce unnecessary transportation (Benyus, 1997).

There are numerous industrial applications of biomimicry wherein companies are conducting research to apply nature's principles to design of products. The Mercedes-Benz Bionic was modeled after a tropical coral reef dwelling fish called the boxfish. The design of the boxfish is extremely aerodynamic, and the Bionic has a low vehicle drag coefficient of 0.19 that, in turn, helps the Bionic travel approximately 70 miles per U.S. gallon. In addition, akin to its marine-dwelling prototype, the Bionic employs the use of hexagonal structures in its shell that have proven to be extremely durable and space efficient when employed in architecture ("Design of New Mercedes-Benz Bionic Car," 2005).

Another company, Sto Corp., has developed Lotusan paint, an exterior paint that employs the self-cleaning, hydrophobic properties of the lotus plant wherein the water molecules touch a surface, immediately bead together, and roll off due to a repulsion between water and the nonpolar substance. In addition, the structure of the plant enables dirt particles to adhere to the water droplet so they can be removed from the plant, thus enabling the self-cleaning properties of the paint. The Lotusan paint claims to be able to extend the surface life of exterior surfaces while simultaneously decreasing cleaning costs for building owners and has proven to be highly resistant to water damage, dirt, mold, and even UV rays (Sto Corp. Lotusan Videos, n.d.). This same technology is also being examined by GE to further understand its potential applications on metal surfaces. Ideally, if able to synthesize into a spray coating, the lotus effect could be useful as a quick fix for deicing aircrafts.

Some of the other examples of biomimicry are as follows:

- Whalepower, a company, implemented tubercles in the wind turbines to reduce drag.
- The front end of the Shinkansen bullet train is modeled after the king-fisher beak, to reduce noise and increase speed and efficiency.
- Sick chimpanzees go to trees from the Veronia genus, and researchers are looking to test the chemical compounds on these trees for treating parasites in humans.
- EvoLogics developed a high-performance underwater modem that emulates dolphins unique frequency modulating acoustics to send early warnings for tsunamis ("What Could Nature Teach Us?" n.d.).

Environmental Stewardship and Sustainability_____

Stewardship means to take care of something. Sustainability is about using resources responsibly so that there is enough left for future generations. What do these terms mean together? How can an individual, an organization, or a community be stewards of the environment so that sustainability is attainable? What actions can you, as an individual, take to make it so?

An organization aims to balance making money with sustainability within its operations. Through this balance, this organization may take into account the needs of future generations. In practice, there are numerous opportunities that consider environmental sustainability. The following is a list of such environmentally sustainable practices:

- *Manufacturing:* Use recycled and toxin-free materials, reuse and recycle transport packaging, incorporate pollution prevention programs, and set energy and water efficiency goals.
- *Suppliers:* Reduce packaging of raw materials and provide greener and less toxic supplies.

- *Product impact:* Reduce overall environmental impact and increase end-of-life recycling.
- *Office operations:* Recycle paper and reduce paper usage, purchase recycled office supplies, and use e-mail.
- *Purchasing:* Set up environmentally preferable purchasing, purchase non-toxic and recycled supplies, request bulk supplies, and screen purchases.
- *Transportation:* Encourage teleconferencing, usage of mass transit, and alternative fuel vehicles for carpooling and minimize trip miles through efficient routing of product and raw material supply.
- *Food service:* Provide reusable dinnerware, implement recycling programs, donate excess food, establish composting programs, and encourage energy and water efficiency.
- *Facility management and housekeeping:* Maximize energy efficiency in lighting, heating, and cooling; install water-saving devices such as low-flow toilets and showerheads; use the least toxic cleaning materials; and employ green building techniques in maintenance.
- *Landscaping:* Evaluate fertilizers, pesticides, and herbicides; landscape to conserve water; monitor watering systems to use only when needed; and establish composting programs.
- *Interactions with the public:* Inform the public and customers about sustainability efforts ("Stewardship Initiative Sustainability Definition," 2002).

This list can be a starting point for any organization to start implementing environmental sustainability within their day-to-day operations. While this list is by no means exhaustive, it can serve as a baseline, and once organizations start realizing cost benefits, further opportunities for savings can be realized.

Environmental Protection Agency's Approach to Environmental Stewardship

Stewardship has had a long history across many cultures. In the United States, communities of American Indians are considered to be the first practitioners of environmental stewardship. In the past decades, the consequences of poor environmental stewardship were often not as dire since the economy and the population was smaller and the technologies were much simpler than they are today. Despite this fact, there have been documented cases of serious human-caused environmental problems (Diamond, 2005). At the present time, both individuals and organizations are starting to realize that ecologically sustainable choices are economically sustainable and in their best interest.

Consider the following statement:

Over the next 50 years, while the world's population is forecast to increase by 50 percent, global economic activity is expected to increase roughly fivefold. Conventional demand studies suggest that global energy consumption is likely to rise nearly threefold and manufacturing activity at least threefold, driven largely by industrialization and infrastructure growth in developing regions. Global throughput of material is also likely to triple, according to conventional projections. (Matthews et al., 2000)

Most people want a cleaner environment, a robust resource base, and a stronger economy that supports all individuals. However, the economy, the resource base, and environmental quality are all influenced by the day-to-day choices made by individuals, companies, communities, and government organizations. These choices range from product design to housing and transportation, from city planning to government procurement and operations, and so on.

Many of these choices are and ought to lie beyond direct control of the government. However, government can help by creating opportunities that enable and encourage environmental stewardship. The EPA and its state partners (at government levels) have launched a series of programs aimed to encourage environmental stewardship.

According to the EPA, its mission "is to protect human health and the natural environment." For a long time, the EPA approached its mission through regulations at the point of discharge. In the 1990s, pollution prevention was added to the earlier approach.

As illustrated in Figure 6.11, this environmental responsibility has evolved from simple compliance to continuous improvement that employs metrics to report on environmental performance. Furthermore, with the use of metrics and targets aimed at reducing the environmental footprint, there has been a further evolution to a "focus on long-standing solutions to promote sustained environmental quality. Environmental stewardship is

Figure 6.11   Evolution of Environmental Stewardship

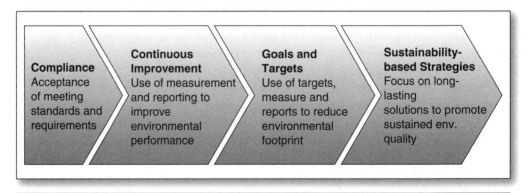

Source: U.S. Environmental Protection Agency Environmental Stewardship Staff Committee (2005).

also attractive since it allows private entities to participate in achieving sustainable environmental results" (U.S. EPA Environmental Stewardship Staff Committee, 2005).

Tools for Sustainability

There are numerous options available for organizations that wish to incorporate principles of sustainability within their operations or strategy. These options range from tools such as EMS, **total quality environmental management (TQEM)** to process evaluators such as **sustainable value stream mapping**. A brief discussion of these tools and process follows next. Depending upon the type of organization, these tools and processes can be employed at various stages of the path toward sustainability.

Environmental Management System

EMS is a tool used to manage an organization's environmental programs in a planned, systematic, and documented way. It is a "continual cycle of planning, implementing, reviewing and improving the processes and actions taken by an organization to meet its business and environmental goals" (EMS, n.d.).

How to Develop an EMS

An EMS is usually built on the **plan-do-check-act cycle (PDCA cycle)**. The diagram shown in Figure 6.12 illustrates this process. The first step is to develop an environmental policy. The next step in the process is planning the EMS and then implementing the EMS. The last step in the process concerns checking the EMS using system checks and controls. The EMS is a process of continual improvement whereby an organization is constantly reviewing and revising the system.

- *Plan:* Planning, including identifying environmental aspects and establishing goals
- *Do:* Implementing, including training and operational controls

Figure 6.12 Plan-Do-Check-Act Cycle

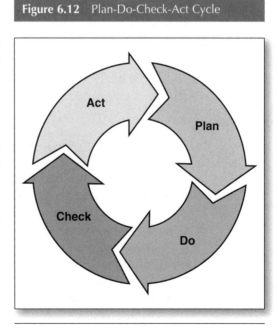

Source: http://en.wikipedia.org/wiki/File:PDCA_Cycle.svg

- *Check:* Checking, including monitoring and corrective action
- *Act:* Reviewing, including progress reviews and acting to make needed changes to the EMS. (EMS, n.d.)

The EMS can be used for most of the organizations, ranging from traditional manufacturing to services to governmental agencies. Some of the key elements of EMS are as follows:

- Policy statement that defines the organizations commitment to the environment
- Identification of significant environmental impacts of the products and services
- Development of objectives and targets for setting of the environmental goals
- Implementation of plans to meet objectives and targets
- Training to get employees on board
- Management review

The EMS can result in numerous benefits in both business and environmental areas. It can do the following:

improve environmental performance, enhance compliance, prevent pollution and conserve resources, reduce/mitigate risks, attract new customers and markets, increase efficiency, reduce costs, enhance employee morale, enhance image with public, regulators, lenders, investors, and achieve/improve employee awareness of environmental issues and responsibilities. (EMS, n.d.)

However, any such system has its set of associated costs, which include costs of internal resources, costs for training of personnel, costs for technical resources, and so on.

Total Quality Environmental Management

There have been other systems that deserve mention. One in particular is the TQEM, a process for applying total quality management approaches to corporate environmental strategies. The TQEM was created by the Global Environmental Management Initiative (GEMI), a coalition of 26 companies including IBM, AT&T, and Kodak. There are four basic elements of TQEM:

1. *Customer identification:* Customer preferences determine environmental quality. The internal customers are comprised of the company's employees, and the external customers are comprised of buyers, environmental groups, and the general public.

2. *Continuous improvement:* Both the management and the employees of a company should work toward the improvement of environmental performance.

3. *Doing the job right first time:* In order to eliminate environmental risks, the employees should isolate and get rid of potential environmental problems.

4. *A systems approach:* All components of the TQEM system need to be designed so that they work together to achieve desired goals ("TQEM," n.d.).

In its TQEM primer, GEMI stated that in order to analyze and condense information, the TQEM tools such as cause and effect diagram, the Pareto chart, the control charts, flowcharts, and histograms can be used ("TQEM: The Primer," 1993).

Sustainable Value Stream Mapping

There are a number of metrics used in measuring environmental performance, such as energy use, water use, air emissions, that are not optimized in a lean process. Value stream mapping analyzes the proportion of process time that added value. However, this tool does not address resources and waste. In order to fill this gap, Simons and Mason (2002) developed sustainable value stream mapping by adding a metric (supply chain carbon dioxide divided by market weight of product) to the mapping process. As an example, Simons and Mason (2002) applied this process tool to food supply chains and recommended producing food closer to the point of consumption (Venkat & Wakeland, 2006).

Sustainable Operating System

The SOS is a process that can be used by organizations to prioritize their goals to achieve sustainability. In this manner, SOS is akin to a process that lets organizations examine the business case for sustainability on a topic by topic basis (Blackburn, 2007). There are four elements to an SOS: (1) the drivers, (2) the efficient enablers, (3) the pathway elements, and (4) the evaluators.

The drivers make sure that the organization is motivated toward sustainability on a continuous basis. The main driver is champion or the leader who puts sustainability on the business agenda and gets the dialogue started. Another important driver is to sell sustainability to the management. Since sustainability is a vague term with numerous connotations, this term must be defined clearly and could be translated into a sustainability policy. The last drivers are the reward and accountability mechanisms that are meant to keep the focus and the motivation on achieving sustainability objectives (Blackburn, 2007).

The efficient enablers make it possible for the organization to assume its sustainability efforts in an efficient manner. The core team and a deployment team are essential to an organizational structure needed in this process. In addition, deployment and integration are the other efficient enablers needed to spread sustainability throughout the organization (Blackburn, 2007).

For the pathway elements, each organization needs to develop its own SOS standards. These could range from previously set standards like OSHAS (Occupational Health and Safety Assessment Series), ISO 9001 or 14001, The Natural Step, and so on. A set of priorities is also needed to sift through the numerous possible actions toward sustainability (Blackburn, 2007).

Three elements of the evaluators assist an organization in keeping track of its progress. These are as follows: creating goal and metrics, measuring and reporting progress, and engaging stakeholders and attaining feedback (Blackburn, 2007).

An organization ought to notice a substantial once the four elements of the SOS are documented and the process is operating within a continuous PDCA cycle (Blackburn, 2007).

Sustainability Balanced Scorecard

The SBSC is based on the balanced scorecard (BSC), a management tool proposed by Kaplan and Norton (1996). The BSC is a tool for organizations that seek to manage the demands of various stakeholders and to translate strategies into action. The BSC contains four perspectives:

1. *The financial perspective:* Measures the financial gains provided to its shareholders

2. *The customer perspective:* Focuses on customer needs and satisfaction

3. *The internal perspective:* Focuses on the performance of the key internal processes

4. *The organization learning:* Focuses on the organization's people and infrastructure (Kaplan & Norton, 1996).

The SBSC provides a broader scope by integrating all three dimensions of sustainability. In addition to the four perspectives of the BSC, a fifth perspective can be included to address stakeholder issues. Since the BSC contains both financial and nonfinancial aspects, it also has the potential to address sustainability management. However, the BSC is only a tool and it is still imperative to define a sustainability policy and strategy.

Hence, the SBSC offers corporations an opportunity to translate sustainability vision and strategies into action. In addition, the SBSC offers the integration of environmental and social aspects and objectives into the core management of companies (Bieker, 2003).

Conclusion

There are numerous strategies and frameworks available to the organizations committed to pursuing sustainability. From thinking perspectives of natural capitalism to The Natural Step, from design parameters of industrial ecology to C2C and biomimicry, from tools such as EMS to SOS and processes such as sustainable value stream mapping to SBSC, there exist a comprehensive set of strategies available to examine impact of activities on the environment, the economy, and the community.

KEY WORDS

Cradle to cradle (C2C)

Environmental management system (EMS)

Four system conditions

Industrial ecology

Ladder of sustainability

Life cycle assessment (LCA)

Plan-do-check-act cycle (PDCA cycle)

Shareholder value

Sustainability Balanced Scorecard (SBSC)

Sustainable operating system (SOS)

Sustainable value creation

Sustainable value stream mapping

Total quality environmental management (TQEM)

DISCUSSION QUESTIONS

1. What are the four drivers and the four quadrants of the sustainable value framework? Can you think of examples of companies in each of the four quadrants?

2. List the seven rungs of sustainability. Discuss which rung might be the easiest and the hardest to attain.

3. In terms of natural capitalism, how can we redesign systems and incentives so that more value is placed on natural resources rather than industrial products?

4. Can you think of an application of industrial ecology within your community? Within your college or university?

5. Brainstorm to conduct a preliminary LCA of bottled water (plastic).

6. How can a computer manufacturer use the C2C principles to design a laptop?

7. Of the 10 biomimicry principles listed, which ones can you apply to your daily life? Can you research any other company that has incorporated biomimicry principles in the design of their products?

8. There are three types of systems listed under systems thinking. Can you think of any organization that is moving from Type II to Type III?

9. Research your local government or city government to determine if they use a form of EMS in their daily operations.

10. Of all the tools and processes mentioned in the last section of this chapter, which one might have the greatest applicability at your workplace? Discuss.

11. Use the four system conditions of The Natural Step to examine some everyday actions, for example:
    - Buying a cup of latte from the corner café
    - Buying a pair of sneakers
    - Purchasing a new laptop
    - Getting a new car

RECOMMENDED CASE STUDIES

Larson, A. (2008). *Wall-to-Wall Carpet Goes Cradle-to-Cradle, UVA-ENT-0084.* Chesapeake, VA: Darden Publishing.

Larson, A. (2008). *Rohner Textiles: Cradle-to-Cradle Innovation and Sustainability, UVA-ENT-0085.* Chesapeake, VA: Darden Publishing.

Lee, D., & L. Bony. (2007). *C2C Design at Herman Miller*, Prod. #:607003-PDF-ENG. Cambridge, MA: Harvard Business Publishing.

RECOMMENDED WEBSITES

http://atkisson.com/wwd_tools.php
www.axisperformance.com/SCORE_overview.html

http://biomimicry.net/
www.epa.gov
www.mcdonough.com/cradle_to_cradle.htm
www.natcap.org
www.naturalstepusa.org

7

Role of the Consumer

LEARNING OBJECTIVES

By the end of this chapter, you should be able to do the following:

- Discuss **consumption** and its link to ecosystem services.
- Evaluate the link between consumption and environment.
- Detail the sustainable choices in food, drink, housing, clothing, and transportation.
- Explain the role of consumers.
- Discuss the **ecological footprint** and compute **carbon footprint.**
- Elaborate on the role of business in promoting **sustainable consumption.**
- Examine the future of consumption.

Chapter Overview

This chapter explores the role of consumers. As the global drivers of population and affluence drive up consumption, there is more and more stress on the limited natural resources. What is the role of individuals, as consumers, in making sustainable choices in the categories that have the greatest ecological impact: food, drink, housing, and transportation. How does one go from reckless consumption toward a more sustainable consumption? Our choices as consumers are one of the most powerful ways of communicating to companies as to what we buy and what we condone. Furthermore, how can business assist in promoting sustainable consumption.

Limits to Consumption

The average U.S. citizen consumes 18 tons of natural resources per person per year and generates an even higher volume of waste. One of the first economists to analyze consumption was John Kenneth Galbraith (1958), whose article "How Much Should a Country Consume?" called for an analysis into problems that might be caused by consumption. Herman Daly (1999) stated that since energy resources are limited, there ought to be limits on consumption. Daly's (1999) work was important since it linked economic growth to a decline in well-being that came from social and environmental sacrifices made in the pursuit of growth. The theoretical work suggests that consumption must be viewed in its social and ecological context.

Global Drivers

Consumption around the world is driven by population growth and economic development and will rise as consumers in emerging economies demand goods and services. The world population hit the 7 billion mark in November 2011, and it is anticipated to reach 9 billion by 2050 (World Business Council for Sustainable Development [WBCSD], 2008). Around 60% of gross domestic product (GDP) is from consumer spending on goods and services. The projected rise in GDP of emerging countries like China, India, and Brazil is expected to bring a corresponding increase in the number of middle-class consumers. According to figures by Goldman Sachs, about 70 million people each year enter into an income equivalent to between $6,000 and $30,000 in purchasing power. If this trend continues, the middle class will comprise almost 80% of the world population (O'Neill, 2008). There is now an emergence of *global middle class*. The combination of two forces—(1) globalization and (2) economic integration—gives consumers increasing access to products and services.

However, there is an inherent inequality. The market pressure created by the affluent spending and consumption comes at a price wherein many are excluded. At the present, 4 billion people earn less than $3,000 per year. Expenditure on food tends to dominate the budgets of these low-income consumers. With a rise in the income levels, the amount spent on food often declines, the amount spent on transportation and telecommunication rises, and the amount spent on housing remains relatively constant. For example, low-income consumers comprise 95% of the population in Africa that incur 71% of expenditure (Hammond, Kramer, Katz, & Walker, 2007). According to estimates by the World Wildlife Fund (WWF), three planets would be required were everyone to consume similar to the average citizen from the United Kingdom and five planets to live like the average North American (WWF, 2006).

However, this consumerism does not necessarily translate to happiness. The New Economics Foundation's (WBCSD, 2008) *Happy Planet Index* discovered that people can live happy lives without using more than their "fair share" of the earth's resources. There is no country that combines high GDP with low life satisfaction though there are many less affluent countries that achieve high life satisfaction (WBCSD, 2008). This is contradictory to the popular notion that money (and consumption) can buy happiness.

Link to Earth's Ecosystems

Global consumption has a direct linkage to the Earth's **ecosystems,** two thirds of which are in decline. According to the Millennium Ecosystem Assessment (MA), 60% of nature's essential resources are degraded (WBCSD, 2008). In addition, almost 30% of the earth's terrestrial area has been turned into urban areas or farms (WBCSD/Earthwatch Institute/World Resources Institute/International Union for the Conservation of Nature [IUCN], 2006). Almost one third of the earth's plants and animals have gone into extinction since 1970 (WWF, 2006). Approximately 10% to 30% of mammal, bird, and amphibian species are threatened with extinction (IUCN, 2007). Studies indicate that current extinction rates could increase by a factor of 10 (WBCSD, 2008).

Biodiversity loss and changes to ecosystem services come from a set of direct drivers: habitat change, climate change, invasive alien species, and pollution (WBCSD, 2008). The sobering fact is that despite all the technological advances, scientists have not been able to create soil or seeds or life. For this reason alone, consumption needs to be curtailed and contained.

Ecological Impact

According to the One Planet Business report, the highest levels of ecological impact is on food and drink followed by household equipment and housing. Food, transportation, and housing have the most significant impacts (WWF UK, 2006). Housing uses the most materials and energy (WWF UK, 2006). For this reason, food, transportation, and housing will be discussed in greater detail in the next section.

Patterns of consumption levels vary considerably by geography, income, and demographics. Sustainability challenges also vary markedly per type of economy (see Figure 7.1). Though poorer countries emit the least amount of greenhouse gases (GHGs), they are most vulnerable to the loss of biodiversity and ecosystems. They are also vulnerable to flooding, reduced access to clean fresh water and health and social problems (Sustainable Consumption Research Exchanges [SCORE!], 2008). Affluent consumers in rich nations need to be aware of their impacts, especially on the disadvantaged populations across the globe.

Consumption Choices

According to Figure 7.2, the highest impact is in the categories of food, drink, and housing. Other categories of significant impact include clothing, recreation, hotels/restaurants, and transportation (WBCSD, 2008).

Figure 7.1   Sustainable Consumption Challenges

Type of Economy	Example Countries	Main Sustainability Challenge
Consumer	United States, Japan, Western Europe	Dramatically lowering resource use while maintaining economic output (Factor 10)
Emerging	China, Southeast Asia	Leapfrogging to sustainable structures of consumption and production without copying Western examples
Developing	African countries, some in South America	Developing dedicated solutions for the "low income segment of the population," providing a basis for sustainable growth

Source: SCORE! (2008).

Given that most of the expenditures are on food, drink, housing, clothing, and transportation, it is worthwhile to explore these choices in more detail. How can consumers make more informed and more sustainable choices in these primary areas of impact?

Figure 7.2   Ecological Footprint Per US $1 Million

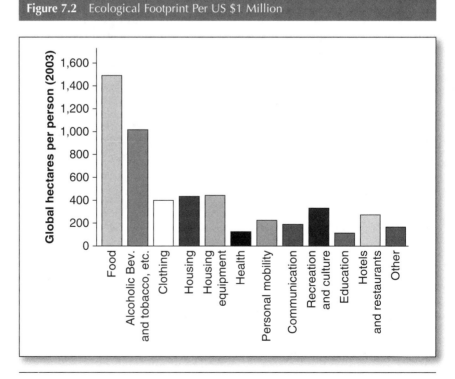

Source: WBCSD (2008).

Food and Drink

There is a synergy that exists in the sense that what is good for an individual is ultimately good for the society and good for the world. Food is fuel for the bodies. How humans feel is directly related to what they eat. In a society, there needs to be demand for organically grown fruits and vegetables. At the same time, farmers who are practicing sustainable ways of farming by conserving water and reducing the use of pesticides and synthetic fertilizers need to be supported. While it is tempting to grab convenient, packaged foods, it is more healthy and sustainable to eat fresh, healthy, and organic food.

Produce

Human bodies require five to nine servings of fruits and vegetables, but produce is exposed to chemicals in the form of pesticides and fertilizers. The best choice is to eat organic produce since it is grown without the use of synthetic pesticides, fertilizers, antibiotics, or added hormones, and as a result, it contains one third of the pesticides found in conventional produce. The chapter on food (Chapter 3) listed the fruits and vegetables that are most exposed to pesticides and the "Clean 15" list that contained the fruits and vegetables that were exposed to an average of two pesticides. Another trend is to buy local from farmers markets or local produce stands. Food that needs to be transported long distances is usually treated with fungicides and shipped before it is fully ripened. The term *food miles* refers to how long the food has traveled before it is consumed. There are benefits of buying local food, and a good option is to join a community supported agriculture (CSA) group in the local area. These CSA farms charge members a fee to purchase shares of each season's harvest. The website www.localharvest.org/ can be used to find a local CSA group.

Meat and Poultry

Beef, chicken, pork, and lamb comprise the main portion of majority of meals. There has been a call for eating lower on the food chain, and there are good reasons for this argument. The commercialization and mass production of meat has lowered the price of meat, but the risks of foodborne illnesses such as E. coli, salmonella, Campylobacter, and Listeria monocytogenes has gone up. Ground meat is especially vulnerable since it is derived from more than one animal. In addition, hormones and antibiotics are routinely given to animals to promote growth, and these residues stay in the meat after processing. Animals suffer severe stress when raised in industrial settings. Oftentimes, the animals in feedlots are cramped, surrounded by waste, and fed an unnatural diet. Choose meat that is free-farmed since it comes from animals raised in pastures without hormones and antibiotics. Meats labeled as grass fed are a good choice since the animals are raised on pasturelands and stored grasses. For poultry and eggs, some labels state *free-farmed* or *cage free* or *free range* implying that the bird was given some outdoor access. In absence of other labels, look for meat labeled **certified organic.**

Seafood

Fish is considered a good source of protein and omega-3 fatty acids, but heavy metal contamination is a concern in eating seafood. In addition, since the advent of commercial fishing, the oceans are being fished out at an alarming and unsustainable rate. Wild fish caught at sea can contain mercury and polychlorinated biphenyls (PCBs). Mercury builds up in the fish muscle so it cannot be removed. Since mercury can harm brain development, pregnant women are advised not to eat fish. Commercial fishing has plundered the oceans, and an estimated 75% of the world's fish species are close to collapse. The worldwide populations of tuna, swordfish, cod, and halibut have been reduced by 90%. Look for seafood that has been certified by the Marine Stewardship Council (MSC) (Garlough, Gordon, & Bauer, 2008). About half of the world's supply of fish now comes from fish farms. Though farming is a feasible solution to the falling wild fish populations, there are certain challenges present. Some of the cages or net pens are overcrowded, and antibiotics or anti-parasite pesticides can spill over to the waterways. Farmed fish can escape from farms and spread disease to the wild fish and interbreed, causing a dilution of the gene pool (Garlough et al., 2008).

Dairy

Milk, cheese, and yogurt are enjoyed in numerous diets. However, the use of hormones and chemicals in cows' milk is a concern. Recombinant bovine growth hormone (rBGH) is a genetically engineered hormone that is injected into cows to increase milk production. This hormone is of concern since it never went through long-term safety testing by the U.S. Food and Drug Administration (FDA). A study in Canada found that this hormone was absorbed by rats; hence, rGBH was not approved in Canada. rGBH also stimulates the production of IGF-1, insulin growth factor, which can cause cell division and tumor growth. The United States is one of the few countries where dairy farmers can use rGBH. Milk that is certified organic is usually free of rGBH (Garlough et al., 2008).

Water

Water is a basic and essential need for all living beings, and it is the most plentiful substance in our bodies and on the planet. Indeed, the longest a human can survive without water is 3 days. There has been much discussion on the environmental damage from bottled water. First of all, the water inside is not regulated as much as tap water, and there is no saying where the water comes from. In many cases, this bottled water is actually more contaminated than tap water. In addition, bottled water contains a host of issues. The flexible plastic water bottles leach phthalates, chemicals that mimic the female hormone estrogen. Estrogenic endocrine disruptors are linked to health problems for both men (low sperm counts, lower energy, and decreased sex drive) and women (early puberty and increased rates of breast and ovarian cancers). In terms of environmental costs, bottled water costs more to transport as 1.5 billion gallons of fuel are needed per year whereas tap water is delivered through an energy efficient infrastructure. The most damaging environmental concern comes from the manufacture of 1.5 million plastic bottles (from petrochemicals) every year, and most of these bottles end up in landfills (Horn, 2006). There have been some products entering the market that are more sustainable. One example is the Green Planet petroleum-free bottle, made from plants. These bottles are compostable and recyclable. Another sustainable solution is filtered water whereby a water filter is attached to the faucet to get rid of the impurities. There are numerous water filters in the market ranging from simple carbon filters and faucet mounted filters to expensive systems like reverse osmosis systems and ultraviolet light filters. For more detail on different types of water, refer to Chapter 2 of this book. In addition, Brown (2009) offers a detailed discussion of water shortages worldwide.

Coffee and Tea

The coffee plant is a rain forest shrub with red berries that mainly grows in Africa and Latin America. Traditionally, coffee plants were grown in shade, under the rain forest canopy, which served as a habitat for migratory birds. Most of these plantations are being moved to full sun farms as the production increases fivefold. Coffee plantations are also referred to as farming sweatshops since the workers and farmers are paid very little for the harvest. In the early 1990s, the coffee producers received 30% of the total coffee income, but this has dropped to 8% or less. As a consumer, look for the certified organic label to ensure that the beans were not treated with synthetic pesticides. **Fair trade certified** coffee was purchased directly from producers or cooperatives, and this practice states that the growers got a higher percentage of their share. Lastly, it is better for the environment to purchase coffee that was *shade grown,* and the two certifications are **Rainforest Alliance** and Bird Friendly (Garlough et al., 2008). Tea production is also subject to similar problems of pesticide usage and low wages for pickers. Though a handful of brands own 90% of the market, organic and fair trade certified teas are increasingly appearing in health food stores and specialty stores.

Beer and Wine

Beer is made from barley, hops, and some yeast and perhaps wheat. The commercial production of these grains involves the use of herbicides, insecticides, fungicides (hops are susceptible to fungus), and fertilizers. Certified organic beer is made with 95% organic ingredients, and the beer must be processed in breweries that do not use harsh acids or chemicals for cleaning. Sales of organic beer have jumped up by 40% in 2005 to $19 billion. Purchasing local beer is also a sustainable choice, and microbreweries are gaining in popularity. Conventionally grown wine grapes are also subject to fumigants, insecticides, fungicides, and herbicides. The pesticide methyl bromide has been used to kill insects, weeds, and nematodes before the planting of vines. Organic wine is made with 95% organic ingredients and does not contain added sulfites. Some wines are also organically processed without the use of synthetic, chemical agents. Depending on the location, locally grown wines might also be available (Garlough et al., 2008).

Housing

A home is a big investment in financial terms, and the housing sector uses the most materials and energy. Home represents a space where leisure time is spent with families and friends. However, it also represents the space where sustainability ideals can be put into practice. Small changes such as filtering the water, recycling and composting, using natural products in our lawn and cleaning, and using energy efficient appliances can all save money and make homes more sustainable.

Better Housekeeping

When homes are cleaned, the idea is to get rid of the dirt, grime, and other germs. What is surprising are the amount of chemicals and toxins hidden within the very cleaners that are used. The most hazardous are drain cleaners, oven cleaners, toilet bowl cleaners, and any other product that contains chlorine or ammonia. In addition, fumes created by chemicals in cleaning products contribute to indoor air pollution.

One of the most common ways to incorporate sustainability at home is to increase the home's efficiency. Some of the simple steps to accomplish this goal include sealing the cracks around doors and windows with sealant to prevent heat loss, turning down the thermostat since a 2-degree change can result in 8% savings in heating or cooling bills, replacing the lightbulbs with compact fluorescent lightbulbs since these are much more efficient than the traditional incandescent bulbs, turning off the lights and appliances when not in use, conserving water by taking quick showers instead of long baths, purchasing recycled paper and being prudent about buying disposable products, and looking for the **Energy Star** label when purchasing appliances (Horn, 2006).

Another step is to recycle. An average consumer generates 4 pounds of trash per day, and this translates to 400 billion pounds a year. In terms of the composition of the trash, 40% of trash is paper and cardboard, 18% is yard waste, 9% is metals, and 8% is plastic and other products. At present, more than 70% of the waste is sent to landfills to be buried and about 27% of the waste is recycled, but this percentage can be improved (Horn, 2006). For cleaning homes, the chemically laden cleaners can be skipped, and almost all cleaning can be accomplished by using baking soda, white vinegar, lemon juice, borax, liquid soap, and so on. As an alternative, nontoxic cleaners such as Method and Seventh Generation can be purchased. Most of the suburban homes have a yard that in the United States consumes more than one third of all the pesticides in the world. A sustainable option is to convert the yard into an organic garden. Use natural fertilizers and pull out weeds by hand (Horn, 2006).

A home can also be redesigned to be more sustainable. Nowadays, most retailers carry products that are green by design. An increasing number of design professionals, from interior designers to architects, understand this concept and are willing to employ the principles into home design. At first thought, it might seem that green home goods are going to be expensive. However, many green options are designed to save money in the long run. Some of the simple tips in designing or redesigning a home to make it more sustainable or green include purchasing Forest Stewardship Council (FSC) certified wood furniture, choosing natural fibers for upholstery and carpets, purchasing window shades made from bamboo or wood, using organic mattresses and comforters, and so on. (Garlough et al., 2008).

Modern appliances are designed to make life easier—from dishwashers to air conditioners and refrigerators—and it is hard to imagine a house without these appliances. However, these appliances also burden the planet in terms of their electricity consumption. At the present time, the current U.S. household dedicates 20% of its energy bill to the powering of appliances and electronics. In addition, the current U.S. household emits 9,900 pounds of carbon dioxide a year. Some tips for appliances and electronics include choosing Energy Star products and appliances, installing a fan to cool the house, defrosting the refrigerator regularly, checking that the air purifier does not emit ozone, washing clothes in cold water cycles, drying clothes on a clothesline or drying rack, using rechargeable batteries and recycling old batteries, turning off the computer when done with work, using power strips in rooms with many appliances and switching off the power strip when appliances are not in use, disposing e-waste responsibly, reusing or recycling, donating old computers to nonprofit organizations, and using LED or solar powered flashlights (Garlough et al., 2008).

Sustainable Building and Retrofitting

A lot of architects and contractors are turning to green construction to satisfy the demand for green homes. Indeed, a new home can be designed in such a way so as to be green, incorporating issues like size, building materials, ventilation, insulation, and energy efficiency. However, many of these elements can be incorporated in the remodeling of a home. From a sustainability point of view, it is better to remodel an existing home than to build a brand-new home.

The first basic step is to insulate for efficiency. The installation of a programmable thermostat can minimize energy usage by shutting off when the house is unoccupied and setting the home into varying temperature zones. Smart landscaping can help with energy savings. In a colder climate, planting a row of trees can block cold winds, and in the summer, a tree can be positioned to block the summer sun. Shades can be used to cool the house in summers and opened to warm the house with natural sunlight in winter. Another idea to cool the house is to open the windows on the northern side of the house. To warm the house in winter, close off unused rooms. Covered porches or awnings can reduce cooling bills along with the installation of fans. Installation of storm windows can help with the insulation in cooler climates (Horn, 2006).

The second step is to use sustainable building materials: Ceramic tiles or natural stone flooring is a more sustainable option than carpets or vinyl. For kitchen cabinets, solid wood cabinetry is a better choice since particleboard is treated with formaldehyde. Some alternative building materials have come on the market in the past few years such as concrete, modular construction, mortarless blocks, straw bale with cement stucco skin, and used and recycled materials from other construction projects (Horn, 2006).

The third step is to look at power sources and determine whether the house can be retrofitted with renewable power sources such as solar, wind, and geothermal. In case of solar power, a home can meet its hot water needs with a solar panel on the roof. A more extensive solar array can meet all the power needs of a home. Residential wind turbines are rather expensive ranging from $6,000 to $20,000. But these costs can be offset if these are used for powering entire communities. In case of geothermal, heat pumps can be installed that cool the house in summers and heat in the winters. The options are discussed in the alternative energy chapter (Chapter 5).

Clothing

The process of clothing manufacturing has many environmental implications. Polyester is made from petroleum, and the required crude oil to make it increases the demand and with it, additional emissions. Cotton also has a significant environmental impact, as it has been subject to pesticides and insecticides. Much of the cotton is exported to China and other countries where it is woven and assembled. Each year, Americans purchase more than 1 billion garments made in China: an average of four pieces of clothing for every U.S. citizen (Claudio, 2007).

Americans throw away 68 pounds of clothing per year. A lot of clothing is donated to charities, but only one fifth is ever used again (Claudio, 2007).

Instead, the charities sell clothing to textile recyclers at 5 to 7 cents per pound. One company, Trans-Americas Trading Company, recycles used clothing into fiber used to stuff upholstery.

Some companies have sought a niche in *eco-fashion*. The International Organization for Standardization (ISO) defines eco-fashion as "identifying the general environmental performance of a product within a product group based on its whole life-cycle in order to contribute to improvements in key environmental measures and to support sustainable consumption patterns" (Claudio, 2007). Patagonia makes fleece clothing from plastic soda bottles, estimating that they have saved more than 86 million bottles from the landfill.

Transportation

It is said that a car is the second most expensive item for a household after the purchase of a home. The transportation choices have direct linkage to the carbon footprint. One of the most impactful decisions is to live near work. Commuting to and from work is expensive in terms of time, energy, and the environment. A job closer to home can lead to better quality of life. Some companies are offering alternatives to commuting such as working from home, teleconferencing, and so on. If a commute to work is unavoidable, consider taking public transportation since it is much more fuel efficient than driving alone. Some communities or organizations also offer carpooling as an alternative (Horn, 2006).

There are some ways to keep cars running more efficiently. Some ways to boost gas mileage are to check that the tires are properly inflated, get a tune-up, replace air filters, and take off the roof rack when not in use (Horn, 2006). When in the market for a new car, consider the hybrid versions, the alternative fuel option, and **flexible fuel** option.

- *Hybrids:* At present, **hybrids** represent the best option in sustainable transportation. Numerous car companies ranging from Chevrolet and Ford to Hyundai and Toyota offer hybrid models. The Prius gets 50 or 60 miles per gallon (mpg). Some of the larger vehicles like the Lexus RX 400h offer hybrid drive, but most of the energy is spent toward performance of the vehicle. The hybrid versions cost more, upwards of $3,500 to $6,000 more than a conventional version. There are tax credits and carpool lanes offered to incentivize the sale of hybrids, but the demand of these vehicles will depend on the consumer demand and price of gasoline.
- *Flexible fuel tanks:* Most General Motors (GM), Ford, and Chrysler cars and trucks can run on a mix of 85% ethanol and 15% gasoline (E85), gasoline only, or a mixture of the two. Though about 2.3 million of these cars are on the road, only a few use this option due to the

difficulty of finding the fuel. There are only about 609 ethanol stations, and most of these are located in the Corn Belt region, with most being located in Minnesota.

- *Biodiesel*: This fuel is renewable and domestically produced. It can be manufactured from animal fats or vegetable fats, and it is safe and biodegradable. A blend of 20% **biodiesel** with 80% petroleum diesel can be used in conventional diesel engines. However, the engines require some modification if biodiesel were to be used in its pure form (Horn, 2006).

Role of Consumers

Given all this information on food, drink, housing, clothing, and transportation, it is still important to understand more about consumer attitudes and behaviors. There are many factors: availability, affordability, convenience, and force of habit (WBCSD, 2008).

There is rising awareness of environmental and social issues. About 96% of Europeans surveyed agreed that protecting the environment is important (Directorate of the Environment, 2008). Almost one in four U.S. adults agree with a set of values that includes "environmentalism, feminism, global issues and spiritual searching" (WBCSD, 2008). The people in this group are well educated, relatively affluent, and are the kind of consumer likely to purchase hybrid cars (WBCSD, 2008).

Globally, a survey of consumer choice and environment in 14 countries found that consumers "feel empowered when it comes to the environment and are taking some action in their daily lives to reduce consumption and waste" (WBCSD, 2008). Another global survey also found that consumers are willing to act on environmental concerns. The largest rise in awareness came from U.S. consumers (WBCSD, 2008).

Furthermore, consumers in both rapidly developing and developed markets report that they would prefer to buy from companies with high reputations in environmental and social responsibility (Directorate of the Environment, 2008).

However, people do not always act on environmental and social concerns. A McKinsey survey globally found that 53% of consumers were concerned about environmental and social issues, and 13% were willing to pay more but currently did not do so (*The McKinsey Quarterly* from WBCSD, 2008).

Barriers to Change

What is the reason for the difference between what people say they are willing to do and their actual consumer behavior? The four most significant factors were as follows: (1) lack of understanding, (2) comfortable lifestyle/greed,

(3) associated higher costs and taxes, and (4) the "tragedy of the commons." The last factor reflects an "I will if you will" mentality (WBCSD, 2008).

Some consumers are prone to the *rebound effect*—a tendency to use products *more* in response to efficiency improvements, reducing the expected benefits (Sussex Energy Group/UK Energy Research Centre, 2007). For example, consumers in the United States reportedly increase their use of air-conditioning by up to 50% when they switch to a green energy supply. Rebound effects have also been observed in home heating and personal transportation (WBCSD, 2008).

In addition, there also exists confusion around numerous labels and environmental claims. Some products are certified by a local or national authority that is internationally recognized and respected. Some of the examples of third-party labels include *organic* (e.g., U.S. Department of Agriculture [USDA], Rainforest Alliance, Soil Association), *healthy* (e.g., National Heart Foundation Approved, low glycemic index/gluten free), *sourced from sustainable sources* (e.g., FSC, Sustainable Forestry Initiative [SFI], MSC), *dolphin friendly* (e.g., Greenseas), *ethically sourced* (e.g., Fairtrade), and *eco-friendly* (e.g., EU Flower) (WBCSD, 2008).

Still, labels help foster sustainable consumption. Many products designed to be environmentally responsible did not meet the basic expectations of the consumer (such as **electric cars** and recycled paper).

Consumers trust each other more than labels or any other source of information (WBCSD, 2008). While consumers do not trust brands, they believe in their purchasing power (WBCSD, 2008). Consumers are also turning to peer-published blogs on the Internet for information. It seems that companies need to be savvy to address the barriers to behavior change in order to effectively communicate the message of their products to the consumers.

Ecological Footprint and Carbon Footprint

By its very nature, human activity has an impact on the planet. However, the idea of sustainable consumption is that if we are mindful of our activities on the planet, we can make decisions to reduce our impact. The two tools most commonly used are the ecological footprint and the carbon footprint.

The ecological footprint, developed by Mathis Wackernagel and William Rees, examines the ecological capacity required to support the consumption of products ("Ecological Footprint," n.d.). In addition, it also measures the waste generated by this consumption. The ecological footprint of the commute from home to work can be calculated. In the same manner, it can be computed for an entire community or an organization.

The ecological footprint varies by development and consumption level. The largest ecological footprint belongs to the U.S. consumer, who uses about 24 acres to support his or her lifestyle. As a comparison, Germans have an ecological footprint of 13 acres compared to Indians, who have an ecological footprint of 2 ("Ecological Footprint," n.d.). Among the wealthier nations, the Europeans and the Japanese can serve as models because they have high quality of life and footprints that are half the size of North Americans. Some of this is related to more efficient use of resources in Europe and Japan. This serves as a reminder that quality of life does not depend on large resource use ("Ecological Footprint," n.d.). For all global citizens to live an American or Canadian lifestyle, it would take "two more earths to satisfy everyone, three more still if population should double, and twelve earths altogether if world-wide standards of living should double over the next forty years" (Lovins, Lovins, & Hawken, 2000).

Humanity's combined footprint is more than the earth's capacity. The challenge of sustainability is to find ways to create fulfilling lives while reducing our impact on the earth. The ecological footprint shows us how much we use so that we can make more sustainable choices.

A carbon footprint provides a measure of the impact of activities on the environment. The primary footprint measures the direct emissions of carbon dioxide from travel choices and energy consumption. The consumer has direct control over these emissions. The secondary footprint is more complex since it measures indirect carbon dioxide emissions from the life cycle of the products used ("Carbon Footprint," n.d.). More consumption translates to a greater footprint. There are web-based calculators that let individuals and corporations estimate their footprint (see the appendix). Some of these calculators compute travel emissions by car or air; the other calculators can compute home emissions. Most of the carbon footprint calculator sites also provide simple tips to reduce the footprint from the perspective of a consumer or a business. Please refer to the mini-case at the end of this chapter to calculate a carbon footprint.

Role of Business

How can businesses help in mainstreaming consumption? Businesses have an important role to play in promoting sustainable consumption by "delivering sustainable value to society and consumers, helping consumers to choose and use their goods and services sustainably, and promoting sustainable lifestyles that help to reduce overall consumption of materials and resource" (WBCSD, 2008). There are three basic business approaches: (1) innovation that develops new and improved products, (2) choice influencing that enables customers to choose products more sustainably, and (3) choice editing that removes unsustainable products and services from the marketplace (WBCSD, 2008).

Innovation

Innovation is a core business function whose goal is to "deliver high levels of emotional and functional value while minimizing resource use and environmental impacts" (WBCSD, 2008). There are four ways in which innovation can assist: (1) eco-efficiency measures, (2) product innovation and design, (3) production and supply chain management, and (4) business model innovation.

Eco-Efficiency

This stands for the goods and services creating more value with less impact. Businesses can achieve this goal through numerous options: minimize packaging, reuse and recycle to minimize the amount of materials wasted, reduce the amount of fuel used for transportation (e.g., by "greening" vehicle fleets and using videoconferencing), reduce resource use, and produce and distribute efficiently.

Product Innovation and Design

Businesses can reformulate products for better performance. As an example, detergent manufacturers (such as Henkel and Procter & Gamble) discovered that 90% of the carbon emissions came from heating the water and operating the dishwasher or washing machine. As a result, the product was reformulated to deliver even better performance at lower temperatures, which in turn would save money for the consumer.

Production and Supply Chain Management

Customer relations is critical to "greening the supply chain" (WBCSD, 2008). Hence, businesses are incorporating green supply chain practices through making standard business practices green. More on greening the supply chain is discussed in Chapter 8.

Business Model Innovation

How does a product or service deliver social benefits? There are numerous strategies that can be employed ranging from differentiation strategies to low-cost, no-frills strategies. Some strategies aim for first mover advantage while others focus on a specific market geography or segment (WBCSD, 2006).

Choice Influencing

Choice influencing is a partnership between business and the consumer, one that ranges from sustainable production and design to consumer selection, use, and disposal. Companies use choice influencing to promote sustainable consumption by responsible marketing, advertising and sponsorship, and partnerships with key groups such as nongovernmental organizations (NGOs) and the media. (WBCSD, 2008).

Marketing and Advertising

The function of marketing is to provide information about sustainable products and services. Using customer surveys and market research, information can be gleaned about consumer attitudes and behaviors. This information is used in pricing, distributing, and making other business decisions. When building a brand, care must be taken so that the claims are authentic and credible so as to not fall into the trap of *greenwashing* (WBCSD, 2008).

Some of the green marketing approaches include the following:

single-issue focus in corporate and brand campaigns (e.g., "carbon neutral" or product carbon labels), screening and optimization of entire portfolio (e.g., reducing "unhealthy" food ingredients such as salt or sugar, and increasing "healthy" ingredients), "green line" of products to gain mindshare (e.g., hybrid cars and some cosmetic products based on natural ingredients), "social cause" products and campaigns (e.g., innovations addressing social challenges), responsible marketing communications (e.g., encouraging responsible use of the product). (WBCSD, 2008)

Choice Editing

Choice editing involves the decisions that impact consumption. Organizations at most levels can be involved in the process of choice editing. At the business level, supply chains can be scrutinized to eliminate components that pose risks to human health or the environment. At the retail level, hazardous products can be eliminated from shelves, and at the government or regulatory level, legislations can be drafted to ban hazardous substances. For successful choice editing, all the stakeholders in the value chain are to develop solutions. Businesses can also play a role in educating consumers on how to lead sustainable lifestyles. Since transparency is essential for trust, a common, robust set of indicators needs to be developed to report performance on economic, environmental, and social performance (WWF UK, 2006). These reporting standards shall be discussed in greater detail in Chapter 10.

Future of Consumption

Sustainable consumption is a systemic challenge in which all the players, from businesses to governments and consumers to civil society have the power to effect change. The consumers need the support of business, governments, and NGOs in order to lead sustainable lifestyles. Businesses have a role to play since they can help define sustainable products and can assist in mainstreaming sustainable consumption (WBCSD, 2006).

Individuals can make a number of incremental improvements in the way they live. Although these differences may seem to make the smallest impact on the environment, the more people who practice living in an eco-friendly manner, the better.

The automobile and mode of transportation is a good place to start. The simple action of consolidating errands can reduce fuel. How many times is it necessary to rush out to the grocery store for one item? A reduction in driving saves on fuel. What many consider a primitive mode of transport—the bicycle—for many in the world, this is the only way they can get around. Not only does it save on fuel but it improves one's cardiovascular health. One can place a basket on the bike, lock it, and go anywhere without having to pay for parking.

The switch to alternative fuel vehicles is also a wise choice. Commuters want to go as far as possible on as little fuel as they can. Hybrid or electric vehicles have increased in popularity not only for their fuel efficiency but also for the reduction in emissions. Do the math: If gasoline goes for $4.00 per gallon and the vehicle is driven for 10,000 miles per year, a 20 mpg auto requires 500 gallons of fuel, while a 30 mpg auto requires 333 gallons. The difference of 167 gallons saves $668 per year. If the vehicle is driven for 15,000 miles, the savings would be over $1,000. The problem, at present, is that the increased cost of a hybrid makes it difficult to justify cost.

Public transportation obviously offers tremendous cost advantages where it is available. Public transportation can save one individual an average $9,700 annually based on July 2012 gasoline rates (American Public Transportation Association [APTA], 2012). As gasoline prices trend upward, these savings become larger in magnitude. The challenge is to find an efficient public transportation option that is both convenient and reliable.

An energy audit of a house is sometimes available from the local energy company. Heat and cooling may escape through poor windows and leaks in the walls and doors. Old furnaces are also less efficient, and a replacement can pay for itself in savings in only a few years. Half of the home energy expenses come from the heating and cooling, and a homeowner should make sure they have as tight a home as possible.

A home conversion to solar heating usually requires a costly retrofit; therefore, one would assume they would live in the home long enough to realize payback on the investment. However, in times of an energy crunch, the home may actually increase in value due to the savings in energy.

Conclusion

We, as individuals and consumers, have a big role in sustainable consumption. Despite the popular myth of retail therapy, well-being is not necessarily correlated with high consumption. As discussed in this chapter, consumers in both the developing and affluent nations have a responsibility to address consumption since we are losing Earth's basic ecosystem services at an unsustainable rate. Consumer choices have a significant impact based on the choices made in the consumption of food, drink, housing, clothing, and transportation. Thought these are primary areas, sustainable choices can be extended to other areas such as recreation, health, communication, and education among others. As shown by the *Happy Planet Index* (WBCSD, 2008), a high consumption level does not guarantee happiness. It might be time to fill life with value instead of stuff.

KEY WORDS

Biodiesel

Carbon footprint

Certified organic

Consumption

Ecological footprint

Ecological impact

Ecosystems

Electric cars

Energy Star

Fair trade certified

Flexible fuel

Food miles

Hybrids

Rainforest Alliance

Sustainable consumption

DISCUSSION QUESTIONS

1. What are the global drivers of consumption? What steps can be taken by affluent and emerging economies to curb consumption?

2. Of all the stresses on the earth's ecosystem, which one seems most pertinent? Discuss.

3. What are the sustainable choices that a consumer can make in food and drink purchases? Which ones make the most sense to you?

4. Go to www.localharvest.org, and find a CSA group closest to you.

5. Why is the common usage of antibacterials detrimental to the environment?

6. Refer to the information on household cleaners. Which product would you stop using given the amount of chemicals contained within?

7. What are some steps to increase the efficiency of a home?

8. What are some simple tips for appliances and electronics? Does your home contain any of these energy saving appliances or electronics?

9. Use Google to find a carbon calculator to compute your carbon footprint. (See also page 291 in Chapter 11.) Compare your footprint to that of others in the class (e.g., www.carbonfootprint.com/calculator.aspx).

10. There are numerous electric cars and hybrids slated to enter the automotive market. Research some of these cars on the web, and discuss which of these cars you would consider.

11. What role can business play in sustainable consumption? Can you think of a company that promotes such practices?

12. What do you think are the biggest hurdles for consumers when it comes to switching to more sustainable consumer habits?

MINI CASE CARBON FOOTPRINT

Three friends—Alyssa, James, and Xavier—were sitting in a café discussing their commuting choices and whether these choices were sustainable. Their discussion follows:

Alyssa: Okay, guys, I live with my parents, and I take the train to school. So in a sense, my footprint should be lowest, right?

James: But your parents have a massive house. Its almost 6,000 square feet! Can you imagine the energy that goes into heating the house in Chicago winters.

Alyssa: Well, you drive your car from the suburbs to the city for school every day! I cannot imagine that being good for the earth.

Xavier: Guys, I have the best deal. I live in an apartment in the city and walk to school. Now that is a perfect solution.

James: Wait a minute, Xavier. You are an international student. Don't you, like, fly to Spain every month or so?

Xavier: I guess so. But I bet it's better than driving around everywhere.

Alyssa: Well, I hardly fly, and I don't even own a car so I bet my lifestyle is the best.

Xavier: I would not be so sure. We see cars and airplanes as emitting carbon dioxide, but there is a lot of energy that goes into homes.

Mini Case Questions

1. Alyssa lives in a 6,000 square foot home with her parents and two siblings in a Chicago suburb. Calculate her home's carbon footprint.

2. James drives a 2010 Jeep Cherokee, and the annual mileage is about 12,000 miles. Calculate his vehicle's carbon footprint.

3. Xavier flies home to Madrid four times a year round trip from Chicago. Calculate his airline carbon footprint.

4. Discuss the results with your classmates. Whose footprint is the highest? The lowest? Are the results surprising to you?

5. Please go to one of these following websites for the carbon footprint computations:

   Cool Climate Network: http://coolclimate.berkeley.edu/uscalc

   The Nature Conservancy: www.nature.org/greenliving/carboncalculator/index.htm

   Terrapass: www.terrapass.com/carbon-footprint-calculator/

   Carbon Footprint: www.carbonfootprint.com/calculator.aspx

RECOMMENDED WEBSITES

http://e-stewards.org/find-a-recycler/

www.hybridcars.com/index.php

www.localharvest.org/

www.lowenergyhouse.com/code-sustainable-homes.html

www.organic.org/

www.thegreenguide.com/

www.wbcsd.org

Appendix

Top Ten Sustainable Steps

Greg Horn, in his book titled *Living Green: A Practical Guide to Simple Sustainability*, offers ten simple steps to become sustainable:

1. *Organic eating:* Organic food tastes better and is much healthier than regular, conventional food. In the US, for each 1 percent increase in organic food consumption, pesticide and herbicide use is reduced by over 10 million pounds.

2. *Carbon neutral:* For a small sum of money, the carbon footprint can be offset. There are numerous carbon calculators, some of which will be discussed in Chapter 11.

3. *Recycling:* This step can cut the waste stream by up to 75 percent. An average US consumer produces 1609 pounds of waste per year. If all the glass, paper and metal was recycled, it would save 162 million tons of materials going into landfills per year.

4. *Disposables:* A switch to a glass from a water bottle and a coffee mug from a Styrofoam cup would save $244 billion bottles and cups made from petrochemical based plastics from ending up in landfills each year.

5. *Natural personal care:* Keep toxic chemicals off human bodies and out of the environment. A simple check—if something is not edible, it should not be applied to the body.

6. *Natural lawn care:* A suburban lawn uses six times the hazardous chemicals per acre than conventional farming. A switch to natural lawn care would result in saving billions of pounds of synthetic fertilizers, pesticides, and herbicides from entering the environment.

7. *Green cleaners:* Each day, about 32 million pounds of chemicals are dumped down the drain from household cleaning chemicals. A switch to green alternatives keeps these chemicals out of the water supply.

8. *Filtered tap water:* The process of filtering removes chlorine and fluoride and comes at a fraction of the cost of purchasing bottled water.

9. *Increased energy efficiency:* Insulation of homes and usage of fuel-efficient cars, such as hybrids, can dramatically reduce use of fossil fuels.

10. *Information:* A subscription to green magazines helps in communication on sustainability resources, tips, and tools. (Horn, 2006)

Household Cleaners

The following is a list of common household cleaners, the lurking chemicals, and the alternatives available.

All-Purpose cleaners: Some of these cleaners contain DEA and TEA and others contain butyl cellosolve that is easily absorbed through the skin and can cause damage to kidneys, liver and reproductive systems. Any product containing ammonia can cause respiratory irritation. As an alternative, buy natural all–purpose cleaners in a health store or make your own all purpose cleaner by dissolving four tablespoons of baking soda in one quart of warm water.

Disinfectants: Most disinfectants contain pesticides to kill bacteria and their effectiveness is questionable since these products cannot kill germs in the air. Most disinfectants contain APEs that are hormone disruptors and Triclosan. A better option is to wash foods thoroughly before cooking and thaw meat in the refrigerator than on the countertop. Soapy water or white vinegar can be used to clean surfaces. Another alternative is to mix half a cup of borax with a gallon of hot water to disinfect.

Glass cleaners: The common window cleaners contain butyl cellosolve, a neurotoxin that can damage liver, kidneys, and red blood cells. In addition, these cleaners also contain ammonia that can irritate airways. As an alternative, glass cleaner can be made with a cup of water mixed with a quarter cup of white vinegar or a tablespoon of lemon juice.

Furniture polish: Many brands contain formaldehyde, a carcinogen, or petroleum distillates that can damage nerves. For dusting and polishing, combine one half cup of white vinegar and few drops of olive oil. Silver can be scrubbed with toothpaste to remove tarnish. Copper can be cleaned with a paste of salt and white vinegar and brass can be cleaned with a paste made one cup flour, one cup white vinegar, and one teaspoon salt. Less toxic brands of furniture cleaners can also be purchased.

Toilet cleaners: Most cleaners contain corrosive agents that are irritating to eyes, [sinuses], and airways. Some cleaners also contain sodium bisulfate that can trigger asthma attacks. For home-made cleaner, mix one cup of borax with one-quarter cup of white vinegar and let it sit for a few hours. Almost 99 percent of bacteria can be killed by ordinary vinegar.

Drain cleaners: The chemicals in these products are the most corrosive containing sodium hydroxide and sodium hypochlorite, both of which can damage eyes and skin permanently and are lethal if ingested. Instead keep drains clear by putting in metal or plastic screens available at hardware stores. In case of a clog, use a snake plumbing tool to get rid of the blockage. To disinfect drains, pour a cup of straight vinegar down twice a week.

Scrubs and cream cleansers: The abrasive agents in scrubs contain silica, harmful when inhaled, or chlorine bleach, that irritates airways. A paste of baking soda and water cleans stains on most countertops, showers, tubs, and toilets.

Soaps and detergents: For dishwashing liquids, choose clear since the dyes can be contaminated with led or arsenic. For laundry detergents, choose fragrance-free and vegetable-based products. Stay clear of antibacterial detergents and products with bleach and harsh fragrances.

Cloth cleaners: Half of the trees cut in the North America are used to make paper products. Wood pulp is also being sourced from South America and China. For home cleaning, use a cloth cleaner made from cotton since these can be used, washed, and reused again. In case paper products cannot be avoided, try to purchase recycled products. (Garlough et al., 2008)

Personal Care

The following is a list of common household cleaners, the lurking chemicals and the alternatives available (Horn, 2006).

1. *Choose natural, organic fiber clothes*: Find clothes made from 100 percent natural fibers like cotton, silk, linen, hemp, or tencel. Some of the examples are Patagonia and Prana.

2. *Purchase chemical-free kids clothing*: Avoid fire retardant clothing that contains polybrominated diphenyl ether (PDBE), which has been linked to development problems with brain and thyroid. Buy bedding, diapers, and clothing that are made from organically grown fibers. For diapers, choose gDiapers that come with a flushable inner lining.

3. *Find green drycleaner*: Green drycleaners are beginning to use nontoxic chemicals and other technologies to replace the harmful chemicals such as perc and hexane.

4. *Buy safe personal care products*: Though the adage of "Don't put it on your skin if you would not eat it" sounds shocking, it simply means that personal care items should be made from natural oils, herbs, vitamins, and minerals. The Food and Drug Administration (FDA) does not regulate cosmetics and only gets involved if a product is proven to be hazardous. Some of the worst products in terms of chemical additives are as follows:

- Antiperspirants
- Sunscreens and sunblocks
- Soaps and shampoos
- Hair dyes and hair spray
- Toothpaste and mouthwash
- Lipstick

(Continued)

(Continued)

- Mascara
- Eye shadow, blush, and face powder
- Perfumes and aftershaves

5. *Filter shower water and bathwater*: Two thirds of the daily chlorine exposure comes from showering. An inexpensive carbon filter that attaches in a shower-head can cut this exposure.

6. *Female natural hygiene products*: Tampons are made from rayon, which is a petrochemical-based fiber, or from cotton that contains pesticide residues. Sanitary napkins also contain fibers bleached with dioxon.

8

Role of the Corporation

LEARNING OBJECTIVES

By the end of this chapter, you should be able to:

- Present the **chrysalis economy.**
- Discuss why sustainability is more than green.
- Define **corporate social responsibility (CSR)**, and link it to sustainability.
- Understand the phases of CSR and how to make a case for CSR.
- Discuss the benefits and challenges of CSR.
- Explain **green supply chains** and sustainable value chains.
- Examine the role of logistics, transportation, and **green procurement.**
- Map out a business case for sustainability.

Chapter Overview

This chapter discusses the role of the corporation. Is the sole responsibility of a corporation to generate profits for its shareholders, or does a business need to do more? What is the impact of a corporation on the community? What are the methodologies available to corporations that would like to be more socially responsible? This chapter focuses on the topics of CSR, green supply chains, and the **business case for sustainability.**

The Chrysalis Economy

The preceding seven chapters of the book presented the renewable resources such as air, water, food, forests, and clean energy. We also discussed sustainable strategies and the role of consumers in sustainable consumption. Next, we turn our attention to the global economy and corporations. What might a sustainable global economy look like?

A sustainable global economy will arise in an era of severe technological, economic, social, and political metamorphosis. The main reason is that the present pattern of wealth creation and distribution is simply unsustainable. The present economy is highly destructive of natural and social capital, and the divide between the rich and the poor is ever widening. Since these patterns of wealth creation will lead to worsening environmental and social problems, there will be increasing pressure to transition to sustainable development (Elkington, 2004).

Figure 8.1 illustrates four main types of companies, or *value webs*, in this path toward a chrysalis economy—(1) **corporate locusts,** (2) **corporate caterpillars,** (3) **corporate butterflies,** and (4) **corporate honeybees.**

Corporate Locusts

These companies operate with an unsustainable business model in that they operate in a manner that overwhelms the carrying capacity of social systems. These companies are termed *destructive locusts* since they destroy social and environmental value, and most of these are found rampant in parts of Africa, Asia, Latin America, and Russia. The key characteristics of corporate locusts are as follows:

- Destruction of natural, human, social, and economic capital
- An unsustainable burn rate
- A business model that is unsustainable in the long run
- Tendency to swarm, overwhelming the carrying capacity of ecosystems
- Incapacity to foresee negative system effects
- An unwillingness to learn from mistakes (Elkington, 2004).

When companies act like corporate locusts, the governments have had to take charge in controlling the worst offenders. In a global economy, the environmental protection regulation needs to be extended beyond formal jurisdictions.

Figure 8.1   Corporate Characteristics

	Low Impact	High Impact
Regenerative (increasing returns)	Butterflies	Honeybees
Degenerative (decreasing returns)	Caterpillars	Locusts

Source: Elkington (2004).

Corporate Caterpillars

The impacts of these companies are more local, and as a result, they are harder to isolate. These caterpillars have the following characteristics:

- Depend on *high burn rate* in the form of renewable capital
- Operate on an unsustainable business model
- Operate in sectors where other companies are moving toward sustainable growth
- Have the potential to transform toward more sustainable growth

In this case, governments need to provide conditions for businesses to evolve while employing regulatory incentives to ensure that the development keeps in pace with environmental and sustainable objectives (Elkington, 2004).

Corporate Butterflies

These are small companies that are easy to spot. These companies are covered in the media and are highly conspicuous. Examples include Patagonia, The Body Shop, Ben & Jerry's, etc. These butterflies have the following characteristics:

- A sustainable business model
- Strong commitment to CSR
- Wide network
- Involvement in symbiotic networks
- High visibility and powerful representation for small companies

Corporate butterflies tend to occur in *pulses*. One trend was in the 1960s with the boom in whole food and renewable energy. Another wave came in 1990s with organic food, ecotourism, and social investments. Governments can help butterflies by encouraging change that would move companies from caterpillar to butterfly stage (Elkington, 2004).

Corporate Honeybees

This is the area that companies, innovators, entrepreneurs, and government agencies and investors will seek out in the coming years. Ideally, in a sustainable global economy, there would be a steady hum of corporate honeybees and economic version of beehives. The impact would be sustainable and strongly regenerative. The honeybees would have the following characteristics:

- A sustainable business model based on innovation
- A set of clear ethics-based business principles

- Strategic sustainable management of natural resources
- Evolution of powerful symbiotic relationships
- Sustainable production of natural, human, social, institutional, and cultural capital
- Capacity to moderate the impacts of corporate caterpillars in its supply chain (Elkington, 2004).

The attention around sustainability will lead to patterns of change in corporate behavior. Some companies might choose to remain degenerative yet try to improve their image by mimicking butterfly and honeybee traits. But no corporation can remain in the locust stage forever. Given the right set of drivers in the form of leadership or stakeholder demand, any corporation can start its transformative journey (Elkington, 2004).

Sustainability Is More Than Green

Of the world's 100 largest economic entities, 63 are corporations, not countries. This immense power calls for greater responsibility as society wants to hold global businesses accountable to meet the challenges facing our planet. What we are seeing are increasing limits on growth in the world and less credit. For this reason, companies need to develop and execute a strategy for sustainability. This is much more than a green strategy. The reason being that sustainability is much bigger than being simply green. Sustainability takes into account every dimension of the business environment: social, economic, and cultural, as well as natural (Werbach, 2009).

In a large picture, a sustainable business means a business that can thrive in the long term. Sustainability is much more than a public relations push. Sustainability is even bigger than an occasional agreement to ongoing efforts to save the planet. If sustainability is to be realized fully and well implemented, it can drive a bottom-line strategy to save costs; a top-line strategy to reach a new consumer base; and a talent strategy to get, keep, and develop creative employees. This kind of true sustainability has four equal components:

1. Social, to address conditions that affect us all, including poverty, violence, injustice, education, public health, and labor and human rights

2. Economic, to help people and businesses meet their economic needs; for people: securing food, water, shelter, and creature comforts; for businesses: turning a profit

3. Environmental, to protect and restore the earth—for example, by controlling climate change, preserving natural resources, and preventing waste

4. Cultural, to protect and value the diversity through which communities manifest their identity and cultivate traditions across generations (Werbach, 2009).

Corporate Social Responsibility

What is the role of a corporation or a company? The actual word *company* comes from Latin—cum and panis, which mean "breaking bread together" (Arndt, 2003). Given that this terminology suggests some synergistic role, what are some of the views on the role of a company in the present age?

Let us consider two opposing views. Milton Friedman, a Nobel laureate, argued against CSR since it distracted business leaders from making money. Indeed, in an article titled "The Social Responsibility of Business Is to Increase Its Profits," he emphatically stated, "There is one and only one social responsibility of business—to use its resources and engage in activities designed to increase its profits" (Friedman, 1970).

Furthermore, he stated, "Few trends could so undermine the very foundations of our free society as the acceptance by corporate officials of a social responsibility other than to make as much money for their stockholders as possible" (Friedman, 1962).

David Packard, Hewlett-Packard (HP) (Carmichael, n.d.), said the following:

> Why are we here? Many people assume, wrongly, that a company exists solely to make money. People get together and exist as a company so that they are able to accomplish something collectively that they could not accomplish separately—they make a contribution to society.

Hence, whereas Milton Friedman stated that the main responsibility for a company was to make money and increase profits, David Packard is of the view that a company needs to do more than just make money: The company needs to contribute to society. It is the latter viewpoint that is becoming more prevalent in that companies need to provide value to society, one that goes beyond the company's bottom line.

CSR is derived from the three title words: (1) corporate, (2) social, and (3) responsibility. Hence, in very general terms, CSR stands for the social role or responsibility that a corporation has toward the society that it operates within. CSR is also known by some other terms, some of which are *corporate or business* responsibility, *business or corporate* citizenship, community relations, corporate stewardship, social responsibility, or strategic philosophy (Werther & Chandler, 2011).

Definition

Sustainable business and CSR are part of a cluster of terms that include sustainable development, socially responsible business, green management, corporate citizenship, and ethical business.

CSR has been defined in terms of sustainability, and sustainability has been defined in terms of CSR. CSR is commonly promoted as a means to achieve sustainability. This view is held both by researchers (Young, 2004) and practitioners (Frame, 2005). Some researchers see CSR and sustainable business as being synonymous (Laine, 2005) while others have stated that sustainability can be viewed as a broader concept compared to CSR and that sustainability "embraces a wider, time-dependent definition of a benefit to society and focuses on results rather than standards of behavior" (Foot & Ross, 2004). At the simplest level, it calls for corporations to behave responsibly and pursue sustainable development goals.

History of Corporate Social Responsibility

According to Wilson (2003), the earliest CSR efforts can be traced back to the early Greek society though Seeger and Hipfel (2007) noted that CSR has been around since the 1930s. The first formal definition of social responsibility was given by Howard R. Bowen (1953) in 1953 and it stated, "It refers to the obligations of businessmen to pursue those policies, to make those decisions, or to follow those lines of action which are desirable in terms of the objectives and values of our society" (Carroll, 1999).

Milton Friedman (1970) is the most cited critic, noting that businesses best serve societies by operating efficiently, hiring workers, paying taxes, and increasing shareholder value. Despite Friedman's criticism, businesses have adopted CSR. Allen (2004) described the uneven evolution of CSR from 1950s to the present day. Business for Social Responsibility (BSR) was formed in 1992 and CSR Europe in 1996.

The past 15 years have been witness to emergence and rapid growth of sustainability initiatives. Sustainable development entered the discourse in 1972 at the UN Conference on the Human Environment at Stockholm. The business community embraced the sustainability concept in 1991 with the formation of the Business Council for Sustainable Development. Since then, sustainability has gained wider acceptance, and the original organization has grown into the World Business Council for Sustainable Development (WBCSD) with 175 international member companies (Drexhage & Murphy, 2010).

According to KPMG, 52% of the largest 250 global companies issued CSR reports in 2005 (Smalheiser, 2006). CSR is about how companies manage the business processes to produce an overall positive impact on society.

Corporate Social Responsibility is the continuing commitment by business to behave ethically and contribute to economic development while improving the quality of life of the workforce and their families as well as of the local community and society at large. (Holme & Watts, 2000, p. 10)

In the United States, early CSR reports often focused on philanthropy. The companies made profits, paid taxes, and then donated a certain share of the profits to charitable causes. As CSR developed, this notion progressed to include protection and improvement of the lives of workers. The current CSR reports cover issues that impact almost every area of operations from hiring and training workers to ethics and governance to responsible purchasing, environmental impact, and supply chain policies (CSR, n.d.). In contrast, the European model looks at operating the core business in a socially responsible way, complemented by investment in communities for solid business case reasons. The application of CSR would vary from culture to culture since there will be a difference in values or priorities across cultures In different act (Baker, 2004).

Phases of Corporate Social Responsibility

CSR's role changes as demands and the expectations of society change. The CSR movement had four main phases. It started with a reactive phase, wherein CSR was viewed as a public relations function intended for damage control when companies made mistakes with the community and the environment. In the second phase, some of these companies started to incorporate process efficiencies in manufacturing and services and started to establish relationships with stakeholders including nongovernmental organizations (NGOs). In the third phase of integration, companies created key performance indicators that were then used to publicly report on various functional business units. The knowledge garnered from this stage fed into the fourth stage of **value creation,** where brand enhancement, product development, and R & D looked for solutions to social issues that impacted the bottom line (Smalheiser, 2006).

The main advantages of a well-executed CSR is that it builds business value in many ways: by enhancing brand image, establishing a cooperative relationship with government, and attracting investors. In addition, a company can attract and retain motivated employees, enter new markets, position the company to partner for governments and NGOs, and improve risk avoidance (Smalheiser, 2006). The following examples illustrate how companies are building business value and gaining strategic advantage.

Examples

Business strategy: How does a company serve global markets in various stages of development in order to secure goodwill and support that would protect its investments and secure a broad credibility? The Marathon Oil Corporation started a malaria eradication and treatment program in Equatorial Guinea in conjunction with the local government and NGOs that led to a massive drop in new incident cases of malaria. In addition, the company installed a workforce program that will enable local people to acquire skills necessary to earn employment at the company.

Overcoming obstacles: Becton, Dickinson and Company (BD), a New Jersey-based technology company making medical devices, also focuses on global health issues. The company has the social networks, expertise, and resources to work closely with local organizations to help treatment of diseases. BD also manufactures single use syringes that minimize the rate of injections caused by reusing these syringes.

Fertile ground: In areas of environmental innovation, General Electric's (GE) *ecomagination* works in areas of product and packaging design, water stewardship, and greenhouse gas (GHG) mitigation. Canada's Domtar Corporation had a history of obtaining timber rights from public lands. As a company committed to sustainable forestry, its operations are based on sustainable forestry standards.

Brand building: As consumers become sensitive to environmental issues, companies attempt to develop new products. Waste Management, the largest trash-removal company in the United States, is also the largest recycler. The company is a leading convertor of waste to energy and operates 17 plants that process 24,000 tons of solid waste per day. It has more than 100 landfill projects that convert methane into clean energy. The company converts its landfill areas to wildlife habitats, thus providing more than 17,000 acres of land devoted to wetlands and wildlife (Smalheiser, 2006).

Making the Case for Corporate Social Responsibility

In general terms, the case of CSR can be made on moral grounds. The point to be made is that since the corporation exists within society, it needs the infrastructure, the employees, and the consumer base from this very society. However, not everyone can be convinced on the moral ground alone. How can the upper management of companies, the C-suite, be convinced that adoption of CSR would be good for their company? Porter and Kramer (2006) made four arguments to support their case: "moral obligation, sustainability, license to operate, and reputation" (p. 81).

The first argument, one of moral obligation, states that companies ought to "do the right thing." Specifically, the message is that businesses "achieve commercial success in ways that honor ethical values and respect people, communities, and the natural environment" (Porter & Kramer, 2006). In areas of financial reporting, moral obligations are easy to understand and apply. However, most corporate social choices involve balancing competing values, interests, and costs. For example, Google's entry into China has resulted in a conflict over censorship and Chinese government mandates. A pharmaceutical company has no direct way of knowing how to allocate its revenues between subsidizing care, developing cures for the future, or providing investor dividends (Porter & Kramer, 2006).

The second argument is derived from sustainability, and it places importance on environmental and community stewardship. Going back to the Brundtland Commission's definition of sustainability, "meeting the needs of the present without compromising the ability of future generations to meet their own needs" usually invokes the triple bottom line (TBL) approach of economic, social, and environmental performance. In this approach, companies ought to operate in ways that improve their long-term performance while avoiding short-term pitfalls arising from environmental or societal concerns. For example, DuPont saved over $2 billion from energy use reductions since 1990, and McDonald's reduced its solid waste by 30% from changes to materials used to wrap its food. However, in some other areas, sustainability is used in vague terms—transparency is more *sustainable* than corruption or philanthropy leading to *sustainability* of a society (Porter & Kramer, 2006).

The third argument comes into play when companies identify a set of social issues pertinent to the stakeholders, engage in a dialogue with the community, and make decisions. This thinking is prevalent in companies that depend on government approval, such as mining or other extractive industries, and in companies whose operations, by nature, are hazardous, such as chemical manufacturing. The inherent challenge is that companies that seek to placate stakeholders run the risk of ceding the control of their CSR agendas to external parties (Porter & Kramer, 2006).

The fourth argument concerns the reputation of the company and also seeks to appease external stakeholders. In industries, like chemical and energy, this strategy is pursued like an insurance policy in case of a crisis. Some companies like Ben and Jerry's, Patagonia, and The Body Shop stand out due to their long-term commitment to social issues. However, the social impact is tough to determine, and there is no way to quantify the benefits of social investment (Porter & Kramer, 2006).

The important point to note is that there needs to be integration between business and society. A healthy society needs successful companies since these companies create jobs, wealth, and innovation that lead to an increase in the standard of living. In turn, a successful company needs a healthy society since education and health care are essential to having a productive workforce. In coming up with corporate social agenda, a company needs to be responsive to its stakeholders and, furthermore, look for ways to achieve social and economic benefits in a strategic manner (Porter & Kramer, 2006).

Porter and Kramer (2006) also classified CSR in two main categories: responsive and strategic. **Responsive corporate social responsibility (CSR)** companies act as good citizens and mitigate harmful value chain impacts. An example of the former role is GE's program to adopt underperforming high schools. GE helps with donations, and the GE managers mentor students. An example of the latter role is B&Q, a chain of home supply centers based in England that has begun to analyze its entire product line against a list of social issues in order to determine which products might pose a social responsibility risk (Porter & Kramer, 2006).

Strategic corporate social responsibility (CSR) aims to identify initiatives whose social and business benefits stand out in scope. It also taps shared value by investments in aspects that strengthen the competitive advantage for the company. For example, Toyota's Prius is a car model that has produced competitive advantage and environmental benefits. Nestle works directly with small farmers in developing countries in order to source basic commodities such as milk, coffee, and cocoa. Another good example is Whole Foods Market, which emphasizes purchasing from local farmers, screening out foods that contain any of 100 common ingredients considered to be environmentally damaging, constructing stores using minimum amount of virgin raw materials, purchasing wind credits, and offsetting all the electricity consumption. Examples also include initiatives from large companies— Sysco aims to preserve small family farms and offer local produce to customers, GE aims to focus on developing water purification technology, and Unilever aims to meet the needs of the poorest populations worldwide (Porter & Kramer, 2006).

Relevance of Corporate Social Responsibility

There are four main environmental forces that are causing CSR to gain relevance: (1) increasing affluence, (2) globalization, (3) ecological sustainability, and (4) brands.

Increasing Affluence

CSR tends to be more prevalent in affluent nations where consumers can afford to be picky in the products they purchase. However, the relevance of CSR is just as important in developing nations as the multinational corporations are being held responsible for their overseas actions. One example is the infamous case of Nike and its subcontractors where CEO Phil Knight was reluctant to accept responsibility for the company's overseas labor practices (Werther & Chandler, 2011).

Globalization

The media are quick to report any *corporate mistakes* to the consumers. In addition, the Internet facilitates instant communication among consumer groups located worldwide, enabling them to coordinate action such as product boycotts. Consumers are better informed and are more diligent when it comes to their choices. For the companies, the market is also being shaped by grassroots campaigns. Hence, it is in the best interest of a corporation to listen to bottom-up concerns and respond in a proactive manner (Werther & Chandler, 2011).

Ecological Sustainability

From growing affluence and change in society's expectations comes an increased concern for the environment. Firms that are perceived to be indifferent to their environmental responsibilities are likely to be criticized and penalized. Some firms have recognized this shift and responded by taking positive steps. For example, Wal-Mart has started integrating some aspects of sustainability into their operations (Werther & Chandler, 2011).

Brands

In the past few years, great strides have been made toward the integration of CSR into the core culture of companies. For example, companies such as Chevron, GE, Microsoft, and HP have made public commitments to CSR and have reported on their CSR performance. Companies also want to be included on *Fortune*'s annual list of the best companies to work for. In Europe, companies are required to report on their social and environmental performance (CSR, n.d.). Brands are highly crucial since a popular brand increases leverage, which in turn impacts sales and revenues. A strong corporate brand is of immeasurable value to the company, and CSR can assist in the branding of a corporate image.

Positive Brand Building

British Petroleum (BP) spent $200 million to reposition itself as an environmentally sound and socially responsible company. BP is in stark contrast to ExxonMobil, which has to constantly battle NGO attacks and consumer boycotts. In response to the 2010 Gulf of Mexico oil spill, BP agreed to pay an estimated $7.8 billion in settlement charges (Fisk, 2012). The Body Shop takes an aggressive stand on fair trade and other social issues and attracts consumers via this fair trade stance. The clothing company Benetton also advertises on social issues that it deems are important to consumers (Werther & Chandler, 2011).

Brand Insurance

Nike faced consumer boycotts and NGO attacks in the mid-1990s. However, Nike has turned itself around and is now known as a committed corporate citizen. It publishes an annual CSR report and has appointed a VP for corporate responsibility. Merck & Co. takes a socially responsible stance when it announced that "medicine is for the patients, not for the profits." The most cited example is Merck donating the medicine Mectizan to combat river blindness, an infectious disease in Africa and Latin America (Werther & Chandler, 2011).

Key Corporate Social Responsibility Areas

What are the main areas that companies tend to report in CSR? The four main areas that emerged from the "Winning With Integrity" framework by Business in the Community in 2000 ("Key CSR Issue Areas," n.d.) are as follows:

Marketplace: What is the value created by the goods and services produced by the company? In turn, what cost does the business impose on the community it operates within and the society at large?

Environment: Can companies begin to tackle their environmental footprint? Can companies control their GHG emissions via efficiency measures? Can companies satisfy customer needs with minimal environmental impact?

Workplace: How does a company attract, recruit, and retain skilled people? There is evidence that people want to work for companies that stand out in corporate reputation, including social responsibility.

Community: Is the company viewed as a good influence on the community? At what level are the employees of the company involved within the community? ("Key CSR Issue Areas," n.d.).

These four key areas of CSR reporting are the ones that emerged as more important. Next, as we analyze some of the common CSR policies, note that most of these policies impact these four areas.

Corporate Social Responsibility Policies

In general terms, CSR refers to running a business while keeping an account of the social and environmental impact of the business. In practical terms, CSR calls for developing policies that incorporate responsible practices within daily business operations and for the reporting on progress actually made toward these practices.

Some of the common CSR policies include the following:

- adoption of internal controls reform in the wake of accounting scandals;
- commitment to diversity in hiring employees and barring discrimination;
- management teams that view employees as assets;
- workplaces that integrate the views of line employees into decision-making processes;
- adoption of operating policies that exceed compliance with social and environmental laws;
- advanced resource productivity, focused on the use of natural resources in a more productive, efficient, and profitable fashion; and
- taking responsibility for conditions under which goods are produced directly or by contract employees (CSR, n.d.).

CSR is only one part of the overall corporate strategy. How can companies achieve progress toward a more competitive environmental approach? Porter and van der Linde (1995) suggested the following four options:

1. Measure direct and indirect environmental impacts

2. Recognize the opportunity cost of underutilized resources

3. Create a bias in favor of innovation-based, productivity-enhancing solutions

4. Become more pro-active in defining relationships with regulators and environmentalists

Benefits of Corporate Social Responsibility

There are numerous businesses that recognize the benefits of CSR. However, those that are investing in CSR face a new set of challenges. CSR can be viewed as a public relations ploy, and there are numerous companies that do the minimum, for example, by funding a development project or two in an area in which they operate. In order to move further, companies need to consider the social and environmental impact of their policies alongside profit when making investment strategy decisions and incorporating management practices. Surveys state that business leaders are called upon to play an increasingly larger role in solving social issues, from education to environment (Bielak, Bobini, & Oppenheim, 2007). The biggest argument against CSR is the familiar one in that there is a lack of tangible economic benefit since both opinion and research on this relationship has been divided.

Businesses have shown that *strategic* CSR supports business objectives along with accruing certain intangible benefits such as increasing brand awareness, attracting talented workforce, and improving relations with regulators. A survey of MBA candidates stated that they look at reputation when considering where to work after graduating. Social responsibility is one of the factors that drive reputation (Butcher, 2009), and 77% of consumers will not buy from companies they distrust (Butcher, 2009). As a result, companies must respond to the demand for more ethical business processes and actions.

An International Business Report by Grant Thornton on CSR states the following:

> Four of the top five [corporate social responsibility] initiatives were directly associated with people and their workplace—active promotion of workforce health and well-being (71 percent of respondents); provision of apprenticeships and work experience (67 percent); promotion of diversity/equality in the workplace (64 percent) and allowing flexible working (62 percent). In many countries [...] a large proportion of respondents say they have taken action on waste management and have also acted to improve energy efficiency. (MacBeath, 2008)

Some of the other areas that companies are focusing on are product life cycle management, strategic sourcing and procurement, logistics, and continuous process improvement.

Business leaders are committed to incorporating CSR into their strategies (Riddleberger & Hittner, 2009). About 60% of the survey respondents stated that they believe CSR has increased in importance over the past year. The hard reality is that many of these businesses are not sure about how to implement changes that would improve business performance and have a beneficial societal impact. As a policy, program, or process, CSR is strategic when it results in supporting the core business activities (Burke & Logsdon, 1996).

The way to support the purpose of CSR within firms is by the concept of value creation. In specific terms, "under what conditions does a firm jointly serve its own strategic business interests and the societal interests of its stakeholders?" (Burke & Logsdon, 1996, p. 495). In the study by Burke and Logsdon (1996), value creation is most effective when the following factors are considered:

- centrality—closeness of fit to the firm's mission and objectives;
- specificity—ability to capture private benefits by firm;
- pro-activity—degree to which the program is planned in anticipation of emerging social trends and in the absence of crises;
- voluntarism—the scope for discretionary decision-making and the lack of externally imposed compliance requirements;
- visibility—observable, recognizable credit by internal and/or external stakeholders for the firm; and
- value creation—identifiable, measurable economic benefits that the firm expects to receive (Cavett-Goodwin, 2007).

For the most positive impact, businesses need to focus on efficient operations balanced with diverse social and environmental ecosystems. CSR is a necessity rather than a choice given the increasing scrutiny from stakeholders (Butcher, 2009).

Most of the current CSR theories are focused on four main aspects: (1) meeting objectives that yield long-term profits, (2) employing business power responsibly, (3) combining social demands and (4) being ethical. The CSR theories can be classified into four groups: (1) instrumental, (2) political, (3) integrative, and (4) value theories (Garriga & Mele, 2004). The instrumental theories are the ones in which the corporation's social activities serve as a means to achieve economic results. The political theories focus on the power of corporations in society and how this power can be employed responsibly. The integrative theories state that the corporation can focus on the satisfaction of social demands. Lastly, the value theories are based on responsibilities of corporations to society (Garriga & Mele, 2004).

Challenges of Corporate Social Responsibility

One weakness of CSR is the lack of measures of performance, something that can lead to unsubstantiated claims. Even the examples provided in the preceding discussion on companies like BP, Marathon Oil Corporation, Nike, and so on are open to debate. However, there is one process that aims to set forth a common set of guidelines, the Global Reporting Initiative (GRI) (www.gri.org). This process incorporates the active participation of various global stakeholders ranging from businesses to environmental and labor organizations. More details on GRI will be discussed in Chapter 10 of this book.

CSR has also been undermined as an initiative. There are three main failings that have attributed to this failure. These points are as follows:

1. CSR has been restricted to the largest companies and to a specific PR department within these companies.

2. CSR has adopted a model akin to the quality management model that results in incremental improvements.

3. CSR does not always make economic sense and, in the short term, companies that push their costs to society are rewarded (Visser, 2001).

Visser proposed a radical, or holistic, CSR that is termed as CSR 2.0. The four DNA codes for this CSR 2.0 are (1) value creation, (2) good governance, (3) societal contribution, and (4) environmental integrity. The strategic goals for each of these are: economic development, institutional effectiveness, stakeholder orientation, and sustainable ecosystems, respectively (Visser, 2001).

Green, Sustainable Supply Chains

A supply chain is the planning and management of all activities involved in manufacture of a product or provision of a service. A green, sustainable supply chain can be defined as follows:

> The process of using environmentally friendly inputs and transforming these inputs through change agents—whose byproducts can improve or be recycled within the existing environment. This process develops outputs that can be reclaimed and re-used at the end of their life-cycle thus, creating a sustainable supply chain. (Penfield, 2007)

The point of a green, sustainable supply chain is to reduce costs while helping the environment.

Though the trend of developing a green supply chain is getting popular, most companies are not sure where to start. Indeed, most of the large corporations have no green supply chain policy in place. A survey conducted by BearingPoint, the management consultant group, found that 35% of companies have already established a green supply chain. The interest in green supply chains is linked to size: "54% of companies with turnover in excess of $700 million claim to have established a Green Supply Chain" (Green Supply Chain Management, n.d.). In the past few years, companies have been attempting to minimize cost, increase efficiency, and improve supply chain visibility. The focus on green supply chains does not have to undermine these prior goals. Some best practices have emerged from the companies that are greening their supply chains.

Align the Green Supply Chain With Business Goals

A company should identify how a transition to a green supply chain can help achieve business goals. For example, if a company wants to reduce its energy costs, it should explore more energy efficient equipment. If the overall goal is one of cost reduction, then the move to a green supply chain should align with the business goal (Murray, 2010).

Use the Green Supply Chain to Improve Processes

Companies that green their supply chain should review all their business processes to determine areas where a greener approach can improve their business. This might identify the inefficiencies along the supply chain, such as wastage of raw materials, underutilized raw materials, and inefficient equipment (Murray, 2010).

Green Suppliers and Material Refurbishment

Companies should aim to find suppliers who have not sacrificed the quality of their product in an attempt to minimize their environmental impact. In this manner, companies can begin to green their supply chains before any material reaches their site. In addition, companies should pay close attention to their return process since a refurbishment program can offer more purchasing options to the customers and widen the customer base while improving the environmental impact of the products (Murray, 2010).

It is important to have strong leadership in place before a transition to a green supply chain can be made. A simple plan to implement a green supply chain will not be realized without the necessary resources, both financial and manpower.

Ten Steps to Create a Sustainable Supply Chain

The supply chain of any product comprises various steps that include resource extraction, transportation, production, packaging, distribution, sales, consumer use, and disposal. Each stage in the supply chain has repercussions on the environment, and a sustainable-minded company would need to account for all these steps along the way. The following steps have been taken by some of the business leaders—Starbucks, Wal-Mart, Disney, Gap, Timberland, and HP—in an attempt to green their supply chains (Kaestner, 2007):

1. *Start with the top:* Top-level management support is critical. With sustainable supply chains, the chief executive, the finance director, and the board need to support the initiative (Baker, 2011). Any large-scale initiative that impacts the whole corporation needs top-level approval.

2. *Make the business case:* The benefits of a sustainable supply chain must be outlined internally to employees and managers and externally for risk reduction and development of a positive brand. The business case is also essential in order to get the top-level support (Baker, 2011). More details on articulating a business case are provided later in the chapter.

3. *Develop a code of conduct:* Various certification schemes need to be assessed to develop a code of conduct. In those instances where the certification schemes do not suffice, internal standards can be developed. As an example, Starbucks developed its own Corporate Average Fuel Economy (CAFE) standards (Kaestner, 2007). Companies can apply these standards internally and also communicate these efforts externally. A two way process—listening and broadcasting—is crucial (Baker, 2011).

4. *Collaborate with critics:* For companies that have been criticized by media, this step is perceived as being sincere. For example, Home Depot worked with the Rainforest Action Network, Starbucks allied with the Rainforest Alliance, and Wal-Mart asked the Environmental Defense Fund (EDF) to open an office in Arkansas (Kaestner, 2007).

5. *Use scorecards to rate suppliers:* Every supplier has its own set of standards and, taken collectively, these standards can lead to confusion. A better alternative is to develop scorecards to rate suppliers in order to improve performance and to document efforts for auditors.

6. *Verify through third-party certification:* Companies need to get third-party verification via an external audit. When companies develop their own standards and audit themselves, the external stakeholders are skeptical of the results.

7. *Team up with competitors:* There is a need for similar supply chain standards within an industry, a goal that competitors could team up to accomplish. Too many standards with different reporting structures lead to unnecessary confusion.

8. *Take corrective action:* Certain companies do not engage their suppliers due to the possibility of failing a compliance audit. Valid certification schemes need to be used to identify and dismiss failing suppliers.

9. *Empower suppliers to build capacity:* Companies ought to engage their suppliers to get them to improve their performance before dismissing them. For example, Starbucks advises farmers to use fewer chemicals to maintain soil health (Kaestner, 2007).

10. *Encourage transparency:* Internal standards and codes of conduct are necessary, but companies need to communicate their efforts publicly

in order to promote awareness. Companies also need to be clear about their own standards, both in the application of standards and in the communication of these standards (Kaestner, 2007).

To develop a sustainable supply chain strategy, it is of utmost importance to get management approval, to develop credible standards by collaborating with nonprofits, to assist suppliers to attain best practices, and to keep customers informed about company efforts. More details on how many companies actually follow these 10 steps are provided in the Green Procurement section. Though these steps might seem overwhelming at first, the benefits of a sustainable supply chain lead to reducing costs while minimizing the impact on the environment.

In an effort to save money and the environment, companies can take a closer look at operation in three areas: (1) facility design, equipment, and systems; (2) **logistics and transportation;** and (3) green procurement. A win-win approach whereby a green retrofit can lead to cost savings can be embraced by the most critical opponents within a corporation.

Facility Design, Equipment, and Systems

Facility Design

Traditional bulbs can be converted to fluorescents for energy savings. Skylights and photo sensors can be used to adjust lighting. Solar panels can be used for heating water and generating power. Geothermal heat pumps (GHPs) (discussed in Chapter 5) can be used for further cost savings. The installation of the right dock seals can also save money by preventing energy loss. An energy provider can identify cost savings for a specific facility (Hill, 2010).

Equipment

Fuel cells, more efficient than internal combustion engines, can reduce carbon dioxide emissions by up to 45%. Conveyer systems can be designed to be energy efficient. Turn off conveyers when not in use, and employ motors and sensors to shut down and power the conveyer systems back up. Automated systems such for storage, retrieval, and transportation might cost less given the trade-off in energy costs. Maintenance needs to be kept on track since delays lead to cost inefficiencies (Hill, 2010).

Systems

Various systems can offer further cost reductions. An important strategic consideration is in locating warehouses and inventories to satisfy customer demands at the lowest transportation and related energy costs. For inventory, picking routines can improve output while reducing energy costs. Warehouse management systems (WMS) can be used to select the right personnel and equipment to reduce travel distances and related energy costs. Also, companies are shifting to reusable packaging, containers, and pallets (Hill, 2010).

In terms of facility and warehouse design, the potential of cost savings from environmental initiatives is immense. The cost savings from reduction of energy wastages is an essential step to start tackling the *low-hanging fruit* for environmental savings. This reduction in energy costs frees up resources for other corporate initiatives.

Logistics and Transportation

Strategic choices in logistics and transportation allow for a greener supply chain without sacrificing the bottom line (Chan & Joy, 2008).

Strategic Consolidation Programs

Logistics companies can ship full truckloads by combining purchase orders. The suppliers and retailers can work to attain further cost efficiencies.

Warehouse Planning

Warehouses can be built in centralized locations to service retailers. An efficient provider operates in an area to provide maximum shipping potential.

Establishing a Strategic Route

Truck routing software is used to maintain efficiency. Also, software packages can integrate a biodiesel mapping system to locate fueling stations that provide alternative fuel.

Alternative Fuel

Biodiesel does not require any engine modifications since a truck can easily switch off between biodiesel and diesel. Numerous logistics providers have switched to biodiesel. As an example, States Logistics Services, Inc., has converted its transportation fleet to run on B99 (blend of 1% petroleum diesel and 99% biodiesel) biodiesel fuel (Doherty, 2011).

Certification Programs

The U.S. Environmental Protection Agency (EPA) sponsors a program to reduce emissions. The SmartWay Transport Program holds carriers responsible for reducing emissions, but third-party logistics providers (3PLs) must also reduce their emissions by selecting greener carriers (Chan & Joy, 2008).

Logistics and transportation play an essential role in the carbon footprint of a corporation. Producing a green product is not enough: The storage and the subsequent transportation of this product has to be designed keeping the environment implications in mind. Logistics companies investing in alternative fuels reduce operational costs. For example, UPS has 1,914 alternative fuel vehicles in its fleet and has one of the most technologically diverse alternative fuel fleets in the industry (Berman, 2011).

Green Procurement

More companies are purchasing greener products. A survey of 450 companies found that there was a 63% increase in green purchasing (Davies, 2009). Other results from the survey are outlined.

Office Supplies, Cleaning Products, and Computers

Information technology was identified as an industry leader. What products are being purchased based upon green criteria? The top three industries were cleaning products (78%), office supplies (57%), and computers and IT hardware (55%). Certification is important since there are many ratings for these product categories, such as the Forest Stewardship Council's (FSC) certification for paper and wood products, *Green Seal* for cleaning products, and the Electronic Product Environmental Assessment Tool (EPEAT) standard for computers (Davies, 2009).

Measuring Green Purchasing

Within purchasing, almost 73% of companies state that green criteria are important. Overall, 59% of companies stated that they have a green procurement policy and that green criteria are included in requests for proposal (RFPs). As recommended in the 10 steps that were given earlier, companies communicate green criteria to their suppliers and evaluate results. About one third of the companies surveyed publish a code of conduct for their suppliers. In addition, companies are also measuring performance using supplier scorecards. In terms of supplier evaluation, larger companies with revenues over $1 billion used ISO 14001 as a leading factor in their evaluations, whereas smaller companies relied on published CSR or sustainability reports (Davies, 2009).

Selling Green

About 84% of companies stated that there is a need for third-party standards or certifications for green products. More companies (50%) identified positive environmental performance as a reason to award or renew a contract versus companies (35%) that canceled a supplier's contract due to poor environmental performance. Though many buyers (61%) prefer independent certifications, about 45% use self-declaration and 33% use references to evaluate their suppliers (Davies, 2009).

In the previously given 10 steps, some advice was offered by leading companies. This section on green purchasing reports the results from a survey that attest to the importance of certifications, standards, codes of conducts, scorecards, and so on. The main point is that companies need to work with suppliers to convert their supply chains to green, sustainable supply chains.

Carbon Disclosure Project's Supply Chain Project

Another good source for finding sustainable and green supply chains is the Carbon Disclosure Project's (CDP) Supply Chain Program. This project aims to drive action on climate change by getting companies and their suppliers involved. CDP facilitates the computation of a corporation's carbon footprint by measuring direct GHG emissions and including the climate change risks and opportunities along the supply chain. For the purposes of disclosure, CDP provides a global process, and the information garnered can be used by senior management in large corporations. For corporations, one of the main reasons to sign as a member is to understand how suppliers are reducing their GHG emissions (Carbon Disclosure Project [CDP], n.d.). More information on CDP is provided in Chapter 10. In the survey on green purchasing, only 13% of companies surveyed ask their suppliers for GHG emissions data (Davies, 2009).

A Business Case for Sustainability

At times, sustainability officers at corporations struggle to articulate the business case, and they attempt to come up with the commercial benefits of social and environmental initiatives. So why is this business case so hard to find? David Bent (2009) provided six pointers on mapping a business case for sustainability:

1. *There is no "one size fits all" business case.* The business case needs to be specific to the company since every company has different issues of sustainability and drivers of shareholder value
   "Lesson: Focus on finding the business justification" (Bent, 2009).

2. *The "societal case" doesn't make a business case.* Companies are making profits from resources that are *unsustainable*, such as bottled water. Though there might be greater overlap between societal case and business case in the future, for now, companies need to focus on their own business case.

"Lesson: Don't expect a justification for all the things the company needs to do" (Bent, 2009).

3. *Opportunity trumps responsibility.* It is easy to get trapped into a check-list-compliance mode that looks at costs alone. However, corporate sustainability is about finding the route to be successful in the future. **"Lesson: Present sustainability as a way of unlocking opportunity for the company now and into the long term"** (Bent, 2009).

4. *The more you look, the more you find.* The process becomes self-fulfilling, and once companies start searching, they find more opportunities (Bent, 2009). Companies usually start with tackling the low hanging fruit of energy savings and find themselves moving on to bigger avenues. **"Lesson: Explore how to make sustainability commercial and improve the company's business case"** (Bent, 2009).

5. *Sustainability professionals and finance professionals speak different languages.* The former discusses benefits to society and the company and the latter is more focused on the financial benefits to the company. Sustainability change agents have to learn to speak to the financial audience as well. **"Lesson: Frame the case for sustainability in terms that the finance director will understand"** (Bent, 2009).

6. *The "no business case, no permission" vicious cycle.* Permissions are needed to get funding from finance to prepare a business case but the permission is not given without a business cycle, leading to a vicious cycle. **"Lesson: Plan small steps to create a virtuous circle of permission and results"** (Bent, 2009).

The present media and government initiatives are packed with initiatives for green businesses, green jobs, and emerging green economies, and these will be a central part of the new world now being created.

For any company that aims to achieve greater sustainability, it must articulate a strategic direction—an overarching goal that is consistent with the company strengths, is connected to its core business, is able to inspire personal contributions of its members, and is attainable within 5 to 15 years.

Conclusion

This chapter presented the role of businesses and corporations. It started with the large picture concept of a chrysalis economy that provides the grounding and argument as to why corporate sustainability is absolutely essential. The next section discussed why the concept of being sustainable is much more than simply being green. Next, we presented a detailed discussion on CSR—its phases, its benefits, and challenges. Then we presented a discussion on green supply chains to illustrate how corporations are attempting to make the supply chains more sustainable. The chapter ended with a discussion of how to make a business case for sustainability.

KEY WORDS

Business case for sustainability

Chrysalis economy

Corporate butterflies

Corporate caterpillars

Corporate honeybees

Corporate locusts

Corporate social responsibility (CSR)

Green procurement

Green supply chains

Logistics and transportation

Responsive corporate social responsibility (CSR)

Strategic CSR

Value creation

DISCUSSION QUESTIONS

1. What is the role of a corporation? Does it exist simply to make money, or should businesses serve the needs of the society as well? Can you provide examples of companies in both cases?

2. Are sustainability and CSR linked together? Explain.

3. What are the four phases of CSR? Use the Internet, and search the CSR reports of any particular company to find what phase it is operating within.

4. What are the four arguments given to make a case for CSR? Which of these would you feel most comfortable in promoting? For example, to a potential recruiter or at your company.

5. Should CSR be responsive or strategic? Discuss with an example.

6. What are the six environmental forces that are causing CSR to be relevant? Which of these forces do you deem to be most relevant?

7. What are the benefits of CSR? Which one of these would be the most attractive to you? Would you prefer working at a company that commits to CSR?

8. What are the 10 steps to creating a sustainable supply chain? Which of these might be applicable at the company you work for?

9. How can companies encourage their suppliers to go green?

10. What is the role of transportation and logistics in a green supply chain? How about the role of green procurement? Are any of these initiatives being undertaken at your company? Your university?

11. Why is it important to make a business case for sustainability? Think of your role as an advocate of sustainability attempting to explain the business case to your peers.

12. What are corporate locusts and corporate caterpillars? Can you think of a corporate locust that is unwilling to change?

13. What are corporate butterflies and corporate honeybees? Can you think of examples where a particular company has gone from being a butterfly to a honeybee?

14. Research the CSR reports of some of the local companies in your area. Evaluate the report critically, given the knowledge gained from this chapter. For example, is the report an exercise in public relations (greenwashing), or did the company commit to some goals and make headway in the pursuit of these goals?

RECOMMENDED CASE STUDIES

1. *Burt's Bees: Balancing Growth and Sustainability,* Product Number 410704-MMC-ENG, Harvard Business School Publishing.

Learning Objective: To understand the leadership challenges of implementing sustainable business practices and how to balance sustainability with growth. Case examines Burt's Bees' sustainability journey and in particular the important element of CSR as essentially a nonmarket strategy; committed companies can set industry standards to corporate acquisitions and how Burt's Bees can continue to pursue its social and environmental endeavors while growing as its own unit and within the larger parent company, Clorox.

2. McDonald's Corporation: Managing a Sustainable Supply Chain, Product Number 907414-PDF-ENG, Harvard Business School Publishing.

Learning Objective: To investigate how a major food service company takes a proactive role in sustainability of the food supply chain? McDonald's seeks to learn from a successful response to Greenpeace's Amazon deforestation campaign in order to make its supply chain more socially and environmentally responsible.

3. Sustainability at Millipore, Product Number 610012-PDF-ENG. Harvard Business School Publishing.

Learning Objective: To expose students to the challenges of conceptualizing *environmental sustainability* at an organization level and differentiating sustainability management from traditional environmental, health, and safety management. The case provides a background of the sustainability movement and reviews major sustainability frameworks (including The Natural Step, Carbon Footprints, and the Sustainability Hierarchy) and prevailing sustainability performance metrics.

RECOMMENDED WEBSITES

www.asyousow.org/csr

www.cdproject.net

www.greenbiz.com

www.hp.com

www.wbcsd.org

9 Role of Governments and Nongovernmental Organizations

Chapter Overview

This chapter presents the role of governments and NGOs in promoting sustainability. We start with the role of governments in advancing sustainability and provide some examples of legislation along with the role of the EPA. Next, we segue into the history and the growth of NGOs and the role of NGO funding as it relates to power. We discuss the role of NGOs in social development, community development, and **sustainable development** and present cases of partnerships between NGOs and businesses. We conclude with a detailed discussion on a specific category of NGOs: the **environmental nongovernmental organizations (ENGOs).**

Role of Governments

What role, if any, should governments play in promoting sustainability? Governments worldwide are beginning to recognize the challenge of sustainability, and this term is being addressed in public policy discussions. Any one government cannot work in this area alone; it is imperative to work with other governments in order to address the issue in a global context. According to a GlobeScan poll of experts, the leading role in achieving sustainability will be played by business (35%), followed by NGOs (30%), and governments (24%) (Bell, 2002). Chapter 8 discussed the role of business in advancing sustainability, and this chapter will discuss the role of governments and NGOs in advancing sustainability.

Governments need to be able to anticipate rising demand for sustainable products and services. Governments can play a key role in aiding the transition toward more efficient, less damaging economies. Those governments that can lead in this role would be able to set the agenda for their economies, industries, and citizens (Peck & Gibson, 2002).

In most developed countries, like the United States and Canada, the government is the largest employer, the largest landowner, and the largest fleet owner. The government is also the largest consumer of energy and has the largest impact on the environment. It stands to reason that governments should incorporate sustainability principles in their internal operations (Bell, 2002).

In developing countries, the role of the government assumes even greater significance. Within the realm of sustainability, the governments ought to encourage companies to address the needs of the world's entire population (Prahalad & Hart, 2002).

According to a KPMG report, the government has four distinct roles in addressing sustainability concerns. These roles are as follows:

1. Policy development

2. Regulation

3. Facilitation

4. Internal sustainability management

As shown in Figure 9.1, each of the policy making, regulating, facilitating, and internal sustainability managing roles of government has its own characteristics and success factors. Combined, these roles have the potential to effectively support sustainability management through setting goals, driving change, and leading by example ("Sustainable Insight," 2009).

Figure 9.1 Four Government Roles to Spur Sustainability

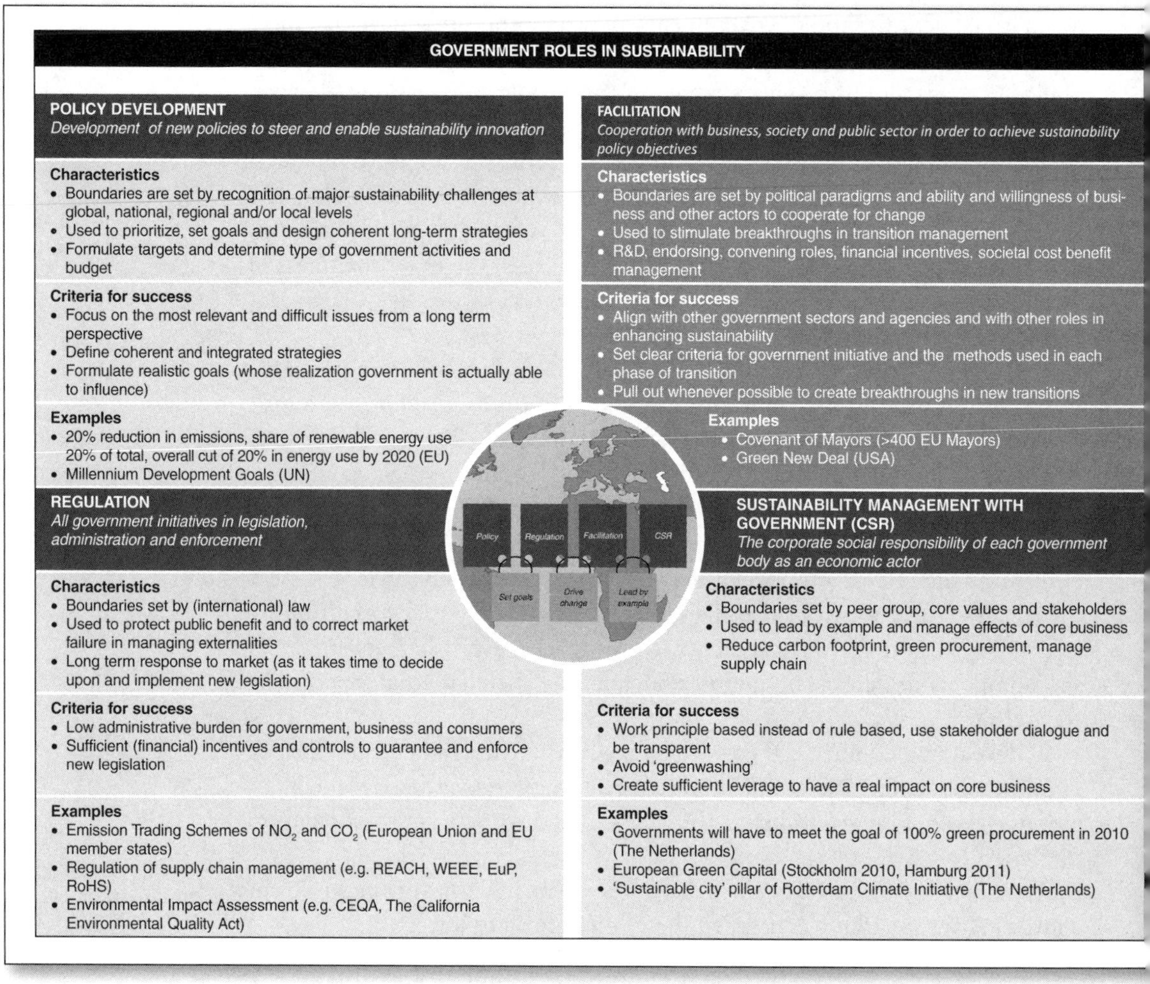

GOVERNMENT ROLES IN SUSTAINABILITY

POLICY DEVELOPMENT
Development of new policies to steer and enable sustainability innovation

Characteristics
- Boundaries are set by recognition of major sustainability challenges at global, national, regional and/or local levels
- Used to prioritize, set goals and design coherent long-term strategies
- Formulate targets and determine type of government activities and budget

Criteria for success
- Focus on the most relevant and difficult issues from a long term perspective
- Define coherent and integrated strategies
- Formulate realistic goals (whose realization government is actually able to influence)

Examples
- 20% reduction in emissions, share of renewable energy use 20% of total, overall cut of 20% in energy use by 2020 (EU)
- Millennium Development Goals (UN)

FACILITATION
Cooperation with business, society and public sector in order to achieve sustainability policy objectives

Characteristics
- Boundaries are set by political paradigms and ability and willingness of business and other actors to cooperate for change
- Used to stimulate breakthroughs in transition management
- R&D, endorsing, convening roles, financial incentives, societal cost benefit management

Criteria for success
- Align with other government sectors and agencies and with other roles in enhancing sustainability
- Set clear criteria for government initiative and the methods used in each phase of transition
- Pull out whenever possible to create breakthroughs in new transitions

Examples
- Covenant of Mayors (>400 EU Mayors)
- Green New Deal (USA)

REGULATION
All government initiatives in legislation, administration and enforcement

Characteristics
- Boundaries set by (international) law
- Used to protect public benefit and to correct market failure in managing externalities
- Long term response to market (as it takes time to decide upon and implement new legislation)

Criteria for success
- Low administrative burden for government, business and consumers
- Sufficient (financial) incentives and controls to guarantee and enforce new legislation

Examples
- Emission Trading Schemes of NO_2 and CO_2 (European Union and EU member states)
- Regulation of supply chain management (e.g. REACH, WEEE, EuP, RoHS)
- Environmental Impact Assessment (e.g. CEQA, The California Environmental Quality Act)

SUSTAINABILITY MANAGEMENT WITH GOVERNMENT (CSR)
The corporate social responsibility of each government body as an economic actor

Characteristics
- Boundaries set by peer group, core values and stakeholders
- Used to lead by example and manage effects of core business
- Reduce carbon footprint, green procurement, manage supply chain

Criteria for success
- Work principle based instead of rule based, use stakeholder dialogue and be transparent
- Avoid 'greenwashing'
- Create sufficient leverage to have a real impact on core business

Examples
- Governments will have to meet the goal of 100% green procurement in 2010 (The Netherlands)
- European Green Capital (Stockholm 2010, Hamburg 2011)
- 'Sustainable city' pillar of Rotterdam Climate Initiative (The Netherlands)

Source: Sustainable Insight (2009).

Changing Role of Governments

Increasingly, governments are called to form partnerships ranging from the ones with other levels of government to ones with civil society organizations (CSOs) and the private sector. In terms of advancing sustainability, the government can also play a significant role. The five roles are discussed as follows:

1. *Vision/Goal setter:* Governments need to provide vision and strategy to incorporate sustainability in public policy. Concepts such as natural capitalism (discussed in Chapter 6), eco-economy (Brown, 2009), and green economy (Milani, 2000) call for grand-scale transformations in systems dealing with energy, waste, water, and governance. Governments would need to develop strategies for a transition to an economy based on sustainability principles.

2. *Leader by example:* Governments can improve the environmental performance of public procurement (Organisation for Economic Co-operation and Development [OECD], 2002), whereby public funds are used in construction of highways and buildings, power generation, transportation, and water and sanitation services. Green procurement can also provide impetus to innovative and environmentally friendly products. As an example, Japan used procurement of low emission automobiles to drive innovation (Bell, 2002).

3. *Facilitator:* Governments need to create "open, competitive, and rightly framed markets" that would include pricing of goods and services, dismantling subsidies, and taxing waste and pollution, etc. However, as Lester Brown (2002, p. 26) pointed out, "not one country has a strategy to build an eco-economy".

4. *Green fiscal authority:* Governments are exploring environmental taxes and market-based instruments for ecological fiscal reform. Though the market solutions can be more amenable to businesses for their flexibility, these approaches might not be the best at pricing certain environmental assets such as clean water (Bell, 2002).

5. *Innovator/Catalyst:* The government needs to play a strategic role in advancing innovation in all sectors of society since the advancement of sustainability will demand changes. There is a strong need for technological and policy innovation (Bell, 2002).

The traditional role of a government is one of an authority figure that protects public interests and regulates industries. This role is changing as governments are working collaboratively with other stakeholders from companies to CSOs. As the roles of governments change, so do their responsibilities. Indeed, the whole future of a sustainable world can be shaped by the policy decisions taken by governments, individually or in collective forums.

Policy Instruments

There are two basic policy instruments that can be employed by governments: (1) direct regulation and (2) market instruments and economic/fiscal measures.

Direct Regulation

The first form of public policy on environment was direct regulation. These approaches are also termed as *command and control* approaches since the taxes are set by the regulatory agency or the government, and the companies need to comply and pay these taxes. Though taxes are controversial and governments have faced pushback to the idea of carbon taxes, regulation is still an effective mechanism to ensure minimum performance from those players that are reluctant to comply.

Market Instruments and Economic/Fiscal Measures

This category includes any set of instruments that reward innovation in sustainability from the private sectors. These instruments can include subsidies, taxes, ecolabeling schemes, and public procurement policies. The idea is that if the private sector is given enough motivation, the sector itself would come up with the best way to solve a problem. One such example was the cap and trade system, wherein the cap on emissions would be set by the regulatory agency, and companies would have an incentive to lower emissions and trade the extra permits. Research does indicate that market mechanisms are efficient, flexible, and more palatable to industry (Dhanda, 1999). More detailed discussion on command and control versus market schemes will be presented in Chapter 11.

In addition, governments can also employ new policy instruments that expand the range of alternatives to regulation and legislation. The task of choosing the best "mix" from this wider array of possible options is not straightforward (Howlett & Ramesh, 1995), and research is ongoing to assess these various alternatives. For example, Italy is experimenting with a scheme that provides the consumer with a modest (1%) sales tax reduction on the price of green products. France, on the other hand, has introduced mandatory corporate sustainability reporting (Bell, 2002).

Role of the Environmental Protection Agency

In the United States, the largest regulatory organization is the EPA, one that from the time of its inception acted as a watchdog for the environment implementing pollution control regulations and ensured that businesses met the legal requirements. As time progressed, the EPA's role has changed from pollution control to pollution prevention. This change has led to implementation of some market-based regulation such as the Acid Rain and NOx cap-and-trade programs to reduce emissions. For the future, EPA is looking at advances in science and technology and government regulations and promoting innovative green business practices ("What Is EPA Doing?" n.d.).

Advances in Science and Technology

These advances in science and technology are important for robust environmental policy. The Office of Research and Development (ORD) at the EPA works to develop long-term solutions. In addition, this office provides technical support to the EPA regional offices and to state and local governments.

Government Regulations and Practices

Executive orders are edicts that are issued by the president. Two executive orders have been aimed at the environment:

Executive Order (EO) 13423 sets policy and goals for federal agencies to "conduct their environmental, transportation, and energy-related activities under the law in support of their respective missions in an environmentally, economically and fiscally sound, integrated, continuously improving, efficient, and sustainable manner" (What Is EPA Doing?" n.d.).

EO 13514 builds upon EO 13423 "to establish an integrated strategy towards sustainability in the Federal Government and to make reduction of greenhouse gas emissions (GHG) a priority for Federal agencies" ("What Is EPA Doing?" n.d.).

The EPA also implements a range of programs to reduce the environmental impact of its operations. These can range from retrofitting old buildings to the construction of newer, more energy efficient buildings. In addition, the Sustainable Facilities Practices Branch publishes the annual reports on energy management and conservation programs.

List of Environmental Protection Agency Programs for Sustainability

There are numerous EPA policies and programs that have helped to shape new ways of manufacturing and doing business (Hecht, 2009). Here are some examples:

Supply Chain and Manufacturing

Green Suppliers Network

Lean Manufacturing

Design for the Environment

Clean Processing

Green Chemistry Program

Nanoscale Materials Stewardship Program

Management and Performance

Sector Strategies Program

Performance Track

Preferential Purchasing

EnergyStar

WaterSense

In addition, the EPA provides resources for sustainable practices. Within the category of urban local sustainability, these programs range from smart growth and urban heat mitigation to waste composting and water resource programs. Within the category of industrial sustainability, the programs range from green engineering and IT to ozone alternatives and safe pesticides ("Science and Technology: Sustainable Practices," n.d.).

These programs aim to shape practices that go beyond controlling pollution to actually changing the strategic thinking of companies. According to the EPA, environmental protection will be created by a vision that inspires businesses and consumers rather than by disincentives to pollute ("What Is EPA Doing?" n.d.).

Local Governments for Sustainability

Much of the work on sustainability has been accomplished at the local level. One of the most comprehensive programs is **Agenda 21**, which calls for involvement at the local, national, and global level. Agenda 21 articulates a series of environmental strategies for the management of natural resources and the monitoring and reduction of chemical and radioactive waste. It also contains socioeconomic plans to improve heath care, to develop sustainable farming development and fair trade policies, and to reduce poverty (Agenda 21, n.d.-b). Furthermore, Agenda 21 requires local governments to develop their own "Local Agenda 21" for sustainable development. Agenda 21 is a large document with 40 chapters. The appendix to this chapter contains Chapter 27 of Agenda 21, one that discusses the role of NGOs.

Another local association is the **International Council for Local Environmental Initiatives (ICLEI)—Local Governments for Sustainability,** comprised of over 1,200 local government members. The members of ICLEI represent 70 countries and more than 569,885,000 people (About ICLEI, n.d.). The programs and projects of ICLEI call for the following:

> participatory, long-term, strategic planning process that address local sustainability while protecting global common goods. This approach links local action to internationally agreed-upon goals and targets such as: Agenda 21, the Rio Conventions on Climate Change, Biodiversity, and Desertification, the Habitat Agenda, the Millennium Development Goal, and the Johannesburg Plan of Implementation. ("Our Themes," n.d.)

Nongovernmental Organizations

Definition

What is an NGO? The term *NGO* stands for nongovernmental organization, and it includes a variety of organizations such as "private voluntary organizations," "civil society organizations," and "nonprofit organization"

(McGann & Johnstone, 2006). The term *NGO* describes a range of groups and organizations from watchdog activist groups and aid agencies to development and policy organizations. Usually, NGOs are defined as organizations that pursue a public interest agenda, rather than commercial interests (Hall-Jones, 2006).

It is believed that the first international NGO was probably the Anti-Slavery Society, formed in 1839. However, the term *NGO* originated at the end of World War II when the United Nations sought to distinguish between private organizations and intergovernmental specialized agencies (Hall-Jones, 2006). NGOs are a complex mixture comprised of alliances and rivalries; businesses and charities; conservatives and radicals. The funding comes from various sources, and though NGOs are usually nonprofit organizations, there are some that operate for profit (Hall-Jones, 2006).

NGOs originate from all over the world and have access to different levels of resources. Some organizations focus on a single policy objective of AIDS while others will aim at larger policy goals of poverty eradication (Hall-Jones, 2006).

History of the Nongovernmental Organizations Movement

The first NGO was the Anti-Slavery Society followed by the Red Cross and Caritas, a movement that arose at the end of the 19th century. Most of the other NGO movements were founded after the two world wars and, hence, were primarily humanitarian in nature. For example, Save the Children was formed after World War I, and CARE was formed after World War II (Hall-Jones, 2006). The decolonization of Africa in the 1960s led to a new way of thinking—one that aimed at causes of poverty rather than its consequences. The armed conflicts of the 1970s and 1980s (Vietnam, Angola, Palestine) led the European NGOs to take on the task of mediators for informal diplomacy. Their support for locals had an impact on the demise of the apartheid regime in South Africa and the dictatorships of Ferdinand Marcos in the Philippines and Augusto Pinochet in Chile. In addition, in the mid-1980s, the World Bank realized that NGOs were more effective and less corrupt than the typical government channels. The food crisis in Ethiopia in 1984 spurred a new market for "humanitarian aid" (Berthoud, 2001).

In the history of the NGO movement's growth, there have been several milestones. One of the first milestones was the role of the solidarity movement in the political transformation in Poland in the 1980s. The next was the impact of environmental activists on the 1992 Earth Summit in Rio de Janeiro. Another milestone was the Fifty Years Is Enough campaign in 1994. This was organized by the South Council and was aimed at the World Bank and International Monetary Fund (IMF) on the belief that these two institutions had been promoting and financing unsustainable development overseas that created poverty and destroyed the environment. The most recent milestone was the organization of the labor, anti-globalization, and environmental groups that protested and disturbed the Seattle World Trade Organization (WTO) meeting in 1999 (McGann & Johnstone, 2006).

Funding

The numbers of NGO organizations have grown dramatically, and NGOs have become a powerful player in global politics, facilitated in part by the increasing funding by public and private grants (McGann & Johnstone, 2006). This funding comes in from all kind of sources and is redirected in every conceivable direction. The world's biggest NGO is the Bill & Melinda Gates Foundation with an endowment of $28.8 billion. The 160 **international nongovernmental organizations (INGOs)** associated with Inter*Action* have combined annual revenues of $2.3 billion (Aall, 2000).

There are some NGOs that are very sophisticated at wooing the media while other unknown NGOs work tirelessly at the grassroots level. Some NGOs are membership-based, such as Amnesty International, that refuse to accept money from political parties, agencies, or governments whereas other NGOs are profit-making organizations focused on lobbying for profit-driven interests (Hall-Jones, 2006)

One trend is that NGOs are becoming dependent on governments for funding and service contracts. For example, 70% of CARE International's budget ($420 million) came from government contributions in 2001, 25% of Oxfam's income came from EU and British government in 1998, and 46% of Médecins Sans Frontières (Doctors Without Borders) income came from government sources. Similarly, World Vision collected goods worth $55 million from the U.S. government (Hall-Jones, 2006).

Numbers and Budgets

INGOs rose in number from 6,000 in 1990 to 26,000 in 1996 ("The Non-Governmental Order," 1999). At present, there are 1.5 million nonprofit organizations in the United States and more than 1 million NGOs in India. Along with the growth in the number of NGOs, the memberships have also been expanding at steady rate ("The Non-Governmental Order," 1999).

Some of the biggest NGOs in terms of size and financial strength are to be found in the humanitarian realm. For example, Oxfam, World Vision, CARE, and Save the Children are all strong brands that belong to extremely large organizations with strong financial power. The biggest NGO—World Vision—had an annual budget of $2.1 billion for 2006 (Karajkov, 2007).

Some of the other NGOs can boast of similar financial resources. Over 70% of the relief funding goes to the biggest NGOs. The biggest eight are comprised of the following organizations (Karajkov, 2007):

1. World Vision, $2.1 billion (2006)

2. Oxfam, $528 million (2004–2005)

3. CARE, $624 million (2005)

4. Save the Children, $863 million (2006)

5. Catholic Relief Services, $694 million (2005)

6. Doctors Without Borders, $568 million (2004)

7. International Rescue Committee, $203 million (2005)

8. Mercy Corps, $185 million (2005)

Growth in Power

The real story is how these organizations have networked and impacted world politics.

Global politics have gone through a drastic shift resulting from the growth of nongovernmental agencies. NGOs or CSOs have moved from being in the background to having a presence in the midst of world politics and, as a result, are exerting their influence and power in policy making at global scale. Some organizations such as Amnesty International and Greenpeace have effectively become NGO brands and have helped make *NGO* a household word. At the 1992 Earth Summit in Rio, there was a large NGO presence. While 1,400 NGO members were involved in the official proceedings, another 17,000 NGO members staged an alternative forum to the meeting. Encouraged by their success, a larger group gathered in Beijing for the Fourth World Conference on Women (McGann & Johnstone, 2006).

How have NGOs gained this global attention? There are various strategies that have been employed. For example, some NGOs organize large-scale protests, capture international headlines, and gain notoriety. The two NGOs that were successful in organizing large-scale action around specific themes were Amnesty International, which focuses on human rights issues, and Greenpeace, which focuses on ecological issues (Berthoud, 2001). There are other NGOs that have organized meetings to challenge the legitimacy of the WTO, the G8, the World Bank, and the IMF. The effectiveness of these NGOs' efforts took the governments and other global multilateral institutions by surprise. In response, these efforts forced the governments to figure out ways to involve NGOs in their decision making. Now that their place in world politics is firmly established, the majority of NGOs have moved from street protests to a policy making role in the boardrooms of the United Nations, WTO, World Bank, and the IMF (McGann & Johnstone, 2006).

What are the factors that have led to the unprecedented growth of NGOs? Research by McGann and Johnstone (2006) have isolated six interrelated forces as follows:

1. *Democratization and the civil society ideal:* The emergence of civil society and the addition of more open societies have both led to an environment that was favorable to the proliferation of NGOs.

2. *Growing demand for information, analysis, and action:* The general public is bombarded with unsystematic and unreliable information. NGOs can collect data to make decisions, a role that is invaluable in developing countries where such information might not readily exist.

3. *Growth of state, nonstate, and interstate actors:* After World War II, there was a global trend toward increased democratization and decentralization that led to an increase in the number of nations or states after World War II. In addition, numerous intergovernmental organizations (United Nations, WTO, World Bank) were created and were granted certain powers and functions. This led to an unprecedented growth in the number of governmental organizations, NGOs, and nation–states.

4. *Improved communications technologies:* The growth of the Internet has led to inexpensive, instant, and largely unregulated flow of information. In addition, the nature of the information age makes it very difficult to restrict the inflow of information from the perspective of authoritarian governments.

5. *Globalization of NGO funding:* The issue of funding is important since many organizations work with small budgets and staffs. In many nations such as in Africa, Asia, and Latin America, there are no tax incentives to fund NGOs. Hence, most of the funding flows from developed countries to developing or transitional countries. However, foreign funding raises questions about the credibility of an organization. Furthermore, the issues of funding, transparency, and accountability become more complicated when NGOs cross national borders.

6. *Paralysis and poor performance of the public sector:* There has been an erosion of confidence in the government leaders and institutions. The never-ending scandals involving public officials combined with poor performance of policy makers have led citizens to question the legitimacy of governments. When the institutions are considered ineffective and the nation–state is distrusted, the NGOs operating on a local, grassroots level have emerged so that these deficiencies can be addressed.

Role of Nongovernmental Organizations

Given this unprecedented growth in the numbers and financial power of NGOs, how has the role changed or matured? What we see is that NGOs can have a huge impact. These NGOs are unfettered, not answerable to specific agendas, and, in many instances, can act independently.

Even though NGOs are highly diverse organizations, the one common goal is that they are not focused on short-term targets, and, hence, they devote themselves to long-term issues like climate change, malaria prevention, or human rights. In addition, public surveys state that NGOs often have public trust, which makes them a useful proxy for societal concerns (Hall-Jones, 2006).

Next, we will discuss four important roles of NGOs. These roles are (1) social development, (2) **sustainable community development**, (3) sustainable development, and (4) **sustainable consumption**.

Social Development

NGOs play an important role in **global social development**—work that has helped facilitate achievements in human development as measured by the UN Human Development Index (HDI) (n.d.).

One of the major strengths of NGOs is their ability to maintain institutional independence and political neutrality. Even though NGOs need to collaborate with governments in numerous instances, failure to maintain neutrality and autonomy may severely compromise the NGOs' legitimacy. Unfortunately, if a government insists upon political allegiance, the NGOs encounter the dilemma of either violating the neutrality position or failing to provide needed services to the population. Indeed, some NGOs have been asked to leave in troubled countries due to political reasons (Asamoah, 2003).

The major advantages that NGOs bring to this role include "flexibility, ability to innovate, grass-roots orientation, humanitarian versus commercial goal orientation, non-profit status, dedication and commitment, and recruitment philosophy" (Asamoah, 2003). The drawbacks in working with NGOs are similar to the advantages that were previously listed. In addition, some other disadvantages include "over-zealousness, restricted local participation, inadequate feasibility studies, conflicts or misunderstandings with host partner, inflexibility in recruitment and procedures, turf wars, inadequately trained personnel, lack of funding to complete projects, lack of transparency, inability to replicate results, and cultural insensitivity" (Asamoah, 2003).

Sustainable Community Development

NGOs have shown leadership in promoting sustainable community development. Due to their particular ideology and nature, NGOs are good at reaching out to the poor and remote communities and mobilizing these populations. They can also empower these populations to regain control of their lives and can work with and strengthen local organizations. In addition, such NGOs can carry out projects more efficiently and at lower costs than government agencies and, most importantly, promote sustainable development (Nikkhah & Redzuan, 2010).

The five dimensions of sustainable community development are as follows:

1. Increasing local economic diversity

2. Self reliance: development of local markets, local production, local processing, greater co-operation among local economic entities

3. Reduction in the use of energy combined with recycling and management of waste products

4. Protection and enhancement of biological diversity and stewardship of natural resources

5. Commitment of sustainable communities to social justice. (Bridger & Luloff, 1999)

Since NGOs are professionally staffed organizations aimed at reduction of human suffering and to the development of poor countries (Streeten, 1997), they have a significant role to play in supporting women, men, and households. The roles for such NGOs include "counseling and support service, awareness raising and advocacy, legal aid and microfinance" (Desai, 2005). The long-term aim for these NGOs is to assist in sustainable community development through activities such as capacity building and self-reliance (Langran, 2002). This can be done by funding projects, contributing to awareness, and promoting the self-organization of various groups (Baccaro, 2001).

A case study in Vietnam illustrates that NGOs play an important role in promoting sustainable community development (Hibbard & Tang, 2004). Usually this is accomplished by providing three basic functions: (1) service delivery (relief, welfare), (2) education, and (3) public policy advocacy (Stromquist, 2002). The idea is that NGOs can promote sustainable community development via three functions: (1) microfinance, (2) capacity building, and (3) self-reliance. NGOs ought to develop local products and local markets; develop social, capital, and human resources; encourage and motivate people to participate in activities; and act as network liaisons between community and systems. In this manner, the long-run goal of sustainable community development would be achieved (Nikkhah & Redzuan, 2010).

Sustainable Development

NGOs have played a significant role in promoting sustainable development at the international level. NGOs are going beyond their primary focus on governments and starting to address large corporations. In this vein, NGOs have focused attention on the social and environmental impacts of business activity, helped in part by advances in information and communications technology. The brands of multinational corporations have also been vulnerable to pressure from activists and from NGOs on the corporation's labor, environmental, or human rights record. As the downstream customers are targeted, even the supply chain partners and suppliers are feeling the pressure (Hall-Jones, 2006).

In response to such concerns, many corporations are embracing a stakeholder approach that looks at the impact of business activity on customers, employees, communities, and other interested groups. There are numerous visible manifestations of this shift. The primary one has been an increased attention to social and environmental affairs. Many corporations are taking responsibility for their actions and are starting to report on the impact of their activities. A secondary shift is more heartening: Many companies have designed management structures that integrate sustainable development concerns (Hall-Jones, 2006).

NGOs can take most of the credit for creating these trends. The question remains as to how the business world should react to NGOs in the future. Should companies gear themselves in preparation of attacks from hostile critics? Should companies engage NGOs to become helpful partners? Depending upon their philosophy, not all NGOs are willing to collaborate with the private sector. Some of NGOs observe at a distance, and monitor, publicize, and criticize cases where companies fail to consider its impacts upon the community. However, other NGOs are willing to allocate some of their resources to working along with business in order to further corporate social responsibility (CSR) (Hall-Jones, 2006).

Agenda 21 of the United Nations has a chapter dedicated to the role of NGOs in partnering for sustainable development. Please refer to the appendix for the full text of this chapter.

Sustainable Consumption

NGOs can also play an important role as partners to business/industry in promoting sustainable consumption. Some of the instances where this partnership has been successful is in categories such as product development, sustainable housing, labeling, World Wildlife Fund (WWF), green purchasing, marine stewardship, and so on. The basic premise is, can NGOs influence behavioral change? Specifically, there are two questions that need to be asked: (1) How are NGOs educating households to change their consumption behavior, and (2) how can NGOs be potential partners to businesses in promoting sustainable consumption (Kong, Saltzmann, Steger, & Ionescu-Somers, 2002)?

A range of projects shows that NGOs are engaging businesses to promote sustainable consumption. Some of the interesting approaches are as follows:

Using Strategic Means to Point Out Problems

NGOs are encouraging households to exercise their power as shareholders. In case shareholder power is substantial, this can raise public awareness and change business policies. For example, Friends of the Earth's (FoE) Green Paycheck Campaign tells individuals how to use their shareholder power and screen their investments so that "money becomes a tool for change" (Kong et al., 2002).

Assessing Environmental Impacts of Products

NGOs rank products and services based on their environmental performance and impacts. The idea is that consumers can then pick and choose what products or brands they would purchase. For example, many consumer organizations have adopted a commitment to sustainability in their mission statements, such as in Austria, Germany, Sweden, Norway, and the Netherlands, and their assessment of products reaches consumers via magazines, websites, and other publications (Kong et al., 2002).

Greening the Supply of Products and Services

NGOs are developing or designing products that will minimize the environmental impacts of consumption. The consumer is simply offered an alternative of more sustainable consumption, and this choice is deemed empowering. For example, the WWF is engaging the retail sector to offer more sustainable food products. It also cooperates with the catering sector to design WWF Weeks for the menu and one permanent WWF dish. This campaign has been successful in increasing demand for organic products in Switzerland (Kong et al., 2002).

Focusing on Market Forces

Creating a green demand that will drive changes in supply, NGOs are providing information through labels that would empower consumers to make informed choices. For example, WWF has worked with the industry to design labeling schemes to help in the launch of independent certification bodies. The Forest Stewardship Council (FSC) was created in 1993 to protect the world's forest by a coalition of NGOs, businesses, and government entities. Unilever and WWF started the Marine Stewardship Council (MSC) to establish a certification scheme for sustainable fishing (Kong et al., 2002).

Forming Extensive Networks of Different Stakeholders

NGOs enter into collaborations with other NGOs and businesses to highlight issues and jointly look for solutions. For example, the Green Purchasing Network (GPN) promotes green purchasing among consumers, businesses, and other governmental organizations in Japan. It consists of 2,150 members including Sony, Fuji, Toyota, Honda, Canon, and Mitsubishi among others (Kong et al., 2002).

Business Partnerships

In the past, corporate philanthropy was the main driver for business–NGO collaboration. The new wave of collaboration is different. The present trend is toward strategic partnerships aimed to address internal operational issues and the external impacts of corporate activity. Within the partnerships, NGOs and trade unions are involved in decisions that impact core business practices. As a result, CSR has evolved from what companies do with their profits to looking at how companies make those profits (Bendell, 2010).

One notable trend has been that of development NGOs promoting sustainable development among other companies. As an example, the British NGO called the Fairtrade Foundation initiated a pilot project to assist companies in developing codes of practice to guide relationships with their suppliers. Another initiative, launched in 1998, contained a broader mandate and came with UK government backing. The Ethical Trading Initiative (ETI) is a network of companies, NGOs, and trade union organizations working together in identifying and promoting good labor practices, including monitoring and independent verification. Some of the members include supermarket chains J. Sainsbury and Tesco, garment industry players Levi Strauss and the Pentland Group, and NGOs Oxfam and Save the Children (Bendell, 2010).

NGOs are helping in the establishment of certification systems that would help companies to monitor, measure, and communicate their social and environmental best practices. As an example, the WWF, an environmental NGO, has helped in the FSC accreditation, certification, and labeling scheme that endorses products from properly managed forests. Rather than waiting for time-consuming regulatory agreements, the NGO spearheaded the creation of a new organization for moving the industry toward sustainability (Bendell, 2010).

Caveats

Not all NGO-business collaborations are always fruitful. As an example, challenges arose in the creation of a certification scheme for banana plantations. In the case of Chiquita's partnership with the Rainforest Alliance, the scheme started with the NGO certifying bananas, but over time, this certification grew to coffee and other fruits. The critics argued that this was a case of greenwashing since the partnership did not tackle the most important issues in banana production (Bendell, 2007).

What can business gain from forging a relationship with an NGO? There are four reasons for this relationship:

Credibility

There is evidence that company-generated social and environmental reports suffer from a credibility gap. The United Nations Environment Programme (UNEP) states that an active dialogue and stakeholder partnership is needed.

Marketing

There has been an increased level of interest in the environmental policies when companies work with NGOs.

Expertise and Innovation

NGOs have expertise in sustainable development issues. For example, retail outlets worked with WWF to come up with the forest stewardship certification.

Networks

Companies can work with NGO networks to tackle sustainability issues in countries where their suppliers are located. Also, international NGO networks can help suppliers gain access to socially and environmentally progressive markets (Bendell, 2010).

This partnership between opposites can be attractive. There are tangible differences between NGOs and businesses, in resources and organization structures, that make NGOs attractive partners for those companies that are seeking to move toward sustainability. What is important to note is that these differences, such as the capacity of NGOs for independent advice and action, ought not be compromised due to any kind of partnership. The relationship of partnerships, by itself, is a very valuable element in bringing about change. Since NGOs bring a different perspective to the boardroom, this partnering can be an attractive proposition (Bendell, 2010).

There have been numerous success stories that pertain to this partnership. For example, the WWF Climate Savers Program discusses how some of the companies are planning to cut their carbon dioxide emissions. Refer to the

WWF website for more details on these partnerships: www.worldwildlife
.org/what/globalmarkets/Climate%20Change/climatesavers2.html.

Environmental Nongovernmental Organizations

ENGOs are the NGOs that work directly for the preservation of the environment. There is a linkage between environmental protection and democracy in that democracy enhances the protection of the environment
(Holden, 2002). Indeed, Principle 10 of the Rio Declaration states,
"Environmental issues are best handled with the participation of all concerned citizens, at the relevant level" (United Nations Conference on
Environment and Development [UNCED], 1992). This viewpoint is further
reiterated by the Johannesburg Declaration that also restates the need for
"broad-based participation in policy formulation, decision-making and
implementation at all levels" as well as the "need [for] more effective,
democratic and accountable international and multilateral institutions"
(United Nations, 2002, Principles 26, 31).

Role of Environmental Nongovernmental Organizations

The ENGOs provide for "popular participation and influence" in environmental politics (Holden, 2002, p. 139). This influence can be noted by the
following two examples: (1) Greenpeace has 2.8 million supporters worldwide (Greenpeace, 2003) and FoE has an estimated 1 million supporters and
66 member groups worldwide with 5,000 local activist groups (FoE
International, 2002, p. 3). In the UK, there are about 4.5 million people that
belong to some sort of ENGO (Connelly & Smith, 2003, p. 85).

According to the World Commission on Environment and Development
(WCED), ENGOs play "an indispensable role . . . in identifying risks, in
assessing environmental impacts and designing and implementing measures
to deal with them, and in maintaining the high degree of public and political
interest required as a basis for action" (WCED, 1987, p. 326).

ENGOs have become key players in environmental politics at all levels
from local to global. As an example, FoE can play an important role from
local planning disputes to global environmental conferences (Pricen & Finger,
1994, pp. 4–6). Hence, ENGOs are vital democratic entities for the promotion of environmental sustainability.

However, ENGOs have also been questioned or criticized on two fronts.
The first criticism is on grounds of efficacy; that is to say that ENGOs have
insufficient influence to promote environmental sustainability. The second
criticism contends that ENGOs are not always democratic institutions. For
example, Greenpeace is a protest organization that aims to shape the views
of the own members rather than represent these views (Bell, 2003).

The Split: From Two Groups to Five

The environmental movement seems to have split into two groups—one that partners with business and the other that does not. Christine McDonald, former media manager of Conservation International (CI), discussed the practice of ENGOs that accept corporate industrial donations without holding them accountable. She further stated that this relationship between ENGOs and corporations has led to the system of co-optation, whereby the result is greenwashing (McDonald, 2008).

There is an ideological distinction between the two camps of environmentalists: the dark greens and the bright greens. NGOs such as Greenpeace and FoE are dark greens in that they call for radical social change and confront the corporations. The bright greens, on the other hand, such as CI and the Environmental Defense Fund (EDF) work within the system, with the partnership of corporations, to solve these environmental problems (Hoffman, 2009).

Research suggests that this gap between purity and pragmatism is getting wider. However, both the camps need to work together since the ability of moderate ENGOs is enhanced by the presence of the radical ENGOs (Conner & Epstein, 2007).

Andrew Hoffman used social networking tools and came up with five different types of ENGOs: (1) isolates, (2) mediators, (3) bridges, (4) independents, and (5) captives. Refer to the Hoffman (2009) for a complete listing of the five categories of ENGOs.

Isolates

The ENGOs in this group refuse to partner with corporations. They form an ideological core that does not concern itself with the corporate sector's issues. Examples are Greenpeace, The Wildlife Society, FoE, and others (Hoffman, 2009).

Mediators

The ENGOs in this group are central to the corporate network and maintain sectoral links. These ENGOs are pragmatic and are able to influence change due to their corporate ties. For example, the only five ENGOs that are part of the U.S. Climate Action partnership are in this group. These are (1) EDF, (2) The Nature Conservancy, (3) Natural Resources Defense Council (NRDC), (4) World Resources Institute, and (5) WWF (Hoffman, 2009).

Bridges

The first of the hybrid groups among the previous two extremes maintains a narrow spectrum of sectoral links. These ENGOs channel between a specific set of corporate sector issues and the rest of the group. For example, the Center for Clean Air Policy is a bridge focused on solving climate, air quality, and energy problems, yet it maintains ties with oil and gas sectors (Hoffman, 2009).

Independents

The second of the hybrid group is located on the periphery of the corporate network but maintains a wide variety of links, which gives them more autonomy than others. These ENGOs are good at generating innovative solutions that involve collaboration among various sectors. An example is the River Network, which helps freshwater protection organizations (Hoffman, 2009).

Captives

The last of the hybrid group is also on the periphery of the corporate network, and their sectoral links are very limited, mostly tied to marine, firearms, and beer and alcohol. These ENGOs have greater credibility with the sectors they engage with, but this role makes them vulnerable to a small subset of biased influence of one set of corporate interests (Hoffman, 2009).

Blessed Unrest

Paul Hawken (2007) described **blessed unrest** as a movement that is made of citizens and organizations that are united by their shared beliefs. This movement includes NGOs, nonprofit organizations, and people who call themselves environmental activists and others who protest labor injustices or support local farming. Hawken (2007) said, "Life is the most fundamental human right and all of the movements within the movement are dedicated to creating the conditions for life, conditions that include livelihood, food, security, peace, a stable environment and freedom from external tyranny" (pp. 67–68).

The book *Blessed Unrest: How the Largest Social Movement in History is Restoring Grace, Justice and Beauty to the World* by Paul Hawken contains an appendix that lists concerns from climate change to child labor and green banking to global governance. In Hawken's estimates, this movement is comprised of 2 million organizations. More importantly, *Blessed Unrest* makes a link between the environment to issues of social justice and culture. Hawken (2007) said, "Sustainability, ensuring the future of life on earth, is an infinite game, the endless expression of generosity on behalf of all" (p. 187).

Conclusion

There are countless NGOs worldwide, and these organizations have played a significant role in social development, sustainable community development, and promoting sustainable consumption. Businesses that wish to reach out to all their stakeholders can benefit from a productive relationship with NGOs. In addition, there is a category of NGOs called ENGOs that focus on environmental concerns. There are a large number of ENGOs ranging from the Audubon Society to WWF.

Lastly, two of the principles of Agenda 21 are relevant to sustainability. These principles are as follows:

1. the right to development must be fulfilled so as to equitably meet developmental and environmental needs of the present and future generations

2. in order to achieve sustainable development, environmental protection shall constitute an integral part of the development process and cannot be considered in isolation from it. (Agenda 21, n.d.-a)

KEY WORDS

Agenda 21

Blessed unrest

Environmental nongovernmental organizations (ENGOs)

Global social development

International Council for Local Environmental Initiatives (ICLEI)—Local Governments for Sustainability

International nongovernmental organizations (INGOs)

Nongovernmental organizations (NGOs)

Sustainable community development

Sustainable consumption

Sustainable development

DISCUSSION QUESTIONS

1. What is the role of government in advancing sustainability? Do you think that governments can serve as leaders in this role?

2. As a web exercise, explore your websites to find information that can be used for sustainability within business and personal use. Is there any information related to sustainability initiatives?

3. When were NGOs created? What were some of the historical reasons that led to this creation?

4. How do NGOs attain their funding? Do some of these sources of funding pose a conflict of interest?

5. Which NGO is the richest in the world? Has this ranking changed in recent years? What are eight biggest NGOs discussed in the chapter?

6. What are the six factors that contributed to the growth of NGOs?

7. How can NGOs promote the following three areas: (1) social develop-ment, (2) community development, and (3) sustainable consumption? Discuss these roles in detail.

8. Should businesses or corporations partner with NGOs? What are the advantages or disadvantages of this relationship?

9. What is an ENGO? What are the five types of ENGOs? Discuss the dif-ferences between these ENGOs.

10. Research any three NGOs mentioned in the chapter. Go to the official website of these NGOs, and discuss the role of each NGO in detail.

11. Can you think of any NGO and business partnership that has been particularly beneficial or disturbing?

12. What is the role of Agenda 21? Can you find a local chapter of Agenda 21 in your community?

RECOMMENDED CASE STUDIES

1. *Transforming the Global Fishing Industry: The Marine Stewardship Council at Full Sail,* Product Number IMD257-PDF-ENG, Harvard Business School Publishing.

Learning Objective: The MSC is an NGO headquartered in London and established by WWF and Unilever in 1997 to set up a certification and ecolabeling system for sustainable fishing. The case describes the MSC's initial and more recent challenges including the Tragedy of the Commons, a wide range of less willing stakeholders, and the complexity of certifying fisheries on sustainability criteria. It also outlines management decisions to meet at least some of the challenges: improved transparency and engage-ment with stakeholders, new governance structures, and certification methodologies.

2. *PROTECTA—Promoting Civil Society in Serbia,* Product Number HKS124-PDF-ENG, Harvard Business School Publishing.

Learning Objective: This case offers students an opportunity to recount the rise of the organization under increasingly trying personal, political, and professional circumstances—namely war and a repressive state. These cir-cumstances call into question some potential ethical concerns regarding man-agement in a hostile political environment. It offers an opportunity for students to make a decision and plot strategy for the organization's future in areas such as leadership transition, finances, and staffing.

RECOMMENDED WEBSITES

www.audubon.org/

www.bsr.org/

www.care.org/

www.conservation.org/

http://crs.org/

www.csrwire.com/

www.doctorswithoutborders.org/

www.epa.gov

www.foe.org/

www.future500.org/

www.greenpeace.org/

www.interaction.org/

www.kiva.org/

www.mercycorps.org/

www.msc.org/

www.oxfam.org/

www.savethechildren.org/

www.theirc.org/

www.un.org/esa/dsd/agenda21/res_agenda21_00.shtml

www.unep.org

www.worldvision.org/

www.wwf.org

Appendix

Table 9.1 Sustainable Development Programs

Country	Sample of Sustainable Development Research Programs
Austria (individual programs)	Austrian Landscape Research; Austrian Program on Technology for Sustainable Development; PFEIL 05 Program for Research and Development in Agriculture, Forestry, Environment and Water Management.
Belgium (umbrella program and sub-programs)	Scientific Support Plan for a Sustainable Development Policy 1 (Sustainable management of the North Sea, global change and sustainable development, Antarctica 4, sustainable mobility, norms for food products, Telsat 4, levers for a sustainable development policy and supporting actions); Scientific Support Plan for a Sustainable Development Policy 2 (Sustainable modes of production and consumption, global change, eco-systems and biodiversity, supporting actions and mixed actions); Scientific Support to an Integration of Notions of Quality and Security of the Production Environments, Processes and Goods in a Context of Sustainable Development.
Germany (umbrella program and sub-programs)	Research on the Environment (Research on sustainable economic management, regional sustainability, research on global change, socioecological research)
The Netherlands (umbrella program with structured and coordinated individual programs)	Economy, Ecology and Technology (EET); Dutch Initiative for Sustainable Development (NIDO); Sustainable Technology Development Project[2] HABIFORM (Expertise network – multiple use of space)
Sweden (individual programs)	Urban and Regional Planning Infrasystems for Sustainable Cities; The Sustainable City; Economics for Sustainable Development; Sustainable Forestry in Southern Sweden; Sustainable Food Production; Sustainable Coastal Zone; Sustainable Management of the Mountain Region; Paths to Sustainable Development – Behavior, Organizations, Structures (Ways Ahead) Innovation Systems Supporting a Sustainable Growth
UK (individual programs)	Environmental Strategy Research Program Towards a Sustainable Urban Environment EPSRC Infrastructure and Environment Program Environment Agency Sustainable Development R&D Program Sustainable Development Commission Sustainable Technologies Initiative – LINK Program

Source: Hargroves & Smith (2005).

Note: The table shows the three main program types for organizing research for sustainable development: (1) umbrella programs, (2) subprograms, and (3) individual programs.

Table 9.2

List of Mediator Nongovernmental Organizations (NGOs)	Soil and Water Conservation Society
	Whitetails Unlimited
CERES	Wildlife Forever
Conservation International (CI)	
Environmental Defense Fund (EDF)	*List of Captive NGOs*
National Audubon Society	African Wildlife Foundation
Natural Resources	Bat Conservation International
Defense Council (NRDC)	Defenders of Wildlife
The Nature Conservancy	Delta Waterfowl Foundation
Wildlife Conservation Society	Dian Fossey Gorilla Fund
Wildlife Habitat Council	Ducks Unlimited
World Resources Institute	Environmental and Energy Study Institute
World Wildlife Fund (WWF)	Fauna & Flora International
	Fish America Foundation
List of Bridge NGOs	International Wildlife Coalition—USA
Center for Clean Air Policy	Izaak Walton League of America
Rainforest Alliance	Jane Goodall Institute
Scenic Hudson	Land Trust Alliance
Student Conservation Association	National Council for Air and Stream Improvement
List of Independent NGOs	National Wildlife Federation
American Forests	Quail Unlimited RARE Sierra Club
American Rivers	The Wilderness Society
Pheasants Forever	Trout Unlimited
Rainforest Action Network	Wildlife Trust
River Network	Worldwatch Institute

Source: Data from Hoffman (2009).

Appendix A: Agenda 21 Chapter 27

Strengthening the Role of Non-Governmental Organizations: Partners for Sustainable Development

Programme Area

Basis for action

1. Non-governmental organizations play a vital role in the shaping and implementation of participatory democracy. Their credibility lies in the responsible and constructive role they play in society. Formal and informal organizations, as well as grass-roots

movements, should be recognized as partners in the implementation of Agenda 21. The nature of the independent role played by non-governmental organizations within a society calls for real participation; therefore, independence is a major attribute of non-governmental organizations and is the precondition of real participation.

2. One of the major challenges facing the world community as it seeks to replace unsustainable development patterns with environmentally sound and sustainable development is the need to activate a sense of common purpose on behalf of all sectors of society. The chances of forging such a sense of purpose will depend on the willingness of all sectors to participate in genuine social partnership and dialogue, while recognizing the independent roles, responsibilities and special capacities of each.

3. Non-governmental organizations, including those non-profit organizations representing groups addressed in the present section of Agenda 21, possess well-established and diverse experience, expertise and capacity in fields which will be of particular importance to the implementation and review of environmentally sound and socially responsible sustainable development, as envisaged throughout Agenda 21. The community of non-governmental organizations, therefore, offers a global network that should be tapped, enabled and strengthened in support of efforts to achieve these common goals.

4. To ensure that the full potential contribution of non-governmental organizations is realized, the fullest possible communication and cooperation between international organizations, national and local governments and non-governmental organizations should be promoted in institutions mandated, and programmes designed to carry out Agenda 21. Non-governmental organizations will also need to foster cooperation and communication among themselves to reinforce their effectiveness as actors in the implementation of sustainable development.

Objectives

5. Society, Governments and international bodies should develop mechanisms to allow non-governmental organizations to play their partnership role responsibly and effectively in the process of environmentally sound and sustainable development.

6. With a view to strengthening the role of non-governmental organizations as social partners, the United Nations system and Governments should initiate a process, in consultation with non-governmental organizations, to review formal procedures and mechanisms for the involvement of these organizations at all levels from policy-making and decision-making to implementation.

7. By 1995, a mutually productive dialogue should be established at the national level between all Governments and non-governmental organizations and their self-organized networks to recognize and strengthen their respective roles in implementing environmentally sound and sustainable development.

8. Governments and international bodies should promote and allow the participation of non-governmental organizations in the conception, establishment and evaluation of official mechanisms and formal procedures designed to review the implementation of Agenda 21 at all levels.

Activities

9. The United Nations system, including international finance and development agencies, and all intergovernmental organizations and forums should, in consultation with non-governmental organizations, take measures to:

   a. Review and report on ways of enhancing existing procedures and mechanisms by which non-governmental organizations contribute to policy design, decision-making, implementation and evaluation at the individual agency level, in inter-agency discussions and in United Nations conferences;

   b. On the basis of subparagraph (a) above, enhance existing or, where they do not exist, establish, mechanisms and procedures within each agency to draw on the expertise and views of non-governmental organizations in policy and programme design, implementation and evaluation;

   c. Review levels of financial and administrative support for non-governmental organizations and the extent and effectiveness of their involvement in project and programme implementation, with a view to augmenting their role as social partners;

   d. Design open and effective means of achieving the participation of non-governmental organizations in the processes established to review and evaluate the implementation of Agenda 21 at all levels;

   e. Promote and allow non-governmental organizations and their self-organized networks to contribute to the review and evaluation of policies and programmes designed to implement Agenda 21, including support for developing country non-governmental organizations and their self-organized networks;

   f. Take into account the findings of non-governmental review systems and evaluation processes in relevant reports of the Secretary-General to the General Assembly, and of all pertinent United Nations organizations and other intergovernmental organizations and forums concerning implementation of Agenda 21, in accordance with the review process for Agenda 21;

   g. Provide access for non-governmental organizations to accurate and timely data and information to promote the effectiveness of their programmes and activities and their roles in support of sustainable development.

10. Governments should take measures to:

    a. Establish or enhance an existing dialogue with non-governmental organizations and their self-organized networks representing various sectors, which could serve to: (i) consider the rights and responsibilities of these organizations; (ii) efficiently channel integrated non-governmental inputs to the governmental policy development process; and (iii) facilitate non-governmental coordination in implementing national policies at the programme level;

    b. Encourage and enable partnership and dialogue between local non-governmental organizations and local authorities in activities aimed at sustainable development;

c. Involve non-governmental organizations in national mechanisms or procedures established to carry out Agenda 21, making the best use of their particular capacities, especially in the fields of education, poverty alleviation and environmental protection and rehabilitation;

d. Take into account the findings of non-governmental monitoring and review mechanisms in the design and evaluation of policies concerning the implementation of Agenda 21 at all levels;

e. Review government education systems to identify ways to include and expand the involvement of non-governmental organizations in the field of formal and informal education and of public awareness;

f. Make available and accessible to non-governmental organizations the data and information necessary for their effective contribution to research and to the design, implementation and evaluation of programmes.

Means of implementation

(a) Financing and cost evaluation

11. Depending on the outcome of review processes and the evolution of views as to how best to build partnership and dialogue between official organizations and groups of non-governmental organizations, relatively limited but unpredictable, costs will be involved at the international and national levels in enhancing consultative procedures and mechanisms. Non-governmental organizations will also require additional funding in support of their establishment of, improvement of or contributions to Agenda 21 monitoring systems. These costs will be significant but cannot be reliably estimated on the basis of existing information.

(b) Capacity-building

12. The organizations of the United Nations system and other intergovernmental organizations and forums, bilateral programmes and the private sector, as appropriate, will need to provide increased financial and administrative support for non-governmental organizations and their self-organized networks, in particular those based in developing countries, that contribute to the monitoring and evaluation of Agenda 21 programmes, and provide training for non-governmental organizations (and assist them to develop their own training programmes) at the international and regional levels to enhance their partnership role in programme design and implementation.

13. Governments will need to promulgate or strengthen, subject to country-specific conditions, any legislative measures necessary to enable the establishment by non-governmental organizations of consultative groups, and to ensure the right of non-governmental organizations to protect the public interest through legal action.

PART IV

Strategies for a Sustainable Future

10

Transparent Reporting, Measurement, and Standards

LEARNING OBJECTIVES

By the end of this chapter, you should be able to do the following:

- Understand the need for reporting and transparency.
- Present voluntary reporting on sustainability.
- Discuss the role of **Global Reporting Initiative (GRI).**
- Compare and contrast the various ISO (International Organization for Standardization) 14001 standards.
- Explain **ISO 26000** standards.
- Discuss the **UN Global Compact.**
- Present some other reports, repositories, and indexes.

Chapter Overview

This chapter discusses the role of reporting and transparency and the importance of these roles for companies. We explain the importance of voluntary reporting on sustainability and the GRI, and we will outline the **ISO standards.** Furthermore, we include a discussion of the UN Global Compact along with the 10 principles underlying the compact. We will end with a discussion on other standards that exist in the marketplace. The appendix to the chapter contains the speech of former UN secretary general Mr. Kofi Annan calling for the UN Global Compact.

Reporting

Why does a company want to report? What are the incentives for companies to share information on their performance? What kinds of reports exist in the marketplace?

Reporting on performance can help a company drive internal change in numerous ways. First, it forces the company to acknowledge sustainability issues and assess if any gaps exist. If these gaps are communicated internally, the company leaders can show managers and employees what needs to be done and rally support for a cause or an action. In this manner, the sustainability report can serve as a part of the check in a standard plan-do-check-act cycle (PDCA cycle). Furthermore, this change can also come about via a benchmarking study whereby data are collected and compared to a best-in-class company. Lastly, the sustainability reports that spur change also invite comments and scrutiny from external stakeholders (Blackburn, 2007).

Reporting on sustainability performance is one of the primary ways for a company to manage its impact on sustainable development. It is now widely accepted that a company has a responsibility to the local community, environment, and social conditions (refer to the appendix: *Global Compact Speech* by Kofi Annan). Reporting is valuable since it allows companies to measure, track, and improve their performance on various issues such as energy consumption, water usage, and so on. As any manager knows, if a company can measure an issue, it can be managed more effectively. In addition, **sustainability reporting** also promoted accountability and transparency. When the company reports information across a public domain, its stakeholders can track the company's performance on themes around the environment, community relations, and so on. A particular company's performance can be compared to other competitors. For example, how does Starbucks compare with Dunkin Donuts? Starbucks has made a commitment to purchase fair trade coffee. Has Dunkin Donuts made a similar commitment?

Why is transparency important? Trust is an important, yet elusive, goal for a company. It would be terribly unwise for a company to report only the achievements or good stories. It is only a matter of time before some stakeholder or media finds the full details. A company would be prudent not to invite suspicions of cover-ups. Hence, the best approach for a company is to report significant achievements and acknowledge weaknesses along with the steps that need to be taken to address these weaknesses (an action plan). By openly sharing information, a company can convey good-faith estimates with regards to sustainability. As an example, the 2003 reports of ABN AMRO, a Netherlands company, shared information in sidebars labeled as dilemmas. These sidebars contained discussions on animal rights, environmental degradation in a developing country, military defense contracts, and other topics. (Blackburn, 2007). There are numerous other companies—for example, Shell and Nike—that keep reporting even in the presence of public criticisms.

What are the reasons that companies give for reporting? Since most of the reporting is voluntary, it is worthwhile to explore the reasons for reporting. A survey conducted in 2002 of 200 business leaders in 50 countries stated the reasons that companies reported on their sustainability performance.

Why Companies Report on Sustainability Performance

1. Drives constructive change in the management of sustainability issues

2. Educates employees on the issues

3. Aligns the organization on areas of needed improvement

4. Hastens the resolution of problems before they magnify

5. Builds stakeholder trust

6. Enhances company reputation for honesty

7. Strengthens relationships with stakeholders

Benefits of Sustainability Reporting

What are the benefits of sustainability reporting to corporate responsibility? A company needs to publish a public sustainability report for the sake of its stakeholders' information needs. In addition, companies need to be focused on issues outside of the company (Brownlie, n.d.).

A survey of business leaders cited the top benefits of sustainability reporting as improving stakeholder relations and management of sustainable development issues. The survey respondents stated that the benefits of social and environmental performance reporting outweigh the costs. A survey by KPMG (Brownlie, n.d.) indicated that businesses adopt sustainability reporting to do the following:

- Reduce operating costs and improve efficiencies.
- Develop innovative products and services for access to new markets.
- Improve reputation and brand value.
- Recruit and retain excellent people.
- Gain better access to investor capital.
- Enhance the public value of the company.
- Reduce liabilities through integrated risk management. (Brownlie, n.d.)

Indeed, if reporting is so beneficial, why are more companies not doing so? This is because the list of reasons for not reporting is much longer (Blackburn, 2007, p. 314)!

Why Companies Do Not Report on Issues

1. Embarrassed about performance

2. Key competitors aren't reporting on the issue; no competitive advantage

3. Afraid of releasing proprietary information that could hurt business

4. Concerned about reporting information that could create a security risk

5. Concerned about possible litigation on the issue

6. Afraid it will stir up certain stakeholders and create public relations problems

7. Afraid the media will criticize the company for its failings

8. Don't fully understand the issue

9. Not aware of the issue

10. Believe that their trade association is adequately addressing the issue

11. Believe the issue isn't significant/material enough to be a priority

12. Not concerned about improving performance on the issue

13. Believe the cost and effort of reporting would be excessive (Blackburn, 2007, p. 315)

Reporting can be mandatory or voluntary in nature. Some companies report voluntarily since these companies find the reasons to do so to be compelling. However, most companies report since they are required to so by law. The mandatory reports can come from a variety of legal requirements. The most common requirement comes about as **pollutant-disclosure laws.** Herein, companies are required to report on the emissions of toxic pollutants. In the United States, the Emergency Planning and Community Right-to-Know Act (EPCRA) was passed in 1986. The EPCRA requires reporting of toxic emissions under Toxics Release Inventory (TRI), and this law led to the passage of other versions of similar legislations. Other countries that have similar registries of emissions include Canada, Czech Republic, Hungary, Norway, Poland, and Yugoslavia. On a global scale, the Organisation for Economic Co-operation and Development (OECD) has been asked to develop registries similar to TRI in member states. Another requirement of mandatory reporting is in the cases when social and environmental information is included in financial reports. For example, in the case of the contaminated disposal sites, the Securities and Exchange Commission (SEC) rules require that companies declare fines in excess of $100,000.

Global Reporting Initiative

There are numerous frameworks for voluntary reporting on sustainability. At present, the GRI standard has become the *de facto* international reporting standard.

GRI was established in 1997 by the partnership of **Ceres** and the **United Nations Environment Programme (UNEP)**. The broad mission was to develop "globally applicable guidelines for reporting on the economic, environmental, and social performance of corporations, governments and nongovernmental organizations (NGOs)" (Stappen, 2009). GRI works as a collaborative effort in that it incorporates the active participation of multiple stakeholders from corporations to nongovernmental organizations (NGOs) worldwide. This multi-stakeholder aspect leads to GRI's broad applicability, and it has become the de facto international standard in sustainability reporting ("What Is GRI," n.d.).

The GRI reporting framework lays out the principles and the indicators that can be employed by organizations wanting to measure and report their economic, social, and environmental performance ("What Is GRI?" n.d.). The sustainability-reporting framework provides guidance for organizations to disclose their sustainability reporting. This framework is relevant to all shapes and sizes of organizations worldwide and is developed through individuals from over 60 countries that represent many institutions. There are guidelines that should be used as the basis for all reporting. The guidelines consist of principles, guidance, and standard disclosures. The core guidelines are the G3 guidelines ("RG: Sustainability Reporting Guidelines," n.d.).

The first draft of the guidelines was released in 1999, and the framework encompassed the triple bottom line (TBL) of economic, environmental, and social issues. These guidelines then evolved into the G2 in 2002. In 2006, the third generation of these guidelines, the G3, was released ("GRI: More Background," n.d.).

After the successful launch of G3, GRI expanded its Reporting Framework and built powerful alliances. GRI partnered with the UN Global Compact, the OECD, and established regional partnerships with Focal Points in Brazil, Australia, China, India, and the United States. In addition, GRI provided educational publications, research and development publications, sector guidelines for industries, coaching and training, software certification, among other publications intended to assist small- and medium-sized organizations. In March 2011, GRI published the G3.1 Guidelines—an update and completion of G3—with expanded guidance on reporting gender, community, and human rights-related performance ("What Is GRI?" n.d.).

GRI works closely with the investor community and has recently released a report examining how companies can frame their **environmental, social, and governance (ESG) disclosures** to meet the needs of investors. The report also includes recommendations that would benefit companies issuing sustainability reports. GRI plays an important role ensuring that the information related to sustainability performance available to the financial markets is consistent and reliable. The GRI report recommends that companies ought to factor in the expectations of both the shareholders and stakeholders and for companies to link these ESG disclosures to business strategy. In addition, the companies ought to do the following:

- Include supporting statements about ESG performance with facts and/ or evidence.
- Contain forward looking contextual information.
- Be concise.
- Cover a balance of positive and negative sustainability performance.
- Relate ESG strategy to current opportunities and risks ("Reaching Investors," n.d.)

Who Reports, and Why?

Of the more than 50,000 multinational corporations, fewer than 1% use the GRI framework in some capacity (Elkington & Lee, 2006). In addition, most of these are comprised of large companies that presumably have higher expectations to the public. Of the largest group, all the companies in chemicals, forestry, and pharmaceuticals sectors report on their corporate social responsibility (CSR).

A growing number of companies do understand the primary importance of corporate reporting, which is one of competitive advantage. Other benefits include better management of environmental, social, and governance impacts and overall risk; enhancement of company brands and reputation; and greater ability to attract and retain customers and talent. There are other companies that adopt a reactive stance and might initiate reporting in order to comply with a checklist or as a public relations strategy. However, these approaches are shortsighted. When a reactive or defensive approach is not linked to the overall strategy, it often is delegated to corporate communications or public relations. Without an overarching direction from the top management, the managers of departments that are responsible for reporting might fail to grasp strategic issues or they might be unwilling or unable to engage in meaningful debates on impacts or challenges (Elkington & Lee, 2006).

Given all this information, is the GRI really helpful as a tool to report on the sustainability performance of a company? A report lists the potential benefits and drawbacks of the GRI.

Benefits of Global Reporting Initiative

- A holistic framework is provided that follows the TBL: social, environmental, and economic aspects.
- The reporting information is consistent across different organizations.
- It is accepted widely across the globe.
- Organizations across the globe can be compared to one another.
- It can be used to measure and benchmark performance.
- Being flexible, it can be implemented incrementally and used across sectors and geographical contexts.
- Support and integration of other tools and standards, such as AA1000 Series, a principle-based set of standards, is included (GRI, n.d.; GRI Guidelines, n.d).

Limitations of Global Reporting Initiative

- Labor-intensive, especially for smaller companies
- Does not measure pollution prevention
- No guidance provided on data collection or preparation of reports
- Limited usage in social enterprise sector
- No accreditation or external evaluation provided
- Reports impacts, not positive outcomes (GRI, n.d.; "GRI Guidelines, n.d.).

To summarize, the GRI is an excellent tool for the companies that want to report on their sustainability performance. According to the 2010 reports, GRI hit the 1,000 report milestone in mid-October, and submissions of new reports keep climbing (60% upsurge in GRI reports in 2010, 2010).

The Occupational Safety and Health Administration and the Voluntary Protection Program

The Occupational Safety and Health Administration (OSHA) is the main federal agency that is charged with the enforcement of safety and health legislation. The Voluntary Protection Program (VPP) was OSHA's first foray into partnerships within industry. It is a cooperative compliance program that is designed to encourage companies to exceed the minimum OSHA safety requirements. The VPP program realizes that compliance with safety regulations alone is not enough and that there needs to be a structured program in place to achieve the goal of working more safely ("What Is VPP?" n.d.).

The VPP aims to promote effective worksite-based safety and health. The program is designed to prevent fatalities, injuries, and illnesses through a system that is built around hazard prevention, worksite analysis, management commitment, and worker involvement and training. In order to participate in the program, employers need to submit an application to OSHA and go through a rigorous onsite evaluation by a team of safety and health professionals ("All About VPP," n.d.).

The Environmental Protection Agency's Voluntary Disclosure Programs

The U.S. Environmental Protection Agency (EPA) also has some voluntary disclosure programs. The EPA Audit Policy, titled "Incentives for Self-Policing: Discovery, Disclosure, Correction and Prevention of Violations," outlines incentives for entities to voluntarily comply with federal environmental laws and regulations. To take advantage of these incentives, the entities "must voluntarily discover, promptly disclose to EPA, expeditiously correct, and prevent recurrence of future environmental violations" ("Compliance Incentives and Auditing," n.d). In most cases, the EPA and the regulated entity work together to discuss mutually acceptable disclosure details, compliance, and audit schedules. An entity has 21 days from the time it discovers a violation has occurred to disclose the violation to the EPA ("Compliance Incentives and Auditing," n.d.).

International Organization for Standardization Standards

The issue of environmental impact is becoming increasingly important globally. The pressure to comply is coming from numerous sources: governments, regulation and trade agencies, customers, employees, and shareholders. In addition, social pressures are also building up from numerous interested parties, such as consumers and environmental nongovernmental organizations (ENGOs). Hence, other standards besides the GRI need to be explored to meet this need for compliance.

ISO 14001

The ISO was started in 1996 and is located in Geneva. The purpose of the ISO standards is to facilitate and support international trade by developing standards that would be accepted and recognized worldwide. The standard is designed to maintain the balance between profitability and reducing environmental impact. These standards are developed by technical committees and tend to have worldwide support since the members on the technical committees represent various national organizations. The purpose of these standards is to put forth a process that can evaluate the lifetime impact of the product on the environment ("ISO Standards for Life Cycle Assessment [LCA]," 2006).

ISO 14001 states how any organization can implement effective environmental management system (EMS). The ISO 14001 is comprised of the following five steps:

1. [Following] general requirements

2. [Adhering to] environmental policy

3. Planning implementation and operation

4. Checking and corrective action

5. [Undergoing] management review. ("ISO 14001 Environment," n.d.)

These steps lead an organization to identify aspects of the business that have an impact on the environment in order to understand the applicable environmental laws. The next stage is to come up with a management process for continual improvement. The system can be periodically assessed, and if compliant, the organization can be registered to ISO 14001 ("ISO 14001 Environment," n.d.).

According to the ISO 14001, a particular company ought to start with an environmental review if it does not have an EMS in place. The four steps involved in setting an environmental review are as follows:

1. Identify the environmental aspects of the organization.

2. Clarify the legal requirements that apply to these environmental aspects.

3. Examine the current environmental management policies, procedures, and practices.

4. Refine the scope of the EMS ("ISO 14001 2004 Introduction," n.d.).

However, if a company does have an EMS in place, then a gap analysis is needed to update to the new standards ("ISO 14001 2004 Introduction," n.d.). One of the broad appeals of the ISO 14001 is with regards to its relevance. The standards can be applied to almost every organization, including the following:

• Single site to large multi-national companies
• High risk companies to low risk service organizations
• Manufacturing, process and the service industries; including local governments
• All industry sectors including public and private sectors
• Original equipment manufacturers and their suppliers ("ISO 14001 Environment," n.d.)

Besides the 14000 series, there are numerous other standards in the series that serve as guidelines. Some of these guidelines are given as follows. A table (Table 10.2) providing the list of the various ISO 14000 standards is provided in the appendix.

• ISO 14004: provides guidance on the development and implementation of environmental management systems
• ISO 14010: provides general principles of environmental auditing (now superseded by ISO 19011)
• ISO 14011: provides specific guidance on auditing an environmental management system (now superseded by ISO 19011)
• ISO 14012: provides guidance on qualification criteria for environmental auditors and lead auditors (now superseded by ISO 19011)
• ISO 14013/5: provides audit program review and assessment material.
• ISO 14020+: provides guidance on labeling issues

- ISO 14030+: provides guidance on performance targets and monitoring within an Environmental Management System
- ISO 14040+: covers life cycle issues. ("Other 14000 Series Standards," 2002)

ISO 14025

Businesses can be more sustainable if they engage in purchasing goods and services that are less damaging to the environment. However, there is a lot of mislabeling of products, and the information is not always accurate or verifiable. To address this concern, the **ISO 14025** states how to create procedures in order to monitor and develop new ecolabeling schemes. It also provides guidance on ecolabeling issues aimed at creating a globally recognized standard. In general terms, the ISO 14025 provides environmental information on products, and in certain relevant cases, it also provides additional information such as the impact on biodiversity, hazard, and risk assessment ("ISO Standard Will Help," 2006).

ISO 14040

A life cycle assessment (LCA) analyzes the environmental impact of a product throughout its life span. ISO has also published and revised LCA standards in order to highlight areas of improvement in the production and usage of products.

The LCA methodology allows the comparison of the environmental performance of products in order to select the least damaging. The term *life cycle* addresses the fact that a fair assessment would include a holistic approach whereby all the steps from the raw material procurement, production, manufacture, distribution, use, and disposal would be evaluated ("ISO Standards for LCA," 2006).

The following general standards and technical reports have been produced in the **ISO 14040** series:

- ISO 14040: Principles and Framework (1997). These standards provide a clear overview of the practice, applications and limitations of LCA to a broad range of potential users and stakeholders, including those with a limited knowledge of LCA.
- ISO 14041: Goal and Scope Definition and Inventory Analysis (1998). This set provides special requirements and guidelines for the preparation of, conduct of, and critical review of, life cycle inventory analysis (the phase of LCA that involves the compilation and quantification of environmentally relevant inputs and outputs of a product system).
- ISO 14042: Life Cycle Impact Assessment (2000). This set of standards provides guidance on the impact assessment phase of LCA (the phase

of LCA aimed at evaluating the significance of potential environmental impacts using the results of the life cycle inventory analysis).

- ISO 14043: Life Cycle Interpretation (2000). This set provides guidance on the interpretation of LCA results in relation to the goal definition phase of the LCA study, involving review of the scope of the LCA, as well as the nature and quality of the data collected. ("The ISO 14040 Series," 2004)

ISO 14064

These sets of standards are aimed at greenhouse gas (GHG) accounting and verification and were established in 2002 in response to an absence of verification protocols and validation for GHG emissions and removals. **ISO 14064** comprises of three standards that detail specifications and guidance. These three can be used independently or as an integrated set of tools. These three standards are as follows:

- ISO 14064-1:2006, Greenhouse gases—Part 1: Specification with guidance at the organization level for the quantification and reporting of greenhouse gas emissions and removals.
- ISO 14064-2:2006, Greenhouse gases—Part 2: Specification with guidance at the project level for the quantification, monitoring and reporting of greenhouse gas emission reductions and removal enhancements.
- ISO 14064-3:2006, Greenhouse gases—Part 3: Specification with guidance for the validation and verification of greenhouse gas assertions. ("New ISO 14064 Standards," 2006)

ISO 26000: Social Responsibility

The ISO 26000 is an international standard that provides an organization with guidance on how to be more socially responsible. This set of standards can be used as a tool to transition from good intentions to good actions. However, this set of standards contains voluntary guidance, not requirements; hence, it cannot be used as a certification standard like ISO 9001:2008 and ISO 14001:2004.

Importance of ISO 26000

Sustainability encompasses the three aspects of a business: (1) to provide goods and services profitably, (2) to preserve the environment, and (3) to operate in a socially responsible manner. As pointed out in the TBL approach, an organization needs to respect the 3 Ps: (1) people, (2) planet, and (3) profit.

Despite all the high-level declarations of principles related to social responsibility and individual social responsibility programs, the challenge is how to put the principles into practice. Furthermore, the term *social responsibility* has numerous connotations, and it can be challenging to put the principles into practice. Moreover, the previous initiatives have tended to focus on CSR while ISO 26000 provides guidance not only for companies but also for public sector organizations of all types (Frost, 2011). The expertise of these standards is also in articulating international agreements based on two levels of consensus: (1) among the principal categories of stakeholders and (2) among countries (Frost, 2011).

Benefits of ISO 26000

ISO 26000 provides guidance on numerous issues such as the trends, core issues, principles, and practices of SR. They also provide guidance on promoting, integrating, and implementing SR within an organization; engaging with stakeholders; and, finally, communicating information about SR (Frost, 2011).

The intent of ISO 26000 is to assist organizations in contributing to sustainable development and to go beyond legal compliance. Furthermore, ISO 26000 promotes common understanding of social responsibility. While applying the ISO 26000, an organization needs to take into consideration diversity in terms of cultural, economic, environmental, legal, political, and societal factors while staying consistent with international norms of behavior (Frost, 2011).

What Benefits Can Be Achieved by Implementing ISO 26000?

The performance on SR can have immense influence on the reputation and competitive advantage for the organization. In addition, the organization can also attract and retain workers, customers, and clients. Social responsibility can influence the morale, commitment, and productivity of employees as well as impact the perceptions of investors and donors. Last but not least, social responsibility has the potential of influencing the relationship with stakeholders ranging from companies and suppliers to governments and from customers to the community within which the organization operates (Frost, 2011).

Challenges

The application of social responsibility can be challenging. The presence of cultural differences, competing priorities, and other unique variables can lead to confusion regarding the *right* action. There are certain areas that are accepted in certain cultures and banned in other cultures. The standards state "a situation's complexity should not be used as an excuse for inaction" ("ISO 26000 and the Definition of Social Responsibility," 2011). The seven principles of socially responsible behavior as outlined in the standard are "accountability, transparency, ethical behavior, respect for stakeholder interests, respect for the rule of law, respect for international norms of behavior, and respect for human rights" ("ISO 26000 and the Definition of Social Responsibility," 2011).

UN Global Compact

The United Nations put forth the UN Global Compact as an initiative to encourage businesses all over the world to adopt sustainable policies and to report on the implementation of these policies. The UN secretary general Kofi Annan, in his address to the World Economic Forum on January 31, 1999, announced the Global Compact. Please refer to the appendix for the text of this statement.

The UN Global Compact is a "strategic policy initiative for businesses that are committed to aligning their operations and strategies with ten universally accepted principles in the areas of human rights, labour, environment and anti-corruption" ("Overview of the UN Global Compact," 2010). It brings companies together with labor groups, UN agencies, and other civil society agencies. Given the social, political, and economic challenges, more and more companies are recognizing the need to partner with governments, NGOs, and the United Nations. This partnership and understanding has led to the growth in the numbers of the Global Compact. At present, the Global Compact is the largest voluntary corporate responsibility initiative in the world with over 8,700 corporate participants and stakeholders from more than 130 countries ("Overview of the UN Global Compact," 2010).

Overall, the Global Compact pursues two complementary objectives:

1. Mainstream the ten principles in business activities around the world.

2. Catalyze actions in support of broader UN goals, including the Millennium Development Goals (MDGs). ("Overview of the UN Global Compact," 2010)

Given these objectives, the Global Compact promotes collaboration to find solutions for the basic challenges facing society. The initiative combines the power and moral authority of the UN with the strengths of the private sector and expertise of the stakeholders. The uniqueness of Global Compact is that it is both global and local, private and public, and voluntary yet accountable ("Overview of the UN Global Compact," 2010).

The benefits of engagement include the following:

- Adopting an established and globally recognized policy framework for the development, implementation, and disclosure of environmental, social, and governance policies and practices.
- Sharing best and emerging practices to advance practical solutions and strategies to common challenges.

- Advancing sustainability solutions in partnership with a range of stakeholders, including UN agencies, governments, civil society, labor, and other non-business interests.
- Linking business units and subsidiaries across the value chain with the Global Compact's Local Networks around the world—many of these in developing and emerging markets.
- Accessing the United Nations' extensive knowledge of and experience with sustainability and development issues.
- Utilizing UN Global Compact management tools and resources, and the opportunity to engage in specialized workstreams in the environmental, social and governance realms. ("Overview of the UN Global Compact," 2010)

Ten Principles

Underlying the ideology of the UN Global Compact are 10 universally applicable principles in the areas of human rights, labor, the environment, and anti-corruption. These principles are derived from the Universal Declaration of Human Rights (UDHR), the International Labor Organization's Declaration on Fundamental Principles and Rights at Work, the Rio Declaration on Environment and Development, and the UN Convention Against Corruption. The UN Global Compact calls for companies to "embrace, support and enact" these principles as core values.

The first two principles in the area of human rights are stated as follows:

- Principle 1: Businesses should support and respect the protection of internationally proclaimed human rights; and
- Principle 2: Businesses should make sure that they are not complicit in human rights abuses. ("The Ten Principles," 2010)

The first two principles address human rights and call upon businesses to respect these rights and to ensure that there are no violations of internationally proclaimed human rights. The UN General Assembly adopted 30 articles of UDHR, and these articles have been voted by a majority of nations.

The next four principles in the area of labor are stated as follows:

- Principle 3: Businesses should uphold the freedom of association and the effective recognition of the right to collective bargaining;
- Principle 4: Businesses should uphold the elimination of all forms of forced and compulsory labor;
- Principle 5: Businesses should uphold the effective abolition of child labor; and
- Principle 6: Businesses should uphold the elimination of discrimination in respect of employment and occupation. ("The Ten Principles," 2010)

These four principles address labor rights and call upon businesses to recognize labor unions, not to engage in coercive behavior, to abolish child labor, and not to discriminate. An example would be the employment of child labor wherein an international corporation might be held accountable even if the supplier in a different country employs underage children.

The following three principles in the area of environment are stated as follows:

- Principle 7: Businesses should support a precautionary approach to environmental challenges;
- Principle 8: Businesses should undertake initiatives to promote greater environmental responsibility; and
- Principle 9: Businesses should encourage the development and diffusion of environmentally friendly technologies. ("The Ten Principles," 2010)

These three principles address the environment and call for businesses to act in a stewardship role for the environment by protecting it and developing green products and processes.

The last principle, in the area of anti-corruption, is stated as follows:

- Principle 10: Businesses should work against corruption in all its forms, including extortion and bribery. ("The Ten Principles," 2010)

The last principle simply calls for businesses not to engage in any form of corruption.

Other Standards and Registries

In the recent years, external stakeholders such as NGOs and financial institutions have started asking companies for information on their environmental performance. For example, over 80% of global Fortune 500 companies publish reports that disclose their sustainability performance. Some of the examples of key reporting formats and sustainability indexes are presented in Table 10.1 and are discussed as follows:

Ceres

This organization is a group of investors, environmental organizations, and other organizations that are working with companies and investors to address sustainability challenges. The primary mission of the organization is "integrating sustainability into capital markets for the health of the planet and its people." In addition, it has laid out a Ceres 20-20 vision whereby it

Table 10.1   Examples of Key Reporting Formats and Sustainability Indices

Organization	Description
Reporting Formats	
GRI (Global Reporting Initiative)—G3 reports	Based on triple bottom line; international standard used by more than 1200 companies for corporate reporting on environmental, social and economic performance www.globalreporting.org
Ceres & Tellus Institute Facility Reporting Project	Consistent and comparable economic, environmental, and social reporting guidance for US facilities www.ceres.org
World Business Council for Sustainable Development	Global association of companies dealing only with business and sustainable development www.wbcsd.org
Reporting Repositories	
Corporate Register	Free directory of CSR, sustainability, and environmental reports issued by the companies worldwide www.corporateregister.com
Carbon Disclosure Project	Voluntary, annual reporting of GHG emissions worldwide www.cdproject.net
SD Indexes	
Dow Jones Sustainability Index (DJSI)	First global index tracking financial performance of leading sustainability-driven companies worldwide www.sustainability-index.com
Corporate Knights Global 100	100 Most Sustainable Companies across the globe as defined by a Canadian media company www.corporateknights.ca

Source: Phyper & MacLean (2009).

aims to achieve a sustainable global economy by the year 2020. The plan has four pillars, each with specific ambitious goals:

1. We need honest accounting that abolishes the folly of free pollution.

2. We need higher standards of business leadership.

3. We need bold solutions that accelerate green innovation.

4. We need smart new policies that reward sustainability performance. ("Our Vision for a Sustainable Global Economy," n.d.)

World Business Council for Sustainable Development

This **World Business Council for Sustainable Development (WBCSD)** global organization is led by the CEOs of about 200 companies. The council provides a space for companies to share information around sustainable development—from shared experiences and best practices to advocacy and information on how to work with governments and NGOs. The members of this council represent 35 countries and 20 industrial sectors and has a global network of 60 national and regional partners. The council focuses on four key areas—(1) energy and climate, (2) development, (3) business role, and (4) ecosystems. The objectives of the council are to do the following:

- Be a leading business advocate on sustainable development;
- Participate in policy development to create the right framework conditions for business to make an effective contribution to sustainable human progress;
- Develop and promote the business case for sustainable development;
- Demonstrate the business contribution to sustainable development solutions and share leading edge practices among members;
- Contribute to a sustainable future for developing nations and nations in transition. (About the WBCSD, n.d.)

Corporate Register

Corporate Register is based in the United Kingdom, and it aims to provide "the global, central reference point for all CSR related information" ("About Corporate Register," n.d.). While a majority of the content is available free to the stakeholders, a fee is charged for advanced users who need more detailed content. Some of the reports that have been provided include the following:

- An online directory of CSR/Sustainability reports
- CSR/Sustainability reporting directories for the three most significant reporting guidelines currently available: The Global Reporting Initiative, AccountAbility AA1000AS, The Global Compact
- Free directory of service providers in the CSR reporting field
- Announcement service for new CSR reports and CSR events
- Global and independent awards for CSR reporting. ("About Corporate Register," n.d.)

The two audiences for this site are the stakeholders who need to track and access CSR-related information, and companies who need to share their CSR reports and news to the global audience ("About Corporate Register," n.d.).

Carbon Disclosure Project

The **Carbon Disclosure Project (CDP)** is a not-for-profit organization that has the largest database of corporate climate change information. The data are collected from organizations that measure and disclose their GHG emissions. At present, about 2,500 organizations in 60 countries measure and disclose their emissions and climate change strategies.

The idea behind the project is that climate change is not a problem that can be contained within national boundaries. Due to this reason, climate change data are gathered from organizations worldwide in order to develop international carbon reporting standards. The reporting organizations set reduction targets and make performance improvements. In turn, these data are made available to the public.

Lord Adair Turner, chairman of the UK Financial Services Authority, said the following:

> The first step towards managing carbon emissions is to measure them because in business what gets measured gets managed. The Carbon Disclosure Project has played a crucial role in encouraging companies to take the first steps in that measurement and management path. (CDP, n.d.)

Dow Jones Sustainability Index

This index tracks the financial performance of sustainability-driven companies worldwide and was the first global index to do so. As of 2009, more than 70 **Dow Jones Sustainability Index (DJSI)** licenses are held by asset managers in 16 countries to manage a variety of financial products. In terms of total volume, these licensees manage over $8 billion based on the DJSI (DJSIs, n.d.).

Corporate Knights Global 100

Corporate Knights is a Canadian media company that publishes an annual ranking of the world's most sustainable companies called the Global 100. The 2012 list is topped by pharmaceutical maker Novo Nordisk, Brazil's Natura Cosmeticos, Norwegian energy company Statoil, the Danish biotech firm Novozymes, and ASML Holding, a Dutch manufacturer of photolithography machines used in the semiconductor industry.

Here are the criteria used to determine the Global 100—a *sustainability* ranking—for 2012:

1. Energy productivity

2. Greenhouse gas (GHG) productivity

3. Water productivity

4. Waste productivity

5. Innovation capacity

6. Percentage (%) taxes paid

7. CEO to average employee pay

8. Safety productivity

9. Employee turnover

10. Leadership diversity

11. Clean capitalism paylink (MacDonald, 2012)

The concern is that more than half of these criteria—numbers 5 through 10—"have nothing to do with sustainability" (MacDonald, 2012). It seems that "sustainability doesn't mean 'sustainability' any more—it just means all the good stuff that business does" (MacDonald, 2012). A ranking on sustainability that considers environmental performance in only half the criteria is misleading at the least.

Caveats of Reporting

What are the potential downsides of voluntary and mandatory reporting? In terms of reporting on nonfinancial performance, too many surveys and metrics can lead to low response rates that can invalidate the accuracy of the results. In addition, poor performers can design their own metrics with attractive titles, give themselves good scores, and deceive stakeholders. Another concern is that increased measurement can decrease social performance. In the case of child labor restrictions, it is assumed that children not working in factories will attend school. However, the alternative can be that the child is employed in a more dangerous industry, such as prostitution. Hence, the unintended consequences of metrics can actually *decrease* overall welfare. This drawback is an issue for many nonfinancial performances (Levine & Chatterji, 2006).

In the case of ISO 14000 standards, can weak monitoring and sanctioning systems minimize shirking behavior and improve environmental performance? Research has shown that the ISO certified facilities do manage to reduce their pollution emissions more than noncertified facilities (Potoski & Prakash, 2005). Other studies have illustrated that global diffusion of ISO 14001 standards could be due to the companies' desire to appear legitimate in the eyes of external stakeholders (Darnall, 2006). External stakeholders also play an important role in assisting firms to gain competitive advantage. Since the ISO 14001 standards focuses on processes instead of outcomes, the involvement of stakeholders facilitates the communication of credible information on the standard. In this manner, by involving external stakeholders, a company can transform certification into an organizational capability (Delmas, 2001).

Conclusion

Reporting, once considered voluntary, is now becoming a de facto requirement for most companies that are concerned about their public image. Fortunately, there are numerous standards that exist for companies to choose from—ranging from international standards such as GRI and ISO 14001 to smaller, local standards such as Ceres and DJSI. In order to illustrate gains in environmental performance, a company needs to be able to report and verify its accomplishments. In this age of media scrutiny and consumer backlash, to not do so would invite criticisms of greenwash that in turn would undermine any efforts made by the organization.

KEY WORDS

Carbon Disclosure Project (CDP)

Ceres

Corporate Knights

Corporate Register

Dow Jones Sustainability Index (DJSI)

Environmental, social, and governance (ESG) disclosures

Global Reporting Initiative (GRI)

ISO 14001

ISO 14025

ISO 14040

ISO 14064

ISO 26000

ISO standards

Pollutant-disclosure laws

Sustainability reporting

UN Global Compact

World Business Council for Sustainable Development (WBCSD)

United Nations Environment Programme (UNEP)

DISCUSSION QUESTIONS

1. What is the purpose of reporting? Why should organizations report on their performance?

2. Should reporting on sustainability be voluntary or required by law? What might be a better approach to get companies to report on sustainability?

3. Discuss the GRI standards. Browse through the list of companies that have published reports with the GRI. Do you think this list is a representative sample of companies?

4. Find a local company that follows the ISO 14000 standards. Discuss how this company implements the ISO 14001 standards.

5. What is the advantage of ISO 26000 standards for companies looking to implement social responsibility issues into their operations?

6. Go to the WBCSD website. Click on the case studies, and select any one case study to discuss.

7. Research the official website of GRI. What local area companies can you find that have published GRI reports?

8. Research a medium to large local company. Does it publish a report on sustainability—for example, a GRI report, CSR report, etc.?

9. Browse through the DJSI. What is the purpose of publishing such indices? What value is provided by this service?

10. What are the top 10 companies in the Global 100 list published by Corporate Knights. Go to the website (www.global100.org/) to determine what companies are on the list. Were you surprised by the results?

11. Which of the 10 principles of the UN Global Compact do you think would be hardest to comply with at the company you work for? Why is this the case?

RECOMMENDED CASE STUDIES

1. *The Rise of the Global Reporting Initiative (GRI) as a Case of Institutional Entrepreneurship, Corporate Social Responsibility Initiative,* Working Paper No. 36. Cambridge, MA: John F. Kennedy School of Government, Harvard University. Authors: Brown, Halina Szejnwalk, Martin de Jong, and Teodorina Lessidrenska, 2007.

2. *Novo Nordisk: A Commitment to Sustainability,* Product Number 412053-PDF-ENG. Harvard Business School Publishing.

Learning Objective: The case describes the early commitment of a European pharmaceutical company, Novo Nordisk, to integrated reporting. Novo Nordisk is one of the pioneers of integrated reporting and it emerged out of its commitment to a TBL "approach to managing the company." The case describes the company's Blueprint or Change Programme designed to facilitate stakeholder engagement and communicate how the company delivered value to business and society. The case also provides an investor perspective on the company's integrated reporting efforts and its plans for how to improve it in the future.

3. Allied Electronics Corporation Ltd: Linking Compensation to Sustainability Metrics, Prod. #: 412075-PDF-ENG, Harvard Business School Publishing.

Learning Objective: Robert Venter, second-generation chief executive of family-owned Allied Electronics Corporation Ltd. (Altron), considered the pros and cons of more clearly linking the firm's compensation system to sustainability performance. Having made a clear commitment to sustainable development, Venter was confident that the commitment was shared across the senior management team. However, there appeared to be more acceptance in the operating units for meeting financial targets than for meeting sustainability targets. Did the existing incentive structure send the correct message about the sustainability-oriented corporate strategy? Looking at the reshaped strategic themes, Venter considered the pros and cons of more clearly linking the firm's compensation system to sustainability performance.

RECOMMENDED WEBSITES

www.cdproject.net

www.ceres.org

www.corporateknights.ca

www.corporateregister.org

www.global100.org

www.globalreporting.org

www.iso.org

www.sustainability-index.com

www.unglobalcompact.org/

www.wbcsd.org

Appendix: Global Compact Speech, Kofi Annan, Secretary General, UN, January 31, 1999

Secretary-General Proposes Global Compact on Human Rights, Labour, Environment, in Address to World Economic Forum in Davos

Following is the address of Secretary-General Kofi Annan to the World Economic Forum in Davos, Switzerland, on 31 January:

I am delighted to join you again at the World Economic Forum. This is my third visit in just over two years as Secretary-General of the United Nations.

On my previous visits, I told you of my hopes for a creative partnership between the United Nations and the private sector. I made the point that the everyday work of the United Nations—whether in peacekeeping, setting technical standards, protecting intellectual property or providing much-needed assistance to developing countries—helps to expand opportunities for business around the world. And I stated quite frankly that, without your know-how and your resources, many of the objectives of the United Nations would remain elusive.

Today, I am pleased to acknowledge that, in the past two years, our relationship has taken great strides. We have shown through cooperative ventures—both at the policy level and on the ground—that the goals of the United Nations and those of business can, indeed, be mutually supportive.

This year, I want to challenge you to join me in taking our relationship to a still higher level. I propose that you, the business leaders gathered in Davos, and we, the United Nations, initiate a global compact of shared values and principles, which will give a human face to the global market.

Globalization is a fact of life. But I believe we have underestimated its fragility. The problem is this. The spread of markets outpaces the ability of societies and their political systems to adjust to them, let alone to guide the course they take. History teaches us that such an imbalance between the economic, social and political realms can never be sustained for very long.

The industrialized countries learned that lesson in their bitter and costly encounter with the Great Depression. In order to restore social harmony and political stability, they adopted social safety nets and other measures, designed to limit economic volatility and compensate the victims of market failures. That consensus made possible successive moves towards liberalization, which brought about the long post-war period of expansion.

Our challenge today is to devise a similar compact on the global scale, to underpin the new global economy. If we succeed in that, we would lay the foundation for an age of global prosperity, comparable to that enjoyed by the industrialized countries in the decades after the Second World War. Specifically, I call on you—individually through your firms, and collectively through your business associations—to embrace, support and enact a set of core values in the areas of human rights, labour standards, and environmental practices.

Why those three? In the first place, because they are all areas where you, as businessmen and women, can make a real difference. Secondly, they are areas in which universal values have already been defined by international agreements, including the Universal Declaration, the International Labour Organization's Declaration on fundamental principles and rights at work, and the Rio Declaration of the United Nations Conference on Environment and Development in 1992. Finally, I choose these three areas because they are ones where I fear that, if we do not act, there may be a threat to the open global market, and especially to the multilateral trade regime.

There is enormous pressure from various interest groups to load the trade regime and investment agreements with restrictions aimed at preserving standards in the three areas I have just mentioned. These are legitimate concerns. But restrictions on trade and investment are not the right means to use when tackling them. Instead, we should find a way to achieve our proclaimed standards by other means. And that is precisely what the compact I am proposing to you is meant to do.

Essentially there are two ways we can do it. One is through the international policy arena. You can encourage States to give us, the multilateral institutions of which they are all members, the resources and the authority we need to do our job.

The United Nations as a whole promotes peace and development, which are prerequisites for successfully meeting social and environmental goals alike. And the International Labour Organization, the United Nations High Commissioner for Human Rights and the United Nations Environmental Programme strive to improve labour conditions, human rights and environmental quality. We hope, in the future, to count you as our allies in these endeavours.

The second way you can promote these values is by taking them directly, by taking action in your own corporate sphere. Many of you are big investors, employers and producers in dozens of different countries across the world. That power brings with it great opportunities—and great responsibilities.

You can uphold human rights and decent labour and environmental standards directly, by your own conduct of your own business.

Indeed, you can use these universal values as the cement binding together your global corporations, since they are values people all over the world will recognize as their own. You can make sure that in your own corporate practices you uphold and respect human rights; and that you are not yourselves complicit in human rights abuses.

Don't wait for every country to introduce laws protecting freedom of association and the right to collective bargaining. You can at least make sure your own employees, and those of your subcontractors, enjoy those rights. You can at least make sure that you yourselves are not employing under-age children or forced labour, either directly or indirectly. And you can make sure that, in your own hiring and firing policies, you do not discriminate on grounds of race, creed, gender or ethnic origin.

You can also support a precautionary approach to environmental challenges. You can undertake initiatives to promote greater environmental responsibility. And you can encourage the development and diffusion of environmentally friendly technologies.

That, ladies and gentlemen, is what I am asking of you. But what, you may be asking yourselves, am I offering in exchange? Indeed, I believe the United Nations system does have something to offer.

The United Nations agencies—the United Nations High Commissioner for Human Rights, the International Labour Organization (ILO), the United Nations Environment

Programme (UNEP)—all stand ready to assist you, if you need help, in incorporating these agreed values and principles into your mission statements and corporate practices. And we are ready to facilitate a dialogue between you and other social groups, to help find viable solutions to the genuine concerns that they have raised. You may find it useful to interact with us through our newly created website, www.un.org/partners, which offers a "one-stop shop" for corporations interested in the United Nations. More important, perhaps, is what we can do in the political arena, to help make the case for and maintain an environment which favours trade and open markets.

I believe what I am proposing to you is a genuine compact, because neither side of it can succeed without the other. Without your active commitment and support, there is a danger that universal values will remain little more than fine words—documents whose anniversaries we can celebrate and make speeches about, but with limited impact on the lives of ordinary people. And unless those values are really seen to be taking hold, I fear we may find it increasingly difficult to make a persuasive case for the open global market.

National markets are held together by shared values. In the face of economic transition and insecurity, people know that if the worst comes to the worst, they can rely on the expectation that certain minimum standards will prevail. But in the global market, people do not yet have that confidence. Until they do have it, the global economy will be fragile and vulnerable—vulnerable to backlash from all the "isms" of our post-cold-war world: protectionism; populism; nationalism; ethnic chauvinism; fanaticism; and terrorism.

What all those "isms" have in common is that they exploit the insecurity and misery of people who feel threatened or victimized by the global market. The more wretched and insecure people there are, the more those "isms" will continue to gain ground. What we have to do is find a way of embedding the global market in a network of shared values. I hope I have suggested some practical ways for us to set about doing just that.

Let us remember that the global markets and multilateral trading system we have today did not come about by accident. They are the result of enlightened policy choices made by governments since 1945. If we want to maintain them in the new century, all of us—governments, corporations, non-governmental organizations, international organizations—have to make the right choices now.

We have to choose between a global market driven only by calculations of short-term profit, and one which has a human face. Between a world which condemns a quarter of the human race to starvation and squalor, and one which offers everyone at least a chance of prosperity, in a healthy environment. Between a selfish free-for-all in which we ignore the fate of the losers, and a future in which the strong and successful accept their responsibilities, showing global vision and leadership.

I am sure you will make the right choice.

Source: UN Press Release SG/SM/6881, 1 February 1999 entitled Secretary-General proposes global compact on human rights, labour, environment, in address to world economic forum in Davos accessed on October 29, 2012, at http://www.un.org/News/Press/docs/1999/19990201.sgsm6881.html

Table Classifying Various ISO 14000 Standards

Table 10.2 ISO Standards			
Plan	Do	Check	Act
Environmental management system implementation	**Conduct life cycle assessment and manage environmental aspects**	**Conduct audits and evaluate environmental performance**	**Communicate and use environmental declarations and claims**
ISO 14050:2009 Environmental management – Vocabulary	ISO 14040:2006 Environmental management – Life cycle assessment – Principles and framework	ISO 14015:2001 Environmental management – Environmental assessment of sites and organizations (EASO)	ISO 14020:2000 Environmental labels and declarations – General principles
ISO 14001:2004 Environmental management systems – Requirements with guidance for use	ISO 14044:2006 Environmental management – Life cycle assessment – Requirements and guidelines	ISO 14031:1999 Environmental management – Environmental performance evaluation – Guidelines	ISO 14021:1999 Enviromental labels and declarations – Self-declared environmental claims (Type II environmental labelling)
ISO 14004:2004 Environmental management systems – General guidelines on principles, systems and support techniques	ISO/TR 14047:2003 Environmental management – Life cycle impact assessment – Examples of application of ISO 14042	Guidelines for quality and/or environmental management systems auditing	ISO 14024:1999 Environmental labels and declarations – Type I environmental labelling – Principles and procedures
ISO/DIS 14005 Environmental management systems – Guidelines for the phased	ISO/TS 14048:2002 Environmental management – Life cycle assessment – Data documentation format		ISO 14025:2006 Environmental labels and declarations – Type III environmental

(Continued)

Table 10.2 (Continued)

Plan	Do	Check	Act
implementation of an environmental management system, including the use of environmental performance evaluation			declarations – Principles and procedures
			ISO/AWI 14033 Environmental management – Quantitative environmental information – Guidelines and examples
Address environmental aspects in products and product standards		**Evaluate greenhouse gas performance**	
ISO Guide 64:2008 Guide for addressing environmental issues in product standards	ISO/TR 14049:2000 Environmental management – Life cycle assessment – Examples of application of ISO 14041 to goal and scope definition and inventory analysis	ISO 14064-3:2006 Greenhouse gases – Part 3: Specification with guidance for the validation and verification of greenhouse gas assertions	ISO 14063:2006 Environmental management – Environmental communication – Guidelines and examples
ISO/CD 14006 Environmental management systems – Guidelines on eco-design	ISO/CD 14051 Environmental management – Material flow cost accounting – General principles and framework	ISO 14065:2007 Greenhouse gases – Requirements for greenhouse gas validation and verification bodies for use in accreditation or other forms of recognition	
	ISO/WD 14045 Eco-efficiency assessment – Principles and requirements		

Plan	Do	Check	Act
	Manage greenhouse gases		
ISO/TR 14062:2002 Environmental management – Integrating environmental aspects into product design and development	ISO 14064-1:2006 Greenhouse gases – Part 1: Specification with guidance at the organization level for quantification and reporting of greenhouse gas emissions and removals	ISO/CD 14066 Greenhouse gases – Competency requirements for greenhouse gas validators and verifiers document	
	ISO 14064-2:2006 Greenhouse gases – Part 2: Specification with guidance at the project level for quantification, monitoring and reporting of greenhouse gas emission reductions or removal enhancements		
	ISO/WD 14067-1 Carbon footprint of products – Part 1: Quantification ISO/WD 14067-2 Carbon footprint of products – Part 2: Communication		
	ISO/AWI 14069 GHG – Quantification and reporting of GHG emissions for organizations (Carbon footprint of organization) – Guidance for the application of ISO 14064–1		

11

Carbon Markets
Offsets and Standards

LEARNING OBJECTIVES

By the end of this chapter, you should be able to do the following:

- Present the concept of carbon neutrality.
- Explain the **Kyoto Protocol.**
- Discuss the details of carbon markets.
- Compare and contrast the various types of offsets.
- Present the market standards.
- Discuss proceedings of **Conference of the Parties (COP17)** Durban.

Chapter Overview

This chapter discusses the concept of carbon neutrality and then presents the state of the carbon markets including the mandate from the Kyoto Protocol. We examine the concept of carbon offsets and provide examples of the market. The purpose of the chapter is to present the logic and the working of carbon markets—especially in the space of market instruments aimed at lowering of carbon emissions. How did this market develop, and where is it headed? Why does this market spark such heated debates? Does it encourage people to change consumption habits or merely provide a quick fix? We will then discuss carbon offsets in detail and extend the discussion to carbon standards.

Carbon Footprint

All of us have a **carbon footprint,** a measure of our energy and resource consumption. The more water we use, the more food we eat, the more energy we consume, the higher our footprint. Many of us love to travel, but to get somewhere requires fuel, whether by car or by plane. Some environ- mentally conscious individuals feel tremendous guilt over consuming resources and assuage this guilt by contributing an offsetting donation of some sort—perhaps to plant a tree somewhere. Critics of this practice argue that it is simply a drop in the proverbial bucket.

Carbon Neutrality

Companies and consumers are pursuing **carbon neutral** status increasingly and at a surprisingly fast rate. The term *carbon neutral* was chosen as the word of the year in 2006 by the *New Oxford American Dictionary,* and thousands of new green companies have emerged in the past couple years (Main, 2007). Yet beyond the clear social value component, how does this movement relate to company performance and the generation of market value? The movement is concerned with lowering carbon waste on the earth. Carbon offsetting builds on this idea by adjusting operations in a company or the activities of individuals to achieve this goal. Yet it is not clear how well the carbon neutral movement delivers what it promises.

There are five basic steps to achieving carbon neutrality. The first step is to assess a carbon footprint. There are numerous web-based calculators that let individuals and corporations estimate their footprint (see the appendix). The second step is to implement emissions reductions measures such as conservation and energy efficiency. Then, the third step is to com- pute the remaining carbon emissions. At the fourth step, offsets are pur- chased for the remaining amount in the previous step. Finally, the fifth step is to communicate carbon neutrality to the market. This step is mostly applicable to public companies or corporations (Trexler Climate + Energy Services, Inc., 2006).

The concept of being carbon neutral offers the participants an opportu- nity to take personal responsibility for the global warming implications of their lifestyles. Rather than merely discussing scenarios of climate change, it offers an opportunity to be part of a solution. In this context, environmental commodity markets and retail markets for voluntary carbon neutrality pro- vide many solutions for participants. Both markets are still seeking broader public interest. For instance, there are no widely accepted standards of what qualifies as an offset. As an intangible commodity, it is difficult for an envi- ronmentally conscious consumer to make a distinction between a high and low quality offset.

Two Basic Options

What are the various options available to reduce emissions? Depending upon the regulatory history, these options can fall under two categories: (1) command and control and (2) market-based options.

Command and Control Strategies

In this category, the policies are either mandated by the government or a regulatory agency in the form of taxes, subsidies, caps, or targets. In this case, the emissions could be taxed or a subsidy is provided to encourage adoption of clean technology. An example is a carbon tax being discussed in the European Union.

Market-Based Solutions

The second category is market-based solutions that are primarily driven by industry or consumers, and these include emission permits, carbon allowances, pollution offsets, and others. An example would be emission permits that are exchanged between companies in order to meet the quota of emissions. The market drives the exchange whereby a highly polluting company could purchase permits to cover its excess emissions, and a clean company could sell the excess permits in the market. Some of the other approaches include allowances and offsets to cover the carbon usage of an individual or a corporation.

Research has shown that market-based solutions might be the most efficient method for cutting emissions and achieving sustainability (Dhanda, 1999). However, one of most common criticisms toward market-based solutions is that these are unethical by nature. The argument goes that these approaches actually allow companies to pay for emissions and get away with their behavior rather than curtailing back and cutting emissions. This is a point of contention for most of the passionate proponents of the environmental movement.

Kyoto Protocol

The **United Nations Framework Convention on Climate Change (UNFCCC)** was created in response to the growing international concern about the effects of global warming due to human activities. The Kyoto Treaty is the Kyoto Protocol to the UNFCCC and was negotiated in December 1997 at the city of Kyoto, Japan. Essentially, the Kyoto Protocol is a legally binding agreement that states that industrialized countries will reduce their collective emissions of greenhouse gases (GHGs), carbon dioxide, methane, nitrous oxide, sulfur hexafluoride, hydrofluorocarbons (HFCs), and perfluorocarbons (PFCs), by 5.2% compared to the year 1990 ("The Kyoto Protocol," n.d.).

The U.S. position on the Kyoto Protocol has been a subject of controversy and frustration amongst the international community. The United States is a member of the UNFCCC, and it signed the Kyoto Protocol in 1998. However, the United States has not ratified the protocol. In other words, the U.S. position is that it supports the protocol but does not want to be held if its emissions targets are not met.

Why does the United States not support the Kyoto Treaty? There are two main reasons. The first reason is that the United States wants the developing countries to be included in the treaty. At present, the United States is the largest emitter of GHGs. However, developing countries like China, Brazil, and India are anticipated to surpass the U.S. emissions in the next 25 to 30 years. Another concern is that the treaty might have a negative impact on the U.S. economy (Mathews, 2000). According to estimates, if the United States were to adhere to carbon reduction targets, the gross domestic product (GDP) losses might be in the range of 1/2 to 2% by 2020 ("The Kyoto Protocol Summary," n.d.).

> Kyoto includes "flexible mechanisms" which allow Annex I economies to meet their greenhouse gas emission limitation by purchasing GHG emission reductions from elsewhere. These can be bought either from financial exchanges, from projects which reduce emissions in non-Annex I economies under the Clean Development Mechanism (CDM), from other Annex 1 countries under the JI, or from Annex I countries with excess allowances. Only CDM Executive Board-accredited Certified Emission Reductions (CER) can be bought and sold in this manner. Under the aegis of the UN, Kyoto established this Bonn-based Clean Development Mechanism Executive Board to assess and approve projects ("CDM Projects") in Non-Annex I economies prior to awarding CERs. (A similar scheme called "Joint Implementation" or "JI" applies in transitional economies mainly covering the former Soviet Union and Eastern Europe). ("The Mechanisms under the Kyoto Protocol," n.d.)

The Kyoto Protocol offers certified emission reductions (CERs) as part of its flexible mechanism. The Kyoto Protocol allows "flexible mechanisms" to Annex I countries to meet limitations by purchasing or buying GHG emission reductions elsewhere. One of these flexible mechanisms is the clean development mechanism (CDM) wherein a CER can be traded by countries in order to meet GHG limitations. There, CERs are board certified and have to follow a rigorous process of assessment and approval. These trades are highly bureaucratic, and as a result, the transaction costs tend to escalate.

The carbon market falls into two categories: (1) the **cap and trade system** and (2) the **offset carbon market**. The cap and trade system includes countries that have ratified the Kyoto Protocol. The companies receive credits that they can sell when they emit less than the set limit. In the offset space, the emissions reductions can be voluntary or compulsory in nature. The compulsory offsets would be those recognized by Kyoto Protocol and are labeled CERs. The voluntary carbon market is voluntary carbon offsets, and the offsets sold are also called gourmet offsets since these offsets are in a class of their own. Clean Air-Cool Planet's (CA-CP) "A Consumer's Guide to Retail Carbon Offset Providers" (Trexler Climate + Energy Services, Inc., 2006) provides a ranking of offsetting companies based on factors like transparency, third-party **certification,** efforts to educate consumers, and proof that they're not selling the same carbon offset more than once. The ranking is an effort to create some **standardization.**

Carbon Offsets

Carbon offsetting occurs when an individual or organization pays a third party to reduce the emissions of GHGs on its behalf. Organizations or individuals as varied as the International Federation of Association Football (FIFA), the musical band the Rolling Stones, and former U.S. vice president Al Gore have served to increase the demand for offsetting (Gore, 2007). The specific way the transaction works involves the buyer paying a dollar amount to the third party to support projects that sequester carbon from the atmosphere. The result is a unit reduction for a given amount of carbon.

In Chicago, many corporations that emitted carbon had joined the Chicago Climate Exchange (CCX), which required them to offset or eliminate 6% of their emissions by 2010. As of 2006, there were 210 in the membership, including Motorola, DuPont, and Ford. Some of the heaviest emitters, such as British Petroleum (BP) and British Airways, had taken the offset model in house by purchasing offsets and passing the costs to consumers or even encouraging customers to engage in their own offsetting. For instance, CCX claimed that many of its members joined to improve their image, to gain insight into a nascent industry, to prepare for future regulation, and to appease their shareholders, customers, and staff (*The Economist,* 2006b). The value to these companies can come in several forms, which are reflected in different kinds of offsetting.

Rationale

The concept of carbon neutrality has been around for at least a decade. One of the very first companies to reduce and neutralize its GHG footprint was Stonyfield Farms. More recently, there has been a surge of interest in carbon neutrality. Rather than a few individuals or companies doing the right thing, this phenomenon has morphed into an environmental commodity market. There are many companies willing to help one calculate carbon footprints and sell offsets (Trexler Climate + Energy Services, Inc., 2006). *BusinessWeek* estimates that the trade in offsets accounts for more than $100 million a year, and it is growing (Revkin, 2007).

The goal is emissions reduction via energy efficiency, conservation, technology, re-engineering, and greener buildings. Only when further reductions can no longer take place due to technology or monetary constraints does the option to buy offsets emerge. The goal, therefore, is really to "offset" what could not be *reduced*. Of course, offsets do not make a difference if reductions are not undertaken, but they also play a role in educating and informing the public about climate change and demonstrating that the issue is ripe for public policy.

Principal Types

Offset providers usually offer three types: carbon dioxide offsets, renewable energy credits (RECs), and cap and trade. Carbon dioxide offsets are sponsored projects usually sold by the ton and designed to reduce or eliminate GHGs in the atmosphere. Common examples of these projects are reforestation projects, carbon sequestration, methane abatement, and the development of energy efficient technologies. Here, the greatest issue is verification of ownership since offsets are saleable numerous times to different parties. Another challenge is one of permanence—whether the change created by the offset will stay intact—especially in the case of carbon sequestration. Even on natural grounds, the carbon absorbed by a tree in its lifetime is released back into the atmosphere once the tree dies (Main, 2007).

RECs are also referred to as green tags. They represent 1 megawatt hour (mWh) of renewable energy production. The most common examples are wind farms, solar farms, and biogas generators. The most relevant inefficiencies in this market are verifiable ownership and whether the project would have taken place without the required investment (Main, 2007). Cap and trade offsets are known as "emission trading schemes," or "pooled carbon commodities." The participants in these offsets commit to reducing GHG emissions to a certain level. Upon reaching this level, further reductions can be sold or traded in form of certificates. Active entities in this area include CCX, CDM under Kyoto, and the European Trading Scheme (ETS). These certificates of cap and trade offsets are traded like stocks.

There has been a flurry of activity in the market for carbon offsets. Participation in this market is voluntary in nature, and the buyers of offsets range from individuals to nonprofit groups to corporate entities. There are also many different sellers of offsets such as firms, charities, nongovernmental organizations (NGOs), community groups, and international agencies. Some examples of various offsets are to plant trees, prevent trees from being cut down, and replace fuel-guzzling stoves. The cost of offsets varies as well from some studies stating that it ranges from a few cents to $27 per ton of carbon dioxide (*The Economist*, 2006b) to other studies claiming it ranges from $5 to $35 per ton of carbon dioxide (Business for Social Responsibility [BSR], 2006).

Carbon Footprint Calculator

As an illustration, let's see how a carbon calculator works. As an example, consider the website Carbon Footprint (www.carbonfootprint.com/). This is one of the numerous carbon calculators available that let an individual (or a business) calculate his or her carbon footprint. This calculator is comprehensive in that it allows one to compute the footprint in each of the following areas: house, flights, car, motorbike, bus and rail, secondary (food consumption, recycling, etc.). Then it computes the results.

For example, if you own a car, you can enter the mileage and choose the vehicle to determine the footprint. As an example, one can find the carbon footprint of one's car as follows:

Mileage: 20,000

Year (of make): 2010

Manufacturer: Honda

Model: Civic

Derivative: 1.8 cylinder, automatic

Upon entering the data, the calculator yields a total car footprint of 6.03 metric tons that, in turn, can then be offset. One can also use this calculator to find the carbon footprint of an upcoming flight. As an example, one can compute the carbon footprint for a flight from Chicago to London as follows:

From: Chicago (ORD)

To: London (LHR)

Via (optional): Direct

Class: Economy

Trips: One

Upon entering this data, the calculator yields 1.13 metric tons per leg for a total of 2.25 metric tons. Furthermore, this website allows one to offset the footprint by purchasing offsets from a range of projects involving reforestation in Kenya (about $30) to Clean Energy Portfolios (about $13). As an example, in this particular case, each ton of carbon dioxide offset results in the planting of one native tree in Kenya or the United Kingdom.

Carbon Offset Examples

The hospitality industry is gaining popularity for its carbon offsetting. Even among the consumers, travelers can neutralize their trips with carbon offsets. This option involves calculating a carbon footprint for flights and road trips and then purchasing offsets that donate money to projects that promise to produce energy without burning fossil fuels. The reduction equals the amount of carbon the trip created per passenger with the goal being to have a carbon neutral journey.

Many companies offer carbon offsets to consumers. For example, Travelocity.com offers an option to neutralize the environmental impact of trips by planting trees. REI Adventures offsets its carbon emissions produced by air, water, and ground transportation through a contract with an external provider. In their case, each trip has "green tags" for RECs. The external provider, Bonneville, claims to be selling 500,000 RECs every year (Conlin, 2007). Though it is unclear how much impact these programs have on climate change, travelers see this option as a way to help tackle climate change without having to give up their trips (Higgins, 2006). Silverjet, a luxury airline, claimed to be the first carbon neutral airline. Silverjet used to offset 1.2 tons of carbon per passenger and put a cash equivalent of $28 into a fund for green projects. Though Silverjet ceased operations in 2008, other companies (HSBC, Google) are continuing this tradition and are making carbon neutrality part of their brand identity (Braden, 2006).

Beyond individual travel, some companies offset travel expenses. For example, HSBC bought more than $3 million in offsets to achieve carbon neutrality for business travel. Swiss Re aims to reduce business travel by encouraging employees to use calling and videoconferencing.

Whereas advocates believe offsetting builds awareness for emissions control, critics think it is an easy way for those who do not want to change consumer or operational habits (Richardson, 2006). This area is largely unregulated, and there is a problem with potential fraud (Velasquez-Manoff, 2007). There is no current certification or monitoring system that can confirm what offsetting companies promised to do. Another major concern is that some of the companies are engaging in *greenwashing,* or attempting to appear green without actually changing the underlying behavior (Braden, 2006).

Pros:

- Makes economic sense
- Easy to adopt
- Social/individual involvement
- Voluntary market
- Corporate image
- Builds awareness

Cons on Moral Grounds:

- Easy on sacrifice and big on consumerism
- No need to change lifestyle
- Purchase forgiveness with money
- Morality argument: allowing wealthy individuals or organizations to buy themselves out of responsibility to reduce emissions

Cons on Policy Side:

- Market in climate neutrality can blunt public support for binding limits on emission or a tax on GHG fuels
- Introduction or development of greener and cleaner technologies might be hindered
- Flawed principle: gives the impression that the people in rich countries need not change their lifestyle to reduce global warming

Market Performance Criteria

The offset market makes economic sense in that market signals lead to economical offset projects. It is an easy market to enter since all that is required is a computation of the carbon footprint and the amount entailed for the offset. There is also an opportunity for social or individual involvement. Furthermore, it is a voluntary market that builds awareness for a pressing global concern. Companies participate to create a positive corporate image (*The Economist*, 2006b; Russell, 2007).

There are two basic concerns with the market. The first is on moral grounds. It can be reasoned that offsets are "easy on sacrifice and big on consumerism." That is, there is no need to change lifestyle since consumers can "purchase forgiveness with money." In essence, the morality argument is about allowing wealthy individuals or organizations to buy themselves out of responsibility to reduce emissions (*The Economist*, 2006a; DePalma, 2006; Friedman, 2007; Revkin, 2007; Richardson, 2006; Russell, 2007).

The second concern is on policy grounds. A market in climate neutrality can blunt public support for binding limits on emissions. It can also tax fuels and hinder the introduction or development of greener and cleaner technologies. In addition, there are concerns that the market is based on a flawed principle in that it gives the impression that the people in rich countries need not change their lifestyle to reduce global warming (Revkin, 2007).

As with any new market, there are numerous uncertainties that exist in the functioning. The first glaring point is the **price differential** of the offsets, and the variation can be rather confusing for consumers. The second point is the uncertainty as to whether the emissions reductions in a project are verifiable or not. In a worst-case scenario, it is possible to double count the offset wherein a provider could sell a single credit numerous times. Since this market is voluntary in nature, the certifications are done arbitrarily, and there is no standardization on these certifications. Buyers and developers of offsets need to set a baseline to be used to predict emissions that would occur in case the project did not go ahead. Finally, some of the projects are questionable in nature due to natural decay and destruction, which leads to the issue of insurance guarantees.

Next, some of these uncertainties in the market as they concern the market performance criteria are detailed. These six uncertainties are (1) **quality of projects**, (2) **additionality**, (3) certification and standardization, (4) **ownership**, (5) price differential, and (6) transparency.

Quality of Projects

Project quality is crucial in the offset market. For example, tree planting was a popular offset project since trees act as carbon sinks through the process of carbon sequestration. However, trees are subject to decay and destruction. This happened to the offset project of a mango plantation in India for the band Coldplay, who had purchased the offset for their on-tour flights. As a result, offset providers are moving away from this option (Russell, 2007). Whereas, forestry used to account for 100% of carbon neutral's portfolio 2 years ago, it is now down to 20%. The destruction of ecosystems accounts for about one fifth of carbon emissions worldwide (Revkin, 2007).

Additionality

It is important to prove to buyers that a project would not have happened without investment. In other words, the energy savings made should be additional to those that are "business as usual" to count as an offset. Under the CDM of the Kyoto Protocol, there are three criteria accepted as basis for project additionality. The project must not be required by current regulation; the technologies are not common practice; and economic, technological, or investment barriers must offset resources. A baseline can predict emissions that would occur if the project did not go ahead. In the CDM market, for instance, there are about 60 methodologies alone. However, a lack of standardization in these methodologies plagues the offset market (Russell, 2007).

Certification and Standardization

There has been an increase in the demand for an independent standard because of diminishing confidence in the burgeoning market. Several standards have been established that can cause confusion. For instance, the GHG reduction certification standard sets the criteria and GHG reduction projects must meet this to gain a Green-e certificate (Green-e Climate Standard, 2007). Some of the criteria include disclosing detailed information, submitting to periodic independent reviews, and being reviewed by independent parties.

This standard has generated concerns that rival international standards will confuse consumers. The aim is to develop a transparent standard about the emissions that are being reduced. One practitioner in the industry (Michael Buick of Climate Care) believes better standards will survive in the longer run (BusinessGreen blog, 2007).

Ownership

Ownership of offsets is unchartered territory. The price range exhibits a wide variation, there is uncertainty whether the emissions reductions in a project are verifiable, and it is possible to sell a single credit numerous times leading to double counting. Hence, buyers must be assured of the sole ownership of purchased offsets. There needs to be an assurance from the offset providers that the same offset is not being sold multiple times and to different parties. Evidence that ownership is not an issue is becoming an important market performance criterion.

Price Differential

The majority of the offsets purchased worldwide are CERs, and the estimated value is $2.7 billion. The CDM market, within which the CERs are traded, is bureaucratic and has high transaction costs. On the other hand, the market in voluntary offsets is fragmented with prices ranging from $1 to $20 per ton of carbon dioxide. The projects supported range from planting trees in Tanzania to building hydroelectricity plants in Bulgaria and the price differential is primarily due to the quality of the offset project.

Transparency

It is becoming more important to ask providers to give clear information and transparent prices for offsets. This idea is transcending current CDM standards based on certified carbon credits. Voluntary offsets go toward small-scale, local community-based renewable energy projects and high transaction costs of CDM rule such projects out. Thus, voluntary offsets can succeed where the CDM fails but those smaller markets still would require a degree of regulation (Russell, 2007).

Standards for Offsets

Carbon offsets are an intangible good and, as such, their value and integrity depend entirely on how they are defined, represented, and guaranteed. What the market lacks are common standards for how such representations and guarantees are made and enforced. (Broekhoff, 2007)

There are over a dozen standards to verify the legitimacy of an offset provider by numerous combinations of metrics, and no one seems to be able to agree on a valid combination by which to measure providers. If there remains no agreement on a set of standards to which offset providers should be held, how can we even begin to judge whether a corporation has achieved carbon neutrality by using any of these providers?

In the end, the market will likely demand uniform standards or registries in order to vouch for the legitimacy of the purchased offsets (Hamilton, Bayon, Turner, & Higgins, 2007). Moreover, there has been an increase in the demand for a consistent and independent standard because of the uncertainties previously outlined that threaten to diminish confidence in the market. The most effective standards will be those that are clear and rigorous and have broad support from a wide spectrum of stakeholders, ranging from carbon offset project developers to offset traders and buyers from environmental nongovernmental organizations (ENGOs) to the financial industry. The types of standards that currently exist in the voluntary emissions reduction market will be discussed followed by an analysis of the offset providers that strive to meet these standards.

There are three types of standards and certifications in the voluntary carbon offset market. The first category of standards certify the quality of an offset and the projects that it supports. Examples of this type of standard would include the **Voluntary Carbon Standard (VCS)** (now the Verified Carbon Standard); the **Gold Standard; Plan Vivo;** and the Climate, Community, and Biodiversity Standard. A second category of standard focuses on the certification of offset sellers, products, services, and their claims relating to carbon neutrality. Standards that include this certification include Green-e GHG Product Standard, Defra's Guidelines, and the Climate Neutral Network. A third category of standards has been developed by the offset retailers themselves in order to ensure quality within their own portfolios. Examples of these types of standards include the Carbon Neutral Company and MyClimate. While the intent of these retailers may be laudable, there seems to be an apparent conflict of interest inherent in a self-imposed standard structure, and accordingly, these standards are likely to phase out as the market matures (Hamilton et al., 2007).

According to a comprehensive analysis conducted by Kollmuss, Zink, and Polycarp (2008), an inclusive, complete, and credible carbon offset standard must include the following three components:

1. *Accounting standards*: To ensure that offsets are "real, additional, and permanent" (p. 14).

2. *Monitoring, verification, and certification standards*: To ensure that the projects perform according to project design and to quantify the actual carbon savings that happen once the project is up and running.

3. *Registration and enforcement systems*: To ensure that carbon offsets are only sold once, to clarify ownership, and to enable trading of offsets. The offsets must include a registry with publicly available information in order to uniquely identify offset projects as well as a system by which to track transparently the ownership of those offsets.

In order to apply the Kollmuss components, the three reports that detailed the standards: (1) the Kollmuss report, itself, (2) a Business for Social Responsibility (BSR) report (2006), and (3) an analysis by Hamilton, Sjardin, Marcello, and Xu (2008) were analyzed. The four standards most commonly listed in the three reports reviewed include the Gold Standard, the VCS 2007, the **Voluntary Offset Standard (VOS)**, and Plan Vivo.

- The Gold Standard requires that each carbon offset project that bears its certification demonstrate social and environmental benefits and have a well-developed stakeholder engagement process. The Gold Standard can be applied to voluntary offset projects as well as to the CDM standard projects under the compulsory Kyoto Protocol system.
- The VCS 2007 focuses only on GHG reduction attributes and, in a significant departure from other schemes, does *not* require projects to

have additional environmental or social benefits. The VCS 2007 is broadly supported by the carbon offset industry (i.e., project developers, large offset buyers, verifiers, projects consultants).

- The VOS is a carbon offset screen that accepts other standards and methodologies using its own specific screening criteria. It currently accepts Gold Standard's voluntary emissions reductions projects, as well as projects that employ CDM procedures but are implemented in countries that have not ratified the Kyoto Protocol and are therefore not eligible for CDM.

- Plan Vivo is an offset project method for small-scale land use, land-use change, and forestry (LULUCF) projects with a focus on promoting sustainable development and improving rural livelihoods and ecosystems. Plan Vivo works very closely with rural communities and emphasizes participatory design, ongoing stakeholder consultation, and the use of native species.

Examination of Offset Providers

In order to best understand the needs of the consumer market in terms of information overloads and gaps, it is vital to engage in a comparative content analysis of published reports that provide information or ratings on offsets. The reports that were publicly available to consumers and free of charge were accessed in order to ensure that these reports would be available to the average person seeking information. Four reports met these criteria:

1. *A Consumer's Guide to Retail Carbon Offset Providers*, by Trexler Climate + Energy Services (2006)

2. *Carbon Offsets in Context*, by the Context Group (2006)

3. *Voluntary Offsets for Air-Travel Carbon Emissions*, by Tufts Climate Initiative (Kollmuss & Bowell, 2006)

4. Carbon Offset Providers Evaluation Matrix, by Carbon Concierge (2008)

The first report was written primarily for the average consumer. It provides several criteria by which it evaluates and ranks 30 retail providers. Each retail provider was then assigned a score between one and ten. The *Consumer's Guide* lists eight companies that scored more than 5.0 on their rankings. These eight companies are as follows:

1. AgCert/DrivingGreen

2. Atmosfair

3. CarbonNeutral Company

4. Climate Care

5. Climate Trust

6. CO2balance

7. NativeEnergy

8. Sustainable Travel/MyClimate

The *Consumer's Guide* identifies the seven evaluative criteria that it used in its ranking, along with the respective weights assigned. These criteria with the weights are found in Table 11.1.

Some of the other criteria that are not used in the ranking process but that are discussed in the report include the cost of the offset to the consumer, the for-profit versus non-for-profit status of the providers, and the proportion of the funding that goes to the offsets. In addition, there is no discussion of the basis for the weights given. The *Consumer's Guide* was one of the first reports compiled on carbon offsets. The report analyzes only 30 companies; however, it was completed in 2006, and since that time, there have been numerous other providers entering the market so the report is unfortunately outdated.

Carbon Offsets in Context identifies 23 organizations. The report shares information gathered from websites and provides information on key activities, role in offset market, type of offset provided, guidelines/verification, and geography of portfolio. In addition, this report also provides information on turnover/total carbon dioxide offset, year since the company was operational, whether the site has a carbon calculator, the cost per ton of carbon, and a list of external partners. The primary drawback of this report is that there is no rationale provided on the selection of the 23 organizations

Table 11.1 The Seven Criteria and Weights Used by *Consumer's Guide*

Consumer's Guide Evaluative Ranking Criteria and Respective Weights	
Providers' prioritization of offset quality	10.0
Buyers ability to transparently evaluate offset quality	9.4
Transparency in provider operations and offset selection	9.2
Providers' understanding of technical aspects of offset quality	9.0
Priority assigned by provider to educating consumers about global warming and global warming policy	7.8
Ancillary environmental and sustainable development benefits of offset portfolios	5.6
Use of third-party project protocols and certification	3.9

Source: Clean Air-Cool Planet (2006).

analyzed; furthermore, there is no mention of any methodology used. It simply lists the 23 companies (mostly taken from the United Kingdom) and the data collected from the respective websites. Hence, it could be viewed as a brief report giving a snapshot on the activities of these 23 companies.

The third report, *Voluntary Offsets for Air-Travel Carbon Emissions,* is specifically directed to consumers interested in companies that offer programs to address the effects of air travel, which severely limits its coverage in terms of providers. The 13 companies that it includes are listed here with the "highest recommended" offered to 4 of 13:

1. Atmosfair (highest recommendation)

2. Better World Club

3. CarbonCounter.org

4. Carbonfund.org

5. The Carbon Neutral Company

6. Cleanairpass

7. Climate Care

8. Climate Friendly (highest recommendation)

9. MyClimate (highest recommendation)

10. NativeEnergy (highest recommendation)

11. Offsetters

12. Solar Electric Light Fund

13. Terrapass

This report evaluated its subject companies along six criteria:

1. Overhead

2. Quality of offsets

3. Standards and verification

4. Air travel emissions calculator

5. Price per ton of carbon offset

6. Transparency

Finally, the *Carbon Offset Providers Evaluation Matrix* rates offset providers using its "evaluation matrix," which is comprised of eight criteria. An offset provider is awarded a score of 3 (poor), 6 (good), or 9 (excellent) based on an overview of each provider's website and—where insufficient information is available online—information from the providers themselves. The eight criteria are as follows:

1. Business and project transparency

2. Offset quality

3. Project location and offset traceability

4. Industry leadership

5. Business model and program services ratio

6. Third-party evaluation

7. Education

8. Social benefit

Results are calculated for 17 providers in North America, and the companies rated highest by this report were Native Energy and Climate Trust. Interestingly, on the whole, the rated providers scored highest in the categories of third-party evaluation and for business and project transparency. The lowest scores were found in project location, offset traceability, and business model and program services ratio. While this report is one of the most current and quite comprehensive in its content, it discusses only 17 North American companies, including three wholesalers, an extremely small segment of today's offset provider market.

Based on this overview, it appears that there is great demand, therefore, for current information on a larger number of providers across common criteria where contentions have generally arisen.

Conference of the Parties (COP17) Durban

The seventeenth session of the COP to the UNFCCC was held at the UN Climate Change Conference in Durban, South Africa, from November 28 through December 11, 2011. This conference attracted over 12,480 participants, which included about 5,400 government officials, about 5,800 representatives of the United Nations and other intergovernmental and civil society organizations (CSOs), and more than 1,200 members of the media. The main purpose of this conference was to come up with a plan for emissions reductions targets and to decide on the future of the Kyoto Protocol. The meetings at COP17 resulted in the establishment of a second commitment period under the Kyoto Protocol and the operationalization of the Green Climate Fund among other outcomes ("Summary and Analysis of COP17," 2011).

Given the frustrations at the earlier Copenhagen conference and the struggle to rescue the multilateral climate regime in Cancun, the negotiators in Durban were successful in resuscitating the Kyoto Protocol. The decisions adopted will most likely lead to negotiations on a more inclusive 21st-century climate regime (Aguilar et al., 2011).

For the first time ever, the new international climate change treaty would include developed as well as the developing countries. The countries have agreed to decide on the modalities of this treaty by 2015 and implement it from 2020. Thus, big emitters like China, India, and the United States will have legal emission commitments post–2020. The developed countries, such as the European Union, Norway, Australia, and New Zealand, agreed to participate in a second commitment period of the Kyoto Protocol. The second commitment period would start from January 1, 2013, and would extend up to either 2017 or 2020 (to be decided at COP18 in Qatar in November 2012). The extent of participation of Japan, Russia, and Canada in the Kyoto Protocol phase II remains unclear, even though they have said clear no before the COP ("Decision Summary," 2011).

Implications for Carbon Markets

Some of the implications of COP17 are as follows:

- *Globally binding treaty*: The participating nations of COP17 will work on a binding treaty and its wording by 2015 though the implementation is planned from 2020 onward.
- *Price of CERs*: The agreement on emission reduction targets and the adoption of project-based mechanisms will impact prices of CERs along with other factors such as demand, supply, and market forces. Some countries might need to increase their emission reduction targets.
- *The Green Climate Fund*: This fund is to be created to support projects, programs, policies, and other activities in developing countries—some of which have already started to pledge funds.
- *Inclusion of China, India, and the United States*: A major aspect of the treaty is that it will include the three biggest emitters of GHGs in the world. However, the caveat is that there will be no binding emission reduction target under the Kyoto Protocol.
- *Weak links*: The stance of Japan, Russia, and Canada remained unclear. These countries have already refused to accept any targets under the second phase of the Kyoto Protocol. In addition, Canada has also withdrawn from the Kyoto Protocol post the Durban round of COP ("Summary and Analysis of COP17," 2011).

Governments agreed to develop a new market-based mechanism to assist developed countries in meeting part of their targets or commitments under the convention. The details of this (Green Climate Fund) will be taken forward in 2012. The adoption decisions from this conference including the

Green Climate Fund as well as the process to launch an agreement with legal force were welcomed by many participants and observers. However, others continued to insist on the urgent need to significantly scale up the level of ambition to address the gap between existing mitigation pledges and the needed emission reductions recommended by science (Aguilar et al., 2011).

As a follow up, the next UNFCCC Climate Change Conference, COP18/CMP8 is scheduled to take place from November 26 to December 7, 2012, in Qatar. It is hoped that decisions on the markets mechanisms will be made along with the quantification of emissions reductions targets ("Summary and Analysis of COP17," 2011).

Conclusion

In this chapter, we have offered a basic understanding of carbon neutrality, the carbon market, carbon offsets, and the standards surrounding the offset market. Given the large and rising number of offset providers in the highly unregulated and often misunderstood carbon offset industry, this chapter highlights areas of concern for consumers and other stakeholders. The chapter offers insight into the standards environment for offset providers since the numerous standards themselves need to be standardized.

Given that there is so much attention being paid to environmental sustainability, the public needs to be educated about the various policy prescriptions. As long as the purchaser of carbon credits remains naive about the process, uninformed about standards, confused by conflicting claims, and overwhelmed by choice, neither the fundamental values of a right to health and to a sustaining physical environment nor the benefits of a balanced, equitable, and fair global carbon emission standard can truly be realized.

KEY WORDS

Additionality

Carbon footprint

Carbon neutral

Certification

Conference of the
    Parties (COP17)

Gold Standard

Kyoto Protocol

Ownership

Plan Vivo

Price differential

Quality of projects

Standardization

United Nations Framework
    Convention on Climate
    Change (UNFCCC)

Voluntary Carbon Standard (VCS)

Voluntary Offset Standard (VOS)

DISCUSSION QUESTIONS

1. What is the logic behind the cap and trade system? Do you think that this mechanism can help in reducing air pollution in the United States?

2. Why do organizations want to go carbon-neutral? What are the reasons behind this goal?

3. What is the present stance of the United States on the Kyoto Protocol? Why has the United States not signed on this agreement?

4. The market solutions are more popular in the United States, and the command-and-control strategies are more popular in Europe. Why is this so?

5. How do carbon offsets work? Would you consider purchasing offsets the next time you travel?

6. Go to the top five carbon offset providers mentioned in Table 11.2, and determine the price of offsetting your next air travel trip. How do the costs compare? What reasons contribute to the difference?

7. Why do we need certification and standardization in the carbon offset markets?

8. Go to the top five carbon offset providers mentioned in Table 11.2. Which of these standards—Gold Standard, the VCS 2007, the VOS, Plan Vivo—are used by these providers?

9. Go to the appendix, and calculate the carbon footprint of your car and your house. What steps can you take to reduce your footprint?

10. In conclusion, do you think carbon offsets are good or bad? Justify your position using factual data.

11. Research Kyoto Protocol on the web and the follow-up conferences in Cancun, Copenhagen, Durban, and Qatar. Do you think that all nations should agree to binding targets or not? Discuss your reasoning.

RECOMMENDED WEBSITES

www.cleanair-coolplanet.org/ConsumersGuidetoCarbonOffsets.pdf

http://unfccc.int/kyoto_protocol/items/2830.php

Appendix: Carbon Calculators

Note: These calculators are only rough estimators. Hence, the same trip can yield different results. Depending upon the trip, these calculators can provide a starting point

Table 11.2 Carbon Footprint Calculators

Airplane Travel Emissions

Companies	Websites	Types
Atmosfair	www.atmosfair.de/index.php?id=5&L=3	Location to location detail, with layovers
Climate Care	www.climatecare.org/living/calculator_info/index.cfm	Location to location, as well as house and car emissions
Offsetters	www.offsetters.ca/calculators_fights.htm	Location to location detail

Business Emissions Calculators

Companies	Websites	Types
Climate Friendly	www.climatefriendly.com/business.php	One of very few business calculators. Includes factory and office electricity, fleet fuel, and corporate air travel

Car Travel Emissions

Companies	Websites	Types
Certified Clean Car	www.certifiedcleancar.com/menu/cleannow/foryou/index.htm	Input exact car make and model
Target Neutral	www.targetneutral.com/TONIC/carbon.do?method=init	Calculate up to 4 cars at once
TerraPass	www.terrapass.com/road/carboncalc.php	Input exact car make and model
Clean Air Pass	www.cleanairpass.com/treecanada	Input exact car make and model

Other Notable Calculators

Companies	Websites	Types
Carbon Counter	www.carboncounter.org/test.php?testPath=estimate&nextStep=1	Calculate "estimated" or "exact" emissions
Sustainable Travel International	www.sustainabletravelinternational.org/offset/index.php?p=hotel	Include hotel emissions
World Land Trust	www.carbonbalanced.org/personal/calculator/calctravel.asp	Includes hotel, boat, flight emissions
Atmos Clear	www.atmosclear.org/calculator_tran.php	Includes household and recreational equipment, from leaf blowers to jet skis

Source: Clean Air-Cool Planet (2006).

12

Designing Sustainable Cities and Communities

Chapter Overview

This chapter reviews the sustainability plans of some of the major cities of the United States, Europe, South America, and Africa. Since businesses must operate within the context of the local community, a community plan is important in aiding the efforts of businesses. Conversely, cities must expect the employers of its citizens to make an effort to follow the plan.

Business must rely on local city services, including water supply and sewage, fire and police protection, trash pickup, educational systems for children, public transportation, and road repair. Most of these services are taken for granted until something goes amiss. Taxpayers complain about increasing property taxes and at the same time complain about decreases in services.

Many aspects of a facility location decision are tied to the effectiveness of local cities and communities in providing services, tax incentives, and amenities. This chapter will look at some major cities across the world and their sustainability programs. These programs impact the local businesses in many ways.

- By reducing energy consumption, they can save money for other needed services.
- By improving green space, they improve the quality of life of their local citizens.

- By reducing air pollution, they improve the health of their citizens.
- By improving mass transit, they not only reduce air pollution, but also save money for the citizens.

Cities studied in this chapter include the following:

United States:

Los Angeles

Salt Lake City

Denver

Phoenix

Boston

New York City

Atlanta

Washington, D.C.

San Francisco

Portland

New Orleans

International Cities:

London

Paris

Hong Kong

Montreal

Vancouver

Mexico City

Mumbai

Johannesburg

Curitiba

Auckland

Melbourne

A City Sustainability Portfolio

Edward Glaeser (2011), in his book *Triumph of the City* wrote the following:

If the future is going to be greener, then it must be more urban. Dense cities offer a means of living that involves less driving and smaller homes to heat and cool. Maybe someday we'll be able to drive and cool our homes with almost no carbon emissions, but until then, there is nothing greener than blacktop.

Glaeser (2011) offered an interesting, counterintuitive argument in defense of city living. He argued convincingly that city living makes ecological sense: "Cities are much better for the environment than leafy living. Residing in a forest might seem to be a good way of showing one's love of nature, but living in a concrete jungle is actually far more ecologically friendly."

Glaeser's statement makes sense due to the aggregation of population and the infrastructure that enable a more efficient use of resources. Any city should have a complete sustainability program, and this should be highlighted on the city webpage. A comprehensive portfolio would include the following:

- A comprehensive water agenda, entailing policies on water conservation and water quality
- Efforts to utilize alternative energy
- A public transportation agenda to increase its support and use of alternative fuel vehicles in the system
- A policy on urban forestry to promote the city's tree coverage
- A health and safety network for its citizens
- Efforts to improve air quality in the city
- A complete recycling program
- The promotion of open spaces, parks, and trails
- Markets for locally and organically produced food

Los Angeles

Los Angeles, the United States' second-most populated city, suffers from several handicaps: geography, pollution, and an underutilized mass transit system. The beautiful weather attracts some 11 million residents, but the layout of the city forces many to drive. The geography of the Los Angeles Basin is such that the polluted air often sits without moving—a problem also experienced in Denver and Salt Lake City. Despite these handicaps, Mayor Villaraigosa set transforming Los Angeles into one of the greenest cities as his goal.

Only 6% of Los Angeles's energy comes from wind power, with the majority of energy coming from coal plants in Arizona and Utah. A major thrust of Southern California Edison is to expand its solar power. All new public buildings must meet Leadership in Energy and Environmental Design (LEED) standards.

Water has always been a valuable commodity in this arid basin. Water conservation is almost routinely practiced in Los Angeles, and low-flow toilets and showerheads are required at all residences.

Sustainability at Los Angeles International Airport

Los Angeles International Airport (LAX) is actively pursing **LEED certification** by making key changes to the airport's construction. Five main categories are the focus:

1. *Water efficiency*—New toilets flush 1.6 gallons of water. The old, replaced toilets flushed 3 gallons. The result is a tremendous water savings.

2. *Energy and atmosphere*—Here, conversion to energy-efficient light fixtures, a new heating and cooling control system, and additional green power are the main efforts.

3. *Indoor environmental quality*—The reduction of chemical smells is addressed through carpeting, and sealants and paints with low **volatile organic compounds (VOCs).**

4. *Materials and resource conservation*—A change to surfaces with recycled content is in process.

5. *Sustainable site development*—LAX has a storm water treatment plant to take pollutants out prior to going into the city's water system, and has an alternative fuel vehicle fleet. ("LAWA Sustainability," 2007)

Sustainability Building Initiative

In 2002, Los Angeles declared its **Sustainable Building Initiative**. Its three-part program included the following:

Policy and Program Development

- Adopted a citywide policy for new municipal buildings to be built as green buildings. All projects over 7,500 square feet must meet the LEED certified standard.

Education, Outreach, and Training

- Established a Green Building Resource Center.
- Expanded buy-in from city departments through education.
- Developed partnerships with trade associations, community-based organizations, and educational institutions.
- Sponsored an annual green building summit.

Demonstration Projects

- Proposed 10 new green building projects, including the renovation of the Griffith Observatory and the Children's Museum.

Water Restrictions

Los Angeles is accustomed to water restrictions for its residences and businesses. In 2009, the city restricted lawn sprinklers to Monday and Thursday only. And on these days, the sprinkling had to be before 9:00 am and after 4:00 pm. It was also illegal to water the sidewalk. Not even the stars on the Hollywood walk of fame sidewalks could be watered. Customers in restaurants could only be served water if they requested it.

Rebates for Home Energy Efficiency

In 2010, Los Angeles offered $100 rebates for citizens who recycled their refrigerators while purchasing Energy Star refrigerators (Krimmel, 2007).

Salt Lake City

Situated in a beautiful setting at the base of the Wasatch Range, Salt Lake City has a strong interest in keeping its natural beauty. Several times each year, Salt Lake City has the malady of an inversion in which a hazy smog settles in on the city and stays for several days, causing poor air quality.

Its two most recent mayors, Rocky Anderson and Ralph Becker, have been active environmentalists and have set the tone for the city to pursue a sustainability code.

The code has 10 key areas:

1. Climate change and air pollution

2. Water quality and conservation

3. Alternative energy production and conservation

4. Mobility and transportation

5. Urban forestry

6. Housing accessibility and diversity

7. Community health and safety

8. Food production and nutrition

9. Recycling, re-use and waste reduction

10. Open space, parks, and trails (Sustainable City Code Revision Project, n.d.)

Salt Lake City built one of the United States' first LEED certified buildings in preparation for the 2002 Olympic Games—the Olympic Oval in Kearns.

A list of the city's accomplishments include the following:

- Passed an ordinance requiring all county buildings to meet LEED standards
- Obtained LEED certification for the Intermodal Hub and Unity Center
- Purchased acres of open space
- Performed technical audits of city buildings, implementing energy saving measures
- Has a climate action plan
- Updated zoning ordinances in accordance with sustainable practices
- Prohibited bottled water in municipal buildings

Utah received a grade of A from the Network for New Energy Choices, as one of the top four states implementing renewable energy (Green Space Today, 2010).

Denver

Denver, the mile-high city, in Colorado, has a similar geographical setup to Salt Lake City, with the major exception being that the mountains are to the west rather than the east. It has similar problems with haze. Denver released its sustainability goals in an action agenda called Greenprint Denver.

The city listed an agenda of 10 goals:

1. Reduce per capita greenhouse gas emissions from 1990 levels by 10% in 2011.

2. Plant thousands of trees to increase the tree canopy from 6% to 18%.

3. Increase recycling by 50% and reduce the total land filled household waste by 30% from 2004 to 2011.

4. Construct solar and methane power plants capable of heating 2500 homes by 2007.

5. Increase residential incentives for energy efficient households.

6. Require that all new city buildings meet LEED Silver ratings.

7. Expand the fleet of city vehicles, using biodiesel.

8. Decrease reliance on automobiles by increasing transit ridership and improvements to bike paths.

9. Improve water quality through maintenance and repair of sanitary and storm sewers, education and outreach.

10. Pursue sustainable economic development by positioning Denver as a regional center for renewable energy and green industries. (Greenprint Denver, 2010)

Denver was recognized by the group SustainLane as one of the top 10 cities in the nation for sustainable practices. It offers the largest bicycle-sharing program in the country, with 500 bicycles used for a trading system at 50 Denver locations. In this system, users can sign up for a 1-day, 7-day, 30-day, or annual membership ($65).

Colorado's green industry brings in 100,000 jobs and $10 billion in annual revenue, according to the American Solar Energy Society (Chakrabarty, 2009).

Phoenix

The biggest environmental issue for Phoenix is water availability. Phoenix is located in the Arizona desert with the least rainfall of any of the major cities in the United States, and water is a prized commodity. The temperature often rises above 110 degrees Fahrenheit in the summer, and watering a green lawn is very expensive. Most yards are covered with rocks, not grass. Because water is such a valuable commodity, the average Phoenician uses 120 gallons of water per day, compared to an average of 160 in other southwestern cities.

On www.grist.org, Lisa Selin Davis (2010) wrote the following:

Phoenix is a less-natural shade of brown; a ring of smoggy pollution known locally as the Brown Cloud shadows the city. And that's not the only affront to the environs here. Anyone flying in can see the patches of fierce green lawns that paint the landscape, along with the swimming pools; the manmade lake in the suburb of Tempe; evaporating 452 million gallons of water each year; the sear of single family homes spilling across the desert; the traffic clogging the ribbons of highways; and the heat snakes squiggling from all that boiling bitumen. The 517-square-mile city—the fifth largest and fourth fastest growing in America—just survived its second-driest winter on record and is deep in drought. So how is it that this poster child for sprawl and environmental ills is being hailed—albeit by its own government—as an exemplar of sustainability?

Phoenix set a climate action plan in 2009. The city set 10 measures to reduce emissions, including renewable energy, energy efficiency, alternative fuels, and landfill methane collection efficiency.

The impetus in this plan was due to the Arizona's risk of global warming. If warming continues at the present rate of 1.4 degrees every 50 years, it would result in a 15% annual reduction in runoff from the Colorado River, a 40% decrease in water basin storage, and a 45% to 56% decline in hydroelectric power. Arizona's forests would be depleted by 15% to 30%, and incidents of skin cancer would increase.

Examples of Phoenix's sustainability programs include the following:

- Adoption of energy conservation standards in building codes
- Residential recycling program
- Pedestrian-friendly zoning code standards

- Light rail service increased by 37 miles
- A heat-island task force to study ways to reduce urban temperatures
- Water conservation, wetlands habitat restoration, and aquifer recharge projects
- Urban forestry program to increase trees
- Recycled asphalt overlay program for noise reduction and street maintenance
- District cooling projects that chill water at night for daytime cooling ("Phoenix: Living Like It Matters," 2008)

One of the novel approaches Phoenix has taken to reduce greenhouse gas (GHG) emissions is by installing energy efficient traffic signals. The conversion to light emitting diode (LED) technology reduces electricity use by 54%. All 500 city buses use clean burning or alternative fuels.

A federal grant created a partnership with Arizona State University and Arizona Public Service to create Energize Phoenix, a program to save energy and create jobs. The first major project was the Green Rail Corridor. Goals of the program include reducing home energy consumption by 30%, commercial energy use by 18%, and carbon emissions by 50,000 metric tons per year while also promoting energy efficiency. The Global Institute of Sustainability at Arizona State University is the research center for this project. ("City of Phoenix Receives $25 Million Grant," 2010).

Boston

Boston amended its zoning codes to require all new construction projects exceeding 50,000 square feet to earn LEED new construction points. Mayor Menino signed an order in 2007 establishing a goal of an 80% reduction in emissions by 2050.

Boston embarked on a social marketing campaign to increase recycling. The Public Works Department campaign was called "Recycle more, trash less." They tested the feasibility of collecting residential recyclables (plastic, metal, and glass) in one container, known as **single stream collection**. The pilot for this approach realized a 52% increase in recycled trash.

The city of Boston received over $300 million in a stimulus package from the **American Recovery and Reinvestment Act (ARRA)** in 2009. The city employed a novel approach to the analysis of the success of this stimulus— the **sustainable return on investment (SROI)**.

The sustainability analysis recognizes the increasing importance of environmental, energy and social factors when evaluating the use of public funding. In fact, ARRA funding requires consideration of: rapid implementation, green industry creation, energy efficiency and security, greenhouse gas reduction, job creation, and return on investment. The competitive funding programs for ARRA funds, whereby Boston competes for funding opportunities with communities across the country, are increasingly requiring a public benefit-cost analysis and estimation of environmental and energy benefits such as reduced greenhouse gas emissions and reduced dependency on oil and gas consumption. Consequently, this study has developed an innovative approach to measuring sustainability benefits and return on investment based on HDR's sustainable return on investment (SROI) approach. Sustainability benefits are measured over time in terms of energy cost savings, emissions reductions, water preservation, travel time savings, safety, and accelerated development value for a subset of Boston's ARRA investments. (Boston Redevelopment Authority, 2010)

Their analysis projected 2,861 new jobs in Massachusetts with an increase of personal income of $245 million and $410 million in added tax revenue. The sustainability benefits included the following:

- 34.4 million fewer kWh of electricity consumed.
- 277,000 reduction of therms of gas used.
- 23,750 hundreds of cubic feet of water preserved.
- 25,150 fewer tons of greenhouse gas emissions.
- $5.7 million per year savings in direct energy bills.
- $2.4 million savings per year in reduced water and sewer costs.
- $0.9 million per year in reduced greenhouse gas emissions. (Boston Redevelopment Authority, 2010)

New York City

On Earth Day 2007, the mayor of New York City, Michael Bloomberg, announced an environmental sustainability plan for New York City: PlaNYC 2030. The plan includes 100 strategies on the environment, economics, and quality of life. Three key areas are (1) air quality, (2) climate change, and (3) transportation.

Strategies to improve air quality include the following:

- Require filters to reduce pollution inside school buses
- Convert taxis to clean and efficient hybrid models
- Enforce anti-idling laws along heavy truck routes
- Require cleaner fuels for the Staten Island Ferry and other private ferries
- Install new boilers in several dozen schools

Strategies geared toward climate change issues include the following:

- Make government buildings more energy-efficient
- Launched energy planning board to coordinate planning on energy supply and demand

- Had volunteers coat rooftops with reflective coating to reduce cooling costs
- Invested $25 million in energy efficiency improvements in the Castle Hill Houses in the Bronx
- Tested high-efficiency LED lights in parks and roadways

Strategies toward improving transportation include the following:

- Implemented bus corridors on existing roads.
- More than 200 miles of bike lanes were installed in the five boroughs.
- Created pedestrian plazas in Herald Square and Times Square. (Kassel, 2009)

Atlanta

The economic and transportation hub of the South, Atlanta sits at 1,000 feet of elevation, the highest elevation of any major city in the South and East. For many years, Atlanta has experienced traffic congestion on its major arteries: I-20, I-75, I-85, and I-285. Georgia 400 was constructed as an alternative route to help ease traffic. Basically, Atlanta is a suburban community with few residents living in the city center. The **Sustainable Atlanta Initiative** in 2007 set goals for a higher quality of life in the city. The core for the quality of life was as follows:

- Clean air
- Zero waste
- Water efficient
- Efficient buildings
- Abundant green space
- Green jobs
- Clean energy
- Social and economic equity
- More accessible transit options
- Walkability (Mahoney, 2008)

The first year of the Sustainability Initiative, the carbon footprint was reduced by 5.6%, measured in metric tons of carbon dioxide. The city seeks grants to fund projects totaling $105 million. The stimulus funds are aimed at replacing inefficient lighting; installing automatic building controls and reflective roofing; upgrading water conservation; and increasing solar thermal and photovoltaic energy.

Atlanta initiated an incentive recycling system in which residents could receive rewards, gift cards, and products in exchange for the use of recycling carts. Other initiatives included the following:

- *Buildings:* An ordinance was passed requiring all new city construction projects to be LEED certified.

- *Planning and land use:* The BeltLine Project converts 22 miles of aban-doned railroad corridors and 2,900 acres of land into a system of transit and greenways.
- *Green space:* A city ordinance maintains the maximum amount of tree cover within the city.
- *Local food:* The city will promote more healthy food and economically viable local farms.
- *Watershed protection:* This plan is to improve water quality through watersheds. The plan is in three phases: (1) water quality monitoring, (2) watershed assessment, and (3) watershed protection plan.
- *Clean air:* Atlanta was one of the cities that endorsed the Kyoto Protocol, which was never passed by the U.S. Congress. The city out-lawed truck or bus idling for more than 15 minutes.

At the Hartsfield–Jackson Airport, the following took place:

- Encouraged airlines to use single engine taxiing when possible
- Encouraged the use of alternative fuel vehicles
- Partnered with Delta Air Lines and the Metropolitan Atlanta Rapid Transit Authority (MARTA) in a remote baggage check-in at the MARTA airport station
- Constructed an end-around taxiway to reduce the arrival times to reach the gates
- Constructed a rental car facility served by an automated people mover

The 4th- and 5th-grade curriculums added a series of lessons and activi-ties to educate students on the environment (Mahoney, 2008).

Washington, D.C.

The nation's capital calls its program the Green DC Agenda. Washington, D.C., follows a five-step methodology proposed by the **International Council for Local Environmental Initiatives (ICLEI)—Local Governments for Sustainability**. The five milestones to follow are as follows:

1. Inventory greenhouse gas emissions.
2. Set an emissions reductions target.
3. Develop a plan.
4. Implement the plan.
5. Monitor implementation progress. (Green DC Agenda, 2010)

The first milestone was reached in 2006. Washington, D.C., discovered that 61% of emissions came from its 500 city facilities, 21% came from the electricity used to pump and treat wastewater, 7% from streetlights and traffic signals, and 7% from the vehicle fleet. The unaccounted 4% apparently comes from politicians.

City operations have reported a number of successes: Government electric customers buy electricity at a reduced rate and purchase 10% renewable energy. D.C. promotes alternative work schedules and flexible commuting options for employees. Approximately 360 vehicles were removed from the fleet to be replaced by alternative fuel vehicles. Geographic information system (GIS) technology was used to plan more efficient trash, recycling, and waste collections.

Ten SmartBike stations with 100 shared bicycles were installed. Forty miles of bike paths and 1,000 bicycle racks were installed. About 69,000 LED streetlights were installed.

Sports fields have been lit with computer-controlled high-efficiency lighting. Parklands have managed pollution with rain gardens, bioswales, and other stormwater techniques (Green DC Agenda, 2010).

San Francisco

Out west, one of the United States' most beautiful cities is situated on an earthquake fault that has several times caused major catastrophes. San Francisco grades its progress in sustainability according to achievements in 14 areas:

- Air quality
- Biodiversity
- Economy and Economic Development
- Environmental Justice
- Food and Agriculture
- Hazardous Materials
- Human Health
- Municipal Expenditures
- Parks, Open Space and Streetscape
- Public Information and Education
- Solid Waste
- Transportation
- Water and Wastewater (SFEnvironment, 2010)

An aspect of the economic plan is to recruit emerging environmental industries. A sustainable tourism industry has been established that includes education, green spaces, and habitat restoration.

San Francisco has financial incentives available for businesses that perform ISO (International Organization for Standardization) 14000 audits, rewarding those that make corrections. The city has perhaps the most expensive housing in the United States and suggests that businesses assist employees in down payments for mortgages.

In the area of community, San Francisco lists these accomplishments:

- Mixed use, affordable housing has been increased.
- Open and green spaces have been increased.
- Neighborhood boards have been established.
- Percentage of local contractors and minority and woman-owned businesses has increased.
- Tax incentives for owners of lots suitable for garden projects have been targeted.
- Recycling and composting centers have been established in multiple locations.
- Neighborhood sustainability resource centers have been set up.
- Household retrofits to reduce energy and water use have increased.
- Purchase of green products and services has increased.

Few cities have an active food policy within their sustainability program. The goals of the San Francisco program are as follows:

- To increase individual, public, and private-sector participation in a sustainable food system.
- To establish and coordinate a community-based policy and educational program to achieve a sustainable food system.
- To ensure access by all people at all times to enough nutritious, affordable, safe and culturally diverse food for an active, healthy life.
- To create, support, and promote regional sustainable agriculture.
- To maximize food and agricultural production within the City itself.
- To recycle all organic residuals, eliminate chemical use in agriculture and landscaping and use sustainable practices that enhance natural biological systems throughout the city. (SFEnvironment, 2010)

Portland

Located in the Pacific Northwest, Portland, Oregon, was rated by SustainLane.com as the top sustainability city in the United States. Portland benefits from a mild, albeit wet, climate and has an environmentally conscious population.

Portland's 2009 plan has six major goals:

Goal One: Establish a citywide sustainability team to manage strategic goal implementation.

The existing team was voluntary and the movement was to staff with city employees.

Goal Two: Enhance and implement the city's green building policy, sustainability initiatives, and practices.

This goal entailed certifying completion of green building projects.

Goal Three: Grow sustainability expertise among community firms.

Here, the intention is to reach minority and women contractors.

Goal Four: Expand sustainable economic development.

Portland intends to offer trade shows, recruit new sustainable businesses, and introduce sustainability institute.

Goal Five: Reduce energy use, climate, and environmental impacts.

The goal is to purchase 100% renewable energy and find new ways to reduce the carbon footprint.

Goal Six: Enhance sustainability culture through education and training. (City of Portland and Multnomah County, 2009)

Portland's Climate Action Plan includes a 40% reduction in emissions by 2030. Portland had an ambitious goal of 90% of residents could either walk or bicycle to meet basic daily, nonwork needs. By 2030, Portland hopes for a 30% reduction in daily vehicle miles traveled.

From 1990 to 2008, the population had increased more than 20%. At the same time, carbon emissions showed a total net loss as the per person emissions dropped from 14.7 to 11.9 metric tons per year. Meanwhile, passenger miles per day per person increased from 17.4 to 18.5 (City of Portland and Multnomah County, 2009).

New Orleans

Hurricane Katrina crippled New Orleans in 2006. After suffering tremendous casualties and property losses, approximately one third of the population relocated out of the city. Forced to rebuild, the city of New Orleans used the opportunity to write a sustainability plan to aid their efforts.

The plan was coauthored by Earthea Nance, the city of New Orleans director of infrastructure and environmental planning; Wynecta Fisher, the city of New Orleans director of environmental affairs; Jeffrey Schwartz, a professor at the Department of Urban Studies and Planning at MIT; and David Quinn, a professor in the Department of Architecture at MIT. They created a road map around six areas:

1. Green Buildings and Energy Efficiency

2. Alternative Energy

3. Waste Reduction, Reuse, and Recycling

4. Transportation and Clean Fuels

5. Environmental Outreach and Justice

6. Flood Risk Reduction ("GreeNOLA: A Strategy for a Sustainable New Orleans," 2012)

An important aspect of the plan was to reorganize city government to add an Energy Office and a Disaster Mitigation Office. One certainty for New Orleans is that due to its geography, it WILL be hit by devastating hurricanes in the future. What is possible is to find ways to mitigate the damage.

New Orleans is pursuing housing certification standards with incentive packages. Louisiana Senate Bill 90 gives tax credits for up to $25,000 for solar energy and thermal systems. New Orleans models the new plan after the best practices in these cities:

- Portland—The low-income weatherization program, with sliding scale fees and rebates
- Houston—Weatherization of inner-city homes by a utility, CenterPoint Energy
- Seattle—BuiltGreen certification
- Chicago—The Chicago construction standard and the Green Permit Program
- Austin—All new homes zero net energy by 2015
- Atlanta—EarthCraft House Program offered

The commercial building program is modeled after Portland and Chicago. Portland's G/Rated program and Chicago's Green Permit program accelerate the permit process for green buildings.

New Orleans cites the best practices of these cities in establishing its alternative energy program:

- Seattle—Seattle City Light achieved zero net emissions through the purchase of renewable energy credits.
- Salt Lake City—Residents can purchase wind power for a flat rate.
- Portland—Oregon Energy Trust uses a surcharge to finance energy incentives.
- Boston—8.6% of the total energy use is through renewable sources.
- Austin—A goal of 30% renewable energy by 2015 has been set.

The state of Louisiana established a Coastal Restoration and Hurricane Protection Authority that focused around four objectives: (1) reduce economic losses of a storm, (2) promote a sustainable coastal ecosystem,

(3) provide habitats to support commercial and recreational activities, and (4) sustain the unique heritage of coastal Louisiana by protecting historic properties and traditional living cultures. The U.S. Army Corps of Engineers is at work to protect the levee that gave way after Katrina. Small secondary levees are being built around critical public or commercial facilities for protection.

Hurricane Katrina gave New Orleans a hard-learned lesson. As one of the United States' most beloved cities, its sustainability plan probably has more cogent meaning, for its survival is at stake.

SustainLane's U.S. City Rankings

1. Portland, OR

2. San Francisco

3. Seattle

4. Chicago

5. New York

6. Boston

7. Minneapolis

8. Philadelphia

9. Oakland

10. Baltimore

11. Denver

12. Milwaukee

13. Austin

14. Sacramento

15. Washington, D.C.

16. Cleveland

17. Honolulu

18. Albuquerque

19. Atlanta

20. Kansas City ("The 2008 US City Rankings," 2012)

The top three of those ranked in each category rated can be found in Table 12.1:

Table 12.1 Top Three City Rankings by Category

Category	1	2	3
Air quality	Honolulu	Portland	New Orleans
Commuting	Washington, D.C.	Boston	New York City
City innovation	Portland	Chicago	Seattle
Energy	San Francisco	Seattle	Portland
Green building	Portland	Washington, D.C.	Atlanta
Green economy	Portland	Seattle	Sacramento
Housing affordability	San Antonio	Fort Worth	Arlington
Knowledge	Portland	Seattle	New York City
Local food	Minneapolis	Cleveland	Boston
Street congestion	Cleveland	Kansas City	New Orleans
Metro transit	New York City	Chicago	Long Beach
Disaster risk	Mesa	Milwaukee	Cleveland
Planning	New York City	San Francisco	Portland
Water quality	Kansas City	Portland	Louisville
Waste management	San Francisco	Long Beach	New York City
Water supply	Chicago	Cleveland	Milwaukee

London

In the United Kingdom, London fog is a combination of pollution and climate, and one study estimated the poor air quality resulted in over 4,000 deaths per year. The air quality is the biggest challenge for London. Proposals from the mayor of London include the following:

1. All buses must meet European emissions standards by 2015.

2. Taxis older than 10 years must be removed by 2015 and replaced with alternative fuel vehicles.

Larger vans and minibuses must meet the Euro 3 standards.

3. Work is to be done with boroughs on traffic management to smooth driving.

4. New developments must be air quality neutral or better.

5. Dust emissions must be reduced from construction sites.

6. Homes and public buildings should be retrofitted to improve energy efficiency.

Public awareness will be raised to encourage all Londoners to reduce their emissions from travel choices to energy efficiency. (Johnson, 2009)

London was especially aware of the need to preserve their green space and make a good presentation at the 2012 Olympic Games. In the mayor's position on green space, he wrote the following:

With the increasing impact of climate change, open space and water are more important than ever. London will make more of its green infrastructure to provide eco system services (the processes operating in the natural environment on which we depend and can often benefit from): to help manage surface water and regulate temperatures, to facilitate walking and cycling, and as a network, for recreation, to support healthier lifestyles, and for peace and reflection. Defra's "Making Space for Water" (March 2005) emphasizes the importance of green space and of restoring rivers to manage the risk of flooding. Reinstating flood plains provides a natural increase in the flood storage capacity of the whole river, which contributes to flood protection downstream. It also creates important new habitats where wildlife can flourish. (Johnson, 2009)

London and Paris shared the 2008 Sustainable Transport Award, based primarily on its 2003 congestion pricing program, which increased motor vehicle fees and taxed fuel-burning vehicles.

Paris

Paris, the beloved city in France—a city with only one skyscraper—has always been concerned with its appearance. Paris presented its sustainable development, environment, and climate plan at the C40 Tokyo Conference in 2008. One goal was to cut traffic in the city by 25% by increasing public transportation by 12%. The Paris Metro and RER systems make it one of the world's easiest cities to commute, unless you are stuck in the roundabout circling the Arc de Triomphe.

Walking and cycling are emphasized, and there are 215,000 subscribers to the Velib bicycle share system, which has 15,000 available bikes. Paris saw good results from 2002 to 2007, with an 11% reduction in car traffic resulting in a 9% drop in carbon dioxide emissions and a 32% drop in nitrogen oxide emissions. Cycling has increased by 48% since 2002.

Washington Post reporter, Alexandra Topping (2007), described their Velib system:

The system is designed to encourage short journeys. After paying your subscription fee and picking up a bike, the first half-hour is free.

The second half-hour costs one euro, the third costs two euros and a fourth would cost an added four euros, to encourage people to stick to the half-hour system.

But you can take a bike out, as many times as you like in a day—and each time it's free for the first 30 minutes. "This is utilitarian way of getting around," explained Velib project manager Celine Lepault. "The Velibs are for everyone, but tourists should realize they are simply a way of getting from A to B. If they want to take a bike for the day, they should hire one from a rental shop."

There are now 14,197 sleek gray bikes around town. They are elegant, sturdy machines made more for cruising than for speed, with three gears, large padded seats and good hand brakes on the "sit-up" handle bars. By the end of the year, there are to be 20,600 bikes at 1,450 stations—or about one station every 900 feet.

The Velib system is complicated and possibly nerve-racking. So why bother? Quite simply, the Velib does exactly as its name promises. It gives you the liberty to discover Paris at your own pace, under your own steam. Most journeys take less than 30 minutes (it takes about 15 minutes to cycle from the Musee d'orsay to the Eiffel Tower, for example), and instead of popping up at the sights like a touristy mole, you discover all the hidden attractions in between.

The highways in France have extremely high tolls that limit traffic. This puts more commuters on trains. Similar to London, congestion pricing has been introduced to the city to curb traffic.

Hong Kong

One of Asia's most beautiful coastal cities, Hong Kong has serious problems with air quality. In 2008, Hong Kong's Council for Sustainable Development reported on approaches to improve the air. Hong Kong packs 7 million people into 1,100 square kilometers, making it four times the population density of Los Angeles.

Total emissions of respirable particulates have been reduced by 60% since May 2003. Hong Kong has been a leader in performing environmental assessments since the early 1990s. The environmental audit prior to the building of the new airport resulted in minimizing environmental damage. Another example was the scrapping of an excavation project from Mirs Bay.

The recommendations of the council included the following:

- High air pollution days will be denoted with a color coded system and designate the worst days as "red," limiting use of private vehicles, non-essential electrical, and diesel equipment. Schools should post-pone outdoor activities on such days.

- Congestion road pricing, similar to London and Paris, will be intro-duced with penalties for vehicles with high pollution outputs.
- Cleaner fuel options should be pursued for public vehicles.
- Increased pedestrian areas will be available.
- Strict building codes to reduce energy consumption will be enforced.
- Mandates for ecolabels for electrical equipment and appliances will be given.
- The government should educate the public in ways to reduce energy consumption.
- A dialogue with Guangdong, China, to tackle cross-boundary emis-sions should be pursued. (Council for Sustainable Development, 2008)

Several companies such as Ikea, 7-11, Wellcome, and Mannings formed the Dairy Farm International Group and embarked in a campaign to educate prekindergarten children on environmental issues. They called these children "little green ambassadors." The four retailers claimed that this program resulted in the reduction of plastic bag consumption by 30 million per year! Every Tuesday at these companies is designated "No plastic bag day."

Montreal

Montreal, the cosmopolitan French–Canadian city, has monitored its air quality since the 1960s. One of the issues has been the popularity of wood burning as a heat source in winter. In the winter of 2007, the number of poor air quality days in the Rivière-des-Prairies district was five times greater than in the downtown area and was even higher than in the refinery section of the city. In the summer, the numbers were reversed. The Rivière-des-Prairies area is a suburban area. Despite public awareness campaigns, the public has been reluctant to give up its wood-burning fires. However, there has been overall improvement. Montreal had 44 poor air quality days in 2007, a 40% decrease from 2003.

While most of the cities surveyed in this chapter showed improvements in the reduction of GHG emissions, Montreal did not, showing an increase between 2002 and 2003 of 4.4%. The explanation is the increasing density of the population in the city, which grew by 5% (185,000 new residents) from 2001 to 2006.

Montreal has a self-service bike rental network, established in 2009. The bike stations are located in every Metro station and can be returned at any other station. Almost half, 46% of Montreal commuters took public transpor-tation, bicycled, or walked to work in 2006. The cycling network contained 502 kilometers of bike paths (about 310 miles).

The Coolest Cities technical report on Canada's six major cities' sustainability performance made the following recommendations for Montreal:

1. Develop systems for consistent, frequent estimates of GHG emissions from urban personal transportation and ensure results are readily available to city departments and to the public.

2. Provide estimates of future GHG emissions for any significant infrastructure or policy development.

3. Ensure land use and transportation plans are implemented, and develop additional initiatives to meet GHG reduction targets.

4. Increase participation of multiple departments and across municipalities in planning and information sharing.

5. Track progress toward meeting GHG reduction targets and estimate the impact of infrastructure. (City of Montreal, 2007)

Montreal will introduce electric trolley buses linked to overhead wires in 2011, and beginning in 2012, all new buses will be hybrids (Bailie & Beckstead, 2010).

Vancouver

Canada's site of the 2010 Winter Olympic Games, Vancouver set up a sustainability framework in 2002. They established this framework with a noble vision:

Metro Vancouver seeks to achieve what humanity aspires to on a global basis—the highest quality of life embracing cultural vitality, economic prosperity, social justice and compassion, all nurtured in and by a beautiful and healthy natural environment. We will achieve this vision by embracing and applying the principles of sustainability, not least of which is an unshakeable commitment to the well being of current and future generations and the health of our planet, in everything we do. As we share our efforts in achieving this vision, we are confident that the inspiration and mutual learning we gain will become vital ingredients in our hopes for a sustainable common future. (Metro Vancouver, 2010)

Notable achievements Vancouver listed since that time include the following:

• Vancouver's Board of Directors made sustainability the region's primary philosophy.
• Received the International Gas Union Grand Prix for its 100-year plan
• Participated in the Johannesburg UN World Summit on Sustainable Development (WSSD)

- Won the Canadian Municipalities Sustainable Community Award for energy co-generation at the Annacis Waste Water Treatment Plant.
- Installed a turbo-generator as a source of sustainable energy recovery at the Burnaby Waste-to-Energy Facility.
- The first waste transfer station built to LEED standards was commissioned.
- Launched the Sustainability Community Breakfast series
- Acquired Burns Blog, an ecological area
- Launched a television series, the *Sustainable Region.*
- Cohosted the World Urban Forum III
- Announced the Affordable Housing Strategy
- Adopted sustainable purchasing policy
- Adopted a corporate policy for the design and construction of green buildings
- Held the first Sustainability Summit, a regional initiative to set a common vision for the future
- Established a regional facility for organic food waste composting.
- First filtered water has been delivered to areas of Metro Vancouver. (Metro Vancouver, 2010)

Vancouver has a goal of carbon neutral new construction by 2030.

Mexico City

One of the world's most populous cities, Mexico City also fights a battle with its air quality. Eighty eight percent of its GHG emissions come from energy consumption. Mexico City set a Green Plan into motion in 2007. The city government does not doubt the evidence of climate change, as it can point to a change in the intensity and seasonality of rains, increased annual temperatures, and increased incidences of severe weather.

The main components of the Green Plan are related to energy, water consumption, transportation, soil conservation, economic development, waste generation, and environmental education. Mexico City government set four objectives:

To influence the behavioral patterns, habits, and attitudes of Mexico City's population so that it will contribute to the mitigation of climate change and enact adaptation measures.

To attract investment and financing for greenhouse gas emission mitigation projects aimed at overcoming obstacles to the implementation of adopted measures.

To position Mexico City and its government as leaders in national and international efforts to mitigate greenhouse gas emissions in the context of the commitments assumed by Mexico in the United Nations Framework Convention on Climate Change (UNFCCC).

To set out guidelines for public policies in the mitigation of and adaptation to climate change in Mexico and to generate a multiplier effect in the country and the world.

The **Mexico City Climate Action Program** has two global aims, the first being the mitigation of GHG emissions and the second, adaptation to climate change:

Aim 1: To reduce carbon dioxide, equivalent emissions by 7 million tons during the 2008 to 2012 period.

Aim 2: To initiate an integrated program for adaptation to climate in Mexico City and have it fully functional by 2012. (Secretaria del Medio Ambiente Gobierno del Distrito Federal, 2008)

The plan to reduce GHG emissions consisted of 26 actionable items:

1. *Sustainable housing:* Installing solar heating, and energy and water saving systems

2. *Sustainable buildings:* Establishing environmental certification

3. *Renewable energy programs:* Promoting solar water heating and solar energy

4. *Energy efficiency in government:* Efficient lighting in buildings; efficient street lighting; efficiency in electrical transportation system

5. *Efficient home lighting program:* Distribution of 10 million compact fluorescent lamps

6. *Improvement of water pump control systems:* Reduction of energy consumption

7. Reduction of emissions from septic systems

8. Energy improvement of water pump equipment

9. Expansion of hydroelectric plants

10. Infrastructure improvement through leak suppression and pipe rehab

11. *Home water savings:* Promoting low-flow toilets and water saving accessories

12. Reduction of mud emissions from biological treatment plant

13. Construction of 300 km of bike paths

14. Implementation of streetcar corridor from historic center to Buenavista

15. Alternative energy for public transportation

16. Replacement of obsolete vehicles with energy efficient units

17. Establish vehicle inspection program for freight trucks

18. Replace medium capacity vehicles with high capacity city vehicles

19. Implement nine transportation corridors with 200 km of restricted lanes

20. Replace taxis with new vehicles

21. Construct Subway Line 12

22. Increase bus transportation for students

23. Construct compost production plant

24. Exploit biogas from landfill

25. Construct integrate recycling center

26. Modernize and automate separation plants, compost plants and transfer centers (Secretaria del Medio Ambiente Gobierno del Distrito Federal, 2008)

Mexico City has shown improvement. In 1990, there were 333 days in which the ozone level was above the national standard of 0.11 parts per million. The minister of the environment was quoted as saying, "We couldn't even see our astonishing volcanoes the Popocatéptl and the Iztaccihuatl because of the polluted air" ("Mexico City Presents," 2011).

By 2009, the number of days had been reduced to 180 and the number of hours per day that the standard was exceeded had dropped to 1.5 hours from 4.9.

Mexico City was the second major city to outlaw plastic bags in stores with San Francisco being the first. Mumbai, India, soon followed suit.

Mumbai

Mumbai is the largest city in India and the financial capital of the country. It has a population of 13 million and a population density of 27,209 per square kilometer. In the "**Mumbai Sustainability and Corporate Citizenship Protocol**," released by Shri Jayant Patil, the Honorable Minister for Finance and Planning, they make this insightful comment:

With its ever increasing population, deteriorating environmental conditions, income disparities, scarcity of land resources, Sustainability of City becomes a major agenda for Mumbai.

This is not possible without striking a balance between Corporate Governance and Public Governance, because these are two faces of the same coin and it is not possible to improve one, without the other. Talking of this balance is easier said than done. This requires a constant dialogue between Corporate Boards, Government, NGOs and Citizens making concerted efforts for creating a buy-in by all the stakeholders.

The code of conduct for Ministries, Government officials and regulators is as important as they are for Corporate Boards, Communities, Customers, and Citizens at large.

We believe Sustainable community development is the ability to make development choices, which respects the relationship between the 3 "E's"—Economy, Ecology, and Equity. (Patil, 2010. Mumbai Sustainability and Corporate Citizenship Protocol" prepared by Asian Center for Corporate Governance & Sustainability.)

In this passage, Mumbai's government is the first to acknowledge a partnership with corporations and businesses, to admit that they cannot accomplish sustainability without support.

Mumbai sets out 12 principles to accomplish these three Es.

1. Water conservation to help meet future needs

2. Air pollution control for better quality of life

3. Effective land utilization

4. Waste management and restoration

5. Increased distribution of wealth throughout the social strata. In this principle Mumbai states the following:

   Ensure that economic activities and institutions at all levels promote human development in an equitable manner. Guarantee people the right of potable water, clean air, food security, uncontaminated soil, shelter and safe sanitation. Recognize the ignored, protect the vulnerable, serve those who suffer and enable them to develop and enhance their capabilities, in order to earn their livelihood in a sustainable manner.

6. Ensure gender equality and equity.

Mumbai makes several notable comments here:

*Eliminate discrimination in all forms as that based on color, race, sex, sexual orientation, religion, language, ethnicity, and social origin.

*Secure the human rights for women and girls and end all violence against them.

*Promote the active participation of women in all aspects of economic, political, civil, social, cultural life as full and equal partners, decision makers, leaders, and beneficiaries.

*Affirm the right of indigenous peoples to their spirituality, knowledge, lands and resources and to their related practice of sustainable livelihoods.

*Uphold the right of all, without discrimination, to a natural and social environment supportive of human dignity, bodily health and spiritual well being with special attention to right of indigenous people and minorities.

7. Empowerment through education.

8. A culture of tolerance, nonviolence, and peace

9. Uphold the conditions of human settlement as a prime necessity of life

10. Transparency and accountability in governance.

11. Right to information

12. Effective implementation of right to information. (Patil, 2010)

Johannesburg

Johannesburg ("Joburg"), South Africa, the site of the WSSD, set out its sustainability program in 2003, in a 100-page document. The predominant themes of the Joburg report concerned open spaces, biodiversity, conservation, water, air, and waste. Joburg is the only metropolitan city in the world not located on a river, estuary, or ocean.

The biggest problem in Joburg is unemployment, which has been as high as 30% in 2003. Joburg listed the following forces in the environmental report:

- Population growth, rapid urbanization, and urban sprawl
- The failure of government to enforce regulations pollution control
- The pressure to meet the basic needs of the population (food, shelter, and energy requirements)
- The need for economic growth and job creation
- Unsustainable and exploitative patterns of resource use by industry, mining, and agriculture
- Increased waste generation (Joburg Department of Development Planning, 2003)

Air quality: Air pollution appears to be most severe in low-income townships due to the use of low-grade coal for heating, untarred roads, and mine dumps.

Water quality: Since Joburg does not have its own water source, it relies on purchasing potable water from nearby regions. The Kip River and Rietspruit catchments show high levels of sewage pollution, and the Kip River has high counts of mining pollution. The poor quality is traced to overloaded sewers, unreported leaks, and misuse of sewer systems. Also, poor storm water management and uncontrolled construction increase erosion and silt problems. However, the overall quality of the drinking water is considered good.

Waste: A significant area of concern is that 93,000 households do not have garbage services. As a result, Joburg has problems with illegal dumping. Recycling is limited to 6% to 8%, low by international standards.

Open spaces: Past planning policies have resulted in limits on the development of new open space. Abandoned mines are considered wasted space and uninhabitable. Joburg is actively pursuing a policy that will increase green space within the city.

Curitiba

A city widely known as one of the first to advertise itself as *green,* Curitiba's reputation led to rapid growth and with that increasing problems of urbanization.

In the 1960s, then with a population of 430,000, Mayor Ivo Arzua assembled a team of architects and urban planners to help minimize urban sprawl. The Curitiba Master Plan was adopted in 1968 and featured a central two-lane street restricted to buses and local traffic between one-way streets. The center of the commercial district, the Rua Quinze de Novembro, was converted to pedestrian-only, and an industrial zone was moved to the outskirts of the city. At the time of the original plan, there was only 5 square feet of open space per resident. By adding parks and preserving green space, today's figure is 559 square feet per resident. Approximately 1.3 million trees were planted, 16 parks created, and 1,000 plazas established (Gnatek, 2003).

The population climbed to 900,000 in the 1980s, so the city expanded the transportation system, protected a number of green areas from development, and established a recycling program.

The city's population continued to climb, reaching 1.4 million by 1992, and the city had attracted Renault, Chrysler, and Audi plants to its industrial portfolio. Buses carrying 270 passengers were added to the transit system. Curitiba hosted the World Cities Forum that year, increasing its reputation as a world leader in sustainable urban planning.

Today, the city has grown to 1.8 million people. The city is very aggressive in helping its residents find employment and offers training centers for $1 in courses such as auto mechanics, hairdressing, typing, and electrical work so that the unemployed can gain skills. Recycling was introduced in Curitiba's schools, and the schoolchildren encouraged their parents to recycle at home. Today, two thirds of the garbage is recycled (Sustainable Communities Network, 2010).

Auckland

In Auckland, New Zealand, the sustainability plan is called the "Auckland One Plan." The major categories of the plan are as follows:

- Responding to climate change
- Doing more with less

- Capitalizing on global economic change
- Managing population growth and demographic change
- Addressing disadvantage

The plan sets out eight goals:

Goal 1: A fair and connected society

Goal 2: Pride in who we are

Goal 3: A unique and outstanding environment

Goal 4: Prosperity through innovation

Goal 5: Self-sustaining Maori communities

Goal 6: A quality, compact urban form

Goal 7: Resilient infrastructure

Goal 8: Effective collaborative leadership

Then, the plan identifies eight "shifts," which are changes that need to be made to support sustainable development ("Auckland Sustainability Framework," 2010).

Melbourne

The **Australian Climate Change Bill** proposes legislation to reduce GHG emissions by at least 20% by 2020. This aggressive target is accompanied with a number of strategies aimed at accomplishing that goal:

- Reduce emissions from coal-fired generators.
- Provide more support for solar power.
- Establish grants for research in energy.
- Introduce a retrofit for households.
- Offer rebates for solar hot water installations.
- Set up a carbon exchange program for offsets.
- Support the electric vehicles market.
- Install cogeneration plants in hospitals.
- Introduce climate change into the public school curriculum. ("Summary of Key Actions," 2010)

The Ten Dirtiest Cities in the World

Mercer Health and Sanitation rated the dirtiest cities in the world according to a health index (Luck, 2008):

1. Baku, Azerbaijan

2. Dhaka, Bangladesh

3. Antananarivo, Madagascar

4. Port-au-Prince, Haiti

5. Mexico City, Mexico

6. Addis Ababa, Ethiopia

7. Mumbai, India

8. Baghdad, Iraq

9. Almaty, Kazakhstan

10. Brazzaville, the Congo (Luck, 2008)

Not surprisingly, the dirtiest cities in the world are found in third world areas. These countries are in need of assistance to attain the basic necessities of life.

Business Implications

Businesses make location decisions—where do they establish a plant or a corporate or regional headquarters—and these decisions are made with a number of factors. The city infrastructure and financial incentives are key factors, as are transportation and labor costs, the economic climate, and quality of life. Companies may elect to move from one city to another due to poor support or a deficiency in any of the important factors. A sustainability portfolio that is actively implemented is a barometer of the city's capabilities and priorities and is an important consideration in any location decision.

The quality of life is impacted by a city's approach to sustainability. Parks and recreation in beautifully designed spaces beautify a city and make for an attractive place to live, but that must be supported by an infrastructure that maintains the face of the city.

It goes both ways—cities help business, but business must also help the city. Once a business establishes itself in a community, it must participate in the efforts to make the city sustainable. The city plays a part in job satisfaction.

LEED Certification

The U.S. Green Building Council (USGBC) has established the LEED certification for green buildings. The certification, as is evident from the many cities that are requiring all government buildings to become certified, has become a standard for U.S. cities.

The basic categories for new construction are as follows:

Sustainable sites	26 points
Water efficiency	10
Energy and atmosphere	35
Materials and resources	14
Indoor environmental quality	15
Innovation and design	6
Regional priority	4
Total	110 points
Certification	40 to 49 points
Silver	50 to 59 points
Gold	60 to 79 points
Platinum	80 points

Conclusion

The majority of major cities across the world have mapped a comprehensive sustainability plan that sets an agenda for the next 10 to 20 years. The plans set ambitious targets, which in most cases exceed the recommendations of the Kyoto Protocol. However, these documents are written by politicians who will undoubtedly be out of office when the final report card is given two or three decades from now.

While many mayors came out in favor of the Kyoto Protocol, they did not actually have a vote, so it was politically safe to support environmental legislation. The movement in Melbourne to actually legislate emissions reductions will not be effective unless they have a mechanism of enforcement, and that may be in the form of luxury taxes on SUVs, taxes on air passengers, and so on.

What is illustrated in this chapter is that these cities have a sustainability plan, and that is an important first step. The second step is to have ways to meet the goals set forth in the plan.

KEY WORDS

American Recovery and Reinvestment Act (ARRA)

Australian Climate Change Bill

International Council for Local Environmental Initiatives (ICLEI)— Local Governments for Sustainability

LEED certification

Mexico City Climate
Action Program

Mumbai Sustainability and
Corporate Citizenship Protocol

Single stream collection

Sustainable Atlanta Initiative

Sustainable Building Initiative

Sustainable return on
investment (SROI)

Volatile organic compounds
(VOCs)

DISCUSSION QUESTIONS

1. Does your city have a sustainability plan? If so, how does it compare to some of the cities reviewed in this chapter?

2. What are the major components of a city sustainability plan?

3. What considerations should smaller cities, with populations ranging from 50,000 to 500,000, make in writing a sustainability plan?

4. Is it necessary for a smaller town to consider a sustainability plan?

5. Compare other airports—for example, Chicago's O'Hare and Atlanta's Hartsfield–Jackson—with the plan at LAX.

6. Why do cities pursue LEED certification for their buildings?

7. Could the shared bike system of Portland and Paris work in congested cities like New York City, Chicago, and San Francisco? Spacious cities like Salt Lake City, Denver, and Jacksonville?

8. How does public transportation figure into a city's sustainability plan?

9. How do cities in desert communities—for example, Phoenix, Las Vegas, and Tucson—differ in their water policies from water-rich cities—for example, Portland, Seattle, and Chicago?

10. Compare the proportions of green space in major cities. How does the protection of parks and recreational locations influence sustainability plans?

11. What are the arguments for and against city living as a way to be more ecologically sound?

RECOMMENDED WEBSITES

www.sustainability.asu.edu

www.usgbc.org

13 GREEN MARKETING

Chapter Overview

Companies must use all of their marketing tools to sell products. Through effective promotion, sales, and distribution, a company will attempt to get their goods into the hands of waiting customers. The basic principles of marketing still apply when it comes to "green" marketing, a term that has come to encompass environmental and socially conscious oriented goods.

This chapter will review the basic principles of green marketing and study the best and worst approaches to promoting these products. We will review the five green *P*s, and discuss the demographic factors of green consumers.

Green Marketing

Companies that seek to leverage their eco-friendly products employ marketing techniques that have several labels. It has been called green marketing (Ottman, 1998), environmental marketing (Coddington, 1993), ecological marketing (Henlon, 1976), eco-marketing (Fuller & Butler, 1998), and finally **sustainable marketing** (Fuller, 1999).

Fuller (1999) defined sustainable marketing as meeting customer needs with an ecologically compatible process of development and distribution.

For our purposes, we will use the term *green marketing*, because it appears to have attained the most use in practice.

All organizations seek to establish a sustainability presence for a number of reasons. It may be because they truly believe in it. It may be because their competitors are involved and they need to keep up, or it might be that their buyers may want to know their stance. Marketing this presence is becoming more and more critical.

For a company to actually market their products as green, there must be a number of considerations, including **authenticity,** commitment, and a programmatic approach.

1. Authenticity—The company should have a genuine claim to the environmentally or ecologically beneficial. Grant (2007) gave a number of marketing claims producers made in the United Kingdom:

   • Organic
   • Carbon neutral
   • Recycled
   • Genetically modified-free
   • Dolphin-friendly
   • Biodegradable
   • Energy efficient
   • Additive-free
   • Not tested on animals
   • Fair-trade
   • Free range
   • Sweatshop-free clothing
   • Vegan
   • Forest Stewardship Council (FSC)-certified (forestry)
   • European eco label
   • UK fuel economy label
   • Energy Star
   • Confidence in textiles
   • Marine Stewardship Council (MSC)

Claims of this type in the United States must pass the muster of the Federal Trade Commission (FTC), which monitors false advertising. The point is that the claim should be genuine, for if it were later found to be false, the resultant public relations would be a nightmare.

2. Commitment—The company itself should actively pursue the quest for sustainability. It should be a universal commitment from the president of the organization down through the ranks.

3. A programmatic approach—Sustainability is much more than recycling aluminum and paper and only watering the lawn on odd-numbered days. A complete program aimed at addressing a complete, holistic approach should be established prior to embarking on green marketing. Failures in one aspect of the triple bottom line (TBL) can make all other good efforts go to waste—for example, selling fair trade coffee, while employing underage workers.

This chapter reviews the principles of green marketing and gives examples of companies that have succeeded or failed in this endeavor. We will review the problems associated with greenwashing, a practice in which firms attempt to make false claims or to distract from other environmental problems. Finally, we will review a number of companies that have successfully employed green marketing.

Marketing has always relied upon a number of factors to help place a product in a customer's hands. It starts with marketing research to discover the attributes a customer wants in a product. Product development then embarks with a design strategy intended to approach that ideal mix of customer attributes. The sales team is charged with targeting the relevant buying groups and securing purchases. Advertising is charged with finding the media outlets that may increase customer demand through effective commercials or ads. The supply chain is responsible for the timely delivery of the product so that the customer is satisfied with the purchase. **Customer relationship management (CRM)** tracks customers' buying habits to maximize the marketing research aspects.

The classic 5 Ps of marketing are product, price, place, promotion, and people. Each of these must be carefully considered if a company is going to use green as their marketing strategy.

1. *Product:* Is the product completely vetted? Are all claims legitimate, proven, and certified? Is the product packaging recyclable?

2. *Price:* If the product costs more to deliver, are customers willing to pay extra for the product, given its environmental superiority over competing products? Marketing research and focus groups will help answer this question.

3. *Place:* What stores would be the most appropriate to capture the demographic who would buy this product? In what area of the country would sales be optimal?

4. *Promotion:* What media outlets would the potential customers be most likely to pay attention to? What nongovernmental organizations (NGOs) might be willing to partner for this particular product?

5. *People:* Do we have the support people who identify with the values presented by this product?

Conventional marketing is out. Green marketing is in. Effectively addressing the needs of consumers with a raised environmental consciousness cannot be achieved with the same assumptions and formulas that guided consumer marketing in the high production-high consumption postwar era. New strategies and innovative product and service offerings are required. (Ottman, 1998, p. 45)

Paths to Develop Sustainable Products

Unruh and Ettenson (2011) stressed a three-pronged approach to green product development. Path #1 was **accentuate,** emphasizing the existing green attributes the company already possesses. They provide the example of the Brita water filter, which took advantage of the move away from plastic water bottles by pointing out the environmental advantages of their filter. However, companies risk public backlash if they have other products in their portfolio that do not pass muster. Unruh and Ettenson gave the example of British Petroleum's (BP) "Beyond Petroleum" campaign, which sought to emphasize other product areas. *Fortune* magazine's reaction was "Here's a novel advertising strategy—pitch your least important product and ignore your most important one" (Murphy, 2002). In light of the BP oil spill in the Gulf of Mexico, it is doubtful BP will push a "Beyond Petroleum" campaign in the immediate future. The only ads BP sponsored in 2010 were apologetic commitments to clean the spill.

Path #2 is to **acquire**—buy firms that improve the green portfolio. Small firms that have sound ecological practices—for example, Ben and Jerry's and Stonyfield Farm—were both purchased by larger firms.

Path #3 is **architect.** Build your own products. The Toyota Prius is an example. Whichever path a company takes, Unruh and Ettenson (2011) pointed out to be cognizant of any environmental "skeletons" in the portfolio that may exist and to ascertain whether new green claims are credible and not candidates for cries of greenwashing—a practice of making hollow environmental claims that do not have merit.

The Rules of Green Marketing

Consultant Jacquelyn Ottman (2010) illustrated five simple rules of green marketing:

1. *Know your customer:* Ottman's example was Whirlpool's introduction of a chlorofluorocarbon (CFC)-free refrigerator. Whirlpool had to increase the price of their refrigerator to a level that customers were not willing to pay.

2. *Empower consumers:* Give them the feeling that the purchase of the product actually makes a difference.

3. *Be transparent:* Skepticism abounds about environmental claims, so the product should have legitimate claims.

4. *Reassure the buyer:* The product should perform the task it is designed to do and not forsake functionality for environmental claims.

5. *Consider your pricing:* Make sure customers feel the extra cost is warranted.

Ottman (2010) gave the example of the Toyota Prius, which offered good design and function in a hybrid automobile. Customers felt assured that they were not sacrificing performance and reducing emissions. Unfortunately, a problem with the accelerator caused a recall and a public relations problem that impacted sales in 2009. A second example given was Tide Coldwater, a detergent that saves energy bills by allowing clothes to be washed in cold water. Again, customers could feel good about this purchase.

Ottman's (2010) tips on implementing these rules include the following:

1. Think and act holistically. Green "thinking" should be part of every product and service decision the company makes.

2. Engage consumers on an emotional level in order to build brand equity. Try to make customers feel good and responsible about their purchase.

3. Communication is critical to success and will help avoid accusations of greenwashing. As stated earlier in this chapter, authenticity is paramount.

4. Eco-innovation can be used to grow top-line sales. With mature product lines, this may be a creative way to prolong the product life cycle by improving the environmental aspects of the product.

5. Aim for an ideal goal of zero environmental impact. Company-wide programs seeking real gains beyond recycling should be considered as a beginning.

A study by Fraj-Andres, Martinez-Salinas, and Matute-Vellejo in 2009 supported the hypothesis that "environmental marketing positively influenced the firm's operational and commercial performance."

Greenwashing

Greenwashing is defined by the firm TerraChoice as "the act of misleading consumers regarding the environmental practices of a company or the environmental benefits of a product or service." In Australia, concerns about false green claims led to the Green Marketing and the Trade Practices Act that states, "Firms which make environmental or green claims should ensure that their claims are scientifically sound and appropriately substantiated." France's consumer protection agency rules that cars should only be depicted in advertisements placing them in traffic scenes, rather than immersed in nature. The U.S. FTC established rules of environmental claims and can fine companies that mislead consumers.

TerraChoice, an environmental marketing consulting firm, listed the "Seven Sins of Greenwashing," The firm went into *big box* retailers to classify all products that made green claims. They found 2,219 products making 4,996 claims.

Some of the highlights of their study include the following:

- From 2007 to 2008, the total number of green products increased by 79%.
- More than 98% of the products committed one of their sins.
- Kids, cosmetics, and cleaning products were the guiltiest of committing a greenwashing sin.
- Less than 1% of all print advertisements in 1987 would be classified as green. By 2008, more than 10% of print ads were classified as green.

The Seven Sins of Greenwashing

1. *Sin of the hidden trade-off:* Suggesting a product is green, but not considering the trade-offs involved. Paper, for example, may be listed as environmentally preferable; however, that disregards the other aspects of the timber industry.

2. *Sin of no proof:* A claim that cannot be substantiated.

3. *Sin of vagueness:* A poorly defined claim. "All natural" can mean just about anything. What does "non-toxic" actually mean?

4. *Sin of irrelevance*—A claim that is unimportant. CFC-free is a frequent claim, but since CFCs are banned anyway, the claim is irrelevant.

5. *Sin of lesser of two evils*—A claim that may be true, but is intended to distract the consumer from other issues. An example is the fuel-efficient SUV, which might get the best mileage in its class, but nowhere close to a smaller sedan.

6. *Sin of fibbing*—Making a completely false claim. This can lead to fines from the FTC.

   Sin of worshipping false labels—Making false endorsement claims. In Canada, one manufacturer of paper towels used a certification-like emblem on its product and claimed, "This product fights global warming." (TerraChoice, 2012)

A website listed what it considered to be America's 10 worst greenwashers:

1. *Kraft's Post Select Cereals:* Advertised as "natural ingredients," but the corn is genetically engineered.

2. *The Council for Biotechnology Information:* Promoted genetically engineered foods through books aimed at children

3. *Tyson chicken:* Claims its chickens are "all natural," when they are treated with antibiotics

4. *The Audubon Nature Institute:* Belongs to the National Wetlands Coalition, an organization lobbying to weaken the Endangered Species Act of 1973 (ESA). The National Wetlands Coalition is a consortium that includes Chevron and ExxonMobil.

5. *Comanche Trace:* Advertises its golf courses as "great habitats," although they deplete natural habitats

6. *Clairol:* Advertises Herbal Essences shampoos as "truly organic" although they include sodium lauryl sulfate, propylene glycol, and D & C red no.33, which don't exactly sound truly organic. To its credit, Clairol does not test on animals.

7. *Americans for Balanced Energy Choices:* For promoting coal as a "clean fuel"

8. *General Motors (GM):* For displaying SUVs in natural habitats to promote its cars as environmentally friendly. GM is a member of the Coalition for Vehicle Choice, an organization that opposes clean air legislation.

9. *American Electric Power:* For making claims about being environmentally friendly, while being one of the nation's biggest polluters.

10. *ExxonMobil:* Advertises that the air we breathe is getting better, while lobbying against the Kyoto Protocol. (Deen, 2012)

Another website, 247wallst.com, had a similar list that included American Electric Power, ExxonMobil, and GM ("The Green Hypocrisy," 2009). In addition, the website added these seven to their list of the worst 10 examples of greenwashing:

1. *General Electric (GE):* That bastion of corporate success launched a $90 million Ecoimagination advertising campaign in 2005. They said that revenue from their Ecoimagination products stood to earn $17 billion in 2008. This probably is to help the public forget that from 1947 to 1977, GE discharged 1.3 million pounds of polychlorinated biphenyls (PCBs) from two facilities into the Hudson River. The U.S. Environmental

Protection Agency (EPA) estimated that the cancer risk from eating fish from the Upper Hudson exceeded the EPA standard by 700 times. In addition, GE was listed by the League of Conservation Voters as one of the companies who support political candidates who consistently vote against clean energy and conservation.

2. *DuPont:* DuPont's marketing campaign, "Open Science," stressed how "DuPont and its partners are tackling the issues of our food shortages, dwindling petroleum, and global warming" ("The Green Hypocrisy," 2009).

Only 3 years earlier, DuPont was fined $16.5 million for violations for failure to report the health risks affiliated with a chemical compound used to make Teflon. Like GE, the marketing campaign seemed designed to help consumers forget past actions.

3. *Archer Daniels Midland (ADM):* Interestingly, this producer of biofuels ethanol and biodiesel was criticized by 247wallst.com with this statement:

> The truth is that both ethanol and biodiesel emit less global warming pollution than burning petroleum-based gasoline. Unfortunately, producing biofuels creates enormous amounts of global warming pollution, so much so that many argue that they offset the benefits gained when the fuel is used to power engines. This is the sin of the hidden trade-off. In this case, a company promotes the green attribute of a product without consideration for other environmental factors. ADM publicly touts biofuels' green benefits, while failing to mention that the energy necessary to grow the corn requires significant amounts of fossil fuels, offsetting the environmental benefits. According to the journal *Science,* "corn-based ethanol, instead of producing a 20% savings, nearly doubles greenhouse emissions over 30 years and increases greenhouse gases (GHGs) for 167 years. Biofuels from switchgrass, if grown on U.S. corn lands, increase emissions by 50%." ("The Green Hypocrisy," 2009)

4. *Waste Management:* 247wallst.com's criticism reads, "According to Elizabeth Royte, a journalist for the Natural Resources Defense Council's [*OnEarth*] since 2005, Waste Management has spent more than $90 million on TV commercials and print advertisement emphasizing the number of trees it saves through recycling, the amount of land it has set aside for wildlife habitats, and how much energy it generates through incineration. However, what the ads fail to disclose is that burning trash doesn't come without a price. Although the technology continues to improve, incinerators still discharge small levels of mercury, lead, and dioxin into the atmosphere." Royte also wrote, "They also generate more carbon dioxide per megawatt-hour of energy generated than do power plants, and their ash is toxic. An

additional consequence of incineration is that it discourages using landfills. Because power plants that use incinerators require a consistent flow of garbage, they are necessarily antagonistic to principles such as recycling, composting, and reducing waste. Waste Management's corporate PAC has donated to two members of the dirty dozen, Mitch McConnell and Sam Graves" (Royte, 2008).

5. International Paper: International Paper helped found the Sustainable Forestry Initiative (SFI) for certification of forestry practices. However, the Sierra Club, the Environmental Defense Fund (EDF), and the Rainforest Action Network have been critical of the certification process as weak and self-serving to member companies and licensees.

6. BP (making this list pre-spill): Although advertising "Beyond Petroleum," according to a 2009 study published by Greenpeace, BP allocated 93% of its research and development to the extraction of oil, gas, and other fossil fuels. Alternative energy research comprised the remaining 7%. The EPA also fined BP $12 million for "failing to fulfill its obligations under the law, putting air quality and public health at risk" ("The Green Hypocrisy," 2009). These violations were against the Clean Air Act and took place in Texas City.

7. Dow Chemical: Dow's campaign, titled the "Human Element," won a national award for the best television commercial in 2008. Meanwhile, Dow was under investigation for its slow cleanup of a polluted spill of the Tittabawassee River in Michigan ("The Green Hypocrisy," 2009).

Some of the companies named as greenwashers, to be certain, are making attempts to change their image through positive actions. Others, however, try to change the public perception simply by advertising.

A 1996 study by Carlson, Grove, Kangun, and Polonsky found differences in environmental advertising in the United States, Great Britain, Australia, and Canada. The researchers found the following:

> Environmental ads originating in the United States tend to communicate less information about tangible environmental benefits that are most beneficial to consumers. If so, U.S. organizations may be creating the illusion of being 'green; when, in fact, they are not making significant contributions and improvements to the physical environment in terms of their products and production processes. Collectively, the ads from Australia, Great Britain, and Canada appear to emphasize process- and product-based claims in their efforts to demonstrate environmental commitment; more than half the claims from each of these countries are substantive. Conversely, the U.S. ads tend to stress associative claims that present a green image or provide environmental facts. (Carlson et al., 1996)

Green Marketing Segments

Ottman (1998) classified consumers as *dark green,* consumers who will pay added costs to buy green products; *light green,* consumers who lean green but are not willing to pay extra costs; and *basic brown,* those who just don't care. Ottman (1998) further classified the dark green consumers into four groups:

1. *Resource conservers:* These consumers wear classic clothing, are prone to carry cloth shopping bags to the grocery store, and would never be found with bottled water. All their appliances are Energy Star, and their lightbulbs are compact fluorescent bulbs. They are conscious of energy consumption and try to minimize. To appeal to these consumers, marketers need to emphasize the longevity and reusability of the products.

2. *Health fanatics:* They eat organic foods, use sunscreen, and buy non-toxic products. Marketers should hone in on the health benefits. Finding shelf space at a natural foods store—for example, Whole Foods—would be a good start.

3. *Animal lovers:* Individuals who may be vegetarian or vegan or may be a member of PETA (People for the Ethical Treatment of Animals) would never buy leather or fur. They often contribute to groups that protect animals. To appeal to these individuals, advertising should be sought in the specialty magazines like *PAWS* magazine, *Animal Fair,* or partner with organizations like the ASPCA (the American Society for the Prevention of Cruelty to Animals).

4. *Outdoor enthusiasts:* Campers and hikers whose idea of a good time is a day at REI. They seek products that reduce their impact on the environment—clothing made from recycled products, for example. To appeal to this group, they should advertise in the *Sierra Club* magazine or *Backpacker* magazine and look for opportunities to partner with national parks.

The Boston consulting firm, Cone LLC, and Boston College Center for Corporate Citizenship surveyed 1,080 consumers and developed five guidelines for green marketing, based upon the responses.

1. Be precise. Claims should be specific and quantify the environmental impact.

2. Be relevant. Show the connection between the product and the environment.

3. Be a resource. Provide appropriate consumer information.

4. Be consistent. Avoid contradictory signals, i.e., the gas-guzzling SUV in nature.

5. Be realistic. Nothing is perfectly green. (Cone LLC, 2008)

_____ The Ogilvy Earth Handbook

Ogilvy Earth, the sustainability arm of the firm Ogilvy & Mather, provides the handbook _From Greenwash to Great_ (Ogilvy Earth, 2010). They divide the marketing campaign into three distinct phases: (1) planning your approach, (2) developing communications, and (3) launching and beyond.

Planning Your Approach

- _Focus on fundamentals:_ Form a team to plan through the supply chain, and map a plan. Hellmann's Mayonnaise switch to the use of free-range eggs is an example.
- _Get out ahead:_ Ogilvy mentioned GE (also listed in the greenwashing villains) and its CEO, who instructed his firm to be aggressive in its sustainability efforts.
- _Partner for content and credibility:_ Look for a third party to join forces with. Clorox, for example, partnered with the Sierra Club.

Developing Communications

- _Make honesty a priority:_ Tell the truth. Period. Patagonia offers a nice touch by illustrating the path an article of clothing takes to get on your body.
- _Find strength in humility:_ "Frame your brand's achievements in a way that acknowledges your limitations and includes a commitment to try harder" (Ogilvy Earth, 2010).
- _Embrace the detail:_ Provide all the details, and be truthful about their implications. One example is Coca-Cola's claim of "30% plant-based 100% recyclable bottles"
- _Show, don't tell:_ Demo your products so customers can witness their performance.

Launching and Beyond

- _Become a first responder:_ Be proactive in responding to criticisms. Greenpeace accused Timberland of "slaughtering the Amazon" for its leather procurement practices. Timberland's response was to partner with Greenpeace for help finding different suppliers.
- _Commit for the long term:_ This is not a short-term solution. (Ogilvy Earth, 2010)

Corporate Examples

Burt's Bees

Burt's Bees, a small company that manufactured a natural body lotion (acquired by Clorox), contrasted its ingredients with competitors' in an advertisement that read, "How do you get all the soft without the suspicious?" It contrasted its ingredients of milk and honey with DMDM hydantoin, a chemical often found in competing body lotions.

Burt's Bees also is packaged from mostly recycled products, so it is a company that is not only cognizant of natural ingredients but minimizing waste (Arvizu, 2008).

McDonald's

McDonald's marketed its green efforts in a campaign called the "Global Best of Green" (2009). It trumpeted its many efforts in sustainability that included the following:

- Switching from bleached to brown napkins in Canada, reducing energy use
- Recycling cooking oil in the United States
- Using less oil in its fryers
- Recognizing store managers as "Energy All Stars" for conserving energy
- Reducing electricity consumption by 11% in France
- Reducing carbon emissions in Mexico by using solar water heaters
- Switching to cardboard salad bowls from plastic in Europe
- Recycling organic waste in Switzerland ("Global Best of Green," 2009)

Amtrak

Amtrak, the U.S. rail system, has advertised its mode of transportation as the most environmentally friendly with justification (see Table 13.1). When compared to auto and plane transportation, train travel consumes the least energy.

Amtrak has pointed out the following benefits to train travel:

- Reduced British thermal units (BTUs) per passenger mile from 2,800 in 2003 to 2,650 in 2006
- Removed 8 million cars from the road and the need for 50,000 air flights per year. One freight train takes 280 trucks or 1,100 cars off the road.

- Committed to a 1% reduction of GHGs from 2003 to 2006, and 0.5% from 2007 to 2010.
- A participant in the Chicago Climate Exchange (CCX), the trading system for GHGs.

Whole Foods

Whole Foods, the grocery chain specializing in organic and natural products, is a brand that is completely in concert with the sustainability ethos. It has become synonymous with the green movement to the point it does not have to emphasize this fact in its advertising, since its consumers have that built-in perception of its products. Here are excerpts from its corporate website:

The 3 Rs: Reduce, Reuse, Recycle

Whole Foods has the three major themes of reduce, reuse, and recycle embodied in its program. Examples of reducing: banned plastic grocery bags, reduced energy consumption in its stores, and implemented paperless ordering systems.

Examples of reusing include the use of biodegradable plates and bowls in the dining area and the donation of packing peanuts to local shipping stores. Examples of recycling include the use of rechargeable batteries, and the use of recycled paper.

Whole Foods uses wind power and solar power. As of 2010, ten Whole Foods stores had received LEED certification and the company received the EPA Green Power Partner of the Year in 2006 and 2007.

REI

REI, the outdoor retailer, is another company whose brand is associated with a care for the environment. The typical REI patron is someone who is active outdoors and enjoys camping, biking, hiking, running, skiing, or mountain climbing.

Their stewardship report highlights their environmental concern and TBL approach.

REI's passion for the outdoors runs deep. Our core purpose is to inspire, educate, and outfit people for a lifetime of outdoor adventure and stewardship.

Stewardship is our commitment to get people outside and leading healthy active lives, caring for our planet by protecting shared natural spaces, and engaging others in making a difference. ("Stewardship at REI," n.d.)

Wal-Mart

Wal-Mart states that its sustainability efforts really began with Hurricane Katrina. As the company responded to the emergency, it realized that it had the power to make a difference in social and environmental issues. Wal-Mart's CEO laid out three goals:

1. To be supplied 100% by renewable energy

2. To create zero waste

3. To sell products that sustain resources and the environment

Since that time, Wal-Mart has made great strides not only in retooling existing stores and greening the supply chain but in designing new stores that are ecologically sound. A senior vice president of sustainability (SVP) position was created, and its current SVP, Andrea Thomas, maintains a blog called "The Green Room" (www.walmartgreenroom.com/) that includes helpful updates for costumers and suppliers.

Best Buy

Best Buy, the Minnesota-based consumer electronics firm, has found a convenient way to market its sustainability advocacy and make money at the same time. By joining forces with the EPA's **Responsible Appliance Disposal (RAD) Program,** Best Buy handles the removal and disposal of old appliances while selling replacement appliances, often with the Energy Star certification.

In 2009, Best Buy collected 120 million pounds of obsolete electronics goods from U.S. consumers. Since old appliances may contain PCBs, CFCs, and other harmful refrigerants, it plays an important and needed role in recycling.

This goes a long way in helping sales, because most consumers cannot physically remove large appliances, and it is easier to have Best Buy take care of removal while installing a replacement. Other companies may offer the same practice, but Best Buy has made it part of their advertising campaigns to increase public awareness.

Abt

On a smaller scale, Abt, a Chicago-based appliance and consumer electronics retailer, applies similar principles to its bigger competitor, Best Buy. It also handles disposables and has a very high sustainability awareness and sets high environmental standards. Among its efforts in this regard are the following:

- The use of natural light in its store. The lighting system uses high output fluorescent lights that are 60% more efficient than standard lighting. Abt makes use of wind and solar energy.

- Paper catalogs have been eliminated in favor of the website.
- There is an on-site cafeteria, and bikes are provided for employees who prefer to go out to lunch, avoiding the use of cars.
- Delivery trucks use biodiesel. Used oil, oil filters, coolant, and batteries are recycled. Water that washes trucks is also recycled, hopefully not in its drinking water!

Fifty Years of Green Marketing

Fast Company's (2012) website (www.fastcompany.com/pics/50-year-history-green-marketing) chronicled the 50-year history of green marketing. Important dates in corporate green marketing include the following:

1969—Santa Barbara oil spill concerns are raised.

1970—First Earth Day

1977—GE ceases dumping PCBs into Hudson River. The Occidental Chemical Love Canal disaster.

1980—Superfund created to clean up hazardous waste sites.

1980s—Volkswagen begins testing solar-powered cars.

1980—ARCO Solar produces more than 1 megawatt of photovoltaic modules.

1984—Union Carbide's fertilizer plant leaks methyl icocyanide in Bhopal, India.

Mid-1980s—Dupont sells substitutes for CFC refrigerants.

1989—Exxon Valdez spills 11 million gallons of crude oil in Prince William Sound.

1990—76% of Americans call themselves "environmentalists."

1990—Apple introduces first environmental policy.

1993—Clorox makes *Fortune*'s list of top companies in environmental management.

1993—Nike launches Reuse-A-Shoe program.

1999—Honda Insight and Toyota Prius are introduced.

2002—Jury rules that Monsanto Chemical is responsible for polluting Anniston, Alabama, with toxic PCBs.

2002—U.S. Department of Agriculture (USDA)-certified organic labeling is introduced.

2007—Home Depot Eco-Options program is introduced.

2009—Wal-Mart institutes sustainability labeling system. ("A 50 Year History of Green Marketing," 2012)

Ecotourism

Many tourists have taken advantage of "ecotourism"—travel that is specifically designed to reduce the impact on the environment. The International Ecotourism Society (TIES) defines ecotourism as "responsible travel to natural areas that conserves the environment and improves the well-being of local people."

The ecotourism principles espoused by TIES (n.d.) are as follows:

- Minimize impact.
- Build environmental and cultural awareness and respect.
- Provide positive experiences for both visitors and hosts.
- Provide direct financial benefits for conservation.
- Provide financial benefits and empowerment for local people.
- Raise sensitivity to host countries' political, environmental, and social climate.

One of the best websites for ecotourism is the *New York Times* travel guide (www.travel.nytimes.com/travel/guides/eco-tourism/overview.html). A recent selection of tours included Quebec, Galapagos, Guyana, Belize, and Costa Rica.

Several travel guides are available for those interested in ecotourism and its benefits. *The Lonely Planet Code Green* (Lorimer, 2006) is but one example of books that are directed at those who intend to travel but are cognizant of treading lightly and leaving a minimal footprint.

The Federal Trade Commission Environmental Standards

The U.S. FTC has established standards regarding environmental marketing claims. Violation of these standards can result in a fine.

The General Principles

In general, the FTC states that the marketing disclosure must be clear and understandable. It must establish whether the claim relates to the product itself, or the packaging. For example, a box of aluminum foil may be labeled *recyclable,* but it is unclear whether the claim relates to the product or the box. If any part of the product is not recyclable, the advertising is considered deceptive.

Overstatements of fact can get a company into trouble. The claim "50% more recycled content" may be true if the product has gone from 2% to 3%, but it is still trivial. Comparative claims also must be valid, when it relates to a competitive product. "The most recycled content of all brands" must be supported.

The claim of *degradable* must have scientific backing to establish a claim. Similarly, claims of *compostable* must be supported with scientific proof. Also, *recyclable* must have evidence. An aluminum can that states, "Please recycle" carries a message that it is recyclable, and this is, in fact, warranted by evidence. However, any product with the same message that cannot be recycled is using deception.

The phrases *ozone safe* and *ozone friendly* can be misrepresented. If a product does no damage to the ozone but still contributes to smog, the claim is deceptive.

The FTC provides numerous examples on its website. Here are several found in the *Guides for the Use of Environmental Marketing Claims* (FTC, 2007):

> A product is advertised as environmentally preferable. This claim is likely to convey to consumers that this product is environmentally superior to other products. If the manufacturer cannot substantiate this broad claim, the claim would be deceptive. The claim would not be deceptive if it were accompanied by clear and prominent qualifying language limiting the environmental superiority representation to the particular product attribute or attributes for which it could be substantiated, provided that no other deceptive implications were created by the context.
>
> A trash bag is marketed as "degradable," with no qualification or other disclosure. The marketer relies on soil burial tests to show that the product will decompose in the presence of water and oxygen. The trash bags are customarily disposed of in incineration facilities or sanitary landfills that are managed in a way that inhibits degradation by minimizing moisture and oxygen. Degradation will be irrelevant for those trash bags that are incinerated and, for those disposed of in landfills, the marketer does not possess adequate substantiation that the bags will degrade in a reasonably short period of time in a landfill. The claim is therefore deceptive.
>
> A nationally marketed lawn and leaf bag is labeled compostable. Also printed on the bag is a disclosure that the bag is not designed for use in home compost piles. The bags are in fact composted in yard trimmings composting programs in many communities around the country, but such programs are not available to a substantial majority of consumers or communities where the bag is sold. The claim is deceptive because reasonable consumers living in areas not served by yard trimmings programs may understand the reference to mean that composting facilities accepting the bags are available in their areas. To avoid deception, the claim should be qualified to indicate the limited availability of such programs, for example, by stating, "Appropriate facilities may

not exist in your area." Other examples of adequate qualification of the claim include providing the approximate percentage of communities or the population for which such programs are available.

A packaged product is labeled with an unqualified claim "recyclable." It is unclear from the type of product and other context whether the claim refers to the product or its package. The unqualified claim is likely to convey to reasonable consumers that both the entire product and its packaging that remain after normal use of the product, except for minor, incidental components, can be recycled. Unless each such message can be substantiated, the claim should be qualified to indicate what portions are recyclable.

A product in a multi-component package, such as a paperboard box in a shrink-wrapped plastic cover, indicates that it has recycled packaging. The paperboard box is made entirely of recycled material, but the plastic cover is not. The claim is deceptive since, without qualification, it suggests that both components are recycled. A claim limited to the paperboard box would not be deceptive.

An advertiser notes that disposal of its product generates "10% less waste." The claim is ambiguous. Depending on contextual factors, it could be a comparison either to the immediately preceding product or to a competitor's product. The 10% less waste reference is deceptive unless the seller clarifies which comparison is intended and substantiates that comparison, or substantiates both possible interpretations of the claim.

The seller of an aerosol product makes an unqualified claim that its product "Contains no CFCs." Although the product does not contain CFCs, it does contain HCFC-22, another ozone depleting ingredient. Because the claim "contains no CFCs" may imply to reasonable consumers that the product does not harm the ozone layer, the claim is deceptive" (FTC, 2007).

The FTC's document contains many similar examples of deceptive and fair claims that companies have made of their products.

Business Implications

Green marketing is something that businesses must be very careful about. Claims have to be justifiable and authentic or a campaign can cause irreparable damage. One might even question whether a company conducts a green campaign because they truly believe in the spirit of the campaign or they simply are after another demographic.

There are consumers out there who will pay more to be ethically, socially, and environmentally proactive. The decision to campaign about a company's activities in this domain should be backed with proof, or else the greenwashing sites will embarrass the company publicly.

Conclusion

Companies may find it advantageous to advertise the environmental advantages of their products, because many of today's consumers will pay attention to their claims. As a result, care and diligence must go into the making of these claims to assure that they are legitimate.

This chapter listed the sins of greenwashing and portions of the general principles of the FTC. Bad publicity is the result of an unwarranted claim, and that can cause loss of goodwill with customers. Therefore, all effort should be made to provide scientific proof to substantiate a claim. Once a company enters the marketplace with an advertisement, it is too late to discover that the product has not been properly vetted and there are holes in the argument of its environmental superiority.

The most important aspect of green marketing is authenticity—to have a valid claim that the company can promote. A company that cannot back up its claims risk being tagged with the label of a *greenwasher.*

KEY WORDS

Accentuate

Acquire

Architect

Authenticity

Customer relationship
    management (CRM)

Five green *P*s

Green marketing

Greenwashing

Responsible Appliance
    Disposal (RAD) Program

Sustainable marketing

DISCUSSION QUESTIONS

1. Define sustainable marketing.

2. What are the basic requirements for successful green marketing?

3. What are the five green *P*s?

4. Describe Ottman's rules of green marketing.

5. What are the seven sins of greenwashing?

6. Select several periodicals, and scan the advertisements for examples of green marketing. Is there any level of greenwashing involved?

7. Examine the comparative advertisements in one industry—that is, automobiles, computers. What degree of green marketing do you find among the competitors?

8. Describe green marketing attempts from companies considered to be in "dirty" industries: steel, chemical, energy, and so on.

9. Discuss the public relations efforts of companies that have experienced significant environmental catastrophes: ExxonMobil, BP, and others.

10. Ecotourism is aimed at environmentally conscious consumers. Locate some advertisements for tours, and note their ecological features.

RECOMMENDED WEBSITES

www.247wallst.com

www.amtrak.com

www.ecotourism.org

www.fastcompany.com

www.greenbiz.com

www.greenmarketing.com

www.greenwashing.com

www.sinsofgreenwashing.org

www.travel.nytimes.com/travel/guides/eco-tourism

www.walmartgreenroom.com

Appendix _____

Green Jobs

LEARNING OBJECTIVES

In this appendix, we will do the following:

- Discuss the overall green economy.
- Study the impact of the green economy on jobs.
- Review the workforce implications on 12 industry sectors

Appendix Overview

There was much discussion in the course of the 2008 U.S. presidential election that new green jobs needed to be created. As typical of any political campaign, the exact nature of these green jobs was rather vague. What were they? What kind of training was necessary to get one of these jobs? What locations offered the most potential for green jobs?

Indeed, many college students will be on the hunt for green employment. What they need is guidance on the types of jobs that are available and how they can qualify for them.

The following is an article written for the U.S. Department of Labor, Employment, and Training Administration by six researchers—Erich Dierdorff, Jennifer Norton, Donald Drewes, Christina Kroustalis, David Rifkin, and Phil Lewis—who answer that very question. Their article will present an overview of the green economy, discuss the greening of occupations, and review the staffing implications in green sectors.

Greening of the World of Work: Implications for O*NET®-SOC and New and Emerging Occupations

Erich C. Dierdorff, Jennifer J. Norton, Donald W. Drewes,
& Christina M. Kroustalis North Carolina State University

David Rivkin & Phil Lewis National Center for O*NET Development

Prepared for

U.S. Department of Labor Employment and
Training Administration Office of Workforce Investment
Division of Workforce System Support Washington, DC

Submitted by

The National Center for O*NET Development February 12, 2009

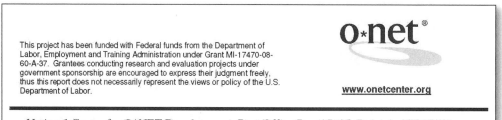

This project has been funded with Federal funds from the Department of
Labor, Employment and Training Administration under Grant MI-17470-08-
60-A-37. Grantees conducting research and evaluation projects under
government sponsorship are encouraged to express their judgment freely,
thus this report does not necessarily represent the views or policy of the U.S.
Department of Labor.

www.onetcenter.org

National Center for O*NET Development, Post Office Box 27625, Raleigh, NC 27611

SECTION I: OCCUPATIONAL IMPLICATIONS OF THE GREEN ECONOMY

Section I-1: Overview of the Green Economy

It is certainly no exaggeration to note that the label "green" has become ubiquitous. Underlying this prevalence is a substantial body of literature focused on all things green. This literature spans multiple disciplines (e.g., labor economics, engineering, environmental science) and is found in a variety of outlets ranging from the popular press to governmental reports to academic journals. The overall conclusion from this burgeoning domain is that the "greening" of our national economy is not only currently underway, but also that it should be met with concerted efforts to significantly increase both intellectual and financial capital investments. Numerous arguments for such amplified attention are frequently proffered to include issues of national security, environmental protection, climate change, and domestic job growth.

Enabling focused investment requires systematic study to better understand and define what it means to be "green." The rush to jump on the "green" bandwagon has outpaced the development of a concept of what it actually means to be green. For example, consider the praise by the popular press of individuals "going green" by using recycled goods and reducing consumption, or specific companies by increasing energy efficiency, or municipalities offering grants for green residential construction projects (e.g., fitting homes with solar panels). In other words, green activities can range from choosing a specific brand of cleaning spray to installing a wind energy farm. To determine the workforce ramifications of this vast array of green activities is a substantial undertaking. The first step is to focus the scope by developing a precise and bounded definition of what the green economy means in the context of jobs or occupations.

A thorough understanding of any job or occupation requires an understanding of the context in which these entities exist. One way to conceptualize the broader context of work is through an economic lens—in the present case, what is referred to as the green economy. Fortunately, there is a general consensus in the extant literature regarding the scope of the green economy, which is summarized in the definition below.

The green economy encompasses the economic activity related to reducing the use of fossil fuels, decreasing pollution and greenhouse gas emissions, increasing the efficiency of energy usage, recycling materials, and developing and adopting renewable sources of energy.

In support of these goals is a range of activities and strategies, including retrofitting buildings to improve energy efficiency, promoting usage of mass transit, producing energy-efficient automobiles, increasing the use of wind or solar power, and developing and producing cellulosic biomass fuels. The significant benefits of green economy activities are significant and described as both macroeconomic (e.g., investment in new technologies, greater productivity) and microeconomic (e.g., income growth, job growth). For instance, analysts concluded that renewable energy and energy efficiency technologies generated over 8 million new jobs and $970 billion in revenue in 2006 alone.

At the heart of green economy activities is technology. That is, technological innovations are what drive the many activities that comprise the green economy. For example, clean energy technologies use the sun, wind, water, and plant matter to produce electricity, heat, and transportation fuel. New green technology also spans a broad range of products, services, and processes that lower performance costs, reduce or eliminate negative ecological impact, and improve the productive and responsible use of natural resources. Thus, understanding the development and application of various green technologies can help to depict the potential workforce implications of green economy activities.

With the broader context of the green economy now delineated, the following section turns attention toward describing how occupations are influenced by this context. In this section, existing definitions of green jobs are reviewed and critiqued in an effort to better establish descriptive boundaries that are of practical use for occupational analysis. Special emphasis is given to the technologies that facilitate or enable the green economy activities discussed above.

Section I-2: The "Greening" of Occupations

Although there is no commonly accepted definition of "green job," the existing literature does offer a variety of definitions. Below are typical examples.

"Green jobs are jobs in the primary industries of a green economy that promote environmental protection and energy independence."

[Green collar jobs are] "well-paid, career-track jobs that contribute directly to preserving or enhancing environmental quality."

"A green collar job is a paid position providing environmentally friendly products or services."

"[Jobs associated with] any activity that generates electricity using renewable or nuclear fuels, agriculture jobs supplying corn or soy for transportation fuel, manufacturing jobs producing goods used in renewable power generation, equipment dealers and wholesalers specializing in renewable energy or energy-efficiency products, construction and installation of energy and pollution management systems, government administration of environmental programs, and supporting jobs in the engineering, legal, research and consulting fields."

For occupational analysis, the definition for a green occupation must focus on what it means to be an occupation and what effects the green economy has (or may have) on occupations. Thus, what is needed is a data reduction approach in defining green jobs or occupations to increase the parsimony and precision of green definitions. Key to accomplishing this task is establishing clear boundary conditions and distinct levels of specificity for any proffered definition.

Occupations are groupings of work roles that span multiple organizations but share common purposes and common requirements of incumbents. More specifically, an occupation can be viewed as a "group of jobs, found at more than one establishment, in which a common set of tasks are performed or are related in terms of similar objectives, methodologies, materials, products, worker actions, or worker characteristics." In addition, an occupation is an entity that exists at a level "above" individual incumbents or positions within an organization, in part because numerous individuals and related jobs reside within a particular occupation.

Defining occupations in this manner is important to the notion of "green jobs" in at least two ways. First, it clearly signals the need to shift the level of specificity from "job" to "occupation" when discussing the workforce implications of the green economy. The current literature focuses almost exclusively on green jobs – or simply green job titles rather than taking a perspective more conducive to workforce development efforts: an occupational perspective. Second, defining occupations in this way places an emphasis on the various work and worker requirements (e.g., tasks, skills, knowledge) requisite to occupational performance. Because many green technologies are still at the development stage and workforce results of the application of these technologies are not yet clear, the extant green economy literature has not taken an occupational-level approach, focusing instead on broader industry-level outputs or products, such as renewable power generation and environmental protection enhancement. This broader focus provides very little information regarding specific green-driven changes in the way individuals work or, the requirements of individuals performing this work.

There is an additional dimension to be accounted for in determining the impact of the green economy on occupations: determining the extent to which green economy effects are (a) creating entirely new occupations, (b) significantly changing the work or worker requirements of existing occupations, or (c) simply increasing the demand for workers in existing occupations. These distinctions are essential for locating, describing, and forecasting potential workforce consequences of the green economy. In the interest of workforce development, it is important to consider how the occupation is either created by green economic activities or changing due to these activities when labeling the occupation as "green." In a recent report for the Texas Workforce Commission, Anderberg pointed out the importance of a systematic approach to describing the effects of the green economy on occupations.

"Conferring the green label to entire constellations of occupations or to discrete tasks and work assignments does not necessarily imbue them with special skill requirements that must be addressed with some new education and training intervention. The skills needed to perform some green work assignments will be absolutely no different than those required to perform tasks and work assignments similar, if not identical, to their non-green predecessor. Other green work assignments may be so radically different than their predecessors that an entire degree—or certificate—granting program needs to be developed to impart the necessary knowledge, skills and abilities."

To summarize, there are two primary implications for occupational analysis in general, and the O*NET system in particular. First, the vast job-level information in the existing green economy literature must be consolidated and interpreted for its meaning at the occupation level. In particular, a focus on occupational requirements (tasks, duties, tools and technology, knowledge, skills, and so forth) is essential for discovering the occupational implications of the green economy.

Second, any analytical or descriptive approach used to determine the occupational implications of the green economy must be sensitive to the varying degrees with which green economy activities shape occupational performance. This entails a definitional approach to "green occupations" that moves beyond labeling (i.e., green as adjective) to encompass the dynamic nature of occupational performance (i.e., greening as verb). A parallel can be seen in the shift away from an emphasis on "organization" to "organizing" in the general management literature in order to address the effects of contextual changes in the 1990s (e.g., flattening of firms, use of teams, project-based work). Thus, a valid approach to defining green occupations is to instead define the "greening of occupations."

The "greening" of occupations refers to the extent to which green economy activities and technologies increase the demand for existing occupations, shape the work and worker requirements needed for occupational performance, or generate unique work and worker requirements.

This definition lends itself to three general categories, each describing the differential consequences of green economy activities and technologies on occupational performance. These categories of occupations are described below and include examples of the effects indicative of each. Note that the term "existing occupation" means it is already included within the O*NET database, whereas "new occupation" means it is not yet included in the database.

Green Increased Demand Occupations. The impact of green economy activities and technologies is an increase in the employment demand for an existing occupation. However, this impact does not entail significant changes in the work and worker requirements of the occupation. The work context may change, but the tasks themselves do not. An example is the increased demand for electrical power line installers and repairers related to energy efficiency and infrastructure upgrades.

Green Enhanced Skills Occupations. The impact of green economy activities and technologies results in a significant change to the work and worker requirements of an existing occupation. This impact may or may not result in an increase in employment demand for the occupation. An example is the occupation architect, where greening has increased knowledge requirements pertaining to energy efficient materials and construction, as well as skills associated with integrating green technology into the aesthetic design of buildings. For example, many architects have pursued Leadership in Energy and Environmental Design (LEED) certifications to ensure the proper application of U.S. Green Building Council principles to building designs. The essential purposes of the occupation remain the same, but tasks, skills, knowledge, and external elements, such as credentials, have been altered.

New and Emerging (N&E) Green Occupations. The impact of green economy activities and technologies is sufficient to create the need for unique work and worker requirements, resulting in the generation of a new occupation. This new occupation could be entirely novel or "born" from an existing occupation. An example would be solar system technicians who must be able not only to install new technology, but also to determine how this technology can best be used on a specific site.

Given these definitions of occupational greening and the related impacts, the next section offers an integrative framework for describing the major green economy activities and their respective technologies. As aforementioned, a focus on green technology is beneficial for occupational analysis precisely because the use and development of such technology is proximal to occupational performance. Thus, understanding how green technology is applied toward various green economy activities can inform the potential impact of these technologies on occupational demands (e.g., employment needs, work and worker requirement changes).

Section I-3: Linking Green Economy Activities _____ and Technology to Occupational Greening

As described previously, the major activities of the green economy include decreasing fossil fuel use and greenhouse gas emissions, increasing energy efficiency and recycling, and developing and adopting renewable energy sources. While useful for describing the general functions of the green economy at a broad level, more precise delineations are necessary for efficiently and effectively determining the potential occupational implications of green technology. A comprehensive review of the current literature reveals 12 distinct sectors of the green economy (presented below).

It is important to note that this list is not meant to be exhaustive, as the green economy is certainly dynamic, but these sectors were mentioned across multiple sources suggesting a consensus of their importance. In addition, these sectors are by no means completely independent; rather, their goals and functions are often inextricably linked to one another. Nonetheless, the precise view of green economy activities that is afforded by these categories allows for a more thorough determination of potential occupational implications. These categories also ensure that occupational research spans the entire spectrum of green economy activities and technologies.

1. Renewable Energy Generation. This sector covers activities related to developing and using energy sources such as solar, wind, geothermal, and biomass. This sector also includes traditional, non-renewable sources of energy undergoing significant green technological changes (e.g., oil, coal, gas, and nuclear).

2. Transportation. This sector covers activities related to increasing efficiency and/or reducing environmental impact of various modes of transportation including trucking, mass transit, freight rail, and so forth.

3. Energy Efficiency. This sector covers activities related to increasing energy efficiency (broadly defined), making energy demand response more effective, constructing "smart grids," and so forth.

4. Green Construction. This sector covers activities related to constructing new green buildings, retrofitting residential and commercial buildings, and installing other green construction technology.

5. Energy Trading. This sector covers financial services related to buying and selling energy as an economic commodity, as well as carbon trading projects.

6. Energy and Carbon Capture and Storage. This sector covers activities related to capturing and storing energy and/or carbon emissions, as well as technologies related to power plants using the integrated gasification combined cycle (IGCC) technique.

7. Research, Design, and Consulting Services. This sector encompasses "indirect jobs" to the green economy which includes activities such as energy consulting or research and other related business services.

8. Environment Protection. This sector covers activities related to environmental remediation, climate change adaptation, and ensuring or enhancing air quality.

9. Agriculture and Forestry. This sector covers activities related to using natural pesticides, efficient land management or farming, and aquaculture.

10. Manufacturing. This sector covers activities related to industrial manufacturing of green technology as well as energy efficient manufacturing processes.

11. Recycling and Waste Reduction. This sector covers activities related to solid waste and wastewater management, treatment, and reduction, as well as processing recyclable materials.

12. Governmental and Regulatory Administration. This sector covers activities by public and private organizations associated with conservation and pollution prevention, regulation enforcement, and policy analysis and advocacy.

Section I-4: Section Summary

To summarize, the term "green" is widely applied to a substantial variety of products, services, and even lifestyle and consumer choices. Many of these applications are hard to apply to occupation analysis or difficult for use in workforce development efforts. Existing definitions of what comprises a "green job" are at a level of specificity that seems too molecular for occupational databases such as the O*NET database. Further, such definitions do not address the degree to which green economy activities differentially impact occupational requirements.

To address these issues, several definitions were presented. Considering the primary purpose of this report is to ascertain the implications of the green economy for existing and new and emerging O*NET occupations, definitions of the green economy and of the term occupation were presented. Next, a finer-grained definition that encompassed the impact of green economy activities and technologies on occupations was described. This definition focused on the "greening" of occupations and included three categories that represented varying degrees of influence that the green economy holds for occupational performance. Finally, to facilitate an examination of how specific occupational greening might occur, a list of 12 green economy sectors was introduced. Each of these sectors is described in more detail in the next section. These descriptions include brief synopses of major activities and associated green technologies, and specifically address any occupational implications associated with the sectors.

Section II: Occupational Staffing Implications by Green Sectors

The 12 green sectors previously presented are described in this section. The primary purpose of these synopses is to provide snapshots of general sector activities, recent trends, and potential implications for occupations. This section therefore provides a backdrop to facilitate interpretations of subsequent report sections presenting specific categories of occupations that are impacted by occupational greening.

These sectors were derived from sectors identified in multiple reports within the existing literature. Some sectors are more specific than those often discussed in the literature. This increased specificity allows a more comprehensive depiction of the potential occupational implications of various green economy activities. It should be noted that these 12 sectors are not necessarily equal in terms of scope, economic activity, and occupational potential. Some are currently far more active than others. For example, estimates for California have shown roughly 74% of the total green economy is attributable to activities in renewable energy generation and energy efficiency. Nevertheless, all have the potential to affect work and its context.

Section II-1: Renewable Energy Generation

This sector is arguably seeing the greatest development and growth within the green economy and is at the heart of most "green" discussions. Government regulations, energy costs, climate change, and the depletion of natural resources are all factors driving growth and change in this sector. As of 2008, 24 states and the District of Columbia have enacted regulations ("renewable portfolio standards") that require a particular portion of electricity to be generated from renewable sources. Such renewable energy sources include wind, solar, geothermal, hydropower, biomass, and hydrogen.

It has been estimated that total net renewable power generation will increase by 30%, which equates to 40% of total domestic power generation. Each of these renewable sources is briefly described below. Also included in this sector are traditional, non-renewable sources of energy undergoing significant green technological changes, such as oil, gas, coal, and nuclear.

Wind

Energy derived from wind is commonly used for a variety of purposes such as generating electricity, charging batteries, pumping water, or grinding grain. Wind is reportedly the fastest growing source of renewable energy, both in the U.S. and worldwide, and it has been estimated that potential wind energy resources exist in 46 of the 50 states. During the past 5 years, wind facility installations have grown at a rate of just under 25% per year.

Currently, wind provides only about .4% of energy consumed in the U.S. but its use is growing rapidly due to continual construction of new wind farms and recent breakthroughs in wind technology. In fact, it has been argued that state-of-the-art windmills of suitable scale for use by electric utilities could generate electricity at less than one-half the cost of gas-fired power. Examples of this new wind technology include 40-story turbines with blades spanning 200 feet, as well as offshore wind farms such as a 130-turbine installation in Nantucket Sound, Massachusetts. In addition, government tax incentives have also boosted the use of wind-driven equipment.

Solar

Solar power is expected to show slow and steady growth as it creates greater interest among users such as metropolitan areas. Currently, more than 850 American companies manufacture, install, and sell solar system components. The U.S. is regarded as the world leader in solar research and manufacturing.

A critical component in the use of solar power is photovoltaic technology, which comprises the electricity-generating layers of silicon between solar panels. Until recently, this equipment has been considered too cost-prohibitive to compete with traditional power generation methods. However, recent research and capital investments are expected to enable solar power to be an economically competitive power source within the next ten years.

In addition to photovoltaic cells, solar power innovations include concentrating solar power (CSP) technologies and low temperature solar collectors. While photovoltaic cells convert sunlight directly into electricity, CSP or solar thermal technologies use reflective materials to increase the concentration of the sun's energy. CSP technologies utilize mirror-covered dishes that rotate throughout the day to track the sun and subsequently heat hydrogen to drive generator pistons that produce electricity. Such dishes are becoming more affordable, and their use has been demonstrated in states such as California.

Geothermal

Energy from this renewable source is obtained from the heat of the Earth tapped at various depths ranging from shallow ground to hot water and rock a few miles below the ground, to deeply buried magma. Hot water or steam sources are typically used to supply steam turbines that, in turn, generate electricity. Forecasts have estimated an 87% increase in geothermal energy production over the next two decades, which should result in approximately 35,000 new jobs in drilling, power plant construction, equipment supply and manufacturing, and operation and maintenance. Geothermal energy is recognized as very reliable and cost-effective. However, geothermal plants must be located in very specific areas, such as those with volcanic activity, tectonic plate shifting, or major hot springs and geysers. Technological innovation is available to help ameliorate issues of location specificity. Hot Dry Rock Geothermal Energy (HDRGE) is one such technology and allows geothermal plants to be located almost anywhere.

Hydropower

Hydroelectric facilities currently generate enough power to supply 28 million households with electricity and, because electricity is generated using water, there is little air pollution. Thus, hydroelectric power is considered to be one of the most reliable, cost-effective, and controllable sources of renewable energy. However, there are some limits on its potential for expanded use beyond that already in operation today. For example, there are very few potential locations for new hydrodams. In addition, droughts that often occur in the Western U.S. can create problems for hydropowered electricity generation. Finally, associated adverse effects of waterway damming, such as altering the habitats of local plant, fish, and animal life, have made them less attractive energy sources.

To counter the adverse environmental effects of hydropower, several new technologies are under development. For example, advanced turbine systems are said to have benefits such as reduced fish mortality, improved compliance with water quality standards, and reductions in carbon dioxide emissions.

Biomass

Biomass resources produce an array of energy-related products including electricity, liquid, solid, and gaseous fuels, heat, chemicals, and other materials. This energy source ranks second to hydropower in renewable U.S. primary energy production. Biomass energy is generated from wood products and byproducts, agricultural byproducts, ethanol, paper pellets, used railroad ties, landfill gas, digester gas, municipal solid waste, and methane. Thus, biomass is often described as "waste-to-energy" fuel. In fact, one production method involving cow manure uses the waste of 10 cows per year to produce enough power to supply the needs of the average American home. Methane from waste landfills is also being used to power facilities such as industrial plants.

Hydrogen

Hydrogen is considered a clean energy carrier similar to electricity and can be made from a variety of methods including nuclear energy and renewable resources. One of the most promising hydrogen-based energy systems is hydrogen fuel cells. Interestingly, fuel cells have existed for more than a century, but because they require a constant supply of hydrogen, the limiting challenge has been how to create, store, and transport the hydrogen. Recognizing this challenge and the potential of hydrogen fuel cells as a source of clean and efficient fuel, the Hydrogen Fuel Initiative was announced in 2003 to promote hydrogen fuel cell vehicles from prototypes to in-use models. It is also expected within the next few years that micro fuel cells will be available to power laptop computers and cellular phones.

Traditional, Non-Renewable Energy Generation

The focus of green energy discussions is generally on renewable and clearly green forms of energy production. However, traditional energy sources are also frequently cited in these discussions. For example, coal, gas, oil, and nuclear power are not typically viewed as renewable sources of energy and can have an impact on the environment, yet there are reasons that these energy sources are often part of the green energy discussion.

First and foremost is the issue of sustainability. While the term sustainability is often seen as synonymous with renewability, it is also used in relation to the ability of a country or a region to supply its own energy needs. Dependence on imported oil can be seen as a barrier to U.S. sustainability in terms of energy production and use. Coal, natural gas, and nuclear power offer the chance to provide homegrown energy sources that reduce the reliance on other countries, thus increasing sustainability and also potentially reducing energy costs.

Second, green production techniques and technologies are being explored and applied to these traditional, non-renewable energy sources, as part of efforts to make the use of this type of energy "greener." Efforts have been made to come up with "clean coal" technology, to use natural gas for large vehicles that cannot be powered by hybrid technology, and to use new drilling techniques for finding oil deposits. Section II-6 discusses carbon capture and sequestration techniques that involve applying green technologies to traditional energy sources. In addition, locating and utilizing energy sources within the U.S. helps to reduce the negative environmental impact caused by shipping products long distances.

Workforce Implications

When considered collectively, the increased potential for growth in renewable sources of energy can be expected to impact employment and occupational expansion. This is generally attributed to the fact that renewable energy production is more labor-intensive than energy source production. It has been estimated that significant investment in the renewable energy segment could result in the creation of more than 650,000 jobs in 10 years and more than 1.4 million jobs by 2025. Other examples of job growth forecasts for the different sources of renewable energy are highlighted below.

- Wind and solar energy production offer 40% more jobs per megawatt of power produced than coal-based production, which is currently the largest fuel source for electricity generation in the U.S.
- The Department of Energy estimates that developing dedicated energy crops could create more than 120,000 jobs by 2012.
- Jobs are being created by the increasing use of ethanol in reformulated gasoline, with some estimating that a 40-million gallon ethanol plant has the potential to create over 1,400 construction jobs and 40 facility operation and maintenance jobs.
- The incorporation of hydrogen fuel cells in automobiles is likely to create a demand for technicians specializing in automotive fuel cell batteries.
- Biomass currently employs roughly 66,000 people with a 200% growth capability related to developing dedicated "energy crops" used for fueling biopower generators.

In terms of the greening of occupations, this sector is likely to have consequences for all three green occupational categories. First, existing occupations that can be classified as green increased demand occupations with growth in employment demand related to renewable energy generation include occupations such as power distributors and dispatchers and power system operators. Second, many occupations are likely to be classified as green enhanced skills occupations with changes in the actual tasks and/or competencies required for occupational performance. For instance, occupations such as power plant operators, electrical engineers, continuous mining machine operators, geological sample test technicians, and mechanical engineers are likely to expand to include new tasks and competencies. Finally, because of the new technologies being used, this sector is likely to witness significant green N&E occupations. Some examples of these novel occupational roles are associated with designing wind turbines or wind farms, assessing wind capacity, technician occupations for wind and geothermal operations, designing or operating biomass or methane facilities, and designing, installing or selling solar equipment.

Section II-2: Transportation

This green economy sector covers activities related to increasing efficiency and/or reducing the environmental impact of various modes of transportation, such as trucking, mass transit, freight rail, and water. Factors directing attention toward this sector include concerns about global warming, fuel shortages and rising costs, and a more general move toward sustainable transportation. The notion of sustainability in transportation centers on systems that meet transportation demands of people, businesses, and general society, while operating efficiently and limiting emissions, waste, consumption of non-renewable resources, land use, and noise production.

A large proportion of the change occurring in this sector is attributed to increased production of renewable transportation fuels, such as ethanol and biodiesel, development and production of new vehicle engines, and reengineered (eco-friendly) transportation systems. For example, with respect to water transportation, environmentally sensitive changes included having ships use electrical service while in port (versus diesel fuel) and using biodiesel for powering container handling equipment.

Several green technologies are playing a significant role in this sector. One example of such technology is auxiliary power units (APU) in transportation trucks, which reduce environmental impact from emissions as well as decrease fuel costs. Another example of green technology in this sector is hydrogen fuel cells. Significant attention has been directed toward hydrogen fuel cell development and use, including federal legislation (e.g., 2005 Energy Policy Act) and grants. However, some individuals, such as T. Boone Pickens, have pointed out that fuel cells may lack the power needed for large transportation vehicles (e.g., 18-wheelers) and thus suggest that other alternative transportation fuels, including natural gas, should be concurrently developed. The U.S. Department of Energy also provides numerous grants to support innovation in green transportation technology, recently offering $14.55 million along with matching private funds to total $29.3 million for alternative vehicle technologies.

Workforce Implications

The workplace implications of growing concerns over environmental and conservation issues in the transportation sector should increase demands for individuals with specialized knowledge and skills related to eco-friendly transportation assessment, planning, and logistics. For instance, a significant transition to the use of hydrogen fuel cells would greatly impact occupations involved in automobile production, design and engineering, as well as those that service transportation vehicles. This impact has been estimated to likely result in roughly 20,000 new jobs related to hydrogen fuel cells by 2050. The increased use of alternative transportation fuels in general has been estimated to likely generate 1.5 million jobs directly related to these fuels, as well as roughly 1.4 million jobs in associated fields such as engineering, law, and research.

In terms of the greening of occupations, existing occupations classified as green increased demand occupations include railroad conductors and locomotive engineers. Many existing occupations are likely to be classified as green enhanced skills occupations with changes in the actual tasks and/or competencies that are required for occupational performance. For example, occupations such as automotive specialty technicians, transportation managers, and electronics engineers are likely to expand to include new tasks and competencies. Examples of green N&E occupations include fuel cell engineers and technicians and automotive engineers and technicians.

Section II-3: Energy Efficiency

This sector of the green economy includes activities related to increasing energy efficiency and making energy demand response more effective. Because this sector is closely related to numerous industries, it often defies clear delineation. For instance, most financial investment in this sector is within segments of larger industries (e.g., vehicles, buildings, lighting, appliances). Although a significant portion of this sector involves reducing waste of energy through systematic retrofitting and upgrading of residential and commercial buildings, those green activities will be addressed in a following sector, "Green Construction."

A number of green technologies have been brought to bear in efforts to increase energy efficiency. For example, light-emitting diodes (LED) are a semiconductor technology whose application to general purpose lighting holds the promise of significant energy savings, with currently available products three to four times more efficient than incandescent bulbs. Another example of green technology in this sector is high-performance window technology consisting of low-emissivity coated glass, gas fills, spacers, and improved frames. These high performance windows typically use materials such as fiberglass, vinyl, argon, and silica to reduce energy loss.

The promotion of "smart electrical grids" is also significantly impacting change within this sector. Smart grids employ a number of more specific technologies to meet several criteria set out by the U.S. Department of Energy including self-healing, resisting attack, higher quality power, accommodating generation and storage options, promoting energy markets, and increasing overall efficiency. Technologies used to build and maintain smart grids generally fall into five broad categories shown below.

- Integrated Communications: Connection components used for real-time information and control.
- Sensing and Measurement: Technologies supporting faster and more accurate response (e.g., remote monitoring, pricing, and demand-side control).
- Advanced Components: Component applications from research such as superconductivity, fault tolerance, or power electronics.
- Advanced Control Methods: Methods for monitoring components, enabling rapid diagnosis and precise solutions to grid events.
- Improved Interfaces and Decision Support: Improved information technology to support faster and more accurate human decision-making.

Workforce Implications

One clear implication from energy efficient technologies and practices is a growing need for individuals with knowledge and skills related to "energy consulting," which represents roughly 40% of this sector's current employment. Another predominant area of employment is related to manufacturing, design, and sales of energy efficient technologies (e.g., low-wattage or zero-wattage lighting products). Finally, occupations that pertain to operations and maintenance have particular relevance to this sector of the green economy. For example, occupations associated with controlling building functions, analyzing energy costs, conserving resources, and enhancing sustainability should see increased demand. Moreover, there is evidence suggesting shortages of skills among the current workforce to meet the future demands of this sector. Such shortages include a lack of reliable installation, maintenance, and inspection services, as well as technical and manufacturing skills.

Green increased demand occupations in this sector are likely to involve growth in employment demand related to energy efficiency-related facility and infrastructure upgrades. For example, occupations such as electrical power line installers and repairers, stationary engineers and boiler operators, and boilermakers are needed for these upgrades. Some occupations may be classified as green enhanced skills occupations with changes in the actual tasks and/or competencies that are required for occupational performance. For instance, occupations such as heating and air conditioning mechanics and installers, and mechanical engineers may expand to include new tasks and competencies. This sector may also see some green N&E occupations related to very specific energy activities being performed on a large scale—for example, new or substantially unique occupations such as occupational roles associated with weatherization or sealing of buildings to improve energy efficiency.

Section II-4: Green Construction

This sector covers activities related to designing and constructing new green buildings, retrofitting residential and commercial buildings, and installing other green construction technology.

It has been well documented that to meet the increased demand for environmentally friendly "green" buildings, construction firms have had to substantially change preconstruction designs and materials. Roughly two-thirds of this sector's activities are undertaken by firms that are engaged in design or construction, with the remainder involved with the production and sales of green construction materials.

The broad goals of increasing energy efficiency in residential and commercial structures are likely to foster growth in this green economy sector. Government-sponsored initiatives are central to promoting green construction. For example, recent efforts by the U.S. Environmental Protection Agency's Energy Star® buildings program and the U.S. Green Building Council's LEED™ rating system develop systems by which the energy and environmental performance of office buildings can be measured and compared to national norms. In addition, the LEED rating system for residential buildings was recently introduced. Several green technologies are also influencing green construction activities. These mainly fall into "mechanical technologies" and include innovations such as on-site electricity generating equipment and blackwater recycling systems.

Workforce Implications

The literature on green construction often cites the benchmark of a 35% reduction in energy consumption by existing commercial and residential buildings over the next three decades. This means that occupations dealing with the manufacture of retrofitting products and their installation will be in demand. Moreover, the increased demand for green retrofitting work will simultaneously promote demand for green building materials, thus increasing the need for occupations in manufacturing industries.

Many existing occupations will be classified as green increased demand occupations, with growth in employment demand related to green construction. That would involve occupations such as carpenters, electricians, cement masons and concrete finishers, and welders, cutters, solderers, and brazers. Similarly, several occupations are likely to be classified as green enhanced skills occupations with changes in the actual tasks and/or competencies required for occupational performance. For example, occupations such as construction managers, civil engineers, and construction and building inspectors, most of whom will be involved in installing and inspecting greener building materials, are likely to expand to include new tasks and competencies. Substantial evidence of green N&E occupations resulting in the creation of new or unique occupations is not clear at this time. However, one example of a green N&E occupation is an energy engineer who develops ways to reduce energy costs in the designing, building, and remodeling stages of construction.

Section II-5: Energy Trading

This green economy sector involves various financial services related to buying and selling energy as an economic commodity, as well as carbon trading projects. At least part of the growth of this sector has stemmed from industry deregulation. Such deregulation has led to the increase of trading electricity as a commodity, also known as "power marketing" or "energy marketing". This business model has been directly adopted by entities commonly referred to as "non-utility generators," typically industrial plants that generate their own power and sell it to utilities or other industrial plants. For example, of the more than 3000 electric utilities in the U.S., over half do not have generating capacity but rather purchase electricity from other utilities. Thus, many electric power plants are seen as commodity-producing investments. In addition to energy marketing, there is a simultaneous push to reduce costs through power conservation.

The other significant portion of this sector is devoted to emission trading, frequently focused on carbon trading. In short, the carbon trading market has developed from caps or limits on the amount of carbon dioxide that can be emitted by a particular entity. Companies or other groups are granted emission permits and must hold an equivalent number of credits that represent the right to emit a specific amount of carbon dioxide. Because of the limiting caps, companies that need to increase their emission allowance need to purchase (trade) credits from other firms.

Workforce Implications

Energy marketing, power conservation, and emissions trading all will have implications for employment and new occupational growth in areas such as auditing, market analysis, brokerage, and so forth. For example, occupations related to both financial analysis and emissions analysis are required for carbon trading.

This sector is not likely to see many green increased demand and green enhanced skills occupations; however, future growth in employment demand related to financial services occupations such as financial analysts and securities, commodities, and financial services sales agents may occur. In addition, this sector may see some green N&E occupations resulting in the creation of new or substantially unique occupations. Some examples of these potentially novel occupational roles are associated with trading or analyzing carbon credits and analyzing and purchasing energy. Growth of these types of occupations, however, may require implementation and application of stricter environmental/pollution regulations similar to those adopted by EU countries.

Section II-6: Energy and Carbon Capture and Storage

This sector covers green economy activities related to capturing and storing energy and/or carbon emissions. The primary force in this sector is the increase in coal-based power plants using integrated gasification combined cycle (IGCC) techniques. The World Coal Institute describes the IGCC technique as follows:

An alternative to achieving efficiency improvements in conventional pulverised coal-fired power stations is through the use of gasification technology. IGCC plants use a gasifier to convert coal (or other carbon-based materials) to syngas, which drives a combined cycle turbine. Coal is combined with oxygen and steam in the gasifier to produce the syngas, which is mainly H2 and carbon monoxide (CO). The gas is then cleaned to remove impurities, such as sulphur, and the syngas is used in a gas turbine to produce electricity. Waste heat from the gas turbine is recovered to create steam, which drives a steam turbine, producing more electricity. The result is a combined cycle system.

The benefit of IGCC plants is that they use less water and emit fewer airborne sulfur oxides, nitrogen oxides, particulates, and mercury than conventional pulverized coal plants. IGCC plants still produce carbon dioxide but this greenhouse gas can be concentrated and removed prior to combustion (i.e., "carbon capture and storage" [CCS]). Although IGCC technology is currently being implemented, most experts agree that CCS is farther behind in terms of development and use.

Workforce Implications

Technologies related to carbon capture and storage could generate increased demand for knowledge and skills needed for processes such as geologic or terrestrial carbon sequestration. In addition, demand for individuals to construct and maintain pipelines for carbon transport may increase.

Overall, this sector may not experience significant greening in the immediate future. There may be some green enhanced skills occupations with changes in the actual tasks and/or competencies that are required for occupational performance. One example of such change is for power plant operators. Some green N&E occupations might also be likely. For example, the creation of a unique role associated with carbon capture and sequestration systems. These technologies are still in the research and development stage, so their ultimate workforce impact remains to be seen.

Section II-7: Research, Design, and Consulting Services

This sector encompasses "indirect jobs" to the green economy and includes activities such as energy consulting or research and other related business services. Although not directly related to green technology, these types of occupations have accounted for a significant portion of employment growth in the green economy. For example, it has been estimated that jobs in this sector have grown by 52% since 1990 as compared to a 38% increase in direct jobs during the same time period.

Workforce Implications

Accomplishing this sector's activities requires knowledge and skills in areas such as engineering business consulting, and sales and marketing. This sector is likely to primarily include green increased demand and green enhanced skills occupations through "indirect jobs" or occupations such as financial analysts, sales representatives, geoscientists, engineering managers, marketing managers, and public relations specialists.

This sector may also see some green N&E occupations, which might result in the creation of new or substantially unique occupations such as occupational roles associated with marketing green products or services as well as research and development engineers of green technology.

Section II-8: Environmental Protection

This sector covers activities related to the environmental remediation, climate change adaption, and ensuring or enhancing air quality. Environmental remediation entails the restoration of a contaminated site to a condition that is not a threat to human or animal health. Numerous technologies are used for remediation efforts including ion exchange, soil washing, chemical precipitation, oxidation, electrolytic treatment, and biological treatments with plants, fungi, and bacteria. Climate change adaptations are "actions taken to help communities and ecosystems moderate, cope with, or take advantage of actual or expected changes in climate conditions." Efforts to enhance air quality generally encompass activities related to minimizing or eliminating various pollutants. According to the U.S. Department of Transportation, these pollutants come from many sources: stationary sources (e.g., factories and power plants), dispersed sources (e.g., dry cleaners and painting operations), mobile sources (e.g., cars, buses, planes, trucks, and trains), and, natural sources (e.g., windblown dust and volcanic eruptions).

Workforce Implications

Federal legislation and regulation have been significant forces in this sector. Below are some examples of such legislation.

- Clean Air Act of 1990: Authorizes the U.S. Environmental Protection Agency (EPA) to establish National Ambient Air Quality Standards (NAAQS) to protect public health and public welfare and to regulate emissions of hazardous air pollutants, as well as provides broader authority to implement and enforce regulations reducing air pollutant emissions.
- Clean Water Act of 1972: Establishes the basic structure for regulating discharges of pollutants into the waters of the United States and regulating quality standards for surface waters.
- Comprehensive Environmental Response, Compensation, and Liability Act of 1980 (and Superfund Amendments and Reauthorization Act [SARA] of 1986): Provides a Federal "Superfund" to clean up uncontrolled or abandoned hazardous-waste sites as well as accidents, spills, and other emergency releases of pollutants and contaminants into the environment. Gives the U.S. EPA the power to seek out those parties responsible for any release and assure their cooperation in the cleanup.

This sector is likely to include green increased demand occupations with growth in employment related to environmental protection in occupations such as environmental scientists and natural sciences managers. Several occupations in this sector are likely to include green enhanced skills occupations with changes in the actual tasks and/or competencies that are required for occupational performance. For instance, occupations such as environmental engineers, hazardous materials removal workers, environmental engineering technicians, atmospheric and space scientists, and soil and water conservationists may expand to include new tasks and competencies. Finally, this sector is very likely to include green N&E occupations resulting in the creation of new or substantially unique occupations. Some examples of these potentially novel occupational roles are associated with specializing in water resources, redevelopment of "brownfields," analyzing climate change, certifying environmental quality, and industrial ecology.

Section II-9: Agriculture and Forestry

This sector covers activities related to the use of natural pesticides, efficient land management or farming, and aquaculture. Related to the use of natural pesticides is the increase in consumer demand for certified organic foods. According to the International Federation of Organic Agriculture Movements, organic farming is a form of agriculture that maintains soil productivity and controls pests by excluding or limiting the use of synthetic fertilizers and pesticides, plant growth regulators, feed additives, and genetically modified organisms. The increase in consumer demand has contributed to the growth of organic farming and the food products from these farms. For example, from 2001 to 2006 the demand for organic products rose 10% to a total $40 billion in sales.

Efficient land use and management has been facilitated by the application of geospatial technology. A new term, "precision farming," refers to the use of geospatial data and information systems to plan, manage, and evaluate farming processes. This technology uses geospatial information to plan specific agricultural methods to be used in localized areas of an individual farm, with the intention of maximizing crop yields.

Related to mitigating environmental impact of agriculture, it has been estimated that agricultural activities are responsible for nearly 30% of total U.S. methane emissions. To help lessen this impact, green technologies such as "super soil systems" have been developed and implemented. Super soil entails on-farm waste treatment whereby the wastes are reduced to solids and treated liquid effluent streams. These solids are then composted off-site to be cured and used as organic fertilizers and soil enhancements. In addition, a byproduct of these systems is methane gas, which can be recycled using "biogas digesters" and then used as fuel for generating electricity.

Workforce Implications

Some of the workforce implications of the activities in this green sector include increased demand for individuals skilled in organic farming methods and the development and research of alternative, non-synthetic pesticides. The use of precision farming techniques requires skills and knowledge related to geospatial technology, such as geographic information systems and global positioning systems. Finally, super soil system technology would create needs for occupations associated with the construction and manufacturing of the system's components (e.g., large tanks used for "digesting"), as well as the installation of these components.

With regard to the greening of occupations, this sector is likely to have at least some consequences for all three categories of occupations. Some existing occupations that will illustrate green increased demand occupations include agricultural workers and inspectors. Examples of occupations likely to illustrate green enhanced skills occupations include farmers and ranchers, landscape architects, and agricultural technicians, all of which are likely to expand to include new tasks and competencies.

Lastly, this sector could include some green N&E occupations where novel occupational roles are generated in areas of precision agriculture and biomass farming in the future.

Section II-10: Manufacturing

This sector covers activities related to industrial manufacturing of green technology as well as energy efficient manufacturing processes. There are two broad facets of green economy activities in the manufacturing sector. The first is the manufacturing of "green" materials that are required by other sectors of the green economy (e.g., renewable energy, construction). The second is the application of techniques and/or technologies to the manufacturing process. This latter category is highly related to previous sectors, such as energy efficiency and carbon capture. According to the Center for Green Manufacturing at the University of Alabama, the purpose of green manufacturing is "to prevent pollution and save energy through the discovery and development of new knowledge that reduces and/or eliminates the use or generation of hazardous substances in the design, manufacture, and application of chemical products or processes."

Workforce Implications

When compared to the other green sectors previously discussed, the primary implication of this sector's activities is the increased demand for existing manufacturing-related occupations. Thus, occupational impact is most likely to be in the forms of green increased demand and green enhanced skills occupations. For example, existing manufacturing occupations such as drilling and boring machine tools setters, operators and tenders, as well as separating, filtering, clarifying, precipitating and still machines setters, operators, and tenders are likely to see employment growth due to green economy activities. Green enhanced skills occupations may include occupations such as industrial engineering technicians, electrical engineering technicians, machinists, and occupational health and safety technicians. Green N&E occupations are likely to be found within this sector in relation to the manufacturing of products designed and developed by engineers in such fields as biochemistry, microsystems engineering, and photonics.

Section II-11: Recycling and Waste Reduction

Sector activities encompass solid waste and wastewater management, treatment, and reduction, as well as processing recyclable materials. This sector includes municipal waste and recycling as well as wastewater treatment and management. Many firms within this sector typically specialize in designing and manufacturing water purification products. Other firms focus more heavily on managing recycling and/or waste treatment operations.

Workforce Implications

Significant investments by state and local government programs to increase recycling have facilitated employment demand. For example, studies conducted in 2003 and 2004 found over 50,000 establishments employing over 1.2 million individuals within recycling area of this sector. Similarly, the U.S. Bureau of Labor Statistics forecasts the demand for occupations related to waste management to increase by 14% between 2006 and 2016. Some green enhanced skills occupations could include employment growth in existing occupations such as plant and systems operators as well as refuse and recyclable materials collectors. Green N&E occupations in this sector could create potentially new occupational roles associated with sustainable design, recycling and reclamation, and coordinating recycling activities.

Section II-12: Governmental and Regulatory Administration

This sector includes activities by public and private organizations associated with conservation and pollution prevention, regulations enforcement, and policy analysis and advocacy.

Within public or governmental organizations, many of this sector's activities involve conservation and pollution prevention efforts and creating and enforcing regulations. In addition, non-profit organizations are frequently involved with policy analysis and advocacy of conservation, climate change, and other energy-related issues. Profit-oriented organizations, such as venture capitalists and private equity firms, are often engaged in financing small- and large-scale renewable energy projects and other green technology projects.

Workforce Implications

An increase in the activities related to this green economy sector would translate into a demand for both specialist-type occupations (e.g., testing specialists, researchers) and more general occupations related to regulation or administration (e.g., compliance managers, policy advisors). With regard to the greening of occupations, this sector is likely to have at least some consequences for all three occupational categories. Some existing occupations that will be classified as green increased demand occupations include agriculture inspectors. In terms of green enhanced skills occupations, occupations such as soil and water conservationists and environmental engineers are likely to expand to include new tasks and competencies. Finally, as stricter regulations are adopted and enforced, this sector could include some green N&E occupations where novel occupational roles are generated in areas of consulting in sustainability, air quality control, consulting in gas emissions permits, and verification of emissions reporting.

Note: The complete article and references can be downloaded from www.Onenet.com

Conclusion

The research team's report is a comprehensive study in the future of green employment. Students who anticipate a career within this field should investigate many of these avenues as they seek employment. With time, job trends and skills will change somewhat, so it is best to stay abreast of hiring patterns through as many outlets that one can find.

The research team identified 12 distinct green sectors and the workforce implications on each of these:

1. Renewable energy generation

2. Nonrenewable energy generation

3. Transportation

4. Energy efficiency

5. Green construction

6. Energy trading

7. Energy and carbon capture and storage

8. Research, design, and consulting services

9. Environmental protection

10. Agriculture and forestry

11. Manufacturing

12. Recycling and waste reduction

Each of these sectors will be affected by the green economy to varying degrees.

DISCUSSION QUESTIONS

1. Review the Sunday newspaper for your city or town. What jobs do you find that could be classified as green?

2. Repeat the exercise for Internet job sites.

3. Locate the city officer for sustainability, and interview him or her about hiring patterns in and around your locale.

4. How do the definitions of green jobs differ?

5. What are the primary green implications for occupational analysis?

6. What are the 12 sectors of the green economy?

7. What is the most reliable source of renewable energy?

8. What are the two most used sources of U.S. energy production?

9. What are the main categories of smart grids?

10. What sectors of the green economy show the most promise for job growth?

RECOMMENDED WEBSITES

www.ejobs.org

www.greenjobs.com

www.greenjobs.net

www.onetcenter.org

www.usgbc.org

References

1992 Conference on Sustainability in Rio de Janeiro. Division for Sustainable Development. (1992). *Rio Declaration on Environment and Development.* www.un.org/esa/dsd/agenda21/

60% upsurge in GRI reports in 2010. (2010, November 3). Retrieved from www.globalreporting.org/information/news-and-press-center/Pages/60-percent-upsurge-in-GRI-reports-in-2010-.aspx

The 2008 US city rankings. (2012). Retrieved from www.sustainlane.com/us-city-rankings/

2009/10 blueprint for sustainability: The future at work. (2010). Ford Motor Company. Retrieved from http://corporate.ford.com/doc/sr09-blueprint-summary.pdf

2011 North American environmental report highlights. (2012). Honda.com. Retrieved from http://corporate.honda.com/environment/2011-report/statement.aspx

Aall, P. R. (2000). *NGOs and conflict management.* Washington, DC: United States Institute of Peace.

About Corporate Register. (n.d.). CorporateRegister.com. Retrieved 2009 from www.corporateregister.com/about.html

About ICLEI. (n.d.). *ICLEI—Local governments for sustainability.* Retrieved March 2011 from www.iclei.org/index.php?id=about

About the World Business Council for Sustainable Development. (n.d.). World Business Council for Sustainable Development. Retrieved August 2012 from www.wbcsd.ch/templates/TemplateWBCSD5/layout.asp?type=p&MenuId=NjA&doOpen=1&ClickMenu=LeftMenu

Advantages of solar energy. (n.d.). Retrieved from www.millionsolarroofs.com/advantagesofsolarenergy.html

Affordable-Alternative-Energy.com. (n.d.). *Nanotechnology and solar energy.* Retrieved from www.affordable-alternative-energy.com/nanotechnology-and-solar-energy.html

Agenda 21. (n.d.-a). *Answers.* Retrieved March 2012 from www.answers.com/topic/agenda-21#ixzz1pIXqZtjU

Agenda 21. (n.d.-b). *Chapter 27: Strengthening the role of non-governmental organizations: Partnering for sustainable development.* Retrieved from http://habitat.igc.org/agenda21/a21–27.htm

Agenda 21 of the United Nations, Section 9.11. (1992). Retrieved from www.un.org/esa/dsd/agenda21/

Aguilar S., Appleton, A., Dafoe, J., Doran, P., Kosolapova, E., McColl, V., et al. (2011). *Summary of the Durban Climate Change Conference.* Retrieved March 2012 from www.iisd.ca/vol12533e.html

AirNow. (n.d.). Retrieved from www.airnow.gov/index.cfm?action=airnow.main

All About VPP. (n.d.). Occupational Safety and Health Administration, U.S. Department of Labor. Retrieved January 2012 from www.osha.gov/dcsp/vpp/all_about_vpp.html

Allen, C. (2004, May 5–8). *A rose by any other name? A discursive typology of the terms business social responsibility and sustainability in New Zealand.* Paper presented at the First International Critical Discourse Analysis Conference, Valencia, Spain.

Allenby, B. R. (1992). Industrial ecology: The materials scientist in an environmentally constrained world. *MRS Bulletin, 17*(3), 46–51.

Alter, L. (2007). *Forest Ethics' naughty and nice list of treekillers.* Treehugger.com. Retrieved from www.treehugger.com/corporate-responsibility/forest-ethics-naughty-and-nice-list-of-treekillers.html

American Public Transportation Association. (2012). *July transit savings report.* Retrieved August 2012 from www.apta.com/mediacenter/pressreleases/2012/Pages/120726_TransitSavings.aspx

Anastasiadis, P., & Metaxas, G. (2010). *Sustainable city and risk management.* Paper presented at the 1st WIETE Annual Conference on Engineering and Technology Education, Pattaya, Thailand. Retrieved from www.wiete.com.au/conferences/1st_wiete/11–07-Metaxas.pdf

Anderson, S., & Cavanagh, J. (2000, December 4). *Top 200: The rise of corporate global power.* Institute for Policy Studies. Retrieved from http://www.corpwatch.org/article.php?id=377

Annan, K. (1999) Global Compact speech, press release SG/SM/6881. Retrieved from www.un.org/News/Press/docs/1999/19990201.sgsm6881.html

Applying the ABCD Method. (n.d.). *The Natural Step.* Retrieved May 29, 2012, from www.naturalstep.org/en/abcd-process

Archer, C., & Jacobson, M. (2003, May 13). Evaluation of global windpower. *Journal of Geophysical Research, 108.*

Arndt, M. (2003, March 24). An ode to "the money-spinner" [Review of the book *The company: A short history of a revolutionary idea*]. *BusinessWeek,* 22–23.

Arvizu, S. (2008, February 14). *Green marketing done right: Burt's Bees new campaign.* Retrieved from www.triplepundit.com

Asamoah, Y. (2003). NGOs, social development and sustainability. *Foreign Aid Rating.* Retrieved September 12, 2010, from www.foreignaid.com/thinktank/articles/NGOsAndSocialDevelopment.html

Ashton, W. S. (2008). Understanding the organization of industrial ecosystems: A social network approach. *Journal of Industrial Ecology, 12*(1), 34–51.

Association of American Railroads. (2007, January). *Overview of American railroads.* Washington, DC: Author.

Auckland sustainability framework. (2010). Retrieved from www.aucklandoneplan.org.nz

Aylwin, J. (2002). The Ralco Dam and the Pehuenche people in Chile: Lessons from an ethno-environmental conflict. Retrieved March 2012 from www.historiaecologica.cl/Ralco%20(Aylwin).pdf

Baccaro, L. (2001). Civil society, NGOs, and decent work policies: Sorting out the issues. Discussion Paper Series, International Institute for Labour Studies, Geneva.

Bailie, A., & Beckstead, C. (2010). *Canada's coolest cities, Montreal and CMA.* Retrieved from www.pembina.org/pub/2026

Baker, M. (2004, June 4). *Corporate Social Responsibility—What does it mean?* Retrieved from www.mallenbaker.net/csr/definition.php

Baker, M. (2011, November 10). *Supply chains: Forging stronger links.* Strategy Management, UK: Ethical Corporation. Retrieved from www.ethicalcorp.com/supply-chains/supply-chains-forging-stronger-links

Balu, R. (2002). Strategic innovation: Hindustan lever. *Fast Company, 47,* 120–125.

Barnhill, D. (2006, October). *Deep ecology.* Retrieved from www.eoearth.org/article/Deep_Ecology

Bell, D. (2003, April 16). *Sustainability through democratisation? Assessing the role of environmental NGOs in a liberal democracy. NGOs, sustainability and democracy*. Paper presented at the Political Studies Association Annual Conference, Leicester.

Bell, D. V. J. (2002). *The role of government in advancing corporate sustainability*. Background paper, York University, Toronto, Canada. Retrieved April 2012 from www.g8.utoronto.ca/scholar/2002/be1111062002.pdf

Bendell, J. (2007). Chiquita, International Institute for Sustainable Development. Retrieved from www.bsdglobal.com/viewcasestudy.aspx?id=109

Bendell, J. (2010). Opposites attract. *International Institute for Sustainable Development*. Retrieved from www.bsdglobal.com/ngo/opposites.aspx

Bent, D. (2009). Six key lessons on mapping out a business case for sustainability initiatives. GreenBiz.com. Retrieved May 2010 from www.greenbiz.com/blog/2009/10/20/six-key-lessons-mapping-out-business-case-sustainability-initiatives#ixzz0mzXDsW3u

Benyus, J. M. (1997). *Biomimicry: Innovation inspired by nature*. New York: William Morrow and Company.

Berinstein, P. (2001). *Alternative energy: Facts, statistics, and issues*. Westport, CT: Oryx Press.

Berman, J. (2011). UPS adds to its alternative fuel vehicle fleet with purchase of 48 LNG powered tractors. *Logistics Management*. Retrieved March 2012 from www.logisticsmgmt.com/view/ups_adds_to_its_alternative_fuel_vehicle_fleet_with_purchase_of_48_lng-powe/sustainability

Bernard, S. M., Samet, J. M., Grambsch, A., Ebi, K. L., & Romieu, I. (2001). The potential impacts of climate variability and change on air pollution—related health effects in the United States. *Environmental Health Perspectives, 109*(Suppl. 2), 199–209.

Berthoud, O. (2001, August). NGOs: Somewhere between compassion, profitability and solidarity. *Envio Digital,* Number 21. Retrieved from www.envio.org.ni/articulo/1526

Bielak, D., Bobini, S. M. J., & Oppenheim, J. (2007). CEOs on strategy and social issues. *McKinsey Quarterly*. Retrieved from www.mckinseyquarterly.com/governance/leadership/ceos_on_strategy_and_social_issues_2056

Biello, D. (2008, April 25). Solar power lightens up with thin-film technology. *Scientific American*. Retrieved from www.scientificamerican.com/article.cfm?id=solar-power-lightens-up-with-thin-film-cells

Bieker, T. (2003, July 13–19). Sustainability management with the balanced scorecard. In S. Karner, I. Oehme, & U. Seebacher (Eds.), *Corporate sustainability*. Conference proceedings at the 5th International Summer Academy on Technology Studies, Deutschlandsberg, Austria.

Blackburn, W. (2007). *The sustainability handbook: The complete management guide to achieving social, economic and environmental responsibility*. Washington, DC: Environmental Law Institute.

Boston Redevelopment Authority. (2010). Economic and sustainability benefits of Boston's ARRA investments. Retrieved from *www.cityofboston.gov/ . . . / SROI%20Analysis%20Report_tcm3–18467.pdf*

Bowen, M. (1953). *Social responsibilities of the businessman*. New York: Harper.

Bourne, J. K., Jr. (2010). The deep dilemma. *National Geographic, 218*(4), 40–61.

The BP Gulf of Mexico oil spill update. (n.d.). TheDailyGreen.com. Retrieved from www.thedailygreen.com/environmental-news/latest/gulf-of-mexico-oil-spill

Braden, P. (2006, September 16). Paying the freight for polluting the air: Europe takes the lead. *The New York Times*, p. 8.

Bridger, J. C., & Luloff, A. E. (1999). Toward an interactional approach to sustainable community development. *Journal of Rural Studies, 15*(4), 377–387.

Broekhoff, D. (2007, July 18). Testimony before the House Select Committee on Energy Independence and Global Warming. *Voluntary carbon offsets: Getting*

what you pay for. U.S. House of Representatives. Retrieved from http://pdf
.wri.org/20070718_broekhoff_testimony.pdf

Bromley, D. W. (2008). Sustainability. In S. N. Durlauf & L. E. Blume (Eds.), *The new Palgrave dictionary of economics* (2nd ed.). New York: Palgrave Macmillan.

Brown, B. (n.d.). Essay: Earth as a natural/physical environmental system. *National Geographic.* Retrieved from www.nationalgeographic.com/xpeditions/guides/geogsummary.pdf

Brown, F. (2009, August 24). Percentage of global population living in cities, by continent. *Guardian.*

Brown, F. (2009, September 2). Meat consumption per capita. *Guardian.* Retrieved from www.guardian.co.uk/environment/datablog/2009/sep/02/meat-consumption-per-capita-climate-change

Brown, L. (2009). *Plan B 4.0: Mobilizing to save civilization.* Earth Policy Institute. New York: Norton.

Brown, L. (2009). *Plan B 4.0: Mobilizing to save civilization.* Washington, DC: Earth Policy Institute.

Brown, L. (2002, March/April). The eco-economic revolution: Getting the market in sync with nature. *The Futurist,* p. 26.

Brown, L. R. (1981). *Building a sustainable society.* New York: Norton.

Browne, Lord J. (2000). *Conservation awards dinner.* Speech presented at the conservation awards dinner, London. Retrieved from www.bp.com/genericarticle.do?categoryId=98&contentId=2000484

Brownlie, M. (n.d.). Bringing concrete expression to corporate responsibility: The fundamental role of sustainability reporting. *Corporate Responsibility.* Retrieved 2009 from www.responsiblepractice.com/english/standards/gri/

Buffington, J., Hart, S., & Milstein, M. (2002). *Tandus 2010: Race to sustainability.* Chapel Hill: Center for Sustainable Enterprises, University of North Carolina.

Burke, L., & Logsdon, J. M. (1996). How corporate social responsibility pays off. *Long Range Planning, 29*(4).

Business for Social Responsibility. (2006, December). Offsetting emissions: A business brief on the voluntary carbon market. *The Ecosystem Marketplace.*

BusinessGreen blog. (2007). Latest offset standard draws criticism. Retrieved from http://blog.businessgreen.com/2007/01/index.html

Butcher, D. (2009). Promoting corporate social responsibility. Retrieved November 8, 2009, from http://news.thomasnet.com/IMT/archives/2009/08/promoting-corporate-social-responsibility-global-view-of-sustainability.html

Carbon Concierge. (2008). *Carbon offset providers evaluation matrix.* Retrieved from www.climatetrust.org/pdfs/COPEM.pdf

Carbon Disclosure Project. (n.d.). Retrieved from www.cdproject.net/en-US/Pages/HomePage.aspx

Carbon footprint. (n.d.). Green Student U. Retrieved August 2012 from www.greenstudentu.com/encyclopedia/carbon_footprint

Carlson, L, Grove, S. J., Kangun, N., & M. Polonsky. (1996, Fall). An international comparison of environmental advertising: Substantive versus associative claims. *Journal of Macromarketing, 57*–68.

Carmichael, E. (n.d.). *Lesson #2: Always leave the doors to innovation open.* Retrieved January 2012 from www.evancarmichael.com/Famous-Entrepreneurs/1947/Lesson-2-Always-Leave-the-Doors-to-Innovation-Open.html

Carroll, A. (1999). Corporate social responsibility. *Business and Society, 38,* 3.

Carson, R. (1962). *Silent spring.* New York: Houghton Mifflin.

Cash, S. B., Goddard, E. W., & Lerohl, M. (2006). Canadian health and food: The links between policy, consumers, and industry. *Canadian Journal of Agricultural Economics, 54,* 605–629.

Cavett-Goodwin, D. *(2007). Making the case for corporate social responsibility.* Culturalshifts.com. Retrieved from http://culturalshifts.com/archives/181

Chakrabarty, G. (2009). *Green industry casts wide net.* Retrieved from www.rocky mountainnews.com/news/January 16, 2009

Chan, S.-S., & Joy, J. *(2008). Logistics and transportation: Key steps to a greener supply chain.* GreenBiz.com. Retrieved May 2010 from www.greenbiz.com/ blog/2008/07/13/logistics-and-transportation-key-steps-greener-supply-chain #ixzz0mzXfqxPv

Chicken industry report. (1997, May 26). *Feedstuffs.*

The Chicago Water Agenda. (2003). City of Chicago. Retrieved from www.cityof chicago.org/city/en/depts/water.html

Chiras, D. D. (2010). *Environmental science* (8th ed.). Sudbury, MA: Jones and Bartlett.

Chiras, D. D., Reginald, J. P., & Owen, O. S. (2002). *Natural resource conservation* (8th ed.). Upper Saddle River, NJ: Prentice Hall.

Christmann, P. (1998). Effects of "best practices" of environmental management on cost advantage: The role of complementary assets. *Academy of Management Journal, 43*(4), 660–680.

City of Montreal. (2007). *Environmental assessment report.* Retrieved from www .rsqa.qc.ca

City of Portland and Multnomah County. (2009). Climate Action Plan 2009. Portland, OR: City of Portland Bureau of Planning and Sustainability.

City of Phoenix receives $25 million grant to create "Energize Phoenix" in partnership with Arizona State University and Arizona Public Service. (2010, April 21).

Clarke, T. (2008). In T. Lohan (Ed.), *Water consciousness* (pp. 194–195). San Francisco: AlterNet Books.

Claudio, L. (2007). Waste couture: Environmental impact of the clothing industry. *Environmental Health Perspectives, 115*(10), 449–454.

Clean Air-Cool Planet. (2006). *A Consumers' Guide to Retail Carbon Offset Providers.* Retrieved from www.cleanair-coolplanet.org/ConsumersGuidetoCarbonOffsets.pdf.

Cleveland, C. (2010, June 9). Exxon Valdez oil spill. *The Encyclopedia of Earth.* Retrieved from www.eoearth.org/article/Exxon_Valdez_oil_spill

Climate and energy. (n.d.). Wal-Mart.com. Retrieved from www.walmartstores/sus tainability

Coal energy. (n.d.). Retrieved from www.odec.ca/projects/2006/wong6j2/coal.html

Coddington, W. (1993). *Environmental marketing.* New York: McGraw-Hill.

Compassion Over Killing. (n.d.). *A COK report: Animal suffering in the broiler industry.* Retrieved from www.chickenindustry.com/cfi/broilerindustryreport/

Compliance incentives and auditing, EPA's audit policy. (n.d.). Retrieved 2012 from www.epa.gov/compliance/incentives/auditing/auditpolicy.html

Cone LLC. (2008). Americans misunderstand environmental marketing messages. Retrieved from www.coneinc.com/content//36

Conlin, J. (2007, February 25). Going green, one spring break at a time. *The New York Times.*

Connelly, J., & Smith, G. (2003). *Politics and the environment: From theory to practice.* London: Routledge.

Conner, A., & Epstein, K. (2007). Harnessing purity and pragmatism. *Stanford Social Innovation Review, 5*(4), 61–66.

Consider the turkey. (2010, November 24). Encyclopaedia Brittanica Advocacy for Animals. Retrieved from http://advocacy.britannica.com/blog/advocacy/2010/11/ consider-the-turkey-3/

The Context Group. (2006). *Carbon offsets in context: Providers + advisors.* Retrieved from www.econtext.co.uk/downloads/carbon_offset.pdf

Corporate Social Responsibility. (n.d.). *CA: As you sow.* Retrieved from www.asyou sow.org/csr/

Costanza, R., Mitsch, W. J., & Daly, J. W., Jr. (2006). A new vision for New Orleans and the Mississippi Delta, applying ecological economics and ecological engineering. *Frontiers in Ecological Environment, 4*(9), 465–472.

Council for Sustainable Development. (2008, February). Report on the better air quality engagement process. Retrieved from www.susdev.org.hk

Country comparison: Infant mortality rate. (2012). CIA: The World Factbook. Retrieved from www.cia.gov/library/publications/the-world-factbook/rankorder/2091rank.html

Counts, A. (1996). *Give us credit.* New York: Times Books.

Craven, G. (2009). *What's the worst that could happen?* New York: Perigee.

Cruise ship pollution: Overview. (n.d.). Oceana.org. Retrieved from www.ocean.org/en/our-work/stop-ocean-pollution/cruise-ship-pollution/overview

Daly, H. (1999, April 26). *The first annual Feasta lecture.* Dublin: Trinity College. Retrieved March 2012 from www.feasta.org/documents/feastareview/daly.htm

Darnall, N. (2006). Why firms mandate ISO 14001 certification. *Business and Society, 45*(3), 354–381.

Davies, J. (2009). What does it mean when procurement goes green? *GreenBiz.com.* Retrieved May 2010 from www.greenbiz.com/blog/2009/11/19/what-does-it-mean-when-procurement-goes-green?page=full#ixzz0mzXs6kxH

Davis, L. S. (2010, June 7). What Phoenix, the poster child for environmental ills, is doing right. Retrieved from www.grist.org/article/Phoenix1/PALL

Dean, C. (2007, May 22). Executives on a mission. *The New York Times.*

Decision summary—Durban Climate Negotiations (COP17). (2011, December 12). Climate Connect Limited. Retrieved March 2012 from www.climate-connect.co.uk/ . . . /Durban%20COP%2017%20Summary . . .

Deen, S. (2012). Don't be fooled: America's ten worst greenwashers. *Alternet.org.* Retrieved from www.alternet.org/environment/13984?page=entire

de La Hamaide, S. (2007, April 26). Bangladesh seeks World Bank loan for solar power. *Reuters.*

Delmas, M. (2001). Stakeholders and competitive advantage: The case of ISO14001. *Production Operation Management, 10*(3), 343–358.

DePalma, A. (2006, April 22). Gas guzzlers find price of forgiveness. *The New York Times.*

Desai, V. (2005). NGOs, gender mainstreaming, and urban poor communities in Mumbai. *Gender & Development* [Special issue: Mainstreaming: A Critical Review], *13*(2).

Design of new Mercedes-Benz Bionic car inspired by fish body shape. (2005). DaimlerChrysler Release. Retrieved December 2011 from http://news.monga bay.com/2005/0710-DaimlerChrysler.html

de Villiers, M. (2001). *Water: The fate of our most precious resource.* Boston: First Mariner Books.

Dhanda, K. (1999). A market-based solution to acid rain: The case of sulfur dioxide (SO2) trading program. *Journal of Public Policy & Marketing, 18*(2), 1–15.

Doherty, K. (2011). Top 20 green supply chain partners. *Food Logistics.* Retrieved August 2012 from www.foodlogistics.com/article/10281442/top-20-green-supply-chain-partners?page=6

Diamond, J. (2005). *Collapse: How societies choose to fail or succeed.* New York: Viking.

Directorate of the Environment. (2008, March). European Commission/Eurobarometer 295, Attitudes of European Citizens towards the Environment.

Dow Jones Sustainability Indexes. (n.d.). SAM (Sustainable Asset Management). Retrieved from www.sustainability-index.com/

Dreo, J. (2006, March 9). Sustainable development. Retrieved from http://en.wiki pedia.org/wiki/File:Sustainable_development.svg

Drexhage, J., & Murphy, D. (2010, September). *International Institute for Sustainable Development, sustainable development: From Brundtland to Rio 2012.* New York: United Nations Headquarters.

Duncan, A. (2001). *The definition of sustainability depends on who is speaking.* Oregon State University Extension Service. Retrieved from http://oregonfuture.oregonstate.edu/part1/pf1_02.html

Duran, R. (n.d.). Eco-industrial parks: Just common sense. *Business Xpansion Journal.* Retrieved from www.bxjmag.com/bxj/article.asp?magarticle_id=281

Earthwatch Institute. (n.d.). *Company biodiversity action plan.* Retrieved from www.businessandbiodiversity.org/action_company_bap.html

Ebert, R. (2009, June 17). *Food, Inc.* RogerEbert.com. Retrieved from http://rogerebert.suntimes.com/apps/pbcs.dll/article?AID=/20090617/REVIEWS/906179985

Ecological footprint. (n.d.). Retrieved October 2009 from www.sustainablesonoma.org/keyconcepts/footprint.html

The Economist. (2006a). Sins of emission. *The Economist, 380,* 8489.

The Economist. (2006b). Upset about offsets. *The Economist, 380,* 8489.

Ehrenfeld, J. R. (2006). Feeding the beast: Sustainability is about more than eco-friendly burger boxes. *Fast Company, 111,* 42–43. Retrieved from www.fastcompany.com/magazine/111/next-essay.html

Elkington, J. (2004). Enter the triple bottom line. Retrieved from www.johnelkington.com/TBL-elkington-chapter.pdf

Elkington, J., & Lee, M. (2006, October 24). Third time's the charm. *Grist.* Retrieved from www.grist.org/biz/fd/2006/10/24/guidelines/

Emerson, R. W. (1983). *Essays & lectures.* New York: The Library of America.

Energy Information Administration. (2012). *International energy statistics.* London: Author.

Environmental Management System. (n.d.). Retrieved from www.epa.gov/EMS/info/index.htm

Environmental responsibility: Doing more with less. (n.d.). McDonalds.com. Retrieved from www.aboutmcdonalds.com/mcd/sustainability/our_focus_areas/environmental_responsibility.html

Environmental stewardship. (n.d.). Starbucks.com. Retrieved from www.starbucks.com/responsibility/environment/

Environmental sustainability: Helping customers and partners shrink their footprints. (n.d.). Cargill.com. Retrieved from www.cargill.com/corporate-responsibility/environmental-sustainability/others-footprints/index.jsp

Epicurious Staff. (2006, November 6). *How to eat fewer pesticides.* Environmental Working Group. Retrieved from www.ewg.org/news/how-eat-fewer-pesticides-0

European Photovoltaic Industry Association. (2009, April). *Global market outlook for photovoltaics until 2013* (pp. 3–4). Brussels, Belgium.

European Wind Energy Association. (2009, February). *Wind now leads EU power sector* [Press release]. Brussels, Belgium: Author.

Fargione, J., Hill, J. Tilman, D., Polasky, S., & Hawthorne, P. (2008). Land clearing and the biofuel carbon debt. *Science, 319*(5867), 1235–1238.

Fast Company Staff. (2012). A 50 year history of green marketing. Retrieved from www.fastcompany.com/pics/50-year-history-green-marketing#1

Federal Trade Commission. (2007). *Guides for the use of environmental marketing claims* (Part 260). Washington DC: Author.

Feenstra, T. L., van Genugten, M. L. L., Hoogenveen, R. T., Wouters, E. F., & Rutten-van Molken, M. P. M. H. (2001). The impact of aging and smoking on the future burden of chronic obstructive pulmonary disease: A model analysis in the Netherlands. *American Journal of Respiratory and Critical Care Medicine, 164*(4), 590–596.

Fettig, T. (2007). Harvesting the wind [Episode 6]. In M. Willoughby (Producer), *e2: Energy* [DVD]. Arlington, VA: PBS Home Video.

Fisk, M. (2012, May 3). BP oil spill judge tentatively approves $7.8 billion pact. *Bloomberg Businessweek.*

Food and Agricultural Organization. (2007). Retrieved from http://faostat.fao.org/site/340/default.aspx

Foot, D. K., & Ross, S. (2004). Social sustainability. In C. Galea (Ed.), *Teaching business sustainability Vol. 1: From theory to practice* (pp. 107–125). Sheffield, UK: Greenleaf.

Forest Stewardship Council. (n.d.). *The 10 principles: Ten rules for responsible forest management*. Retrieved from www.fsc.org/the-ten-principles.103.htm

Foroudastan, S., & Dees, O. (2006). Solar power and sustainability in developing countries. *International Conference on Renewable Energy for Developing Countries*. Retrieved from www.mtsu.edu/ . . . /Solar%20Power%20and%20 Sustainability%20in%20Developing%2

Fossil Fuel. (n.d.). *The advantages of coal*. Retrieved from http://fossil-fuel.co.uk/coal/advantages-of-coal

The four system conditions (n.d). *The Natural Step*. Retrieved May 29, 2012, from www.naturalstep.org/en/the-system-conditions

Fraj-Andres, E., Martinez-Salinas, E., & Matute-Vellejo, J. (2009). A multidimensional approach to the influence of environmental marketing and orientation on the firm's organisational performance. *Journal of Business Ethics, 88*, 263–286.

Frame, B. (2005). Corporate social responsibility: A challenge for the donor community. *Development in Practice, 15*(3/4), 422–432.

Friedman, M. (1962). *Capitalism and freedom*. Chicago: University of Chicago Press.

Friedman, M. (1970, September 13). The social responsibility of business is to increase its profits. *New York Times Magazine*, pp. 32–33, 122–126.

Friedman, T. L. (2007, July 8). Live bad, go green. *The New York Times*.

Friends of the Earth International. (2002). *Annual report 2001: Friends of the Earth International*. Amsterdam: Author.

Frost, R. (2011). The essentials. *ISO Focus+, The Magazine of the International Organization for Standardization, 2*(3). Retrieved from www.iso.org/iso/iso_focusplus_march_2011_social-responsibility.pdf

Fuller, D. (1999). *Sustainable marketing*. Thousand Oaks, CA: Sage.

Fuller, D., & Butler, D. D. (1998). Eco-marketing: A waste management perspective. In E. J. Wilson & W. C. Black (Eds.), *Developments in marketing science* (Vol. 17). Proceedings of the Academy of Marketing Science.

The funnel. (n.d.). *The Natural Step*. Retrieved May 29, 2012, from www.natural step.org/the-funnel

Galbraith, J. K. (1958). How much should a country consume? In H. Jarrett (Ed.), *Perspectives on conservation: Essays on America's natural resources* (pp. 89–99). Baltimore: Johns Hopkins University Press.

Gardner, T. (2010, May 26). *Global CO2 emissions to rise 43 percent by 2035: EIA*. Planet Ark. Retrieved August 12, 2010, from http://planetark.org/enviro-news/item/58178

Garner, A., & Keoleian, G. (1995). *Industrial ecology: An introduction, pollution prevention and industrial ecology*. Retrieved from www.umich.edu/~nppcpub/resources/compendia/INDEpdfs/INDEintro.pdf

Garlough, D., Gordon, W., & Bauer, S. (2008) Green guide: The complete reference for consuming wisely. Washington, DC: National Geographic Society.

Garriga, E., & Mele, D. (2004). Corporate social responsibility theories: Mapping the territory. *Journal of Business Ethics, 53*, 51–71.

General Motors sustainability report. (n.d.). Retrieved from www.gmsustainability.com

Genetically engineered foods. (n.d.). WholeFoodsMarket.com. Retrieved from http://wholefoodsmarket.com/values/genetically-engineered.php. Courtesy of Whole Foods Market. "Whole Foods Market" is a registered trademark of Whole Foods Market IP, L. P.

Geothermal Heat Pumps. (2011). Energy Efficiency and Renewable Energy. Retrieved from www.energysavers.gov/your_home/space_heating_cooling/index.cfm/mytopic=12640

Getting to know us. (n.d.). McDonalds.com. Retrieved from www.aboutmcdonalds.com/mcd/our_company.html

Gilman, R. (1991). *Eco-villages and sustainable communities.* Context Institute, Retrieved from www.context.org/iclib/ic25/gilman/

Gipe, P. (2004). *Wind power for home, farm, and business: Renewable energy for the new millennium.* White River Junction, VT: Chelsea Green Publishing Company.

Glaeser, E. (2011). *Triumph of the city.* New York: Penguin Press.

Glanz, J. (2009, December 11). Geothermal power. *The New York Times.* Retrieved from http://topics.nytimes.com/top/news/business/energy-environment/geothermal-power/index.html

Gleick, P. H. et al. (2008). The world's water 2008–2009. *The biennial report on freshwater resources.* Washington, DC: Island Press.

Glickman, D. (1996, September 13). *Secretary's memorandum, 9500–6, sustainable development.* Baltimore, MD: U.S. Department of Agriculture, Office of the Secretary.

Global Best of Green. (2009). *Retrieved from www.usasean.org/cr/members-reports/McD.pdf*

Global Reporting Initiative. (n.d.). *Pollution prevention P2, EPA.* Retrieved from www.epa.gov/p2/pubs/resources/p2meas_gri.htm

Global Reporting Initiative Guidelines. (n.d.). Retrieved November 2009 from www.proveandimprove.org/tools/griguidelines.php

Global Reporting Initiative: More background. (n.d.). United Nations Environment Programme, Division of Technology, Industry, and Economics Sustainable Consumption & Production Branch. Retrieved October 2009 from www.unep.fr/scp/gri/background.htm

Global responsibility report. (2012). Walmart.com. Retrieved from www.walmartstores.com/sustainability/7951.aspx

Global strategy on diet, physical activity, and health. (n.d.). World Health Organization. Retrieved from www.who.int/dietphysicalactivity/diet/en/index.html

The Global Warming Statistics. (n.d.). Global warming statistics. Retrieved from www.theglobalwarmingstatistics.org/the-global-warming-statistics

Global strategy on diet, physical activity, and health. (n.d.). World Health Organization. Retrieved from www.who.int/dietphysicalactivity/diet/en/index.html

Global Wind Energy Council. (2009). *Global wind 2008 report,* Renewable Energy House. Brussels, Belgium: Author. Retrieved from *www.gwec.net/index.php?id=153*

Gnatek, T. (2003). *Curitiba's urban experiment.* Retrieved from www.pbs.org/frontlineworld/fellows/brazil1203

Gold, M. V. (1999). *Sustainable agriculture: Definition and terms.* Baltimore, MD: U.S. Department of Agriculture.

Gore, A. (2007, July 7). So, Al Gore, what's the one thing we can all do to tackle climate change? *The Independent.* Retrieved from www.independent.co.uk/environment/climate-change/so-al-gore-whats-the-one-thing-we-can-all-do-to-tackle-climate-change-456269.html

Graedel, T. E., & Allenby, B. R. (2009). *Industrial ecology and sustainable engineering.* Englewood Cliffs, NJ: Prentice Hall.

Grant, J. (2007). The green marketing manifesto. West Sussex, England: Wiley.

GreenBiz Staff. (2007a, June 28). *Case studies in sustainable grocery supply chains.* Greenbiz.com. Retrieved July 19, 2007, from www.greenbiz.com/toolbox/printer.cfm?LinkAdvID=83325

GreenBiz Staff. (2007b, July). *$100K award for sustainability opens for nominations*. Greenbiz.com. Retrieved from www.greenbiz.com/news/news_third.cfm?NewsID=35812

GreenBiz Staff. (2007c, August 8). *Businesses embracing green procurement, survey finds*. Greenbiz.com. Retrieved from www.climatebiz.com/sections/news_detail.cfm?NewsID=35700

GreenBiz Staff. (2007d, October 22). *Sonoco helps manufacturers cut landfill waste*. Greenbiz.com. Retrieved from www.greenbiz.com/news/printer.cfm?NewsID=36132

GreenBiz Staff. (2008, January 16). *BT- and Cisco-sponsored paper says sustainability breeds innovation and profitability*. Greenbiz.com. Retrieved April 2012 from www.greenbiz.com/print/1601

Green DC Agenda. (2010, June). Green.dc.agenda. Retrieved from www.green.dc.gov

Green-e Climate Standard. (2007). The Green-e Greenhouse Gas Emission Reduction Product Certification Program Standard. Retrieved from http://resource-solutions.org/mv/docs/Ge_GHG_Product_Standard_V1.pdf

The green hypocrisy: America's corporate environment champions pollute the world. (2009, April 2). Retrieved from http://247wallst.com/2009/04/02/the-%E2%80%9Cgreen%E2%80%9D-hypocrisy-america%E2%80%99s-corporate-environment-champions-pollute-the-world/

GreeNOLA: A strategy for a sustainable New Orleans. (2012). Retrieved from www.nola.gov/residents/ . . . /~/ . . . /greenolawithldrfcoverpage.ashx

Green Living Tips. (2010, January, 19). *Green business—The triple bottom line*. Greenlivingtips.com. Retrieved January 26, 2010, from www.greenlivingtips.com/articles/264/1/Triple-bottom-line.html

Greenpeace. (2003). Greenpeace: About us. Retrieved July 4, 2003, from www.greenpeace.org/aboutus/

Greenprint Denver. (2010, June 1). Retrieved from www.greenprintdenver.com

Green Supply Chain Management. (n.d.). Bearing point management and technology consultants. Retrieved from www.bearingpoint.com/en-other/7–5266/green-supply-chain-management/?

Green Space Today. (2010, June 1). Hear from Salt Lake City Mayor Ralph Becker. (2010, June 1). Retrieved from www.greenspacetoday.com

Guerin, B. (2007, February 8). European blowback for Asian biofuels. *Asia Times*.

Hamel, G. (2000). *Leading the revolution*. Boston: Harvard Business School Press.

Hall-Jones, P. (2006). The rise and rise of NGOs. *Public Service International*. Retrieved from www.world-psi.org/Template.cfm?Section=Home&CONTENTID=11738&TEMPLATE=/ContentManagement/ContentDisplay.cfm

Hamilton, K., Bayon, R., Turner, G., & Higgins, D. (2007). *State of the voluntary carbon markets 2007: Picking up steam*. San Francisco: Ecosystem Marketplace & New Carbon Finance. Retrieved from http://ecosystemmarketplace.com/documents/acrobat/StateoftheVoluntaryCarbonMarket18July_Final.pdf

Hamilton, K., Sjardin, M., Marcello, T., & Xu, G. (2008). Forging a frontier: State of the voluntary carbon markets. San Francisco: Ecosystem Marketplace & New Carbon Finance. Retrieved from http://ecosystemmarketplace.com/documents/cms_documents/2008_StateofVoluntaryCarbonMarket.4.pdf

Hammond, A., Kramer, W., Katz, R., & Walker, C. (2007). *The next 4 billion: Market size and business strategy at the base of the pyramid*. World Resources Institute and International Finance Corporation/World Bank Group: Washington, DC.

Harack, B. & Laskowski, K. (2010, November 29). *31 ways to reduce paper usage*. Retrieved from www.visionofearth.org/live-green/31-ways-to-reduce-paper-usage/

Hargroves, K., & Smith, M. (2005). *The natural advantage of nations: Business opportunities, innovation, and governance in the 21st century*. London: The Natural Edge Project, Earthscan.

Hart, S., & Milstein, M. (2003). Creating sustainable value. *Academy of Management Executive, 17*, 2.

Harwood, R. R. (1990). A history of sustainable agriculture. In C. A. Edwards, R. Lal, J. P. Madden, R. H. Miller, & G. House (Eds.), *Sustainable agricultural systems* (pp. 3–19). Ankeny, IA: Soil and Water Conservation Society.

Hauserman, J. (2007). Florida's coastal and ocean future, a blueprint for economic and environmental leadership. New York: National Resources Defense Council. Reprinted with permission from the National Resources Defense Council.

Hawken, P. (2007). *Blessed unrest: How the largest social movement in history is restoring grace, justice and beauty to the world.* London: Penguin Books.

Hawken, P. (1994). *Ecology of commerce.* New York: HarperCollins.

Hecht, A. (2009, January). *Government perspectives on sustainability. Chemical Engineering Progress.* Retrieved from http://72.3.180.220/uploadedFiles/Energy_Website/Publications/Government_Perspectives_on_Sustainability.pdf.pdf

Henlon, K. E. (1976). *Ecological marketing.* Columbus, OH: Grid.

Henrik-Robert, K. (2010). *The Natural Step.* Retrieved from www.naturalstep.org/

Hibbard, M., & Tang, C. C. (2004). Sustainable community development: A social approach from Vietnam. *Community Development Society, 35*(2), 87–105.

Higgins, M. (2006, October 15). How to keep flying and staying green. *The New York Times,* p. 6.

Hill, J., Nelson, E., Tilman, D., Polasky, S., & Tiffany, D. (2006). Environmental, economic, and energetic costs and benefits of biodiesel and ethanol biofuels. *Proceedings of the National Academy of Sciences of the United States of America, 103*(30), 11206–11210.

Hill, J. M. (2010). Getting started with greening your supply chain. *GreenBiz.com.* Retrieved May 2010 from www.greenbiz.com/blog/2010/04/12/getting-started-greening-your-supply-chain?page=full#ixzz0mzWjYprU

Hoffman, A. J. (2009, Spring). Shades of green. *Stanford Social Innovation Review,* 40–49.

Holden, B. (2002). *Democracy and global warming.* London: Continuum.

Holliday, C. (2001). Sustainable growth, the DuPont way. *Harvard Business Review, 79*(8), 129–132.

Holme, L., & Watts, R. (2000). Corporate social responsibility: Making good business sense. *The World Business Council for Sustainable Development, 10.* Retrieved from www.wbcsd.org/includes/getTarget.asp?type=d&id=ODc5Nw

Holmes, J. (n.d.). *Sustainability and the triple bottom line.* Retrieved from http://enterprisedevelop.com/resources/pdf/EDG%20Sustainable%20Enterprise%20.pdf

Horn, G. (2006). *Living green: A practical guide to simple sustainability.* Topanga, CA: Freedom Press.

House-Energy. (n.d.). Solar energy costs payback. Retrieved from www.house-energy.com/

Howlett, M., & Ramesh, M. (1995). *Studying public policy: Policy cycles and policy subsystems.* Toronto: Oxford University Press.

Huff, E. (2011). Solar cell breakthrough achieves 90% efficiency at fraction of costs. NaturalNews.com. Retrieved March 2012 from www.naturalnews.com/028691_solar_cells_efficiency.html#ixzz10egw80Eo

Human Development Index. (n.d.). Human development reports, United National Development Programme. Retrieved August 2012 from http://hdr.undp.org/en/statistics/hdi/

Hunter, M. L. (Ed.). (1999). *Maintaining biodiversity in forest ecosystems.* Cambridge: Cambridge University Press.

Hydropower: Going with the flow. (2012). National Geographic Society. Retrieved from http://environment.nationalgeographic.com/environment/global-warming/hydropower-profile/

Hydropower development: The economic impact of hydropower. (2010). Economy Watch. Retrieved from www.economywatch.com/renewable-energy/hydro power-development-economic-impact.html

In classrooms, not fields. (2011, March). Cargill.com. Retrieved from www.cargill .com/connections/cargill-and-care-classrooms/index.jsp

Industrial Ecology. (2009). Retrieved from www.industrialecology.nl/

The International Ecotourism Society. (n.d.). *What is ecotourism?* Retrieved from www.ecotoursim.org/what-is-ecotourism

International Energy Agency. (2006). *World energy outlook.* Retrieved from www .iea.org/textbase/nppdf/free/2006/we02006.pdf

International Energy Agency. (2008). *World energy outlook.* Retrieved from www .iea.org/textbase/nppdf/free/2008/we02008.pdf

International Union for the Conservation of Nature. (2007). Red list 1996–2007. Retrieved from www.iucnredlist.org/info/2007RL_Stats_Table%201.pdf

ISO 14001 2004 introduction. (n.d.) Praxiom Research Group Limited. Retrieved 2009 from www.praxiom.com/iso-14001-intro.htm

ISO 14001 environment. (n.d.). British Standards Institute. Retrieved 2009 from www.bsigroup.com/en/Assessment-and-certification-services/management-sys tems/Standards-and-Schemes/ISO-14001/

The ISO 14040 series. (2004). ECO SMEs: Services for Green Products. Retrieved March 2011 from www.ecosmes.net/cm/navContents?1 =EN&navID=lcaSmesS tandardReg&subNavID=1&pagID=2

ISO 26000 and the definition of social responsibility. (2011). Retrieved March 2012 from www.triplepundit.com/2011/03/iso-26000-definition-social-responsibility

ISO standard will help purchasers by clarifying environmental labels. (2006, July 10). *ISO News.* Retrieved March 2011 from www.iso.org/iso/news.htm? refid=Ref1020

ISO standards for life cycle assessment to promote sustainable development. (2006, July 7). Retrieved March 2011 from www.iso.org/iso/news.htm?refid=Ref1019

The IUCN red list of threatened species. (2012). Retrieved from www.iucnredlist.org

Joburg Department of Development Planning, Transportation and Environment, Environmental Planning and Management Unit, City of Johannesburg. (2003). *State of the environment report.*

Johnson, B. (2009). *Better green and water spaces.* Retrieved from www.london/gov .uk/greatoutdoors/bettergreen/

Jonnes, J. (2011). What is a tree worth? *The Wilson Quarterly.* Retrieved from www .wilsonquarterly.com

Kaestner, N. (2007). Ten steps to create a sustainable supply chain. GreenBiz.com. Retrieved May 2010 from www.greenbiz.com/blog/2007/05/23/ten-steps-create-sustainable-supply-chain#ixzz0mVBGfTlh

Kaplan R., & Norton D. (1996). *The balanced scorecard: Translating strategies into action.* Boston: Harvard Business School Press.

Karajkov, R. (2007, July 16). The power of N.G.O.s: They're big but how big? *Worldpress.org.* Retrieved from www.worldpress.org/Americas/2864.cfm

Kassel, R. (2009, October 29). Moving the city along the road to sustainability. *GothamGazette.com.* Retrieved from http://old.gothamgazette.com/article/ 20091029/7/3077/

Kenner, R. (2010). *Food, Inc.* [Motion picture]. Los Angeles: Magnolia Pictures.

Key corporate social responsibility issue areas. (n. d.). *Business Respect.* Retrieved May 2010 from www.businessrespect.net/issues.php

Kirschner, A. (2010). Understanding poverty and unemployment on the Olympic peninsula—after the spotted owl. *The Social Science Journal.* Doi: 10.1016/ j.socij. 2009.11.002

Kollmuss, A., & Bowell, B. (2006, December). *Voluntary offsets for air-travel carbon emissions, Tufts Climate Initiative.* Retrieved from http://sustainability.tufts.edu/pdf/TCI_Carbon_Offsets_Paper_April-207.pdf

Kollmuss, A., Zink, H., & Polycarp, C. (2008). *Making sense of the voluntary carbon market: A comparison of carbon offset standards.* Germany: World Wildlife Fund.

Kong, N., Saltzmann, O., Steger, U., & Ionescu-Somers, A. (2002). Moving business/industry towards sustainable consumption: The role of NGOs. *European Management Journal, 20*(2), 109–127.

Kraft Foods sustainability goals & agriculture fact sheet (2011, May). Kraft Foods. Retrieved from www.kraftfoodscompany.com/SiteCollectionImages/Image Repository/news/mmr05112011/2011.05%20FACT%20Goals%20Ag%20 Sustainability%20Release%20FINAL.pdf

Krimmel, M. (2007, February 12). *Transforming Los Angeles into a sustainable city.* Retrieved from www.worldchanging.com/archives/

The Kyoto Protocol. (n.d.). Retrieved March 2012 from www.kyotoprotocol.com/

The Kyoto Protocol summary. (n.d.). Earth's Friends. Retrieved March 2012 from www.earthsfriends.com/kyoto-protocol-summary

Laine, M. (2005). Meanings of the term "sustainable development" in Finnish corporate disclosures. *Accounting Forum, 29*, 395–413.

Land Rover. (n.d.). Retrieved from www.landrover.com/gb/en/lr/aboutland-rover/sustainability/

Langran, L. V. (2002). *Empowerment and the limits of change: NGOs and health decentralization in the Philippines.* Unpublished doctoral dissertation, University of Toronto.

Lasley, F. A., Jones, H. B., Jr., Easterling, E. H., & Christensen, L. A. (1988). The U.S. broiler industry. Commodity Economics Division, Economic Research Service, U.S. Department of Agriculture. Agricultural Economic Report. No. 591. Retrieved from *naldc.nal.usda.gov/download/CAT10407135/PDF*

LAWA sustainability. (2007, Summer). *Centerlines,* pp. 17–19.

Lemonick, M. (2009, March 9). Top 10 myths about sustainability. *Scientific American.*

Leopold, A. (1948). A land ethic. *Sand County Almanac.* Retrieved from http://home.btconnect.com/tipiglen/landethic.html

Levine, D. I., & Chatterji, A. K. (2006). Breaking down the wall of codes: Evaluating non-financial performance measurement. *California Management Review, 48*(2), 29–51.

Licht, F. O. (2009). World fuel ethanol production. *World Ethanol and Biofuels Report, 7*(18).

Life cycle assessment: Principles and practice. (2006). Retrieved June 2012 from www.epa.gov/nrmrl/std/lca/lca.html

Life cycle initiative publications. (n.d.). Retrieved October 2009 from http://jp1.estis .net/sites/lcinit/default.asp?site=lcinit&page_id=138F5949–6997–4BE6-A553– 585E92C22EE4#lcirap

Lohan, T. (2008). *Water consciousness.* San Francisco: AlterNet Books.

Logistics. (n.d.). Wal-Mart.com. Retrieved from www.walmartstores/sustainability

Lomborg, B. (2001). *The skeptical environmentalist.* Cambridge: Cambridge University Press.

Lorimer, K, (2006). *Lonely Planet Green Guide.* Victoria, Australia: Lonely Planet.

Louaillier, K. (2008). 5 myths about bottled water. In T. Lohan (Ed.), *Water consciousness* (pp. 58–71). San Francisco: AlterNet Books.

Love, G. J., Lan, S.-P., & Shy, C. M. (1982). A study of acute respiratory disease in families exposed to different levels of air pollution in the Great Salt Lake Basin,

Utah, 1971–1972 and 1972–1973. *Environmental Health Perspectives, 44,* 169–174.

Lovins, A., Lovins, H., & Hawken, P. (2000). *Natural capitalism: The next Industrial Revolution.* New York: Little, Brown.

Lowe's (n.d.). *Lowe's policy on sustainability.* Retrieved from www.lowes.com/cd_Lowes+Policy+on+Sustainability_1286385507_

Luck, T. (2008, February 4). The world's dirtiest cities. *Forbes.*

MacBeath, A. (2008). Corporate social responsibility: A necessity not a choice. *Grant Thornton.* Retrieved from www.internationalbusinessreport.*com/files/ibr%202008%20-%20corporate%20social%20responsibility%20report%20final%20(150%20dpi)%20web%20enabled.pdf*

MacDonald, C. (2012, January 30). *Global 100 flawed on corporate sustainability.* Business Ethics, Canadian Business. Retrieved August 2012 from www.canadianbusiness.com/blog/business_ethics/68267—global-100-flawed-on-corporate-sustainability

Macmillan, T. (2007). *Meat consumption: Trends and environmental implications.* Brighton, United Kingdom: Food Ethics Council.

Mahara, D., & Mukwita, A. (2002, August 28). Zambia rejects gene-altered U.S. corn. *Los Angeles Times.*

Mahoney, M. (2008). City of Atlanta energy and climate initiatives. *City of Atlanta.* Retrieved from *www.environmentaltrademission.org/ . . . /ETM%20-%20 Presentation%)*

Main, E. (2007). Shifting into neutral. *The Green Guide.* Retrieved from www.thegreenguide.com/doc/119/neutral

Marino, V. (2007, April 29). A starring role for "green" construction. *The New York Times.*

Marx, S. (2001). *Review of natural capitalism.* Retrieved from http://cla.calpoly.edu/~smarx/Nature/NatCap/natcap.html

Mathews, M. S. (2000). The Kyoto Protocol to the United Nations Framework Convention on climate change: Survey of its deficiencies and why the United States should not ratify this treaty. *Dickinson Journal of Environmental Law and Policy, 9*(1), 193–226.

Matthews, E., Amann, C., Bringezu, S., Fischer-Kowalksi, M., Kleijn, R., Ottke, C., et al. (2000). *The weight of nations: Material outflows from industrial economies* (p. V). Washington, DC: World Resources Institute. Retrieved from http://materials.wri.org/pubs_description.cfm?PubID=3023

Mayo Clinic Staff. (2011, October 12). Water: How much should you drink every day? Mayo Clinic. Retrieved from www.mayoclinic.com/health/water/NU00283

McComb, B. C. (2008). *Wildlife habitat management.* Boca Raton, FL: CRC Press.

McDonald, C. (2008). *Green Inc.: An environmental insider reveals how a good cause has gone bad.* Guilford, CT: Globe Pequot.

McDonough, W., & Braungart, M. (2002). *Cradle to cradle: Remaking the way we make things.* New York: North Point Press.

McPherson, E. G., Nowak, D. J., & Rowntree, R. A. (Eds.). (1994). Chicago's urban ecosystem: Results of the Chicago Urban Forest Climate Project. Radnor, PA: U.S. Department of Agriculture, Forest Service.

McGann, J., & Johnstone, M. (2006). The power shift and the NGO credibility crisis. *The International Journal of Not-for-Profit Law, 8*(2).

The mechanisms under the Kyoto Protocol: Emissions trading, the clean development mechanism, and joint implementation. (n.d.). United Nations Framework Convention on Climate Change. Retrieved March 2010 from http://unfccc.int/kyoto_protocol/mechanisms/items/1673.php

MeetGreen. (n.d.). Retrieved from www.meetgreen.com/

Metro Vancouver. (2010). *Metro Vancouver sustainability framework.*

Mexico City presents comprehensive plan to tackle environmental issues. (2011). Retrieved from www.citymayors.com/environment/mexico-green-plan.html

Milani, B. (2000). *Designing the green economy*. Lanham, MD: Rowman & Littlefield.

Mitchell, J. (1970). Big yellow taxi. On *Ladies of the canyon* [Record]. New York: Warner Brothers and Siquomb Publishing Co. Big Yellow Taxi" Words and Music by Joni Mitchell. © 1970 (Renewed) Crazy Crow Music. All Rights Administered by SONY/ATV MUSIC PUBLISHING, 8 Music Square West, Nashville, TN 37203. All Rights Reserved.

Monsanto. (n.d.). *Biotechnology*. Retrieved from www.monsanto.com/products/pages/biotechnology.aspx

Montreal Process Working Group. (1999, December). *The Montreal Process: Forests for the future*. Retrieved from www.rinya.maff.go.jp/mpci/rep-pub/1999/broch_e.html#5

Morikawa, M., Morrison, J., & Gleick, P. (2007). Corporate Reporting on Water, 2007. Retrieved from *www.pacinst.org/reports/water_reporting/corporate_reporting_on_water.pdf*

Morton, O. (2006, September 7). Solar energy: A new day dawning?: Silicon Valley sunrise. *Nature, 443*, 19–22.

Mountain Association for Community Economic Development. (n.d.). Retrieved from http://archive.rec.org/REC/Programs/Sustainablecities/what.html

Murphy, C. (2002, September 30). Is BP beyond petroleum? Hardly. *Fortune*.

Murray, J. (2007, October 22). Study finds greener companies outperform rivals. *BusinessGreen*. Retrieved from www.greenbiz.com/news/2007/10/21/study-finds-greener-companies-outperform-rivals

Murray, M. (2010). Green supply chain best practices. *About.com: Logistics/supply chain*. Retrieved May 2010 from http://logistics.about.com/od/greensupplychain/a/GSC_Best_Prac.htm

Naess, A. (1989). *Ecology, community and lifestyle: Outline of an ecosophy* (D. Rothenberg, Trans. Ed.). Cambridge: Cambridge University Press.

National Renewable Energy Laboratory, U.S. Department of Energy. (2008, October 20). Photovoltaic Solar Resource of the United States. Retrieved from http://www.nrel.gov/gis/images/map_pv_national_lo-res.jpg

Nelson, G. (1970). *America's last chance* (p. 8). Waukesha, WI: Country Beautiful.

Nelson, L. (2007). Solar-water heating resurgence ahead? *Solar Today, 21*(3), 28.

New ISO 14064 standards provide tools for assessing and supporting greenhouse gas reduction and emissions trading. (2006, March 3). Retrieved from http://www.iso.org/iso/news.htm?refid=Ref994

The New York Times. (2012, May 30). Wind power. Retrieved from http://topics.nytimes.com/top/news/business/energy-environment/wind-power/index.html

Nestle, M. (2006). *What to eat*. New York: North Point Press.

Nikkhah, H. A., & Redzuan, M. B. (2010). Role of NGOs in promoting empowerment for sustainable community development. *Journal of Human Ecology, 30*(2), 85–92.

The non-governmental order: Will NGOs democratize, or merely disrupt, global governance? (1999, December 9). *The Economist*. Retrieved from www.economist.com/node/266250

Office Depot. (n.d.). *Environmental stewardship*. Retrieved from www.community.officedepot.com/paperproc.asp

Ogilvy Earth. (2010). *From greenwash to great: A practical guide to green marketing*. New York: Ogilvy Mather.

O'Neill, J. (2008, July 15). Boom time for the global bourgeoisie. *Financial Times*.

Oregon Environmental Council. (2010). *A sustainable economy*. Retrieved from www.oeconline.org/our-work/economy

Organisation for Economic Co-operation and Development. (2002). *OECD governments agree to take the lead on buying "green"* [Press release]. Retrieved from www.oecd.org

Orr, D. W. (1992). *Ecological literacy: Education and the transition to a postmodern world. SUNY series in constructive postmodern thought*. Albany: State University of New York Press.

Other 14000 Series standards. (2002). Retrieved March 2011 from www.iso14000 -iso14001-environmental-management.com/iso14000.htm

Ottman, J. (1998). *Green marketing.* New York: BookSurge.

Ottman, J. (2010, February 6). A smart new way to segment green consumers. *Greenmarketing.com.*

Our themes. (n.d.). *ICLEI—Local governments for sustainability.* Retrieved March 2011 from www.iclei.org/index.php?id=global-themes

Our vision for a sustainable global economy. (n.d.). Ceres. Retrieved August 2012 from: www.ceres.org/about-us/what-we-do/our-vision/our-vision

Overend, R. P., & Milbrandt, A. (2007). Potential carbon emissions reductions from biomass by 2030. In C. F. Kutscher (Ed.), *Tackling climate change in the U.S.— Potential carbon emissions reductions from energy efficiency and renewable energy by 2030.* Boulder, CO: American Solar Energy Society.

Overview of the UN Global Compact. (2010). United Nations Global Compact. Retrieved April 2011 from www.unglobalcompact.org/AboutTheGC/

Pachauri, R. K., & Reisinger, A. (Eds.). (2007). *IPCC fourth assessment report: Climate change 2007.* Geneva, Switzerland: IPCC.

Palmer, J. (2008, October 11). Renewable energy: The tide is turning. *New Scientist.*

Patel, R. (2007). *Stuffed and starved.* Brooklyn, NY: Melville House Publishing.

Patil, J. R. (2010). Mumbai sustainability and corporate citizenship protocol, government of Maharashtra. Asian Centre for Corporate Governance and Sustainability.

PBS. (n.d.). Silence of the bees. Retrieved from www.pbs.org/wnet/nature/episodes/silence-of-the-bees/introduction/38/

Peck, S., & Gibson, R. (2002). Pushing the revolution. *Alternatives Journal, 26*(1).

PEFC. (n.d.). *Forest certification.* Retrieved from www.pefc.org/index.php/certification-services/forest

Penfield, P. (2007). *The green supply chain, material handling industry of America.* Retrieved 2012 from www.mhia.org/news/industry/7056/the-green-supply-chain

Perlack, R. D., Wright, L. L., Turhollow, A. F., Graham, R. L., Stokes, B. J., & Erbach, D. C. (2005, April). *Biomass as feedstock for a bioenergy and bioproducts industry: The technical feasibility of a billion-ton annual supply.* Oak Ridge, TN: Oak Ridge National Laboratory.

Phoenix: Living like it matters. (2008). Retrieved from phoenix.gov/webcms/groups/internet/@inter/@env/ . . . /web . . . /021142.pdf

Phyper, J. D., & MacLean, P. (2009). *Good to green.* New York: Wiley.

Pollan, M. (2006). *The omnivore's dilemma.* New York: Penguin.

Pope, C. A. (1989). Respiratory disease associated with community air pollution and a steel mill, Utah Valley. *American Journal of Public Health, 79*(5), 623–628.

Population growth rate. (2001). World Bank. Retrieved from www.worldbank.org/depweb/english/modules/social/pgr/index.html

Porter, M. E., & Kramer, M. R. (2006, December). Strategy and society: The link between competitive advantage and corporate social responsibility. *Harvard Business Review,* 78–92.

Porter, M. E., & van der Linde, C. (1995, September–October). Green and competitive. *Harvard Business Review,* 120–134.

Portney, P. R., & Mullahy, J. (1990). Urban air quality and chronic respiratory disease. *Regional Science and Urban Economics, 20*(3), 407–418.

Potoski, M., & Prakash, A. (2005). Covenants with weak swords: ISO 14001 and facilities' environmental performance. *Journal of Policy Analysis and Management, 24*(4), 745–769.

Poultry marketplace. (n.d.). Agriculture and Agri-Food Canada. Retrieved February 28, 2012, from www.agr.gc.ca/poultry/consm_eng.htm

Power, M. E., Tilman, D., Estes, J. A., Menge, B. A., Bond, W. J., Mills, L. S., et al. (1996). Challenges in the quest for keystones. *BioScience, 46,* 609–620.

Prahalad, C. K., & Hart, S. L. (2002). The fortune at the bottom of the pyramid. *strategy+business.* Retrieved March 2011 from www.cs.berkeley.edu/%7Ebrewer/ict4b/Fortune-BoP.pdf

Presidio Buzz. (2009, February 23). *Nuclear energy: Pros and cons.* Retrieved from www.triplepundit.com/2009/02/nuclear-energy-pros-and-cons/

Pricen, T., & Finger, M. (1994). Introduction. In T. Pricen & M. Finger (Eds.), *Environmental NGOs in world politics.* London: Routledge.

Profiling food consumption in America. (2009). In *Factbook* (Chp. 2). Retrieved from www.usda.gov

Public sector sustainability under the spotlight. (1999, April). *Government sustainability.* Retrieved from www.governmentsustainability.co.uk/

PV costs down significantly from 1998–2007. (2009, February 23). *Renewable Energy World.*

PV costs set to plunge for 2009/10. (2008, December 23). *Renewable Energy World.*

Raoh, V. A., Whytt, R. M., Garfinkel, R., Andrews, H., Hoepner, L., Reyes, A., et al. (2004). Development effects of exposure to environmental tobacco smoke and material hardship among inner-city children. *Neurotoxicology and Teratology, 26,* 373–385.

Reaching investors: Communicating value through ESG disclosures. (n.d.). Reporting Practices, GRI. The Netherlands: Global Reporting Initiative. Retrieved from www.globalreporting.org

Revkin, A. (2007, April 29). Carbon-neutral is hip, but is it green? *The New York Times.*

RG: Sustainability Reporting Guidelines. (n.d.). Version 3.1, The Netherlands: Global Reporting Initiative. Retrieved from www.globalreporting.org

Richardson, A. (2006). Carbon credits—Paying to pollute? *3rd Degree.* Retrieved from http://3degree.cci.ecu.edu.au/articles/view/781

Riddleberger, E., & Hittner, J. (2009). Leading a sustainable enterprise, IBM Institute for Business Value. Retrieved from ftp://ftp.software.ibm.com/common/ssi/pm/xb/n/gbe03226usen/GBE03226USEN.PDF

Rogers, P. P., Jalal, K. F., Lohani, B. N., Owens, G. M., Yu, C.-C., Duornaund, C. M., et al. (1997). Measuring environmental quality in Asia. Manila, Philippines: Asian Development Bank.

Royte, E. (2008). *Disney (waste) land.* Retrieved from www.onearth.org/article/disney-wasteland

Rural Areas Get Increased Hydro Power Capacity (2007, May 7). *Xinhua.*

Russell, J. (2007). Are emissions offsets a carbon con? *Ethical Corporation.* Retrieved from www.greenbiz.com/news/reviews_third.cfm?NewsID=34804

Rydaker, A. (2007, April 16). Biomass for electricity & heat production. Paper presented at Bioenergy North America, Chicago.

Schlosser, E. (2005). *Fast food nation: The dark side of the all-American meal.* New York: Harper.

Schmer, M. R., Vogel, K. P., Mitchell, R. B., & Perrin, R. K. (2008). Net energy of cellulosic ethanol from switchgrass. *Proceedings of the National Academy of Sciences of the United States of America, 105*(2), 464–469.

Science and technology: Sustainable practices. (n.d.). United States Environmental Protection Agency. Retrieved March 15, 2012, from www.epa.gov/gateway/science/sustainable.html

Seafood sustainability. (n.d.). WholeFoodsMarket.com. Retrieved from http://wholefoodsmarket.com/values/seafood.php

Searchinger, T., Heimlich, R., Houghton, R. A., Dong, F., Elobeid, A., Fabiosa, J., et al. (2008). Use of U.S. croplands for biofuels increases greenhouse gases through emissions from land-use change. *Science, 319*(5867), 1238–1240.

Secretaria del Medio Ambiente Gobierno del Distrito Federal. (2008). Mexico City Climate Action Program 2008–2012 summary, 2008. Retrieved from www.sma .df.gob.mx/sma/links/download/ . . . /paccm_summary.pdf

Seeger, M., & Hipfel, S. (2007). Legal versus ethical Arguments: Contexts for corporate social responsibility. In G. Cheney, J. Roper, & S. May (Eds.), *The debate over corporate social responsibility.* New York: Oxford University Press.

Senge, P. (2000). *Systems thinking primer for natural capitalism.* Retrieved from www.sustainer.org/pubs/NatCapPrimer.pdf

Senge, P. (with Smith, B., Kruschwitz, N., Laur, J., & Schley, S.) (2008). *The necessary revolution: How individuals and organizations are working together to create a sustainable world.* Random House Digital.

Sessions, G. (Ed.). (1995). *Deep ecology for the 21st century.* Boston: Shambala.

Seuss, Dr. (1971). *The lorax.* New York: Random House.

SFEnvironment. (2010). *Sustainability plan report card.* Retrieved from sfenvironment.org.

Sharma, S., & Vredenburg, H. (1998). Proactive corporate environmental strategy and the development of competitively valuable organizational capabilities. *Strategic Management Journal, 19*(8), 729–753.

Shuster, E. (2009, January). *Tracking new coal-fired power plants.* Pittsburgh, PA: Department of Energy, National Energy Technology Laboratory.

Simons, D., & Mason, R. (2002). *Environmental and transport supply chain evaluation with sustainable value stream mapping.* Proceedings of the 7th Logistics Research Network Conference, Birmingham, AL.

Smalheiser, K. (2006, November 13). Value driven leadership: Responsible companies committed to tackling global societal woes have discovered they gain strategic advantage [Special advertising feature]. Retrieved from www.timeincnewsgroup custompub.com/sections/061113_CSRv2.pdf

Sokka, L. (2010). Analyzing the environmental benefits of industrial symbiosis. *Journal of Industrial Ecology, 15*(1), 137–155.

Sow housing. (2012, February 13). McDonalds.com. Retrieved from www.aboutmc donalds.com/mcd/sustainability/library/policies_programs/sustainable_supply_ chain/animal_welfare/sow_housing.html

Stappen, R. K. (2009). Global Reporting Initiative, Forum: Science and Innovation for Sustainable Development, Advancing Science, Serving Society (ASSS). Retrieved August 2012 from http://sustsci.aaas.org/content.html?contentid=693

State of the Air, American Lung Association. (2012a). *Cleanest cities.* Retrieved from www.stateoftheair.org/2012/city-rankings/cleanest-cities.html

State of the Air, American Lung Association. (2012b). *Most polluted cities.* Retrieved from www.stateoftheair.org/2012/city-rankings/most-polluted-cities.html

Steelworks. (2007, April 24). Steel industry exploring new CO2-reducing steel making processes. Retrieved from www.uss.com/corp/environment/documents/Steel%20 Industry%20Exploring%20New%20CO2-Reducing%20Steel%20Making% 20Processes.pdf

Stewardship initiative sustainability definition. (2002). Retrieved from www.p2pays .org/ref/38/37967.pdf : With permission from NC DENR's Division of Environmental Assistance and Outreach.

Stewardship at REI. (n.d.). REI. Retrieved from www.rei.com/stewardship.html

Sto Corp. Lotusan Videos. (n.d.). Retrieved December 2011 from www.stocorp.com/ index.php/en/20090714306/videos-product/sto-videos/menu-id-271.html

Streeten, P. (1997). Non-governmental organizations and development. *Annals of the American Academy of Political and Social Science, 554,* 193–210.

Stromquist, N. P. (2002). NGOs in a new paradigm of civil society. *Current Issues in Comparitive Education, 1*(1), 62–67.

Sturgis, S., (2009, September 30). Growth in renewable energy outpaces nuclear, fossil fuels. *Grist Magazine.*

Summary and analysis of COP17—The UN Climate Change Conference at Durban, Sustainable Solutions for the Environment. (2011). Retrieved from www.emer gent-ventures.com/ . . . /Summary-and-Analysis-of-COP17.pdf

Summary of key actions in taking action for Victoria's future, Melbourne, Australia. (2010). Retrieved from www.climatechange.vic.gov.au/__ . . . /Victorian-Climate-Change-White-Paper

A survey of organizations, providers and research involved in the effort to understand and deal with climate change. (n.d.). Retrieved from www.kyotoprotocol.com

Sussex Energy Group/UK Energy Research Centre. (2007). *The rebound effect: An assessment of the evidence for economy-wide energy savings from improved energy efficiency.*

Sustainable agriculture. (2009). Subchapter 1: Findings, Purposes, and Definitions, U.S. Code, Title 7, Chapter 64. Agricultural Research, Extension and Teaching.

Sustainable City Code Revision Project. (n.d.). Retrieved from www.mayorsinnovation .org/pdf/5SaltLakeCity.pdf

Sustainable Communities Network. (2010). *Brazil.* Retrieved from www.sustainable. org/casestudies/INTL_af_curitiba.html

Sustainable Consumption Research Exchanges. (2008). *System innovation for sustainability 1: Perspectives on radical changes to sustainable consumption and production.*

Sustainable Measures. (2010). *Definitions of sustainability.* Retrieved from www .sustainablemeasures.com/node/35

Sustainability and our future. (n.d.). WholeMarketFoods.com. Retrieved from www .wholefoodsmarket.com/values/sustainability.php

Sustainable insight. (2009, April). *KPMG Global Sustainability Services.* Retrieved February 20, 2010, from www.kpmg.com/GR/en/IssuesAndInsights/ArticlesPubli cations/Sustainability/Pages/Sustainable-Insight-April-2009.aspx

Sustainability moves centre-stage as international pressure grows. (2007, May). *Bioenergy Business, 1*(4).

Swart, R., Amman, M., Raes, F., & Tuinstra, W. (2004). A good climate for clean air: Linkages between climate change and air pollution: An editorial essay. *Climate Change, 66*(3), 263–269.

Swedish Energy Agency. (2008, December). *Energy in Sweden 2008 (pp. 96, 111).* Sweden: Eskilstuna.

Tavanti, M. (2010). *A guidance document for developing a university sustainability master plan at DePaul.* Chicago: The Sustainability Initiatives Task Force, DePaul University. Retrieved from http://sustainabledepaul.blogspot.com/p/ defining-sustainability.html

The ten principles. (2010). United Nations Global Compact. Retrieved April 2011 from www.unglobalcompact.org/AboutTheGC/TheTenPrinciples/ index.html

TerraChoice. (2012). The sins of greenwashing. Retrieved from http://sinsofgreen washing.org/

Thompson, I., & Angelstam, P. (1999). Special species. In M. L. Hunter (Ed.), *Maintaining biodiversity in forest ecosystems.* Cambridge: Cambridge University Press.

Thoreau, H. D. (1854). *Walden.* Boston: Ticknor & Fields.

Time for Change. (n.d.). Pros and cons of nuclear power. Retrieved October 2011 from http://timeforchange.org/pros-and-cons-of-nuclear-power-and-sustainability

Topping, A. (2007, September 23). Free wheeling. *The Washington Post.* Retrieved from www.washingtonpost.com/wp dyn/content/article/2007/09/21/AR20070 92100543.html

Total quality environmental management. (n.d.). BSD Global. Retrieved December 2011 from www.iisd.org/business/tools/systems_TQEM.asp

Total quality environmental management: The primer. (1993). Global Environmental Management Institute. (1993). Retrieved from www.gemi.org/resources/TQE_101.pdf

Toyota 2010 North America environmental report. (2010). Toyota.com. Retrieved from www.toyota.com/about/environmentreport2010/

Turk, J. (1989). *Introduction to environmental studies* (3rd ed.). Philadelphia: Saunders College Publishing.

Tyrvainen, L., Silvennoinen, H., & Kole, O. (2003). Ecological and aesthetic values in urban forests. *Urban Forestry & Urban Greening, 1*(3), 135–149.

UN Department of Economic and Social Affairs. (n.d.). *Agenda 21.* Retrieved June 2012 from www.un.org/esa/dsd/agenda21/

Understanding the AQI. (n.d.). *AirNow.* Retrieved from www.airnow.gov/index.cfm?action=aqibasics.aqi

Union of Concerned Scientists. (2003). Farming the wind: Wind power and agriculture fact sheet. Cambridge, MA: Author.

United Nations. (2002). *Report of the World Summit on Sustainable Development.* New York: Author.

United Nations Conference on Environment and Development. (1992). *Earth Summit 1992.* London: Regency.

United Nations Educational, Scientific, and Cultural Organization. (n.d.). *Education for sustainable development.* Retrieved from www.unesco.org/en/esd/

United Nations Educational, Scientific, and Cultural Organization. (2002). *Education for sustainability.* Paris: Author. Retrieved from portal.unesco.org/en/files/5202/ . . . learnt . . . /lessons_learnt.doc

Unruh, G., & Ettenson, R. (2011, May). Growing green: Three smart paths to developing sustainable products. In G. Unruh & R. Ettenson (Eds.), *Greening your business profitably.* Boston: Harvard Business Review Press.

Urbina, I. (2011, February 26). Regulation lax as gas wells' tainted water hits rivers. *The New York Times.*

U.S. Census Bureau. (2012). Table 373: Selected national air pollutant emissions: 1970 to 2008. *2012 statistical abstract, geography and environment: Air quality.* Washington, DC: Author.

U.S. Department of Agriculture Forest Service. (n.d.). *Urban and community forestry.* Retrieved from www.fs.fed.us/ucf/program.html

U.S. Department of Agriculture. (n.d.). Retrieved from www.usda.gov/wps/portal/usda/usdahome?navid=ORGANIC_CERTIFICATION

U.S. Department of Energy. (2010a, November). *Fuel cell technologies program: Production.* Retrieved from www1.eere.energy.gov/hydrogenandfuelcells/pdfs/doe_h2_production.pdf

U.S. Department of Energy. (2010b, November). *Hydrogen and fuel cells technology program.* Retrieved from www1.eere.energy.gov/hydrogenandfuelcells/pdfs/doe_h2_fuelcell_factsheet.pdf

U.S. Department of Energy. (2011a, January). *Hydrogen and fuel cell technologies program: Storage.* Retrieved from www1.eere.energy.gov/hydrogenandfuelcells/pdfs/doe_h2_storage.pdf

U.S. Department of Energy. (2011b, February). *Safety, codes, and standards.* Retrieved from www1.eere.energy.gov/hydrogenandfuelcells/pdfs/doe_h2_safety.pdf

U.S. Department of Energy. (2011c, August 12). *Biodiesel.* Retrieved from www.eere.energy.gov/basics/renewable_energy/biodiesel.html

U.S. Department of Energy. (2011d, August 12). *Ethanol.* Retrieved from www.eere.energy.gov/basics/renewable_energy/ethanol.html

U.S. Department of Energy. (2011e, August 12). *Ocean thermal energy conversion.* Retrieved from www.eere.energy.gov/basics/renewable_energy/ocean_thermal_energy_conv.html

U.S. Department of Energy. (2011f, August 12). *Renewable energy technologies.* Retrieved from www.eere.energy.gov/basics/renewable_energy/

U.S. Department of Energy. (2011g, August 12). *Tidal energy.* Retrieved from www .eere.energy.gov/basics/renewable_energy/tidal_energy.html

U.S. Department of Energy. (2011h, August 12). *Wave energy.* Retrieved from www .eere.energy.gov/basics/renewable_energy/wave_energy.html

U.S. Department of Energy. (2012a, February 27). *Advancing distributed energy storage.* https://solarhighpen.energy.gov/article/advancing_distributed_energy_storage

U.S. Department of Energy. (2012b, July 30). *Ethanol feedstocks.* Retrieved from www.afdc.energy.gov/afdc/ethanol/feedstocks_starch_sugar.html

U.S. Department of Energy Hydrogen Program. (n.d.). *Hydrogen & our energy future.* Retrieved from www1.eere.energy.gov/hydrogenandfuelcells/pdfs/hydro genenergyfuture_web.pdf

U.S. Energy Information Administration. (2010). Electric power monthly. Retrieved from www.eia.doe.gov/cneaf/electricity/epm/table1_1.html

U.S. Environmental Protection Agency. (2003, October). *Municipal solid waste in the United States: 2001 facts and figures.* Retrieved from www.epa.gov/osw/ nonhaz/municipal/pubs/msw2001.pdf

U.S. Environmental Protection Agency. (2012, March 6). *Basic information about estuaries: Why are estuaries important?* Retrieved from http://water.epa.gov/ type/oceb/nep/about.cfm#protect

U.S. Environmental Protection Agency Environmental Stewardship Staff Committee. (2005). Technical Report prepared by EPA Environmental Stewardship Staff Committee for the EPA Innovation Action Council. Retrieved from www.epa .gov/innovation/pdf/techrpt.pdf

Velasquez-Manoff, M. (2007). Do carbon offsets live up to their promise? *The Christian Science Monitor.* Retrieved from www.csmonitor.com/2007/0110/ p13s02-sten.htm

Velazquez, L., Munguia, N., Platt, A., & Taddei, J. (2006). Sustainable university: What can be the matter? *Journal of Cleaner Production, 14*(9–11), 810–819.

Venkat, K., & Wakeland, W. (2006). *Is lean necessarily green?* Proceedings of the 50th annual meeting of the ISSS, Rohnert Park, California. Retrieved from www.cleanmetrics.com/pages/ISSS06-IsLeanNecessarilyGreen.pdf

Vergano, D. (2007, May 22). Study: Worldwide carbon dioxide emissions soar. *USA Today.*

Visser, W. (2001). The age of responsibility: CSR 2.0 and the new DNA of business. *Journal of Business Systems, Governance and Ethics, 5*(3).

Wald, M. (2009, March 17). Stimulus money puts clean coal projects on a faster track. *The New York Times.*

Watkiss, P. (2005). The validity of food miles as an indicator of sustainable development. London: AEA Technology Environment.

Werbach. A. (2009). When sustainability means more than green. [Article summary of the book *Strategy for sustainability: A business manifesto*]. *McKinsey Quarterly, 4,* 74–79. Retrieved from www.mckinseyquarterly.com/When_sus tainabillity_means_more_than_green_2404

Werther, W., & Chandler, D. (2011). *Strategic corporate social responsibility: Stakeholders in a global environment.* Thousand Oaks, CA: Sage.

Westinghouse. (n.d.). *What is nuclear energy?* Retrieved October 2011 from www .westinghousenuclear.com/Community/WhatIsNuclearEnergy.shtm

What could nature teach us? (n.d.). BioMimicry Institute. Retrieved March 2012 from www.biomimicryinstitute.org/case_studies.php

What is EPA doing? (n.d.). United States Environmental Protection Agency. Retrieved March 2011 from www.epa.gov/sustainability/basicinfo.htm

What is GRI? (n.d.). Global Reporting Initiative. Retrieved February 2012 from www .globalreporting.org/information/about-gri/what-is-GRI/Pages/default.aspx

What is nonpoint source pollution? (n.d.). U.S. Environmental Protection Agency. Retrieved June 2012 from http://water.epa.gov/polwaste/nps/whatis.cfm

What is wilderness? (2009). Retrieved from www.wildernesswatch.org/resources/wilderness.html

What is VPP? (n.d.). The Oregon Voluntary Protection Program, Department of Consumer and Business Services. Salem, OR: Oregon Occupational Safety & Health Division. Retrieved from cbs.state.or.us

Why buy local? (2009, January 9). Sustainable Table. Retrieved from www.sustainabletable.org/issues/whybuylocal/#fn9

Wilderness Society. (2012). *Gaylord Nelson.* Retrieved from http://wilderness.org/content/gaylord-nelson

The Wilderness Society. (n.d.). *Our campaigns.* Retrieved from http://wilderness.org/campaigns

Wilson, E. O. (2002). *The future of life.* New York: Random House.

Wilson, M. (2003, March/April). Corporate Responsibility: What is it and where does it come from? *Ivey Business Journal,* 1–5.

World Alliance for Decentralized Energy. (2004, June). *Bagasse cogeneration— Global review and potential* (p. 32). Washington, DC: Author.

World Business Council for Sustainable Development. (2009, March). *What a way to run the world: WBCSD annual review 2008.* Retrieved from http://www.wbcsd.ch/DocRoot/gUpF06N8whsB1rFquh4k/rapport_annuel_08.pdf

World Business Council for Sustainable Development. (2008). *Sustainable consumption facts and trends: From a business perspective.* Switzerland: Author.

World Business Council for Sustainable Development. (2006). From Challenge to Opportunity: The role of business in tomorrow's society. Switzerland: Author.

World Business Council for Sustainable Development/Earthwatch Institute/World Resources Institute/International Union for the Conservation of Nature. (2006). *Business and ecosystems.*

World Business Council for Sustainable Development/GlobeScan. (2007). *Survey of sustainability experts.*

World Commission on Environment and Development. (1987). *Our common future.* Oxford: Oxford University Press.

World Resources Institute. (2003, April 10–11). *World Resources Institute* (pp. 3–4). Washington, DC: Author.

Worldwatch Institute. (n.d.). Window to prevent catastrophic climate change closing; EU should press for immediate U.S. action. Retrieved January 6, 2012, from www.worldwatch.org/node/5340

World Wildlife Fund. (2006). *Living planet report.*

World Wildlife Fund UK. (2006). *One planet business.*

World Wind Energy Association. (2009). *World wind energy report.* Bonn, Germany: Author. Retrieved from www.wwindea.org/home/ . . . /worldwindenergyreport2008_s.pd . . . worldwindenergyreport2008_s.pdf

Young, R. (2004). Dilemmas and advances in corporate social responsibility in Brazil, The work of Ethos Institute. *National Resources Forum,* 28, 291–301.

Zeller Jr., T. (2009, February 27). Wave power for San Francisco? *The New York Times.* Retrieved from http://green.blogs.nytimes.com/2009/02/27/wave-power-for-san-francisco/

Zero waste. (n.d.). Wal-Mart.com. Retrieved from www.walmartstores/sustainability

Zumbo, J. (n.d.). Wolves. YellowstoneNationalPark.com. Retrieved from www.yellowstonenationalpark.com/wolves.htm

Index

About the Authors ___

Scott Young is professor and chairman of the Department of Management, Drehaus College of Business at DePaul University. He is also an invited Professor at American University of Paris. Previously, he was associate dean for Academic Programs at the University of Utah. Awards and honors he has won include the Doctoral Faculty Teaching Award; Outstanding Teacher, University of Utah College of Business; and Joseph Rosenblatt Award for Innovative Education, University of Utah. Professor Young has published numerous articles in journals such as the *International Journal of Operations and Production Management, Review of Business, International Journal of Production Research, Journal of Operations Management, Journal of World Business, Information and Management, International Business Review, Production and Inventory Management Journal, Production and Operations Management, International Journal of Purchasing and Materials Management,* and the *Journal of Education for Business.* In addition, he is the author of *Managing Global Operations* (with Winter Nie) and *Essentials of Operations Management.*

Scott lives in Wilmette, Illinois, with his wife, Luciana, and daughters, Gianna and Gabriella. He is an avid distance runner, with 34 marathons to his credit, and enjoys writing nonfiction.

Kanwalroop Kathy Dhanda is associate professor in the Department of Management, Drehaus College of Business at DePaul University. Previously, Kathy was an assistant professor in the School of Business Administration at the University of Portland, Oregon, where she was awarded the Outstanding Graduate Professor Award and the Pamplin Fellow Award. She is also an invited professor at AUT University in New Zealand and American University in Paris.

Kathy's academic scholarship focuses on sustainability issues with a primary emphasis in the areas of environmental modelling, carbon markets, emissions trading, corporate social responsibility, and reverse logistics. She has been published in *Operations Research, Journal of Business Ethics, Academy of Management Perspectives, Energy Economics, Journal of*

Public Policy and Marketing Policy Watch, Organization & Environment, Journal of Environmental Economics and Management, as well as other journals. She is also the coauthor of *Environmental Networks: A Framework for Economic Decision-Making and Policy Analysis* (with Edward Elgar).

Kathy graduated cum laude from Angelo State University and received her doctorate degree in management science from the University of Massachusetts at Amherst. She lives in the northern suburbs of Chicago with her husband, Adrian, and her two children, Arman and Ariana. She loves to read, travel, and cook spicy food.

$SAGE researchmethods

The essential online tool for researchers from the world's leading methods publisher

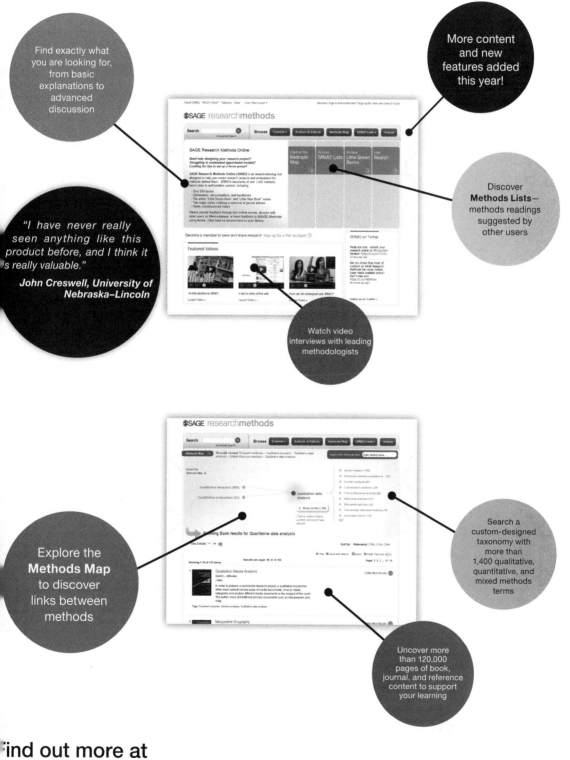

Find exactly what you are looking for, from basic explanations to advanced discussion

More content and new features added this year!

"I have never really seen anything like this product before, and I think it 's really valuable."

John Creswell, University of Nebraska–Lincoln

Discover **Methods Lists**— methods readings suggested by other users

Watch video interviews with leading methodologists

Explore the **Methods Map** to discover links between methods

Search a custom-designed taxonomy with more than 1,400 qualitative, quantitative, and mixed methods terms

Uncover more than 120,000 pages of book, journal, and reference content to support your learning

ind out more at
ww.sageresearchmethods.com